Integrated Approach to Web Performance Testing:
A Practitioner's Guide

B. M. Subraya
Infosys Technologies Limited, Mysore, India

IRM Press
Publisher of innovative scholarly and professional
information technology titles in the cyberage
Hershey • London • Melbourne • Singapore

Acquisitions Editor:	Michelle Potter
Development Editor:	Kristin Roth
Senior Managing Editor:	Amanda Appicello
Managing Editor:	Jennifer Neidig
Copy Editor:	April Schmidt
Typesetter:	Jennifer Neidig
Cover Design:	Lisa Tosheff
Printed at:	Integrated Book Technology

Published in the United States of America by
    IRM Press (an imprint of Idea Group Inc.)
    701 E. Chocolate Avenue, Suite 200
    Hershey PA 17033-1240
    Tel: 717-533-8845
    Fax: 717-533-8661
    E-mail: cust@idea-group.com
    Web site: http://www.irm-press.com

and in the United Kingdom by
    IRM Press (an imprint of Idea Group Inc.)
    3 Henrietta Street
    Covent Garden
    London WC2E 8LU
    Tel: 44 20 7240 0856
    Fax: 44 20 7379 0609
    Web site: http://www.eurospanonline.com

Library of Congress Cataloging-in-Publication Data

Integrated approach to web performance testing : a practitioner's guide
  / B.M. Subraya, editor.
     p. cm.
  Includes bibliographical references and index.
  Summary: "This book provides an integrated approach and guidelines
 to performance testing of Web based systems"--Provided by publisher.
  ISBN 1-59140-785-0 (hbk.) -- ISBN 1-59140-786-9 (pbk.) -- ISBN
 1-59140-787-7 (ebook)
  1. Web services. 2. Application software--Development. 3. Computer software--Testing.   I. Subraya, B. M., 1954-
  TK5105.88813.I55 2005
  006.7--dc22
                                        2005023877

British Cataloguing in Publication Data
A Cataloguing in Publication record for this book is available from the British Library.

All work contributed to this book is new, previously-unpublished material. The views expressed in this book are those of the authors, but not necessarily of the publisher.

Integrated Approach to Web Performance Testing:
A Practitioner's Guide

Table of Contents

Foreword

Globalization, aided by technology innovation and newer, faster communication channels are changing the basis of competition across industries today. To compete, firms must rapidly respond and adapt to a changing market and create responsive, flexible links across their value chains.

In this environment, the advent of *Web-based systems* has created a range of opportunities for organizations. Web-based systems and applications are enabling businesses to improve workflow costs and efficiencies across their supply chains, streamline and integrate their business processes, and collaborate with value-chain partners to deliver a strong value proposition to their customers.

Ensuring the robustness and reliability of Web-enabled systems has, therefore, become an increasingly critical function. *Integrated Approach to Web Performance Testing: A Practitioner's Guide* addresses the realities of performance testing in Web systems and provides an approach for integrating testing with the software development life cycle.

By offering a mix of theory and practical examples, Subraya provides the reader with a detailed understanding of performance testing issues in a Web environment. He offers an experience-based guidance of the testing process, detailing the approach from the definition of test requirements to design, simulation and benchmarking, and building, executing and analyzing testing strategies and plans. The book also details key processes and issues involved in test automation, as well as performance monitoring and tuning for specific technologies.

The chapters are filled with real-life examples, as well as illustrative working code, to facilitate the reader's understanding of different facets of the testing process. The discussion of testing methodology is anchored by a running case study which helps illustrate the application of test plans, strategies, and techniques. The case study and examples help demonstrate various approaches in developing performance testing strategies, benchmark designs, operation profiles and workloads. By bringing an experiential understanding into aspects of Web performance testing, the author is able to offer useful tips to effectively plan and execute testing activity. In addition, the book offers various guidelines and checklists to help practitioners conduct and analyze results using the various testing tools available for Web based applications.

The book provides a highly systematic approach to performance testing and offers an expert's eye view of the testing and functionality of Web systems. Subraya is careful to provide broad, initial groundwork for the subject in his first three chapters, which makes this text accessible even to the beginner.

Integrated Approach to Web Performance Testing: A Practitioner's Guide will prove to be a valuable tool for testing professionals, as well as for students, academicians and researchers.

N. R. Narayana Murthy, Chairman and Chief Mentor
Infosys Technologies Ltd.

Preface

In the current scenario where Information and Communication Technology (ICT) integration has become affordable, most organizations are looking at every single application to be Web-enabled. The functional aspects of an application get reasonable treatment, and also abundant literature is available for the same, whereas no books or insufficient literature is available on the performance aspects of such applications. However, the requirement for developing or creating systems that perform well in the Web commerce scenario is uncontestable.

The proliferation of Internet applications in recent years is a testimony to the evolving demands of business on technology. However, software life cycle methodologies do not yet seem to consider application performance as a critical parameter until late in the developmental process. Often, this impacts cost and delivery schedules negatively, leading to extensive rework and also results in unsatisfactory application performance. In addition, the field of performance testing is still in its infancy, and the various activities involved do not seem to be well understood among practitioners.

Today, Web based software systems are both popular and pervasive across the world in most areas of business as well as in personal life. However, the software system development processes and the performance testing processes do not seem to be well integrated in terms of ensuring adequate match between required and actual performance, especially since the latter activity is usually carried out very late in the developmental life cycle. Further, for practitioners, it is critical to understand the intricacies of environments, platforms, and technologies and their impact on the application performance. Given the wide spectrum of technologies and tools employed in the implementation of systems for different platforms, and a variety of tools used for performance testing, it is important to understand which of the parameters associated with each one of these is significant in terms of their effect on the system performance.

This book fulfills this void and provides an integrated approach and guidelines to performance testing of Web based systems. Based upon a mix of theoretical and practical concepts, this work provides a detailed understanding of the various aspects of performance testing in relation to the different phases of the software development life cycle, using a rich mixture of examples, checklists, templates, and working code to illustrate the different facets of application performance. This book enables a practical approach to be adapted in making appropriate choices of tools, methodologies, and project management for performance testing.

The material presented in the book is substantially based on the experience gained by studying performance testing issues in more than 20 IT application development projects for leading global/fortune 500 clients at Infosys Technologies Limited (a leading CMM level-5 global company specializing in software consulting, www.infosys.com) since 2000. This has been further reinforced through the delivery of more than 10 international preconference tutorials and more than 18 internal workshops at Infosys. Research studies conducted in this area by me has led to eight publications in various national and international conferences. Feedback from participants in tutorials and workshops in addition to those from reviewers has been used extensively to continuously refine the concepts, examples, case studies, and so forth presented in the work to make it useful for designers and architects.

Using a running case study, this book elucidates the concept of performance life cycle for applications in relation to the development life cycle; this is subsequently specialized through an identification of performance related activities corresponding to each stage of the developmental life cycle. Performance test results from the case study are discussed in detail to illustrate various aspects of application performance in relation to hardware resources, network bandwidth, and the effects of layering in the application. Finally, guidelines, checklists, and tips are provided to help practitioners address, plan, schedule, conduct, and analyze performance test results using commonly available commercial performance testing tools for applications built with different technologies on different platforms, together with enabling them to identify and resolve bottlenecks in application performance.

This book is written primarily for technical architects, analysts, project managers, and software professionals who are involved in development and management of projects. By using various techniques described in this book, they can systematically improve the planning and execution of their performance testing based projects. This book could also be used as a text in a software testing course or it can be introduced as an elective course for graduate level students. The book is targeted toward two types of readers: the novice and those who have been exposed to performance testing. The first three chapters are devoted mainly to a novice reader who needs a strong foundation with necessary ingredients on performance testing. The book provides many benefits to different categories of professionals.

The benefits from this book would include:

- A method to capture performance related data during requirement analysis;
- A process and method to plan and design for performance tests;
- A process and guidelines for analyzing and interpreting performance test data;
- Guidelines for identifying bottlenecks in application performance and remedial measures;
- Guidelines for optimal tuning of performance related parameters for applications developed using a sample set of different technologies.

Chapter 1 starts with an overview of software testing and explains the difference between Web application testing and client server testing, particularly performance testing, and sets the context for this book. This chapter also discusses the implications of poor performance and the need for performance testing and sets an abstract goal. Though the performance testing objective is to ensure the best field level performance of the application before deployment, it is better to set subgoals at each level of testing phases. To meet such goals, one needs to understand the basic definition of various types of performance testing like load testing, stress testing, and their differences. What type of testing is required to meet the goal or what kind of comprehensive performance testing is required to ensure an optimal result best understood by the LESS approach which is discussed in this chapter? Finally, the myths on performance testing which are always hogging around project managers while investing on tools and time required to complete the testing is removed in this chapter.

Once the importance of the performance of an application is known, it is necessary to understand how various factors affect the performance. The factors could be many and varied from different perspectives like technology, project management, scripting language, and so forth.

Chapter 2 discusses more on these factors that affect the performance. For instance, technical peculiarities like too many scripting languages, mushrooming of browsers, and Rapid Application Development approach affect the performance of the application. Further, different environments like client server environment may affect the performance of the application. A firewall is one of the important components which is needed to secure the application, but it slows down the performance of the application. Likewise, all possible aspects affecting the performance are discussed in this chapter.

Performance testing is not to be construed as features testing even though it has a definite linkage with the latter. In fact, performance testing begins from where the feature testing ends, that is, once all the desired functional requirements expected from the system are fully met. Both features and performance testing are in one way or another impacted by the various technologies and languages.

Chapter 3 provides insight about the technology aspects, including the software languages necessary for Web development. Without understanding the technology, working on performance testing is difficult. Hence, the topic on reference technology will help readers to understand and to appreciate the performance testing discussed in later chapters. This chapter also discusses various issues like network performance, technology, and user's perception.

Once the basic building blocks on concepts about performance testing and its importance on Web application are ready, the reader is comfortable to dwell on the process of conducting the performance testing as a practitioner would.

Customarily, designers address performance issues close to the end of the project life cycle, when the system is available for testing in its entirety or in significantly large modular chunks. This, however, poses a difficult problem, since it exposes the project to a potentially large risk related to the effort involved in both identifying as well as rectifying possible problems in the system at a very late stage in the life cycle. A more balanced approach would tend to distribute such risks by addressing these issues at different levels of abstraction (intended to result in increased clarity with time), multiple times (leading to greater effectiveness and comprehensiveness in testing application performance), and at different stages during the life cycle. The very first component of activities related to preparation for such testing is in collecting and analyzing requirements related to the performance of the system alongside those related to its features and functions.

The main objectives of Chapter 4 is to define goals of performance testing, remove ambiguities in performance goals, determine the complexity involved in performance testing, define performance measurements and metrics, list risk factors, and define the strategy for performance testing.

Real performance testing depends on how accurately the testers simulate the production environment with respect to the application's behavior. To simulate the behavior of the Web site accurately, benchmarks are used. The benchmark is a standard representation of the applications expected behavior or the likely real world operating conditions. It is typically essential to estimate usage patterns of the application before conducting the performance test. The behavior of the Web site varies with time, peak or normal, and hence the benchmarks do also. This means, there is no single metric possible. The benchmark should not be too general as it may not be useful in particular. The accuracy of the benchmark drives the effectiveness of the performance testing.

Chapter 5 highlights the complexity of identifying proper business benchmarks and deriving the operation pattern and workload from them. Types of workload and their complexities, number of workloads required and their design, sequencing various transactions within the workload and their importance, and required tools for creating the workload are some of the highlights of this chapter.

Design provides only the guidelines, but the build phase really implements the design so that execution of the test can be carried out later. Developing a good testing process guides the build phase properly.

Chapter 6 provides in-depth information on the build phase. The first activity in the build phase is to plan the various activities for testing. Preparing a test plan for performance testing is entirely a different ball game when compared to the functional test plan. A comprehensive test plan comprises test objectives, system profile, performance measurement criteria, usage model, test environment, testing process, and various constraints. However, building a comprehensive test plan addressing all the issues is as important as executing the test itself. The build phase also includes planning a test environment. Developing a test script involves identifying the tool, building proper logics, sequencing transactions, identifying the user groups, and optimizing the script code. Chapter 6 also drives the practitioners to prepare for the test execution. Once the preparation for test execution is ready, the system is ready for test execution.

Chapter 7 discusses more on practical aspects of test execution, wherein we address issues like, entry/exit criteria (not the same criteria as in functionality testing), scheduling problems, categorizing and setting performance parameters, and various risks involved. Practitioners can use this chapter as guidelines for their project during performance test execution.

Once the test execution is completed, the next task is to analyze the results. This is performed in post-test execution phase which is discussed in Chapter 8. The post-test execution phase is tedious and has multifaceted activity. Testers normally underestimate the complexity involved in this phase and face the uphill tasks while tuning the system for better performance. This chapter mainly discusses the revisit to the specific test execution through logs, defines a method/ strategy for analysis, compares the results with standard benchmarks, and identifies the areas of improvement. Guidelines for performance tuning are also discussed here. The chapter mainly helps the practitioner who is keen on test execution and analysis of results.

By now, most practitioners understand the complexity of the performance testing and the inability to conduct such a test manually. Managing the performance testing manually and handling performance issues are next to impossible. Automation is the only solution for any performance testing project, with the best tools available on the market. There is a need for automation and the automation process. Test automation is not just using some tools, and the common assumption is that the tool solves the performance problems. Testers are not aware of the complexities involved in test automation.

Chapter 9 is dedicated to set up a process for test automation and highlights various issues involved in test automation. Some of the strategies to succeed in test automation, based on the author's vast experience in performance testing, are also discussed in this chapter. Practitioners always face problems while selecting a proper automation tool. We present a set of characteristics of a good tool and a survey of available tools in the market. The chapter summarizes by presenting the guidelines for test automation.

Any application should be performance conscious; its performance must be monitored continuously. Monitoring of performance is a necessary part of the preventive maintenance of the application. By monitoring, we obtain performance data which are useful in diagnosing performance problems under operational conditions. This data could be used for tuning for optimal performance. Monitoring is an activity which is normally carried out specific to technology.

In Chapter 10, we highlight performance monitoring and tuning related to Java and .NET. The first nine chapters together described the performance testing from concept to reality whereas Chapter 10 highlights aspects of monitoring and tuning to specific technologies. This chapter provides an overview of monitoring and tuning applications with frameworks in Java and .Net technologies. Readers must have basic exposure to Java and .NET technology before understanding this chapter.

To help practitioners, a quick reference guide is provided. Appendix A discusses the performance tuning guidelines. Performance tuning guidelines for a Web server (Apache), a database (Oracle), and an object oriented technology (Java) are presented. Along with this, .NET coding guidelines and procedure to execute Microsoft's performance monitoring tool, PERFMON, are also discussed. Characteristics of a good performance testing tool and a comparative study of various tools are presented in Appendix B. Further, some templates on performance requirement and test plan are provided in Appendix C for easy reference.

Though guidelines on planning, execution, and result analysis are discussed in various chapters, they are better understood if discussed with a case study. Accordingly, a detailed case study on banking function is taken and discussed. Appendix D highlights various aspects of the case study and brings concepts to practices. A virtual bank is considered and simple routine business functions are considered. Here more emphasis is given on performance and thus only relevant business functions which impact performance are considered. This case study provides the performance requirement document and basic design document on performance testing. Only a sample workload, one test run, and relevant results are presented and discussed. The case study will help practitioners validate their understanding from the book.

This book addresses only the performance testing aspects, not performance engineering like capacity planning.

Acknowledgments

This book is dedicated to my wife, Yamuna, and son, Gaurav, for their loving support and inspiration.

I would like to acknowledge and thank Infosys Technologies Ltd. for supporting and promoting this project. I am deeply indebted to Mr. Narayana Murthy NR, Chairman and Chief Mentor, Infosys Technologies Ltd., for his persistent support and encouragement during the project. I owe enormous thanks to him for writing the Foreword for this book. I would like to specially thank SV Subrahmanya, Infosys, who was instrumental in motivating and encouraging me to work toward the completion of the book. A special thanks goes to JK Suresh, Infosys, who was and is always a source of inspiration for me. I am grateful to him for sharing several valuable inputs and for participating in interactions pertinent to the subject. A special acknowledgement goes to Dr. MP Ravindra for his encouragement and timely intervention on various interactions during the course of the project.

Creating a book is a Herculean task that requires immense effort from many people. I owe enormous thanks to Kiran RK and Sunitha for assisting in going through the chapters. Mr. Kiran was instrumental in aiding the consolidation of many aspects of practitioner's requirement from concept to reality. Sujith Mathew deserves special thanks for reviewing and proffering valuable inputs on various chapters. Subramanya deserves high praise and accolades for keeping me abreast on the latest happenings in this field and helping in the preparation of the manuscript. I would also like to commend Siva Subramanyam for his valuable feedbacks on Chapter 10 and his timely corrections.

A large part of the pragmatics of this book is derived from my involvement with complex projects developed in Infosys and the experience sharing with many participants of tutorials in international conferences. I have had the opportunity to interact with hundreds of professional software engineers and project managers of Infosys and I thank them all for their help in making this book relevant to real-world problems. I sincerely appreciate Joseph Juliano's contribution to the case study during the analysis of results. Special thanks to Bhaskar Hegde, Uday Deshpande, Prafulla Wani, Ajit Ravindran Nair, Sundar KS, Narasimha Murthy, Nagendra R Setty, Seema Acharya and Rajagopalan P for their contribution to the book at various stages.

Thanks are also due to all my colleagues of Education and Research, Infosys for their continual moral support, especially colleagues at the Global Education Center.

Besides the reviewers from Idea Group Inc., the only other person who read every chapter of the book prior to technical review was Shivakumar M of Bharath Earth Movers Ltd. I wish to express heartfelt gratitude to Shivakumar for scrupulously reviewing the first draft of every chapter in this book.

Finally, I would like to thank my family and friends for their perpetual support. Special thanks to my son, Gaurav for his company on scores of occasions including several late nights of writing. Last but not the least, I owe special thanks to my parents for their blessings.

B. M. Subraya
Mysore, India
January 2006

Chapter 1

Web-Based Systems and Performance Testing

For many years, the World Wide Web (Web) functioned quite well without any concern about the quality of performance. The designers of the Web page, as well as the users were not much worried about the performance attributes. The Web, in the initial stages of development, was primarily meant to be an information provider rather than a medium to transact business, into which it has grown. The expectations from the users were also limited only to seek the information available on the Web. Thanks to the ever growing population of Web surfers (now in the millions), information found on the Web underwent a dimensional change in terms of nature, content, and depth.

The emergence of portals providing extensive, as well as intensive information on desired subjects transformed the attitude of users of the Web. They are interested in inquiring about a subject and, based on replies to such queries, make decisions affecting their careers, businesses, and the quality of their life. The advent of electronic commerce (e-commerce) (see *Ecommerce definition,* 2003) has further enhanced user Web interface, as it seeks to redefine business transactions hitherto carried out between business to business (B2B) (see Varon, 2004) and business to customer (B2C) organizations (see Patton, 2004). Perhaps it may even reach a stage where all the daily chores of an individual may be guided by a Web-based system.

Today, Web-based transactions manifest in different forms. They include, among other things, surfing the news portal for latest events, e-buying a product in a shopping mall, reserving an airticket online at a competitive price, or even participating in an e-auctioning program. In all these transactions, irrespective of users' online objectives, the Web users expect not only accuracy but also speed in executing them. That is to say, the customer loyalty to a Web site greatly depends on these two attributes, speed and accuracy. If the Web site design sacrifices speed for accuracy or vice versa, the users of such Web site lose interest in it and seek greener pastures. Thus, in order to retain its existing customers and also add new customers to it, the quality of performance of the Web site must be ensured, apart from accuracy in terms of speed of response and consistency in behavior. Above all, the user must be privileged to access the Web site at any time of the day throughout the year.

Perhaps, no other professional is better privileged than a software professional in appreciating the performance of Web sites, both from user and designer perspectives. From the user perspective, the parameters for evaluating the performance of the Web site are only Web site availability and response time. Factors such as server outages or slow pages have no significance in the mind of the user, even if the person happens to be a software professional. On the other hand, the same person as a Web master expects the server to exhibit high throughput with minimum resource utilization. To generalize, performance of Web-based systems is seen as a thorough combination of 24×7 (24 hours in a day times 7 days in a week) Web site availability, low response time, high throughput, and minimum resource utilization. This book discusses the importance of the performance of Web applications and how to conduct performance testing (PT) efficiently and analyze results for possible bottlenecks.

Web Systems and Poor Performance

From users' perspectives, as said earlier, the performance of Web systems is seen only as a thorough combination of 24×7 Web site availability, low response time, high throughput, and minimum resource utilization at client side. In such a situation, it is worthwhile to discuss the typical reactions of the user for the poor performance variation of the Web site.

How Web Users React on Web Application's Poor Performance

The immediate reaction of the user to server outages or slow pages on the Web is the feeling of frustration. Of course, the level of frustration depends mainly on the user's psychology and may manifest into:

- Temporarily stop accessing the Web page and try after a lapse of time;
- Abandon the site for some days (in terms of days or months and rarely years);
- Not to return to the site forever (sounds a bit unrealistic, but possibilities cannot be ignored);
- Discourage others from accessing the Web site.

The Web users want the site to be up whenever they visit it. In addition, they want to *feel* that the access is fast. A Web site which is fast for one user may not be fast enough for another user.

User's Previous Experience with Internet Speed

A user who is comfortable with a response time of 15 seconds may feel the response time of 10 seconds as ultra fast; however, the user who is used to accessing sites with response time of 5 seconds will be frustrated with response time of 10 seconds. Here user's experience counts more than the concerned Web sites.

User's Knowledge on Internet

Those users having working knowledge on the Internet are well aware of the tendency of response time degradation in Web sites. This enables them to either wait patiently for the Web site to respond or try to access the site after some time.

User's Level of Patience

This is something that has to do with the human mind. According to psychologists, the level of patience in a human being, unlike body temperature, is neither measurable nor a constant quantum. On the other hand, it differs from person to person depending upon personality, upbringing, levels of maturity, and accomplishment. The user with a lesser level of patience will quickly abandon the site if the response is slow and may not return to it immediately. However, the user with higher levels of patience will be mature enough to bear with slow pages of the Web site.

User's Knowledge About the Application

The perception of the user about the performance of the Web site also depends upon knowledge about the application accessed on the Web. If the user is aware about the intricacies and complexities involved in the architecture of the application, then the user will be favorably inclined with regard to the slow response time of the Web site.

User's Need for the Web Site

The user will bear with the performance of the Web site, however bad it is, if the user believes that it is the only place where the required information can be obtained.

Stakeholder's Expectations on Performance

The system developers, sponsors, and owners have a definite stake or interest in the Web site. The expectations of these stakeholders of the Web site are more exhaustive than that of the users of the Web site. Their expectations may be in terms of:

- 24×7 Web site availability;
- Quick response time when a query is performed;
- High throughput when a user is Involved in multiple transactions;
- Adequate memory usage of both client and server;
- Adequate CPU usage of various systems used for the transactions;
- Adequate bandwidth usage of networks used for the application;
- Maximum transaction density per second;
- Revenue generated from the Web site from the business perspective.

In addition, the aspects relating to security and user friendly interface, though they have an expending impact on available resources, will also add to the expectations of the stakeholders. Of course, the degree of sophistication to be incorporated on these aspects varies with the nature of application.

Classification of Web Sties

Classification of Web sites based on performance is a subjective exercise. This is because the demand or expectations from a Web site vary from not only user to user but on the type of Web sites with which each user is associated. A study on commercial Web sites by James Ho, "Evaluating the World Wide Web: A Global Study of Commercial Sites" (1997), classifies the Web sites into three types (see Ho, 2003):

- Sites to promote products and services;
- Sites with a provision of data and information;
- Sites processing business transactions.

Another classification is based on the degree of interactivity the Web site offers. Thomas A. Powell (1998) classifies Web sites into five categories as shown in Table 1.0. Based on complexities and interactivity, he categorizes Web sites into static, dynamic, and interactive ones, and they differ in features.

Table 1.0. Classification of Web sites based on complexity and interactivity

Sites	Features
Static Web sites	The Web sites contain basic, plain HTML pages. The only interactivity offered to user is to click the links to download the pages
Static with form based interactivity	Web sites contain pages with forms, which are used for collecting information from the user. The information could be personal details, comments or requests.
Sites with dynamic data access	Web site provides front end to access elements from database. Users can search a catalogue or perform queries on the content of a database. The results of the search or query is displayed through HTML pages
Dynamically generated Web sites	Web sites displaying customized pages for every user. The pages are created based on the execution of scripts.
Web-based software applications	Web sites, which are part of a business, process that work in a highly interactive manner.

This classification helps to understand the nature of the system and to adopt a better testing process. These two classifications provide two distinctions in which the Web sites could be classified. Together they provide information about degree of interactivity and complexity of Web sites.

The Need for Performance Testing

Before getting into the details regarding the need for performance testing, it is worthwhile to know whether an organization can survive long term without performance testing. A thoughtful survey of 117 organizations to investigate the existence of PT provides a pattern between project's success and need for PT (see Computer World, 1999). Table 1.1 explains how user acceptance of the system is highly dependent on PT.

The need for speed is a key factor on the Internet (see Zimmerman, 2003). Whether users are on a high speed connection or a low speed dial up modem, everyone on the Internet expects speed. Most of the research reports justify the fact that speed alone is the main factor accessing the Web site.

To illustrate, *eMarketer* (November 1998) reports that a user will bail out from a site if pages take too long to load. A typical load time against percentage of users waiting is tabulated in Table 1.2 (see *To be successful, a Web site must be effective*, 2003). To illustrate, 51% of the users wait no more than 15 seconds to load a specific page.

Zona Research Group (see Ho, 2003) reported that the bail out rate increases greatly when pages take more than 7 to 8 seconds to load. This report popularized the *8 second rule*, which holds that if a Web page does not download within 8 seconds, users will go elsewhere. This only signifies that the average user is concerned with the quality of the content in the Web as long as the downloading time is restricted to only a few seconds. If it is more, they tend to bail out of the Web site. To account for various modem and

Table 1.1. Survey of 117 organizations to investigate the existence of performance testing

Performance Testing practices	Organization in which PT is considered	
	Was accepted	*Was not accepted*
Reviewed or Simulated (performance during requirements analysis and design)	21%	0%
Testing conducted at early stages of SDLC	35%	38%
Testing conducted at later stages of SDLC	38%	26%
Did post deployment testing	0%	8%
Did not do performance or load testing at all	6%	60%

Table 1.2. Bail out statistics according to eMarketer *reports*

Load Time	Percentage of Users Waiting
10 seconds	84%
15 seconds	51%
20 seconds	26%
30 seconds	5%

Table 1.3. Expected load time against modem speed

Modem Speed	Expected Load time
14.4 Kilobytes Modem	11.5 seconds
33.6 Kilobytes Modem	7.5 seconds
56 Kilobytes Modem	5.2 seconds
Cable/DSL Modem	2.2 seconds
T1 and Above	0.8 seconds

Table 1.4. Monthly loss from slow page loading

Speed	Lost sales in millions
14.4 Kilobytes	$73
28.8 Kilobytes	$97
56 Kilobytes	$100
ISDN	$14
T1	$38

transfer speeds, *Zona Research* provides expected load time against modem speed as shown in Table 1.3 (see Chen, 2003). The findings demonstrate that T1 lines are fast compared to modems.

Furthermore, *Zona Research* cautions about the impact of violating the *8 second rule* (see Submit Corner, 2003). It says violation of the *8 second rule* inflicts more losses than slow modems. According to this finding, U.S. e-commerce is incurring a loss as high as $44.35 billion each year due to slow pages as shown in Table1.4 (see Zona Research, Inc., 2003). ISDN or T1 lines are good for e-commerce.

Table 1.5. Annual losses due to violation of eight second rule

Industry	Lost sales in millions
Securities trading	$40
Travel & Tourism	$34
Publishing	$14
Groceries	$9
Personal Finance	$5
Music	$4
Box office receipts	$3
Textiles/Apparel	$3

Table 1.6. User's view on response time

Response time	User's view
< 0.1 second	User feels that the system is reacting instantaneously.
<1.0 second	User experiences a slight delay but he is still focused on the current Web site.
< 10 seconds	This is the maximum time a user keeps the focus on a Web site, but his attention is already in *distract zone*.
>10 seconds	User is most likely to be distracted from the current Web site and looses interest.

Industry wise annual losses (see Table 1.5) due to violation of the eight second rule show the concern on slow downloading pages as reported by Zona Research Group (2003). Table 1.5 shows how different categories of loading pages affect the business.

TurboSanta (see Upsdell, 2003) reports (December 1999) that the average home page load time among the Web's top 120 retailers is about five seconds.

Jacob Neilson (2000) (see *Response times: The three important limits,* 2003) says the goal must be to ensure customers the right answers to their mouse clicks within a few seconds at anytime. He suggests that 95% of requests must be processed in less than 10 seconds to win customer confidence as shown in Table 1.6.

Zona Research (2003) estimates that businesses lose US$25 billion a year because of Web site visitors tendency not to wait for the long pages to load. However, Jupiter Media Metrix say (see Sherman, 2004) that 40% of surfers in the U.S. return or revisit the Web sites loading their pages in a few seconds.

Appliant (Chen, 2003) surveyed 1,500 of the most popular Web sites, including AltaVista, AOL, eBay, MSN, and Yahoo. Unlike prior studies which were based on robot-based test traffic, this study was conducted by downloading each home page, counting content components, measuring document sizes, and then computing best case download times for a typical end user connection via a 28.8 Kilobytes/second modem.

The findings of the study revealed that the average home page uses 63 Kilobytes for images, 28 Kilobytes for HTML, 12 Kilobytes for other file contents, and have a best case first load time of 32 seconds. In other words, the average American user waits for about 30 seconds the first time they look at a new home page. According to this research, the

Table 1.7. User's connection speeds as reported by Neilsen/Netratings

Connection Speed	Users
14.4 Kilo baud or less	3.2%
28.8-33.6 Kilo baud	9.3%
56.6 Kilo baud	51.6%
High speed 128 Kilo baud or more	35.9%

Note: The data presented here primarily pertains to the USA and Canada. The Nielsen/NetRatings further estimated the relationship between the number of pages accessed via connecting speed as shown in Table 1.8. High speed connections provide better page access than low speed modems.

Table 1.8. Percentage of page accesses observed in accordance

Connection Speed	Page accesses
14.4 Kilobaud or less	0.7%
28.8-33.6 Kilobaud	2.0%
56.6 Kilobaud	10.9%
High speed 128 Kilobaud or more	86.5%

average load time for AltaVista, AOL, eBay, MSN, and Yahoo home pages is about 25 seconds.

Web sites such as AltaVista and AOL receive many repeat visits with load time benefiting from documenting the cache in the browser. The best case of "cached download time", assuming browsers retain all cacheable document components, for the five first tier sites is 4 seconds which is faster than the 1,500 site average load time of 7.8 seconds. This estimation always addresses best case scenarios only. However, actual performance also depends on factors such as network conditions and Web server load time. Based on this report and Web site user experience, a new rule of 30 seconds has emerged as opposed to the initial eight second rule of Zona Research.

In addition, it is also noted by Appliant Research that some of the Web sites in the US targeting the business audience are less concerned with the performance of dial up systems. This is also reinforced by the findings of Neilsen/NetRatings (February 2003) (see *High speed connections,* 2003) that high speed connections are quite common among business users (compared with home users) in many of the developed countries. However, knowing connection speeds of target users is an important aspect in determining the user's expectation on performance. Many people still use lower speed modems. Table 1.7 provides the percentage of users with reference to the speed of modems.

A survey by Pew Internet (April 2004) strengthens the views of Neilsen/NetRatings report. The survey was conducted in 2003 and 2004 and found that 60% of dial up users were not interested in switching to a broadband connection. This shows that some users are perfectly satisfied with their slow connections. These statistics alert PT professionals to not ignore users with slower connections while planning the effort required for performance testing.

In addition, following news snippets emphasizes the importance of Web site performance:

"Google is a little unusual among dot coms because it competes based on performance, not glitter", says David C. Croson, professor of operations and information. "It's simply the best at search, period. It finds pages that other search engines can't find. And when you search 30 times a day, as I do, performance is what matters." (see *Google success*, 2003, http://news.com)

"These days, online shopping sites are straining under the holiday load", says Keynote Systems. The company's e-Commerce Transaction Performance Index shows major online shopping sites experienced performance problems during the week beginning December 1. The index — which measures the response time and success rate for executing a typical multistep online retail transaction on 13 of the most active e-commerce sites (such as Amazon, Best Buy, Target, and Wal-Mart) — dipped at times during the week to as low as 80% success rate, meaning that consumers could complete only 8 out of 10 transactions, says ARM Research Group. (see Reports Keynote, 2004)

*"We always knew we had a **bottleneck**", says David Hayne, a marketing coordinator at Urban Outfitters who is responsible for the retailer's Web site technology. "The company's Web application servers have to refer to a back end product database — which was not designed to handle Web processing — to display pages, Hayne says. The process slowed Web page views considerably."* (see *Web shops fight fraud*, 2004)

*"If a site is always available but slow, a company is not achieving its objectives from a customer standpoint," says Jeff Banker, vice president of **Gomez Networks**, one of the many firms that monitor site performance. "If a site is fast yet unavailable infrequently, it's still meeting expectations." Banker points to **eBay** — which has experienced infrequent but prolonged outages — to support his assertion that users will stick with sites they find valuable.*

"Availability is assumed at this point, like the dial tone on a phone," Banker says. "But performance is often lousy, and that affects business."

"We don't have downtime, but if we have performance problems, we get a lot of heat," Dodge says. (see Zimmerman, 2003)

User tolerance for slow performance varies by site and the importance of the information they're seeking, says Bruce Linton, president of performance monitor WebHancer.

These snippets demonstrate the need for effective and efficient PT on Web sites before deployment.

When to Detect Performance Bottlenecks

Detecting a bottleneck (see Barber, 2004) in the Web site does not call for a super human effort, nor is it an art restricted to a few. On the other hand, the cause for the occurrence of a bottleneck in the Web may be outside the scope of many users. When a user accesses the Web site for the first time, the user may be expecting the display of the requested Web page. Instead, more often than not, the user may be confounded with the display of an error message as shown in Figure 1.1. The display of error message can be construed as an indication for a possible bottleneck in Web architecture.

There may be several causes for creeping of errors or bottlenecks in displaying the desired page. For instance, it may be due to malfunction of any of the components in the Web architecture. It may be on account of the operating system, browser settings, browser version, or due to the add on components. Problems relating to server or client resources, third party components, and also configuration of the Web, application or database servers, bandwidth, and traffic complicate the generation of bottlenecks in the Web. To illustrate, when a person tries to access a Web-based application using 28.8 Kilobytes per second dial-up connection, the person may fail to download a page. But the same page can be downloaded successfully by using T1 lines. Here the main bottleneck is bandwidth. What is important to know is that by just looking at an error message, it is impossible to identify the area and root cause of the bottleneck except for the fact that there is a bottleneck that needs to be addressed.

Figure 1.1. Web page with an error

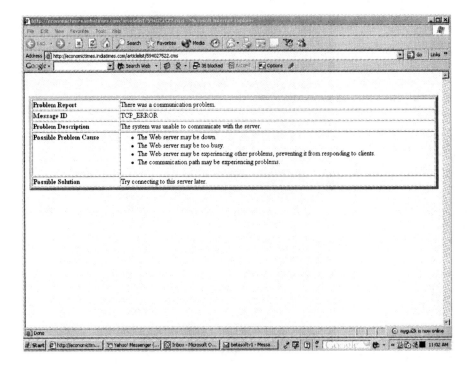

Like bandwidth, server configuration may lead to a bottleneck in the Web. If the virtual directory of Web/application server is not properly configured, the requested scripts, data, or file will not be serviced properly. Similarly, the issues of compatibility — between the Web and application servers — do play a role in optimizing the response time. To illustrate, if the application server is configured to execute the scripts in a certain directory and the Web server is configured in such a way that the directory does not allow executing the scripts in that directory, the requested application would suffer from the issue of compatibility leading to bottleneck in the system. In the same way, the browser settings, like the issue of compatibility between the servers, may be a root cause for a bottleneck, if it is disabled to execute certain scripts like Java scripts.

The foregoing paragraphs very clearly bring out the fact that the cause for a bottleneck in the Web system may be due to several factors. It need not necessarily be due to slow response of the network or the down time of the server, though many times, the users complain about the poor performance of the Web site due to these two factors alone. It is in this context that testing the performance of the Web system gains significance so that the true cause for the poor response can be identified. In fact, this forms the core objective for PT and, needless to say, in the absence of it, the real cause will be camouflaged, much to the chagrin of stakeholders, in the cloak of user's perception without any antidote for poor performance.

One of the effective techniques often used in pedagogy to find the extent of understanding by the student is the questionnaire method. The application of the same in the domain of PT will help in finding out the real cause for poor performance of the Web system. Some of the questions that need to be addressed are:

- Is it the problem of slow response time?
- Is it the problem of unavailability?
- Is it the problem of frequent time outs?
- Is it the problem of unexpected page display?
- Is it the problem of irritating pop up advertisements?
- Is it the problem of bad organization of the content?
- Is the entire Web site slow or just a particular transaction?
- Is the site slow for the entire user base or to certain groups of users?
- Does a set of users report the same problem frequently?

If so, analyze by:

- Investigating their location of use;
- Investigating their link speed;

- Investigating their type of connection;
- Investigating the specific interactivity.

PT helps in finding answers for questions like:

- Will the system be able to handle increases in Web traffic without compromising system response time, security, reliability, and accuracy?
- At what point will the performance degrade, and which component will be responsible for the degradation?
- What impact will performance degradation have on company sales and technical support costs?
- What could be the problem? Is it due to the server, network, database, or the application itself?
- How to predict the performance problem before hand. How to resolve the matter before that could occur.
- If the predicted problem cannot be resolved within time, what could be the alternative?
- Is it necessary to monitor all the hardware components such as router, firewall, servers, network links, or is just the end to end monitoring sufficient?

PT helps, in general, to build confidence of the owners of the Web site to attract more customers.

General Perception about Performance Testing

PT is viewed in different ways based on the goals set for performance measurements. If the requirement is concentrated on specific characteristics of the system such as response time, throughput, capacity, resource utilization, and so forth, then the perception on PT also differs.

Response Time Testing

Response time (see *Response times: The three important limits,* 2003) represents the user's perception of how fast the system reacts for a user request or query. The reaction may be slow or fast based on the type of activity and time required to process the request.

Response time testing is conducted to know how long the system takes to complete a requested task or group of tasks.

Acceptance of a particular response time, as said earlier, is a factor related to human psychology. Expectations differ from user to user. A user who has worked with 5 seconds response time will get frustrated with 10 seconds response time. Though, the reasonable response time differs from application to application and user to user, but industry norms are as follows:

- For a multimedia interactive system, response time should be 0.1 second or less, 90% of the time.

- For online systems where tasks are interrelated, response time should be less than 0.5 second, 90% of the time.

- For an online system where users do multiple tasks simultaneously, response time should be 1 second or less, 90% of the time.

The consistency of response time is measured in several test runs if the performance is calculated specifically in terms of response time.

Throughput Testing

Throughput testing measures the throughput of a server in the Web-based system. It is a measure of number of bytes serviced per unit time. Throughput of various servers in the system architecture can be measured as kilobits/second, database queries/minute, transactions/hour, or any other time bound characteristics.

Capacity Testing

Capacity testing (see Miller, 2005) measures the overall capacity of the system and determines at what point response time and throughput become unacceptable. Capacity testing is conducted with normal load to determine the extra capacity where stress capacity is determined by overloading the system until it fails, which is also called a stress load to determine the maximum capacity of a system.

Myths on Performance Testing

Perception on PT differs from user to user, designer to designer, and system to system. However, due to lack of knowledge, people understand PT in many ways leading to confusion among the user as well as developer community. Some of the myths on PT are:

- Client server performance problems can usually be fixed by simply plugging in a more powerful processor.

- If features work correctly, users do not mind a somewhat slow response.

- No elaborate plans are required for testing; it is intuitively obvious how to measure the system's performance.

- Needs just a few hours to check performance before deployment.

- PT does not require expensive tools.

- Anyone can measure and analyze the performance; it does not require any specialized skills.

However, the real picture on PT is entirely different. It is a complex and time consuming task. Testing on only a few parameters on performance do not yield proper results. Complex parameters and different approaches are required to test the system properly.

Performance Testing: "LESS" Approach

Performance of Web applications must be viewed from different objectives: fast response against a query, optimal utilization of resources, all time availability, future scalability, stability, and reliability. However, most of the time, one or few objectives are addressed while conducting performance testing. While conducting PT with any objective in mind, the ingredients to the testing system are the same. The ingredients could be number of concurrent users, business pattern, hardware and software resources, test duration, and volume of data. The result from such performance tests could be response time, throughput, and resource utilization. Based on these results, some of the indirect results like reliability, capacity, and scalability of the system are measured. These results help in drawing a conclusion or making a logical judgment on the basis of circumstantial evidence and prior conclusions rather than just on the basis of direct observation. Such reasoning is required to justify whether the system is stable/unstable, available/ unavailable, or reliable/unreliable. This can be achieved by conducting the LESS (Load, Endurance, Stress, and Spike) (see Menascé, 2003; Anwar & Saleem, 2004) testing approach.

Load Testing

Load testing (see Menascé, 2003) is a term which finds a wide usage in industry circles for performance testing. Here, load means the number of concurrent users or the traffic in the system. Load testing is used to determine whether the system is capable of handling various anticipated activities performed concurrently by different users. This is done by using a test tool to map different types of activities; then through simulation, different real life conditions are created and in each of these simulated situations, the mapped activities are performed concurrently by a set of simulated users. Users' thinking time during input to the system is also captured. All normal scenarios are simulated and subjected to testing. Load testing is performed to justify whether the system is performing well for the specified limit of load.

To illustrate this, consider a Web-based application for online shopping which is to be load tested for a duration of 12 hours. The anticipated user base for the application is 1,000 concurrent users during peak hours. A typical transaction would be that of a user who connects to the site, looks around for something to buy, completes the purchase (or does not purchase anything), and then disconnects from the site.

Load testing for the application needs to be carried out for various loads of such transactions. This can be done in steps of 50, 100, 250, and 500 concurrent users and so on till the anticipated limit of 1,000 concurrent users is reached. Figure 1.2 depicts a system being tested for 10 and 100 constant load of users for a period of 12 hours. The graph indicates that during these 12 hours there is a constant of 10 or 100 active transactions. For load testing, the inputs to the system have to be maintained so that there are a constant number of active users. During the execution of the load test, the goal is to check whether the system is performing well for the specified load or not. To achieve this, system performance should be captured at periodic intervals of the load test. Performance parameters like response time, throughput, memory usage, and so forth should be measured and recorded. This will give a clear picture of the health of the system. The system may be capable of accommodating more than 1,000 concurrent users. But, verifying that is not under the scope of load testing. Load testing ensures the level of confidence with which the customer uses the system efficiently under normal conditions.

Endurance Testing

Endurance testing deals with the reliability of the system. This type of testing is conducted for different durations to find out the health of the system in terms of its consistent performance. Endurance testing is conducted either on a normal load or on a stress load. However, the duration of the test is the focus of the test. Tests are executed for hours or sometimes even days. A system may be able to handle the surge in number of transactions, but if the surge continues for some hours, then the system may breakdown. Endurance testing can reveal system defects such as slow memory leaks or the accrual of uncommitted database transactions in a rollback buffer which impact system resources.

When an online application is subjected to endurance testing, the system is tested for a longer duration than the usual testing duration. Unlike other testing where the execution is held for a lesser duration, endurance testing is conducted for long duration sometimes more than 36 hours. Figure 1.3 depicts the endurance test on a system with different loads of 10 active users and also a peak load of 1,000 active users running for a duration of 48 hours. This attempt can make the system become unreliable and can lead to problems such as memory leaks. Stressing the system for an extended period reveals the tolerance level of the system. Again, system performance should be captured at periodic intervals of the test. Performance parameters like response time, throughput, memory usage, and so forth should be measured and recorded.

Figure 1.2. Load vs. time during load testing

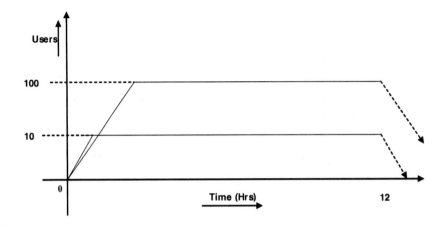

Figure 1.3. Load vs. time during endurance testing

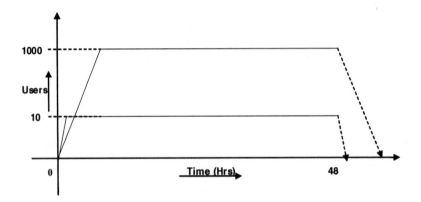

Stress Testing

Though load testing and stress testing (see Anwar & Saleem, 2004) are used synonymously for performance related efforts, their goals are different. Load testing is conducted to check whether the system is capable of handling an anticipated load where as
stress testing helps to identify the load that the system can handle before breaking down
or degrading drastically. Stress testing goes one step beyond the load testing and
identifies the system's capability to handle the peak load. In stress testing, think time
is not important as the system is stressed with more concurrent users beyond the
expected load.

Let us take the same example of an online shopping application which needs to undergo stress testing. Here, unlike load testing where testing was conducted for specified user load, stress testing is conducted for a number of concurrent users beyond the specified limit. It determines the maximum number of concurrent users an online system can service without degrading beyond the anticipated limit of 1,000 concurrent users. However, there is a possibility that the maximum load that can be handled by the system may be found to be same as the anticipated limit.

Figure 1.4 depicts a scenario where the stable load of the system is a load of 1,000 active users. In this stable state, the system is continuously introduced with a surge of 200 users. System performance should be captured at periodic intervals. The performance should be monitored to see if there is any degradation.

If the test completes successfully, then the system should be load tested for 1,200 concurrent users. System performance should be monitored to see if all parameters are stable. If it is not stable, then we understand that the load of 1,200 is not the stable condition for the system. It could be 1,000 or between 1,000 and 1,200, which has to be determined. If it is stable at 1,200, then we move on to the next level of stress testing.

The next level will have a higher surge of users, maybe a surge of 500 more continuous users. This should be introduced keeping 1,200 as the stable condition for the system; again the performance of the system is monitored. This procedure is carried on, and at some increased stress, the system will show signs of degradation. This clearly shows the amount of stress the system can take under the conditions that the system was set up for. System degradation can also be understood here. A system can degrade gracefully and stop or maintain its stable state; on the other hand, it can instantly crash, bringing down the complete system. Stress testing determines the behavior of the system as user load increases (Figure 1.5). It checks whether the system is going to degrade gracefully (Figure 1.5A) or crash (Figure 1.5B) when it goes beyond the acceptable limit.

Figure 1.4. Stress testing during a stable state

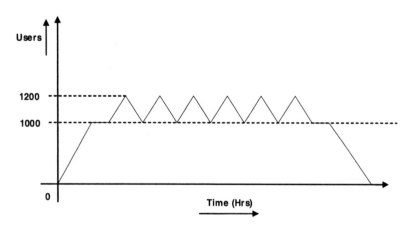

Spike Testing

Spike testing is conducted to test the system suddenly for a short duration. Each surge the system has to face is called a spike.

This can be done with a constant level of spikes over the system's stable load of users as shown in Figure 1.4, that is, spikes of 200 users over the stable state of 1,000 users. On the other hand, it can be tested for the system for variable spikes as shown in Figure 1.6. This testing ensures whether the system will be stable and responsive under unexpected variations in load. If an unexpected surge appears in the user base, the performance of the system should degrade gracefully rather than come crashing down all of a sudden.

In the online shopping application example, there could be variable level of activities throughout the day (24 hours). We can anticipate that the activities will be at a peak during midday as compared to the rest of the day. Figure 1.6 depicts the different spikes when the system is tested across 24 hours with a surge in activities during midday.

A spike is an unexpected load which stresses the system. Unlike increasing the load incrementally and going beyond the specified limit gradually as in case of stress testing, spike testing starts with a less number of users, say one user and then 50 concurrent users and then suddenly the user base is increased. This can make the system become unstable since the system might not be prepared to service a sudden surge of concurrent users. In this case, the possibility of system crashing is very high.

LESS is a comprehensive approach to address the challenges discussed so far in performance testing. While individual tests may satisfy a particular user expectation, this approach provides a multidimensional view about the performance of the system as a whole in terms of response time, optimal resource utilization, and scaling up of more users. Table 1.9 highlights how the LESS approach slowly ramps up concurrent users and duration to address all performance issues.

Difference between the Components of LESS

The LESS approach ensures complete performance testing, but the process comprises more resources and time. The other approach, in terms of cost advantage, is to conduct individual tests instead of conducting all the tests envisaged in the LESS approach. The serious drawback in restricting performance evaluation to individual tests is that each one of them provides only one dimension of performance, ignoring the rest. Each test is performed by a black box method; that is, they accept inputs and produce outputs without knowing the internal structure of the system under test (SUT). On the other hand, each component in LESS addresses different goals. This means load testing is to check the system with an expected load, stress testing to check the maximum load that the system can support, spike testing to determine how the system behaves at sudden load

Figure 1.5. System degradation during stress testing

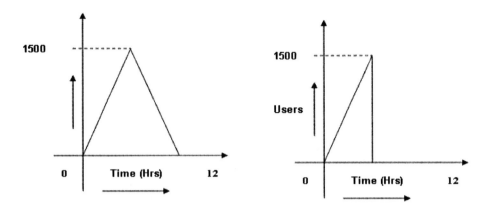

Figure 1.5a. Graceful degradation   *Figure 1.5b. Instant degradation*

surge, and endurance testing to ensure how the system behaves if the stress load is exerted on a system for a longer time. Table 1.10 provides the basic objectives of these testing efforts. Each test targets different goals.

Another important difference among these components is in terms of inputs to the system during the testing period. Table 1.11 highlights the variation in inputs for various types of performance related testing. Load and stress testing differ in number of concurrent users. Load testing is performed for a constant number of users where as stress testing is carried out with a variable number of concurrent users.

Stress testing provides two scenarios. In the first scenario, the variable factor is the number of users within the bandwidth to check the capacity of the system, keeping other inputs constant. In another scenario, hardware/software resources are varied to stress the system, keeping other inputs constant.

Spike testing deals with the surge in the load for short duration with uncertainty in input business pattern. The uncertainty in the business pattern depends on external factors to the system like sudden change in business, political change affecting the business, or any other unforeseen circumstances.

In endurance testing, load is increased beyond the expectation for a long duration of time, and the SUT is observed for its reliability. Here there is a need to choose the specific business pattern which may impact the performance during the endurance testing.

By adopting the LESS approach, it is easy to understand the performance behavior of the system from different points of view. The inference drawn from such tests will help to verify the availability, stability, and reliability of the system. Table 1.12 provides the inferences drawn from the LESS approach which indicates that LESS ensures complete performance testing.

Figure 1.6. Load vs. spike testing

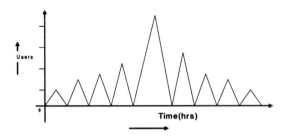

Table 1.9. LESS with ramp up of concurrent users

Types of testing	Number of concurrent users and ramping up	Duration
Load Testing	1 User → 50 Users →100 Users →250 Users →500 Users............. →1000Users	12 Hours
Stress Testing	1 User → 50 Users →100 Users →250 Users →500Users............. →1000Users →Beyond 1000Users........... →Maximum Users	12 Hours
Spike Testing	1 User→ 50Users→ Beyond 1000 Users	12 Hours → 10 Hours → 8 Hours... Hour....Minutes
Endurance Testing	Maximum Users	12 Hours -> .....Longer duration(days)

Although **LESS** provides a comprehensive approach for performance testing, some more additional tests needs to be performed.

Additional testing efforts are required to integrate with PT to enhance user satisfaction and add more value to user requirements. The following section briefly explains configuration testing and scalability testing as additional testing efforts along with a note on contention and security testing.

Configuration Testing

Configuration testing is integrated with PT to identify how the response time and throughput vary as the configuration of infrastructure varies and to determine the reliability and failure rates.

Configuration tests are conducted to determine the impact of adding or modifying resources. This process verifies whether a system works the same, or at least in a similar manner, across different platforms, Database Management Systems (DBMS), Network Operating Systems (NOS), network cards, disk drives, memory and central processing unit (CPU) settings, and execution or running of other applications concurrently.

Table 1.10. Perfomance testing goals of LESS components

Load testing	• Testing for anticipated user base • Verifies whether system is capable of handling load under specified limit
Stress testing	• Testing beyond the anticipated user base, i.e., unreasonable load • Identifies the maximum load a system can handle • Checks whether the system degrades gracefully or crashes suddenly
Spike testing	• Testing for unexpected user base • Verifies stability of the system
Endurance testing	• Testing for stress load for longer duration • Verifies reliability and sustainability of the system

Table 1.11. LESS components and input variations

Types of Testing	Number of Users	Business Pattern	Hardware/Software Resources	Duration	Volume of Data
Load Testing	Constant	Constant	Constant	Constant	Constant
Stress Testing	Variable	Constant	Constant/variable	Constant	Constant
Spike Testing	Variable	Variable	Constant	Variable	Constant
Endurance Testing	Constant	Variable	Constant	Variable	Constant

Table 1.12. Inference from LESS approach

LESS Components	Inference drawn after the test
Load Testing	Whether the Web system is available? If yes, is the available system stable?
Stress Testing	Whether the Web system is available? If yes, is the available system is stable? If Yes, is it moving towards unstable state?
Spike Testing	Whether the Web system is available? If Yes, whether available system is unstable?
Endurance Testing	Whether the Web system is available? If Yes, is the available system is stable? If Yes, is it reliable and sustainable?

Compatibility testing is a term which is used synonymously with configuration testing since compatibility issues are the matter of interest here.

Scalability Testing

Scalability testing integrates very well with PT. The purpose of scalability testing is to determine whether the application automatically scales to meet the growing user load. To illustrate, in a typical practical situation, the Web master may expect a five-fold load increase on the server in the next two years. Using scalability testing will enable the Web master to know whether the existing resources will suffice to maintain the same level of performance or if it is necessary to upgrade the server. Suppose through scalability testing it is revealed that increased gradation is required; then resource planning may be initiated for increasing the CPU frequency or to add more RAM to maintain the same performance with increase in loads as the case may be.

Thus scalability testing enables simulation of the use of resource variables such as the CPU frequency, number and type of servers, and size of available RAM to determine when it becomes necessary to introduce additional servers to handle the increasing load.

Contention testing can also be considered as an additional test which integrates with PT effort. This process deals with evaluating complex problems such as deadlock conditions, concurrency problems at kernel level. Additionally, security testing can also be considered as an additional test along with PT for mission critical Web sites. It is worth noting that the discussion of these two testing efforts is beyond the scope of this book.

Performance Testing Life Cycle

Software Development Life Cycle (SDLC) (see Drake, 2004) is a well known terminology in software engineering wherein we study mainly the different phases of development of software by using different methods/frameworks. Similarly, functional testing life cycle, a subset of SDLC, is also a well proven process and known among testing communities. However, PT Life Cycle (PTLC) is a new term, which is relevant for testing Web-based systems. PTLC is an indispensable part of SDLC. Since performance issues must be addressed at each level of SDLC, there is a need to relook into the SDLC and how performance issues are addressed. This helps in promoting allocation of more time and effort for performance testing.

Performance Testing in Traditional Development Life Cycle

The traditional SDLC defines testing phase as one of its sub activity and the scope is limited. Testing itself is a late activity in SDLC as shown in Figure 1.7. This activity consists of many sub activities. One such activity is system testing which in turn drives the performance testing. Thus PT is isolated as a single phase with in testing as illustrated in Figure 1.7. Like in functional testing, PT is also a late activity and causes many problems. For instance, performance problems in the requirements and design phase may incur outrageous costs. These problems are noticed late; hence a new approach is needed.

Figure 1.7. Scope for performance testing in traditional development life cycle(s)

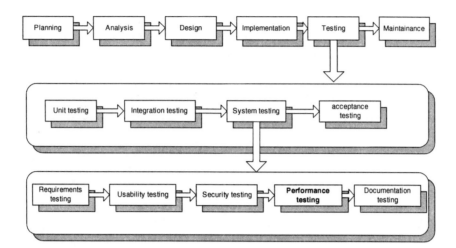

Performance Testing in Modern Development Life Cycle

The traditional SDLC has undergone many changes based on users needs. Most of the users want the system development to be completed with in a short time. Many users expect them to be part of the system development and want to see the system as it evolves. In such cases, PT activity must be initiated along with SDLC and Software Testing Life Cycle (STLC). Figure 1.8 shows the different phases of STLC along with PTLC. A typical PTLC consists of analyzing service level agreement, defining performance requirements, creating test design, building performance test scripts, how these test scripts are executed, and finally the analysis phase. Each phase in SDLC has a component of PTLC. The following chapters in this book elaborate the concept of adopting PT throughout the development life cycle.

Performance Testing vs. Functional Testing

Functionality and performance are two different entities which drive the success of a system. Though both types of testing aim at the same goal of satisfying the requirement, they differ in the objectives, expectations, and method of conducting the test.

Functional testing is conducted to verify the correctness of the operations of the software. The features and functions are tested before performance testing. The purpose is to verify that the internal operations of the product are working according to desired

Figure 1.8. Different phases of STLC and PTLC

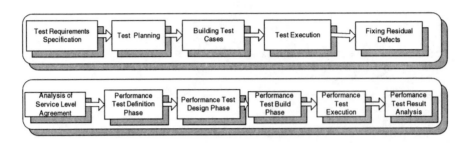

specifications. Functional testing typically tests accuracy of the application and how it behaves with different operating systems. Testing objectives are well defined and straightforward. To illustrate, if an application has a feature to open a file, expected outcome is clear. If the file opens successfully and correctly, it passes the test. If the file does not open correctly, it fails.

PT is relatively complex because the performance of the system itself is subjective. What one user might perceive as slow might be good enough for another user. Unlike the functional testing, PT objectives are quite straightforward and they vary widely depending on business conditions. Software that is functionally correct but is not in compliance to performance requirements is unacceptable to the users. PT is designed to test the overall performance of the system at high load and stress conditions. PT occurs through out the software development life cycle to isolate performance related constraints. Even at unit level, the performance of the individual module may be assessed as the internal logic of software that is being tested.

However, the true performance of the system is identified when the software is fully integrated and ready for production. Performance test requires both hardware and software environment to measure the resource utilization. By capturing the resource utilization statistics, the performance tester can uncover situations that lead to degra-dation and possible system failure.

Performance of a system is generally measured in terms of response time for the user activity. To illustrate, a customer likes to withdraw money from an Automated Teller Machine (ATM) counter of a specific bank. Customer inserts debit/credit card and waits for the response. If the system takes more than 5 minutes (say) to deliver the cash, customer may not appreciate the system. In this situation, though, the system is functioning (delivering cash) according to requirements. It fails in terms of performance (takes more than 5 minutes to complete the transaction).

Which Systems are Vulnerable to Performance Problems?

Both client-server and Web-based applications are vulnerable to performance problems but in varying degrees of intensity. However, the risks involved with a poor performance are too high in the case of Web-based applications.

Client Server Applications

Client-server architectures represent a significant challenge for software testers. The distributed nature of client/server environments, the performance issues associated with transaction processing, the potential presence of a number of different hardware platforms, the complexities of network communication, the need to service multiple clients from a centralized database, and coordination requirements imposed on the server all combine to make testing of client-server architectures and the software that resides within them considerably more difficult than stand alone applications. In fact, recent industry studies indicate a significant increase in testing time and cost when client-server environments are developed.

Web-Based Applications

Web-based applications have evolved from the client-server applications. The client-server concepts are maintained through a Web-client and a Web server. These are software applications which interact with users or other systems using Hyper Text Transfer Protocol (HTTP). For a user, Web client is a browser such as Internet Explorer or Netscape Navigator; for another software application it is an HTTP user agent which acts as an automated browser.

The use of Web applications can range from simple to highly complex tasks. With the advent of e-commerce practice, business enterprises are simplifying the processes and speeding up the transactions using Web as an effective medium. Web-based applications are extensively used for both B2B and B2C e-commerce. The e-commerce technology used for Web applications is developing rapidly. More open system culture is followed and systems are vulnerable to performance problems. Simple applications are being developed with a Common Gateway Interface (CGI) typically running on the Web server itself and often connecting to a database which is again on the same server. Modern Web applications are mounted on complex business logic tiers such as Web server, application server, database server, firewall, router, and switches. Each tier is exposed and vulnerable to performance problems.

Benefits from Performance Testing

PT provides a mechanism to study the behavior of the system. It builds up a confidence to host Web system commercially. Robustness of the system is studied which is useful for maintaining the sustainability of the system. Some of the other benefits are:

- Improved quality from a user's perspective;
- Reduced cost of change;
- Reduced system costs;
- Increased profits;
- Early identification of major application defects and architectural issues;
- Guaranteed customer satisfaction;
- Clarity on resource utilization;
- PT also removes many myths associated with the users and builds confidence.

Constraints of Performance Testing

PT is a complex and time consuming activity. The testing process should start from the requirements collection phase itself. PT requires simulating several hundred concurrent users. This requires automated tools that are expensive. A proper environment like bandwidth, system configuration, and concurrent users hinders in providing adequate performance results. Production environment cannot be simulated as it requires investments. A subdued environment may not produce the relevant results. Skill set to plan and conduct PT is not adequately available. It is a late activity, and duration available for testing is not adequate. However, testing the system for an optimal performance is a challenge and an opportunity.

Summary

The World Wide Web is an irresistible entity when it comes to business and information access in the modern world. All business systems utilize WWW to perform effectively in their own domains of business. A world wide survey shows that business systems are unacceptable if the system is not high performance conscious. Ensuring high performance is the main criteria for Web users to repeatedly use the same site for their business. The performance of any system is attributed to many parameters like response time to a user query, high throughput from the system and availability at all times. To ensure this, each system must undergo performance testing before its deployment. PT could be conducted in many ways such as in load, endurance, stress, and spike testing. All applications must follow their own life cycles like functional testing. If the PT life cycle is followed systematically, one can ensure the performance of the Web site that satisfies the customer.

References

The 8 second rule by submit corner. (2003). Retrieved December 13, 2003, from http://www.submitcorner.com/Guide/Bandwidth/001.shtml

Anwar, K., & Saleem, A. (2004). *Web application stress test & data analysis.* Retrieved November 15, 2004, from http://www.webstar.co.uk/Stress.pdf

Barber, S. (2004). *Identifying the critical failure or bottleneck.* Retrieved November 15, 2004, from http://www-128.ibm.com/developerworks/rational/library/4259.html

Chen, B. (2003). The 30-second rule. *Network World, 7/22/02.* Retrieved December 26, 2003, from http://www.nwfusion.com/columnists/2002/0722chen.html

Drake, T. (2004). *Testing software based systems: The final frontier.* Retrieved December 8, 2004, from http://www.softwaretechnews.com/stn3-3/final-frontier.html

Ecommerce definition. (2003). Retrieved June 20, 2003, from http://www.web-design-uk.biz/ecommerce/ecommerce_definition.htm

Google success. (2003). Retrieved June 14, 2004, from http://news.com.com/Searching+for+Google's+success/2009-1023_3-273704.html

High speed connections. (2003). Retrieved December 13, 2003, fromhttp://www.compar.com/infopool/articles/news1vs14.html

Ho, J. (2003). *Evaluating the World Wide Web: A global study of commercial sites.* Retrieved August 20, 2003, from http://www.ascusc.org/jcmc/vol3/issue1/ho.html

Menascé, D. A. (2003). *Load testing of Web sites.* George Mason University. Retrieved August 17, 2003, from http://cs.gmu.edu/~menasce/papers/IEEE-IC-LoadTesting-July-2002.pdf

Miller, E. (2005). *Website loading and capacity analysis.* Software Research Inc., CA. Retrieved January 5, 2005, from http://www.soft.com/eValid/Technology/White.Papers/wpaper.loading.pdf

Online holiday shopping sites still straining under the load. (2004). Reports Keynote. Retrieved June 14, 2003, from http://www.keynote.com/news_events/releases_2003/03dec10.html

Patton, S. (2004). *The ABCs of B2C.* Retrieved November 16, 2004, from http://www.cio.com/ec/edit/b2cabc.html

Response times: The three important limits. (2003). Retrieved December 10, 2003, fromhttp://www3.sympatico.ca/bkeevil/onlinesig/map.html

Sherman, C. (2004). *Jupiter Media Metrix releases new search specific traffic figures.* Retrieved June 17, 2004, from http://searchenginewatch.com/searchday/article.php/2159341

To be successful, a Web site must be effective. (2003). Retrieved August 20, 2003, from http://www.orion-hitek.com/Tips.htm

Upsdell, C. A. (2003). *Resources: Load times.* Retrieved November 15, 2003, fromhttp://www.upsdell.com/BrowserNews/res_load.htm

Varon, H. (2004). *The ABCs of B2B.* Retrieved November 14, 2004, from http://www.cio.com/research/ec/edit/b2babc.html

Web shops fight fraud. (2004). Retrieved June 14, 2004, from http://www.pcworld.com/news/article/0,aid,113875,00.asp

Zimmerman, C. (2003). *Performance vs. uptime: Sites see need for speed.* Retrieved February 19, 2003, from http://www.internetweek.com/newslead01/lead043001.htm

Zimmerman, C. (2003). *Performance vs. uptime.* Retrieved December 15, 2003, from http://www.varbiz.com/sections/university/web_integration/seminar.jhtml;jsessionid=PHH1EWBL5HLPWQSNDBCSKH0CJUMEKJVN?articleId=18835826&_requestid=409533

Zona Research, Inc. (2003). *The economic impacts of unacceptable Web site download speeds.* Retrieved November 15, 2003, from http://also.co.uk/docs/speed.pdf

Additional Sources

Menasc'e, D., Almeida, V. A. F. (1998). *Capacity planning for Web performance: Metrics, models, & methods.* Prentice Hall.

Pierre, J. M. (n.d.). *On the automated classification of Web sites.* Retrieved June 17, 2004, from http://www.sukidog.com/jpierre/etai.pdf

Towards the measurement of public Web sites: A tool for classification. (n.d.). Retrieved October 17, 2004, from http://www.singstat.gov.sg/conferences/ec/f114.pdf

Ware, S., Tracy, M., Slothouber, L., & Barker, R. (1997). *Professional Web site optimization.* Wrox Press Inc.

Chapter 2

Performance Testing:
Factors that
Impact Performance

It is an accepted fact that no system is perfect from the viewpoint of performance. Problems pertaining to performance affect all types of systems, regardless as to whether they are client/server or Web application systems. It is imperative to understand the factors affecting performance of the system before embarking on the task of tackling them. The constraints affecting the performance may be many but can be broadly classified into (i) technical and (ii) project related factors. The former is very much pronounced in the case of Web-based systems, as the relevant technology has not attained the stage of maturity to address the issues on its own. On the other hand, the project managers struggle to develop an optimal system within the existing technology framework. This in turn, generates many project related factors sub optimizing the performance. Likewise, many factors affecting the performance of the system are discussed in this chapter. The subsequent chapters deal at length with the methods and strategies to tackle these factors.

Project Peculiarities

Management of projects broadly encompasses planning activities during the phases of development and implementation of a system. For instance, the planning at the systems development stage calls for selection of appropriate technology, skill sets, and software.

Defective planning at this stage would have a severe impact on the performance of the final product. The planning stage includes understanding various techniques available for development, skill sets required as well as the use of effective software tools. Therefore, the sooner these peculiarities are understood and addressed, the lesser the possibility of severe performance problems.

Rapid Application Development Approach

The fast changing technology coupled with ever increasing competition had a radical change in the perception of customers toward the product under development. They want to have a feel of the product as it evolves during the development. They would like to be involved in the development phases, and more importantly, they desire to launch the product in the market at an earliest point in time. This, in turn, leads to a pressure on the software development team to reduce the development cycle time for the product. Rapid Application Development (RAD) approach is now increasingly applied for rapid prototyping. Although RAD is based on the typical classic life cycle model of software engineering, its emphasis is more on prototyping and involves iterative design and development phases.

RAD approach follows traditional SDLC steps, but the phases are combined. Since the product has to be released in a tight time interval, thorough involvement of dedicated and well trained developers is required. Some of the issues that need to be addressed in RAD approach, particularly from the angles of performance, are (see Ames, 2005):

- Shorter development time in development may lead to release of low quality product due to lack of concentration on performance.
- Chances of missing information due to the rapid approach may disqualify the performance objectives.
- Inconsistent internal designs like too much of cluttering of objects, sequence of screen navigation (for instance, navigating from one screen to another screen, out of which one screen may be having connections with a database and another screen may contain the presentation of data which is retrieved from the database[filling a combo box, etc.]) may be observed over time, after the product is deployed.
- High possibility of violating coding standards, and unoptimized code may consume too many resources.
- Module reuse for future projects may not be possible due to the project specific design.
- Module may not be flexible for graceful scaling.
- System may collapse for sudden surge in user base.

In RAD, the importance is given to the functionality of the system, rather than to its performance, presumably due to the short development cycle time (see *Software lifecycles*, 2004). There may be instances wherein the product may be released without testing for its performance. In some cases, the projects may be subjected to the testing of performance, but a compromise may be made regarding the methodology to be adopted.

Technical Peculiarities

Technical peculiarities have a severe impact on the overall performance of the system. Choice of technology platform for the product plays an important role in its performance. To illustrate, developing the product on a new and untried technology with the belief that it would boost the performance may lead to other contraindications in terms of other quality attributes such as security, consistency, compatibility, and integrity. As an example, client side scripting is a new technology which can be used to reduce the number of interactions with the server. But the browser level scripting does not ensure total security. This may result in a possibility of exposing sensitive data to malicious access. Likewise, many challenges have to be faced by the development team on the technology front. These are described in the following sections.

Security Threat

Security threats to Web applications can make users worry about online transactions. Their privileged information may be leaked to the outside world. They may lose their credit card information to others and lose money.

While developing Web applications, the major focus is on the functionality rather than on security. If the Web users are able to see a security lapse in the system, then the product loses its market in spite of other interesting features because users no longer trust the Web site. Thus, a significant impact on performance of the site is directly related to the security of the applications. Threats such as SQL injection, cross browser scripting, sniffing can access the valuable, sensitive information of the user. Security and performance are usually at odds with each other. Current implementations of security on the Web have been adopted at the extreme end of the spectrum, where strong cryptographic protocols (see Paulson, 2004) are employed at the expense of performance. The SSL protocol is not only computationally intensive, but it makes Web caching impossible, thus misses out on potential performance gains.

Developer's Negligence on Performance

It is a common practice among many developers not to optimize the code at the development stage. To illustrate, a developer may use more buffer space against a variable in the program than is actually required. This additional reserved space may later impact the performance of the system by denying space for others. Since both optimized and unoptimized code exhibit the same functional behavior, an optimized code is preferred for better performance of the system.

Unoptimized code may utilize scarce system resources such as memory and processor unnecessarily. Such coding practice may lead to severe performance bottlenecks such as memory leaks, array bound errors, inefficient buffering, too many processing cycles, larger number of HTTP transactions, too many file transfers between memory and disk, and so on. These problems are difficult to trace once the code is packaged for deployment.

Complex User Interface

Web users appreciate an elegant, simple user interface. A complex interface would promote a user to abandon the site due to the difficulties in interacting with the site. More complexity also impacts the performance of the site. Only the necessary user identification information should be made mandatory, and all other fields should be optional. Users do not like lengthy, complex interfaces which are irritating to use.

Web Site Contents

In the early days of Internet evolution, Web contents were static information and online traffic was comparatively light. Now, Web contents are dynamic, warranting powerful Web servers and robust techniques to handle data transfer. Database driven Web sites such as e-commerce applications typically display dynamic contents. The visual appearance of the Web page depends on the code executed, which in turn is based on the data stored in the tables. These dynamic Web pages require more processing power that puts stress on the server.

Hyper Text Markup Language (HTML)/Text

Plain HTML/Text (see WHL2004) has negligible impact on the performance of the Web application. Storing them does not require too much space compared to other contents of the site. The organization of the text and the font may have some effect on the quality of the site. Displaying large text pages on Web sites is not good from the user point of

Table 2.0. HTML/Text type contents in a Web page

HTML/Text	
JS	JavaScript
HTML	Hyper text markup language
XML	eXtensible Markup Language
VB Script	Visual Basic Script
CSS	Cascading Style Sheets

Table 2.1. Images that Web page may contain

Images	
JPG/JPEG	Joint Photographic Experts Group
GIF	Graphic Interchange Format
PNG	Portable Network Graphics
BMP	Bitmap

view. Overall, HTML/Text does not impact much on the server resources. Table 2.0 shows the HTML/Text type of contents available in a Web page.

Images

Images (see *Image file formats*, 2004) require more network bandwidth, storage, and CPU power than the text information. Using too many colors in images requires more storage and bandwidth. Inappropriate file formats of images can impair performance. Various performance aware techniques for the storage of images are available which require a proper evaluation for an optimized Web site. Table 2.1 shows the type of images that a Web page may contain.

Multimedia

Multimedia (see Lemay, 2004) components such as audio and video applications embedded in Web pages will have an impact on the performance of the Web site. Sound, bounded with text, takes significantly more time to download than the plain text pages. The type of encoding techniques used to store the audio and video files will have an impact on the quality and the size of the page. Proper selection of encoding techniques depending on the multimedia data can exhibit optimized Web pages. The performance of the multimedia embedded pages depends on the playback applications supported by the browsers. Table 2.2 gives sample multimedia files that a Web page may contain.

Executable Applications

The executable applications embedded in HTML pages, documents present in a Web site, also impact the overall performance of the site. Appropriate storage format and an

Table 2.2. Multimedia files that a Web page may contain

MPG	Moving Pictures Expert Group (MPEG
SWF	Flash Files
AVI	Video files

Table 2.3. Executable files that Web page may contain

PDF	Portable Document Format
XIP	Executable in Place
ZIP	WinZip Compressed files
TAR	Tape Archive

appropriate display format are needed to ensure the quality and size of the pages. Some of the executable files associated with the Web page are shown in Table 2.3.

Client Environment

The environment of the client system has a significant bearing on the performance of the product. Though the contents are stored at the server end, users always closely interact with client systems to get the required information. Clients must be properly configured and connected. They must have required hardware resources with the necessary operating system. Since a designer of Web applications has no control over the client system and its resources, Web applications must work with heterogeneous clients. Thus the client's environment may consist of different browsers, divergent platforms, and different types of security settings, multisize caching, different communication protocols, and different network topology, all having a significant influence on the performance of the product.

Different Browsers and Their Impact

Recent years have witnessed an in break in the number of browsers (see *People use different browsers*, 2004). Unfortunately, a majority of them are not conforming to the WWW standards. Even the population of available standard browsers in the Internet is sizable. The architecture underlying the browser and the security issues to be addressed vary from browser to browser. Due to these constraints, it is a difficult task to develop a Web product which is compatible with all standard browsers. The best example is that of the compatibility problems observed in 2000 by the Web users who have Internet Explorer (IE) and Netscape Navigator as their browsers. Users browsing with Netscape were safe from malicious access whereas users browsing with IE and Netscape installed on their machines were exposed to security threats. This happened due to the privileges granted by Microsoft's IE browser to run a script placed on the Web user's machine by Netscape Communicator. Due to the browser security issues, the number of online transactions drastically decreased on the Internet.

Sometimes problems arising due to usage of multiple browsers may have an impact on performance. The scripts running on one browser may not run on another browser. These browser problems can be eliminated by writing two different pages for the same functionality. Browser redirect script could be used depending on the browser privileges. One more option is to use server scripting to understand the type of browser and display the page accordingly. Incomplete scripts on the browser may impact the performance.

A browser is an important tool to access Web sites and resides on the client machine. As already said, not all the browsers available on the Internet are in conformance with WWW standards. A nonstandard browser may not be compatible for accessing all Web sites. A typical browser could be configured in many ways for optimal performance. Client machines can also be set up with different browsers to simulate the operating environment. A typical testing environment will have clients with multiple browsers. For instance, if the load has to be tested for 2,000 users, then simulation may be made for 1,000 users browsing through IE, 500 users with Netscape Navigator, and balance 500 with Java. Multiple versions could also be simulated. This is required as different versions of the browsers display the screen differently. Not just the browser, client machines can also be set with a mix of hardware and software components. It is difficult to predict the client environment for Web applications. Users of Web applications are unknown and can access from different geographical locations with different hardware and software setups. Therefore setting up an environment with a thorough mix of clients is advisable.

Different Platforms

Configuring clients across different platforms such as Windows 2000, Windows NT, Windows 98, and Linux are needed for a typical test environment. These operating systems contain the TCP/IP stack and the information required to communicate with the Internet. Each operating system implements the stack differently.

Protocol's Impact on Performance

TCP/IP is the basic protocol needed for communicating with the Internet. It is a point to point protocol which allows the client to communicate across the Internet to different types of systems and computers. SMTP (Simple Mail Transfer Protocol) and POP (Post Office Protocol) can be used to send and receive mails in some clients. The rest can be set with IMAP (Internet Mail Access Protocol) for remote mail access activities.

Variants of protocols (see Protocol, 2003) like TCP and HTTP affect performance. Main TCP variants are Reno, NewReno, and Tahoe, which have negligible impact on performance. Throughput of the TCP connection is reduced when maximum segment size of a TCP is increased. This is because the average value of the congestion window of the sender will decrease, which in turn increases the probability of a packet loss. Network traffic can be stopped because of the Initial Congestion Window (ICW) size of a TCP sender. ICW is the amount of the data the sender is allowed to send at the beginning of the connection.

HTTP parameters include parallel or simple connections, persistent connections, and pipelining. An HTTP persistent connection allows the already established connection to stay open beyond a single request response exchange. Persistent connections reduce the need for multiple TCP connections to be set up and separate down, avoiding the high overhead for the typically short Web transaction or downloads. By sending multiple requests on the same persistent connection without waiting for other individual responses from the server, performance bottleneck can be further reduced; this type of connection management by pipelining avoids the roundtrip delay of waiting for each of the responses before sending additional requests. For larger transfers, Selective ACKnowledgment (SACK) could be useful with HTTP 1.1. Web performances are improved and hence reduce page download time by this type of connection management (see Farkas & Huang, 2003).

Server Environment

Server and network setup of a Web-based system plays a major role in performance testing. Since all the applications are hosted in servers and the output of the applications are transferred to the clients via network, these form the heart of the functioning as well as performance of the system.

Servers are the repository of the services which are needed by the clients. These servers can have files, Structured Query Language (SQL) information, objects, data, information about work, and HTTP services. Different types of servers are shown in Table 2.4 designed for specific services. For instance all transaction services execute SQL requests at the server side.

Server environment plays a dominant role in performance. Setting up a proper server environment for PT is as important as in the production site.

Table 2.4. Types of servers and their services

Type of Server	Services
File Server	Provides file sharing services which is requested by client over a network. They are useful for sharing repositories like documents, images and other large data objects.
Database Server	Client passes SQL requests as message to the database server. The results of each SQL command are returned over the network. The code that processes the SQL request and the data reside on the same server.
Transaction Server	Transaction server and the client invoke remote procedures that are residing on the server with SQL database engine. These remote procedures on the server execute a group of SQL statements called transactions. The network exchange consists of a single requests/reply message.
Object Server	The client Server application is written as a set of communicating objects. Client and server communicate by means of objects using Object Request Broker(ORB)
Groupware Server	This addresses the management of semi structured information such as text ,image mail, bulletin
Web Server	The client and server talks using Remote Procedure Call (RPC) like HTTP. This Protocol defines a simple set of commands; parameters are passed as strings, with no provision for typed data.

Server Farm

The ever increasing traffic in the Web and the complexity of Web applications have warranted a need for multiple servers. A *server farm* is a group of networked servers that are housed in one location. A server farm streamlines internal processes by distributing the workload between the individual components of the farm and expedites computing processes by harnessing the power of multiple servers. The farms rely on load balancing software that accomplishes such tasks as tracking demand for processing power from different machines, prioritizing the tasks, and scheduling and rescheduling them depending on priority and demand that users put on the network. When one server in the farm fails, another can step in as a backup.

As the performance of a Web site soars due to the increase in user base, the system architects encounter the need for more servers. They realize that a single server is not sufficient to handle the increasing load. The obvious alternative is to deploy multiple servers or server farms to serve the same content. Thus, identical applications are run on a handful of servers to handle the increasing Web traffic.

However, the need for multiple servers can be due to another issue such as the application becoming too complex to handle with a single server. The limited resources of the single server becomes a bottleneck, and the solution is to either upgrade the server, to introduce a super server, or to introduce a few more servers which can share the increased complexity.

New generation super servers are fully loaded machines with greater processing power and scalability. These include multiprocessors, high speed disk arrays for intensive I/O operations, and fault tolerant features. Multiprocessors improve throughput and application speed of the server. Increasing the number of processors improves the scalability. The use of multiple servers helps in increasing the processing power and also in adding more services to the client.

Load Balancing at Server Farm

A server farm is referred to as a server cluster, computer farm, or ranch. A server farm (see EWP2004) is a group of networked servers that are housed in one location. A server farm streamlines internal processes by distributing the workload between the individual components of the farm and expedites computing processes by harnessing the power of multiple servers. The farms rely on load balancing software that accomplishes such tasks as tracking demand for processing power from different machines, prioritizing the tasks, and scheduling and rescheduling them depending on priority and demand that users put on the network. When one server in the farm fails, another can step in as a backup.

When the load balancer (see Bourke, 2003) receives requests from users, it redirects the requests to the appropriate server. The selection of the server depends on many factors like traffic on the server, capability, and ease of management. Also, with the use of load balancer, the service can be kept up as long as there is at least a single server active in the server farm.

Load balancer is configured to probe the servers at regular intervals to detect and remove the inactive server from server farm and adds the server as soon as the server is up again. Load balancer can be used to detect temporary failures such as network issues, system crashes, server overload, and technical intervention. It removes the faulty server from the server farm and redirects the request to another server hosting the same content.

Performance is a key feature to look for in a load balancer, and significant improvements can be observed by adding a load balancer into the Web architecture. Along with performance, many more benefits could be derived like:

- Availability of Web site is enhanced.
- Improves accessibility to Web site and becomes faster.
- Traffic management is easier.
- Application level routing is possible.
- Content management is made easier.
- System becomes more robust and secured.
- Improves the overall Web server performance.
- Improves the reliability and scalability of the Web-based systems.
- Monitors response time and number of current connections to the specific server.
- Automatic fail over: If a server fails, automatic switch over is easier.
- Fault tolerant pairs can be deployed.

File Transfer Between Servers

Maintaining the same data across multiple servers is an important task. All servers should have identical latest versions of Web pages. To make this happen, Web designers traditionally rely on File Transfer Protocol (FTP) to copy entire files and directories from one server to another. With Web contents becoming more advanced in presentation, extensive use of multimedia files and graphics, transfer of large files is becoming more complex and time consuming. Such transfer of large files via FTP when users are accessing the site will slow down the response time. Also, it consumes a lot of network bandwidth and other network resources resulting in negative impacts on performance.

Location of the Server

Location of the server in the Web architecture also has an impact on the performance of the Web application. The Web server can be connected to LAN or to a subnet, placed inside a firewall. Finally, it has to be balanced between security and performance.

Web Server Connected to LAN

The Internet is directly connected to a corporate Local Area Network (LAN) (see *Local area network*, 2004) through a router which may employ packet filtering capabilities. Here the Web server may be a part of LAN, directly connected to the Internet Service Provider (ISP), which is providing Internet connection as depicted in Figure 2.1.

The architecture is quite simple but not convenient from the performance point of view. The LAN traffic and Web traffic share the same network, and there is a possibility of congestion. The total bandwidth available for the Web server is limited, and if the server is busy, Web traffic will block the entire segment and disturb the corporate activities. This kind of architecture suits less loaded LAN such as implemented in educational organizations.

Web Server Connected to a Subnet

When the server is connected to a subnet (see Cooney, 2004) shown in Figure 2.2, traffic on LAN and the Web are separated. The switch acts as a bridge between subnet and LAN. This architecture shows an improvement compared to the architecture where the server is placed in the corporate LAN. Although the separation of corporate traffic and Web traffic brings a boost in performance, bandwidth is still limited.

Web Server Placed in a LAN Inside a Firewall

When the server is located in the LAN behind a firewall as shown in Figure 2.3, the architecture will have some performance degradation. This degradation results because of the introduction of a layer in the communication path. Also we have a Web server which is a fat server within the LAN. This issue might be negligible and is accepted in lieu of the level of security that the firewall provides to the LAN.

Web Server Placed in a LAN Outside a Firewall

Here we can see considerable improvement in performance on the LAN because the Web server, which is a fat server, resides outside the firewall as shown in Figure 2.4. The traffic is also reduced. But on the other side of the firewall, there will be a security issue which is a major concern.

Renting Server Space

The simplest and least expensive method of obtaining an Internet presence may be renting a space on a server of an ISP. This eliminates the responsibility of hardware and

Figure 2.1. Webserver connected to a LAN

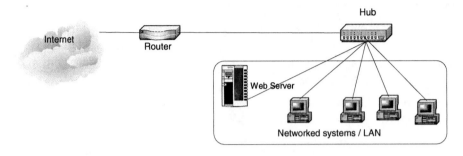

software configuration and maintenance. Renting space is not suitable for dynamic sites since they interact with the corporate database. Renting space on a server at an ISP is a less flexible method and more suitable for Web sites with static content. It is Important to evaluate the capacity of the rental server.

Remote Hosting a Server

Some ISPs allow organizations to physically locate their servers. This is more flexible than renting the space. This technique is more inexpensive than owning a server and suitable to the organization that wants to have more control over the server than is possible with rental space. Hosting a site at a remote server keeps the public traffic separate from LAN traffic. It is important to know that the ISP's Internet connection and LAN should be studied before hosting the server. Configuring remote administration services allows a control on the server hosted from a remote location.

Network Operating Systems (NOS)

Network Operating System (see *Network operating system*, 2004) is middleware which creates a single system image out of different entities in the architecture. NOS makes the network transparent to the users. The types of transparency include location transparency, namespace transparency, logon transparency, replication transparency, local/remote access transparency, distributed time transparency, failure transparency, and administration transparency. This high level of exposure to different types of services introduces a different challenge to performance testing.

Figure 2.2. Webserver connected to subnet

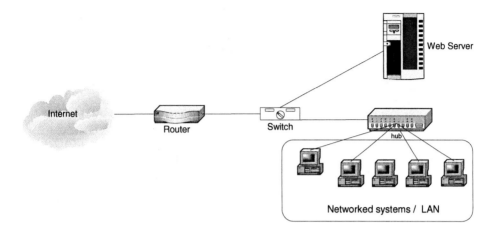

Figure 2.3. Webserver placed in a LAN inside a firewall

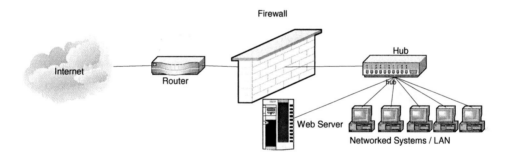

Storage Area Networks (SAN)

SAN is a dedicated network to connect storage related resources. These storage resources are connected to servers which in turn are connected to the network. Implementation of SAN in the Web architecture impacts performance of the system.

These SAN systems may be RAID (Redundant Array of Independent Disks) arrays, tape backups, tape or CD-ROM libraries and are connected by a hub or switch to bus adapters or storage controllers on hosts. A SAN assumes storage processes such as I/O and backups, freeing network bandwidth for applications and thus enhancing network performance.

A Storage Operating System (SOS) allows users to view and share all storage devices without corruption risks. Effective SOS software permits backups and data recovery in

Figure 2.4. Webserver placed outside a firewall

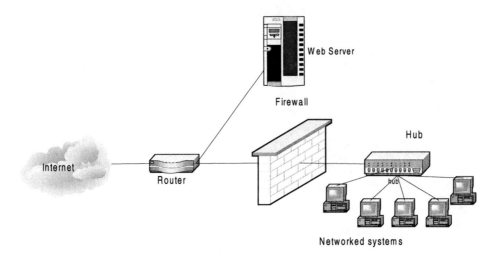

a multiplatform environment and permits storage management via multiple protocols for remote services.

SAN accelerates I/O performance helping to reduce the burden from servers in tiered client server architecture; SAN enables advanced storage management features like high speed remote backup and mirroring. Some of the characteristics of SAN are (see http://www.breocade.com/san/pdf/whitepapers/Architecture.pdf):

- SAN is known for high interconnection data rates.

- Storage limitation is eliminated due to high scalability of SAN.

- Centralized data storage operations make the storage management easier.

- The improper configuring and monitoring can give negative impact on performance of the system.

- SANs provide high bandwidth with zero latency.

- It eliminates I/O bottlenecks from networks.

- It allows all servers in a network to access all storage devices.

- It provides high reliability through the dual port redundancy inherent in optical fiber channel.

- Disk I/O is a limiting factor in Web server performance. Since SAN technology streamlines disk I/O, Web servers become more efficient.

Technology Dependency

The server technology selected to develop the Web pages has a tremendous impact on the performance of the site. Since the server technology mainly interacts with the servers in the architecture, such as Web server, application server, and database server, compatibility of software systems that are used among different servers become major factors affecting performance. To illustrate, in Apache Server, PHP applications run faster than Active Server Pages (ASP) applications. However, ASP based applications run faster in IIS than on any other servers.

Network Environment

Network environment is an indispensable part of Internet and Web systems, without which e-business is a dream. In such situation, it is necessary to analyze the performance of each component constituting the network environment. The following section explains briefly the network components and their respective influence on overall performance of the system. Further, the ISPs and all connection standards will have different levels of influence over the performance.

Internet Service Providers (ISP)

ISP have a major impact on Web performance. Their geographical location, type of networks owned, and speed play a role in assessing their performance. Performance impact on ISPs depends on the following factors:

- Knowing their network topology and how they have been implemented;
- Knowing their external links helps to analyze multiple connections;
- Knowing their routers and redundant equipment;
- Knowing their link speed;
- Knowing their network operations center.

Selecting an ISP with a good backbone network minimizes the number of node hops, which in turn improves performance.

Leased Phone Lines/Dialup

Leased phone lines or dialup connections are most commonly in use by Internet seekers. The bandwidth provided by this connection standard varies depending on the modem capacity. A sophisticated and established telephone network has 64 Kilobits/second (Kbps) of bandwidth whereas other setups have either 28.8 Kbps or 33.6 Kbps throughput modem connection. Dialup connections work on the basis of analog to digital conversion upstream and digital to analog conversion downstream. Both leased analog phone lines and continuously open dialup connections are expensive since users are billed for unacceptable performance too.

Cable Modem

Cable modems (see *What is a cable modem?*, 2004), another type of connection, are better than analog telephone lines. The general speed expected from cable modems is 30 Mbps. If the cable operator is an ISP, the Web user will get greater bandwidth. If the cable operator is not an ISP, then there is a possibility of cross talk and noise problems, which have an impact on performance.

ISDN

The Integrated Services Digital Network (ISDN) (see Becker, 2004) is a digital data transmitting connection standard which propagates with high bandwidth. ISDN uses a standard for transmitting voice, video, and data at the same time over fiber optic telephone lines known as B channels. It is a 64 Kbps channel used for transmitting data. There are two classes in this with an identical bandwidth and distinct number of channels to transfer the data. Basic Rate Interface (BRI) ISDN has two B channels of 64 Kbps whereas Primary Rate Interface (PRI) ISDN has 24 B channels of 64 Kbps. Cost of B channels increases with the number, but performance increases linearly with the increase in number of B channels.

Leased Lines (T1, T3)

The leased lines (see *Leased lines (T1 and T3)*, 2004) are dedicated to carry traffic between two specific points. The T1 leased lines (E1 in Europe) are suitable for organizations needing more bandwidth for short live time. These are based on digital point to point data transfer where cable length is limited to n3 miles. Among the popular leased lines T1/DS1 has a bandwidth of 1.544 Mbps and E1 of 2.048 Mbps. There is also a flexible leased line connection standard referred to as Fractional DS1 which operates with a range of 64 Kbps to 1.544 Mbps bandwidth. High bandwidth lines such as T3/DS3 operate at 44.736 Mbps bandwidth. Though they promise good performance, employing such leased line is an expensive proposition. Thus, the bandwidth definitely impacts performance.

Frame Relay

Frame relay (see Cisco Systems, 2004) is a competitive technology which provides adequate performance for light to heavy Web traffic. The ISPs and the organization that needs the Internet should connect to frame relay network. Once they are connected, a Permanent Virtual Circuit (PVC) is established between frame ISP and organization. Here the Information is broken into small variable sized frames and transmitted over PVC. There is another form of frame relay, which promises better performance than the PVC based connection, that is, Switched Virtual Circuit (SVC). The SVC does not establish a permanent connection between frame ISP and organization; instead it works with a switch which disconnects the circuit when the Internet is not needed. Frame relay networks operate at a bandwidth of 64 kilobits to 536 Megabits/sec. Minimum allocated bandwidth for PVC or SVC is known as committed information rate.

Asynchronous Transfer Mode (ATM)

In recent years, high speed ATM (see Hyper Learning Center, 2004) connections have proven to be cost effective for high traffic Web servers. ATM connection is a packet switched network with a fixed size; small packets called CELLs carry the data. A typical ATM CELL contains 48 bytes of data and 5 bytes of header information. The total fixed size of a CELL is 53 bytes with header containing information about whether the data are sensitive to delay or errors. To illustrate, voice traffic is sensitive to delay but can tolerate errors whereas data traffic is more sensitive to errors than delay. Additionally, the header contains information about network congestion which helps in moderating network traffic. ATM connection standard has data rate ranging from 1.5 Mbps (T1 level) to 622 Mbps (SONET OC 12) and above. It is a fact that high performance switches for ATM traffic eliminate performance loss of store forward devices.

Switched Multimegabit Data Service (SMDS)

SMDS (see Cisco Systems, 2004) is an Internet connection standard wherein variable length frames are physically transmitted over an ATM-like cell layer. This type of connection gives much variety of different bandwidths from 56 Kbps to 34 Mbps. It has been observed that performance is superior over frame relay with a high quality connection link and low retransmission. Unlike frame relay, there is no concept of permanent virtual circuit, and here connections are made and broken according to the requirement.

Web Caching

Caching (see Nottingham, 2004) is the temporary storage of frequently accessed data in higher speed media (typically SRAM or RAM) used for more efficient retrieval. Web caching stores frequently used objects closer to the client through browser, proxy, or server caches. Storing "fresh" objects closer to users avoids round trips to the origin server, reducing bandwidth consumption, server load, and most importantly, latency.

Caching is not just for static sites; even dynamic sites can benefit from caching. Graphics and multimedia typically do not change as frequently as (X)HTML files. Graphics that seldom change, like logos, headers, and navigation bars, can be given longer expiration times while resources that change more frequently, like XHTML and XML files, can be given shorter expiration times. Designing a site with caching in mind targets different classes of resources to give them different expiration times with only a few lines of code.

A Web cache sits between one or more Web servers (also known as origin servers) and a client or many clients, and watches requests received, saving copies of the responses like HTML pages, images, and files (collectively known as representations) for itself. Then, if there is another request received for the same URL, it can use the already stored response in the cache, instead of asking the origin of the server for fresh retrieval.

There are two main reasons Web caches are used: to reduce latency and to reduce network traffic. According to Internet research specialists, one of the common and major performance problems observed by Web users is "slow response time". Further research on the cause of this problem shows that high network traffic has been found to be the culprit. This congestion has been observed more and more in the current graphic and multimedia enriched sites.

Caching is implemented by storing data at three different locations in the following ways:

- User cache or browser caching at client side (see Nottingham, 2004);
- Proxy cache (see Nottingham, 2004) or just a cache at a dedicated server which exists between client and main server;
- Server cache (see Nottingham, 2004) or site caching at server side.

Client Caching

The browser cache works according to fairly simple rules. It will check to make sure that the representations are fresh, usually once a session (that is, once in the current invocation of the browser).

This cache is especially useful when users hit the "back" button or click a link to see a page they have just looked at. Also, if the same navigation images are used throughout the site, they will be served from browser caches almost instantaneously.

Almost all of the browsers support client side caching. Here the client system normally stores the Web pages on a time basis. Recently accessed pages are available in the content of the client cache. This technique may not result in great performance improvement. The overheads observed in client caching are:

- The chances of the user accessing the same pages are quite slim.

- Most of the time, a significant amount of duplicate information is found on the client side.

- Chances of accessing outdated information are always high.

In general, the client may not result in great performance improvement.

Proxy Caching

A dedicated server called "proxy server" is placed in between the client and the main server. Frequently accessed Web pages are stored at the proxy server. When a client requests a page, the proxy server services the request if the requested page is in the cache, or else it forwards the request to the main server. When the page is retrieved from the main server, the proxy server first caches the page and sends the same page to the user.

The overheads due to proxy caching are attributed to:

- Generally proxy is integrated with the firewall. A significant delay can occur due to the presence of a firewall between the client and the proxy server.

- Cache validation and expiration model have to be implemented to get rid of outdated information.

- Many browsers do not allow automatic redirection to the main server if proxy fails.

Compared to client caching, proxy caching improves the performance, but overheads on the server are greater.

Server Caching

To provide fast access to users, many organizations have adopted caching on multiple servers. Server caching is a technique of introducing a fast memory wherein set of library files; such as, HTML documents are stored so that access becomes fast and easy. These files are designed and optimized for fast read and write access, and data are short lived.

Users can retrieve frequently used static pages much faster if they are cached. This allows files to be quickly located in the cache rather than downloading them from memory of the server each time. The same technique can be used for dynamic pages if the request for a particular page displays the same results every time, or the data do not change frequently. Rather than locating and executing the code and reproducing the result in an HTML version, the server can send the page from its cache, which avoids repetitive work and also results in faster access.

Server side caching improves performance by executing only necessary code on the server. The server cache stores the output of frequent dynamic requests. Once the HTML contents are saved in cache, a filter detects frequent requests to the same dynamic page, intercepts the requests, and responds with a cached output, enabling faster access. This caching technique saves performance oriented entities such as bandwidth, server load, page load time, and processing cycles. Caching at the server side helps in:

- Less bandwidth consumption as fewer requests and responses are passed through the network;

- Less server load as the server handles fewer requests;

- Less page load time since pages are accessed from faster cache;

- Less processing cycles because the need for accessing database and applying business logic is eliminated;

- Some server caching techniques are enhanced with page compression which removes blank space inside HTML and enables files to be zipped to a smaller size. Such compressed pages download much faster;

- Incorporating prediction techniques on ability to cache for the server cache can also improve Web accessibility. This technique helps in identifying uncached contents at earlier stages and avoids Web caches from spending a significant amount of time on processing uncacheable contents.

In general, caching is a powerful technique to increase the performance of the system (see King, 2004).

The main server is enabled with a set of cache servers. These cache servers are used to manage frequently accessed data/Web pages. While using server cache, some overheads like load balancing between the servers of a generic host name and chances of outdated information at some server caches need to be addressed.

Apart from the basic caching techniques, a rapid research and improvement (see King, 2004) in caching have been observed in recent years. Once the page resides inside the cache, it loses its security context and compromises any sensitive information stored inside the page. Caching secured sites is a real challenge.

Challenges Ahead

Though this chapter highlighted the various factors that impact performance testing, many challenges need to be addressed during PT. Some of the challenges are:

- Unoptimized Web content leads to poor performance;

- Improper process for software development which suffers in quality of the Web site and hence poor performance;

- Unrealistic deadlines lead to poor design and implementation;

- Slow connections of Web sites lead to network traffic and hence poor response time;

- Imbalanced load on servers affecting the performance;

- Using improper technology leads to poor architecture and response time.

Most of the above topics will be discussed in subsequent chapters.

Summary

Chapter 1 emphasizes the need for performance testing whereas various factors impacting system performance were discussed more elaborately in this chapter. The affective factors differ from client server technology to Internet technology. Since Web systems work on Internet technology, the impact is based on networks, servers, and technology in which the system is subjected to be implemented. However, apart from these, certain peculiarities like project as well technical will impact more on performance. This is because the technology as well as skill sets available have not reached the maturity level for optimized design and implementation. Knowledge on these topics is a must for testers and development teams to implement a high performing system. Conducting performance testing on such a system is a challenge and an opportunity.

References

Ames, A. K. (2005). *A review of coding standards and related*. Retrieved January 15, 2005, from http://www.soe.ucsc.edu/~sasha/proj/codestand.pdf

Becker, R. (2004). *ISDN tutorial*. Retrieved November 11, 2004, from http://www.ralphb.net/ISDN/

Bourke, T. (2003). *It's always the load balancer*. Retrieved March 16, 2003, from http://sysadmin.oreilly.com/news/slb_0301.html

Cisco Systems. (2004). *Frame relay*. Retrieved November 25, 2004, from http://www.cisco.com/univercd/cc/td/doc/cisintwk/ito_doc/frame.htm

Cisco Systems. (2004). *Switched Multimegabit Data Service (SMDS) tutorial*. Retrieved November 17, 2004, from http://www.cisco.com/univercd/cc/td/doc/cisintwk/ito_doc/smds.pdf

Cooney, R. (2004). *Subnet addressing.* Retrieved November 11, 2004, from http://www.nwc.com/unixworld/tutorial/001.html

The essential elements of storage networking. (2004). Architecture. Retrieved November 20, 2004, from http://www.brocade.com/san/pdf/whitepapers/Architecture.pdf

Farkas, K., & Huang, P. (2003). *Impact of TCP variants on HTTP performance.* Retrieved June 13, 2003, from http://www.tik.ee.ethz.ch/~farkas/publications/hot_HSNWKS2002.pdf.

Hyper Learning Center. (2004). *Asynchronous Transfer Mode (ATM) tutorial.* Retrieved September 14, 2004, from http://www.cne.gmu.edu/modules/atm/Texttut.html

HyperText Markup Language (HTML) Home Page. (2004). Retrieved August 20, 2004, from http://www.w3.org/MarkUp/

Image file formats. (2004). Retrieved August 20, 2004, from http://dx.sheridan.com/advisor/file_formats.html

King, A. (2004). *Use server cache control to improve performance.* Retrieved November 25, 2004, from http://www.websiteoptimization.com/speed/tweak/cache/

Leased lines (T1 and T3). (2004). Retrieved December 15, 2004, from http://compnetworking.about.com/cs/t1t3/

Lemay, L. (2004). *Multimedia on the Web.* Retrieved August 21, 2004, from http://www.ucl.ac.uk/calt/vdml/help/mmediaonweb.do

Local area network. (2004). Retrieved December 14, 2004, from http://searchnetworking.techtarget.com/sDefinition/0,,sid7_gci212495,00.html

Network operating system. (2004). Retrieved December 15, 2004, from http://e-comm.webopedia.com/TERM/N/network_operating_system_NOS.html

Nottingham, M. (2004). *Caching tutorial.* Retrieved November 20, 2004, from http://www.mnot.net/cache_docs/

Paulson, L. C. (2004). *The inductive approach to verifying cryptographic protocols.* Retrieved June 11, 2004, from http://www.cl.cam.ac.uk/users/lcp/papers/Auth/jcs.pdf

People use different browsers. (2004). Retrieved September 15, 2004, from http://www.netmechanic.com/browser-photo/tour/BrowserList.htm

Protocol. (2003). Retrieved June 13, 2003, from http://searchnetworking.techtarget.com/sDefinition/0,,sid7_gci212839,00.html

Software lifecycles. (2004). Retrieved June 11, 2004, from http://www2.umassd.edu/CISW3/coursepages/pages/cis311/LectureMat/process/lifecycles/lifecycles.html

What is a cable modem? (2004). Retrieved June 11, 2004, from http://www.cable-modems.org/tutorial/

Wikipedia. (2004). *Server farm.* Retrieved November 17, 2004, from http://en.wikipedia.org/wiki/Server_farm

Additional Sources

Anderson, P., & James, G. (2004). Performance soars, features vary. *Network World*, 1999. Retrieved June 11, 2004, from http://www.nwfusion.com/reviews/0614rev.html

Engalschall, R. S., Ware, M. Tracy, L. Slothouber, & R. Barker (1997). *Website balancing: Practical approaches for distributing HTTP traffic.* Professional Web site Optimization, Wrox Press Inc.

Hall, R. (2002). *Comprehensive analysis of FTSE 100 websites reveals alarming performance assues.* Retrieved June 11, 2004, from http://www.parallel.ltd.uk/documents/ pr_ftse100_sites_020502.pdf

Killelea, P. (2002). *Web performance tuning.* O'Reilly and Associates.

Load balancing. (n.d.). Retrieved December 15, 2003, from http://www.webopedia.com/TERM/L/load_balancing.html

Menansce, D. A., & Almeida, V. A. F. (1998). Capacity planning for Web performance: Metrics, models, and methods.

Mills, W. N., Krueger III, L., Chiu, W., Halim, N., Hellerstein, J. L., & Squillante, M. S. (2001). *Metrics for W.N. Serdar Yegulalp.* Website Stress-Testing.

Mulzer, M. (2001). *Using server-side caching to increase Web site performance and scalability.*

Performance tuning of Web-based applications. (2004). Retrieved November 20, 2004, from http:// www.research.ibm.com/PM/cmg2kmetric.doc

Sarangi, A., & Agarwal, R. (2003). *Capacity planning for testing Web sites.* Retrieved August 12, 2003, from http://www.softwaredioxide.com/Channels/events/testing2001/Proceedings/ajit_infosys.pdf

WWW standards. (n.d.). Retrieved July 12, 2004, from http://www.w3.org/

Chapter 3

Performance Testing:
Reference Technology
and Languages

Performance testing (PT) is not to be construed as features testing even though it has a definite link with the latter. In fact, PT begins from where the feature testing ends. It presupposes successful completion of features testing, meaning that all the desired functional requirements expected from the system are fully met. However, it is worth noting that conducting PT without features testing is often fraught with great difficulties. This is because the residual defects in the system, which otherwise would have been known in features testing, would give misleading results about the performance. Previous chapters emphasized the need for PT and various factors that have impact the performance of Web-based applications. This chapter provides an insight about the technology aspects, including the software languages, necessary for Web development. Needless to add, that technology as well as software languages have a critical impact on the performance of the system.

Client Server and
Web-Based Technology

The evolution of networking in recent decades has set an interesting challenge for the growth of software science. This evolution is the result of fomenting many new as well as radical ideas over a period of time and manifesting them into invention of new technologies. The ensuing section emphasizes the evolution of Web-based technology as a successor to client-server technology.

Client Server Technology

Client server technology (see *Client/server software architectures – An overview*, 2004) is the combination of two simple but distinct processes, that is, client and server process as shown in Figure 3.1. It works on the principle of the request-response mechanism wherein the client process requests a specific service from the server and the server process responds to the client by servicing the request. Client programs usually manage the user interface of the application. The client also manages the local resources such as the monitor, keyboard, workstation, and CPU. A significant volume of processing is done locally at the client side. A server fulfills the client's request by performing the desired task. Such tasks include database retrieval and updates, servicing file requests, managing data integrity, and sending responses to client requests. The server process may run on another machine on the network.

In a broader vision, a server process acts as a software engine that manages shared resources such as databases, printers, modems, or high-powered processors. Client and server have fundamentally different requirements for computing resources such as processor speeds, memory, disk speeds and capacities, and input/output devices.

In such an environment, the performance of the overall system is the function of the performance of both client and server processes. Testing the performance of the system calls for testing not only the client and server but also the network connecting both the entities. The hardware platform and operating system of a client and server are not usually the same. Generally, their environment is heterogeneous and multivendor based. Client and server processes communicate through a well-defined set of standard application program interfaces (APIs) and Remote Procedure Calls (RPCs) (see Marshall, 2004), which enable smooth and interoperable data transfer.

Figure 3.1. Simple client-server technology

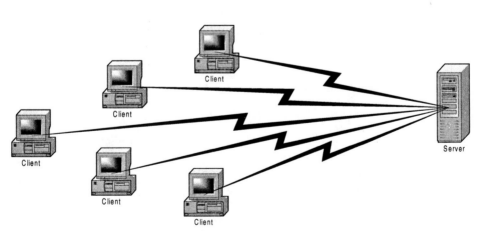

An important characteristic of a client-server system is scalability, and it provides for horizontal as well as vertical scaling. Horizontal scaling means adding or removing client workstations from the network. Vertical scaling means migrating to a larger and faster server machine or multiservers. Horizontal scaling has less impact on performance than vertical scaling.

Following are the typical servers employed in the architecture to serve specified clients.

- **File Servers:** A repository of documents, images, engineering drawings and other large data objects. With a file server, the client sends requests for files or file records over a network to the file server. This form of data service requires large bandwidth.

- **Database Servers:** In database servers, clients send requests created by Structured Query Language (SQL) as messages to the server, and the results of the query are returned over the network. The SQL instructions are processed at the server level as the data are also available. Only the results are transferred to the client.

- **Transaction Servers:** In transaction servers, clients invoke remote procedures that reside on servers which may also contain an SQL database engine. The applications based on transaction servers are called Online Transaction Processing (OLTP) and tend to be mission-critical applications with response time of one to three seconds and require tight controls over the security and integrity of the database.

- **Groupware Servers:** A server containing facilities to manage semi-structured information such as text, images, mail, bulletin boards, and the flow of work.

- **Object Servers:** A server for which the client-server applications are written as different sets of communication objects, thereby client objects communicate with server objects using an Object Request Broker (ORB) (CORBA® BASICS, 2003).

- **IRC Servers:** An option for those seeking real-time discussion capabilities, Internet Relay Chat (IRC) consists of various separate networks (or "nets") of servers that allow users to connect to each other through an IRC network.

- **Proxy Servers:** Proxy server is placed between a client program (typically a Web browser) and an external server (typically another server on the Web) to filter requests, improve performance, and share connections in Web-based technology.

Web-based technology is an extension of client-server technology. This is similar to client-server technology and based on a request-response mechanism between clients and servers as shown in Figure 3.2.

Client machines employ browser interfaces such as Netscape Navigator or Internet Explorer to facilitate users to interact with servers. They also contain the presentation components like HTML pages. Clients manage local resources like monitor, keyboard, workstation, and CPU. It is not mandatory that all the client machines should have the same hardware environment.

Figure 3.2. Clients and servers in Web technology

Typical Web architecture involves Web Server, Application Server, and Database Server. All these servers could be employed in a single machine or established in different machines. There could be a presence of load balancer to distribute and balance the incoming load for Web servers.

Web servers act as interfaces between client and application servers. They understand customer usage patterns, build communities among members, and control access to application content and user information. The popular Web servers are Apache Tomcat Server (see Tomcat site, 2004) and Microsoft Internet Information Server (IIS) (see *Internet Information Services*, 2004).

The application server acts as an interface between the Web server and the database server. The server side executables run at the application server. The popular application servers are Oracle 9*i* Application Server, BEA's Web Logic, and IBM's WebSphere (see Application Server Matrix, 2004).

Database servers provide storage space for all Web applications. Stand alone queries can run these database servers which help in maintaining the data properly. The popular databases are DB2 (see *DB2 product family*, 2004), Oracle (see Oracle, 2003), Sybase (see Sybase, 2003), and SQL Server (see *SQL Server*, 2004).

Difference Between Wired Client Server Technology and Web Technology

Web is a relatively advanced and complex technology compared to wired client-server technology. So there is a significant difference between testing wired client-server and Web applications. Automated testing of wired client-server as well as Web applications is both an opportunity and a challenge.

In wired client-server applications, design uncertainties are greater: architecture is specific and customized; client is fixed; design must be client specific; drivers are custom specific. In Web applications, uncertainties are greater at run time: clients are unknown; client can use any browser or platform.

In wired client-server applications, both the client and the server are the critical items for testing. Fine-tuning needs to be done at both ends, even though network is not an issue,

Table 3.0. Difference between client-server and Web technology

Wired Client–Server Technology	Web-Based Technology
Number of clients is predictable or known (normally less than 100 clients)	Number of clients is difficult to predict (millions of clients)
Client and server are the entities to be tested	Client, server, and network are the entities to be tested
Both server and client locations are fixed and known to the user	Server location is certain; client locations are uncertain
Designed and implemented on intranet environment	Designed and implemented for Internet environment
Server-to-server interaction is prohibited	Server-to-server interaction is normal
Low multimedia type of data transaction	Rich multimedia type of data transaction

as it is an intranet environment. In the case of Web-based applications, the network (Internet, routers, ISPs, etc.) is also to be tuned along with the server. Server side tuning is more complex, as multiple types of servers are involved (Web server, application servers, etc.). Each server exhibits its own properties Table 3.0 provides the major differences between the two technologies.

Both technologies are used for e-commerce applications based on customer requirements.

Web Server and Application Server

Today's business environment demands Web and e-commerce applications that accelerate entry into new markets, help find new ways to reach and retain customers, and allow the introduction of new products and services quickly. To build and deploy these new solutions, we need a proven, reliable e-commerce platform that can connect and empower all types of users while integrating corporate data, mainframe applications, and other enterprise applications in a powerful, flexible, end-to-end e-commerce solution. The solution must provide the performance, scalability, and high availability needed to handle the most critical enterprise applications. A good Web and application server environment provides suitable solutions.

Web Server

A Web server is a server that serves pages for viewing in a Web browser. A Web server typically communicates through HTTP protocol. When the Web server receives an HTTP request, the server responds by sending back an HTML page. When a request comes to the Web server, the Web server simply passes the request to the concerned program. The Web servers do not provide any functionality beyond simply providing an environment in which the server side program can execute and pass back the generated responses.

The server side programs usually provide functions such as transaction processing, database connectivity, and messaging. To process a request, a Web server may respond with a static HTML page or image, send a redirect, or delegate the dynamic response generation to some other program such as Common Gateway Interface (CGI) scripts, Java Server Pages (JSP), Servlets, ASPs (Active Server Pages), or some other server side technology. Such server side programs generate a response, most often in HTML, for viewing in a Web browser.

While a Web server may not support transactions or database connection pooling, it may employ various strategies for fault tolerance and scalability such as load balancing, caching, and clustering features often present in application servers. Most of the servers provide these functions.

Microsoft Internet Information Server (IIS)

MS IIS for Windows is designed for users developing a Web service. IIS replaces the former default Web service, the MS Personal Web Service (PWS), on home and professional versions of Windows (see Information Server Overview and Architecture, 2005). IIS runs in Windows XP, Windows Server OS like Microsoft Windows NT, and Microsoft Windows 2000 series.

As there is an explosive growth of the Internet and an increasing interest in the usage of TCP/IP based information protocols. The software components of IIS are mostly contained in the Application Layer of TCP/IP. The Inetinfo.exe process is the main IIS process; all of the other Internet processes run inside the memory allocated by this process by default. However, it is possible to separate processes from the Inetinfo.exe memory space via the Internet Service Manager as show in Figure 3.3.

Infocomm.dll and Isatq.dll run inside the Inetinfo.exe space and provide many essential services for all the Internet server processes. For example, Infocom.dll provides security, SSL authentication, and caching services. The Isatq.dll (Internet Server Asynchronous Thread Queue Dynamic Link Library) provides TCP port monitoring, bandwidth throttling, and thread queue management services for the Internet server.

Several other services run inside the memory space of the Inetinfo.exe process. They are HTTP, SMTP, NNTP, and FTP services. In addition, the Internet server administration (Isadmin) process runs in the application layer, providing an interface for the administration of the Internet services. Isadmin includes the Distributed Component Object Model (DCOM) facility for the metabase, which allows remote management of the Internet server via command-line scripts.

Internet Server Application Programming Interface (ISAPI) extensions, ISAPI filters, and Common Gateway Interface (CGI) scripts run via the Web (HTTP) service. ISAPI and CGI scripts provide services (and a scripting interface) to animate and automate Web pages. In addition, these scripts can implement additional security measures for the Web server or individual Web pages. We cover scripts in greater detail in later sections.

The interface to the rest of the TCP/IP stack is the Windows Sockets Layer, which is a programming interface separating the protocol from the Internet server applications. Just below the Windows Sockets is the Transport Layer. Inside the Transport Layer is TCP,

Figure 3.3. IIS architecture

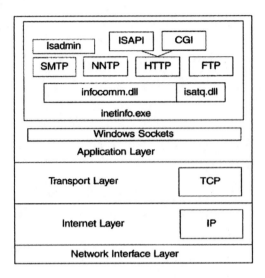

which provides reliable data transmission services for the Internet server. All IIS 4.0 applications send their communications over TCP. The Internet Layer houses the IP, which provides the addressing scheme for communications on the Internet or the internal network. The bottom layer of TCP/IP is the Network Interface Layer, which includes both the hardware and software responsible for transmitting the data to the wire or electronic transfer medium.

For more information on IIS, see http://microsoft.com/iis.

Apache Web Server

In the early days of the Web, the National Center for Super Computing Applications (NCSA) created a Web server that became the number one Web server in early 1995. However, the primary developer of the NCSA Web server left NCSA about the same time, and the server project began to stall. In the meantime, people who were using the NCSA Web server began to exchange their own patches for the server and soon realized that a forum to manage the patches was necessary. The Apache Group was born. The group used the NCSA Web server code and gave birth to a new Web server called Apache. Originally derived from the core code of the NCSA Web server and a bunch of patches, the Apache server is now the talk of the Web server community (see *Apache: The number one Web server*, 2005).

Some of the Apache features are:

- Apache not only runs on most flavors of Unix, but it also runs on Windows 2000/ NT/9x and many other desktop and server-class operating systems such as Amiga OS 3.x and OS/2;

- Support for the latest HTTP 1.1 protocol;

- Support for CGI (Common Gateway Interface);

- Support for HTTP authentication;

- Support for PHP scripting;

- Java Servlet support;

- Integrated Proxy server;

- Support for Server-Side Includes (SSI);

- Support for Secured Socket Layer (SSL).

For more information, see http://apache.org.

These Web servers are popular and provide optimal solutions for Web-based application development.

Application Server

While a Web server mainly deals with sending HTML for display in a Web browser, an application server provides access to business logic by client application programs.

Application servers provide the platforms for the execution of transactional, server-side applications in the online world. They are the modern cousins of traditional Transaction Processing Monitors (TPMs) like CICS. Application servers play a central role in enabling electronic commerce in the Web context. They are built on the basis of more standardized protocols and APIs than were the traditional TPMs. The emergence of Java, XML, and OMG standards has played a significant role in this regard. One of the most important features of application servers is their ability to integrate the modern application environments with legacy data sources like IMS, CICS, VSAM, and so forth. They provide a number of connectors for this purpose, typically using asynchronous transactional messaging technologies like MQ Series and JMS. Traditional TPM-style requirements for industrial strength features like scalability, availability, reliability, and high performance are equally important for application servers also. Security and authentication issues are additional important requirements in the web context. Application servers support DBMS not only as storage engines for user data but also as repositories for tracking their own state.

An application server (see Application Server Matrix, 2004) exposes business logic to client applications through various protocols, possibly including HTTP. The application program in turn uses this logic in the same way, as it would call a method or a function. This function does not say anything about display or how the client must use the information. Such application server clients can include GUIs (Graphical User Interface) running on a PC, a Web server, or even other application servers. The information traveling back and forth between an application server and its client is not restricted to simple display markup. Instead, the information could be any program logic. Since the logic takes the form of data and method calls and not static HTML, the client can employ the exposed business logic.

In most cases, the server exposes this business logic through a component Application Program Interface (API), such as the Enterprise Java Bean (EJB) component model found on J2EE (Java 2 Enterprise Edition) application servers. Moreover, the application server manages its own resources. Such gate-keeping duties include security, transaction processing, and resource pooling and messaging. Like a Web server, an application server may also employ various scalability and fault-tolerance techniques. Some of the popular application servers are:

Web Logic Application Server (BEA)

Web Logic from BEA (see BEA Weblogic platform, 2004) works at the middle tier with client tier at front end and supported with DBMS, enterprise application, and mainframe applications as backend tier. The client tier is supported with Web browser, java client, and so on. Web logic is an industry leading e-commerce transaction platform. It allows the practitioners to quickly develop and deploy reliable, secure, scalable, and manage-able applications. It manages system level details so that application developer can concentrate on business logic and presentation.

WebSphere® Application Server

WebSphere® Application Server from IBM (see IBM WebSphere, 2004) is the industry's premier Java™ based application platform, integrating enterprise data and transactions for the dynamic e-business world. Each configuration (version V6.0 and above) available delivers a rich application deployment environment with application services that provide enhanced capabilities for transaction management as well as the security, performance, availability, connectivity, and scalability expected from the WebSphere family of products.

It provides full J2EE V1.4 compatibility as well as Web services support. It also provides rapid development and deployment features that reduce development cycle time and maximize the ability to use existing skills and resources.

Oracle9i Application Server

Oracle9i Application Server (see Oracle Application Server, 2004) makes it easy to consolidate multiple Web sites and applications into portals. It provides performance enhancing caching technology for turbo-charging Web sites. There are two types of caching in the new application server namely:

- **Web Caching:** Web caching allows site managers to store frequently accessed static and dynamic pages in a buffer in front of the application server, reducing response times. It also provides load-balancing and a patent-pending surge-protection feature to ensure reliability and performance during peak site activity.

- **Database Caching:** Database caching replicates frequently accessed tables from the back-end database to a relational cache in Oracle9i application servers' middle tier, reducing access times. If the Web cache does not have the requested information, it can quickly access it from the database cache without contacting the original database.

Oracle9i application server supports wireless access to Web applications. It provides business intelligence to Web sites and application servers for more efficient resource management. Oracle9i application server supports application and business process integration using the Oracle Integration Server, which supports a JDBC interface, Java Messaging Services (JMS), and workflow automation. It also provides access to legacy applications. It includes Oracle Forms Server for developing and deploying forms-based back-office applications. The Oracle Mod PL/SQL Cartridge lets developers run existing Oracle PL/SQL applications without modification. And for simplified file management, Oracle9iAS's Internet File System provides a unified file system across diverse server hardware and operating systems. It also supports Real Application Clusters and Cache Fusion Technology.

Sun ONE Application Server

The Sun ONE Application Server from Sun Microsystems (see Sun ONE Application Framework, 2004) provides a robust, J2EE technology-based platform for the development, deployment, and management of e-commerce application services to a broad range of servers, clients, and devices. The Sun ONE Application Server is compliant with J2EE 1.3 technology. Scalability (horizontal and vertical), high availability, reliability, performance, and standards compliance are the key goals of this architecture. Because it combines existing Sun ONE products and technologies with the J2EE 1.3 Reference Implementation (J2EE 1.3 RI), the Sun ONE Application Server architecture is built upon proven technologies.

Orion Application Server

Orion Application Server from Evermind (see Orion Application Server, 2005), in the current version 1.2.9, supports parts of the future EJB2 standard, including Message Driven Beans. The Orion application server comes with its own Web server, but it can also be persuaded to work with Apache. It is free for development and noncommercial use.

Many application servers have built-in features of Web servers. Such servers exhibit features of both application and Web servers. While application servers contain Web server functionality, developers rarely deploy separate application servers. Instead, when needed, they often deploy stand-alone Web servers along with application servers. Such a separation of functionality aids performance because simple Web requests have no impact on application server performance.

Evolution of Multi-Tier Architecture

Multi-tiered architecture (Smith, 2004) involves client-server technology. There are several architectures involved with a client-server technology such as two-tier and three-tier architectures. However, there are some legacy systems which still run on single-tier architecture.

A multi-tiered architecture is one where the functionality of the application is spread across multiple layers or tiers, each typically executing in its own server.

Multi-tier architecture breaks applications into various layers such as:

- User Interface which bridges the communication between the user and the application;
- Business Layer associated with all business rules necessary to run the application;
- Data layer addresses the data required for managing business transaction;
- Stored Procedures provide efficient mechanism to speed up the application;
- Data Services help to streamline the data which will be used for business;
- Message Queues formalize the message before getting processed.

These layers help to run the applications efficiently.

Single-Tier Architecture

Typical single-tier architecture of the client-server technology is shown in Figure 3.4. In the legacy single-tier architecture, applications run on a single layer; that is, the user interface, business rules, and database are maintained and executed together at a single server. Here, a single machine is designed to take two logical roles: server and client.

An example could be the Oracle® configuration where users at dumb terminals interact with the SQL*Plus (see SQL *Plus Quick Reference, 2003) command line interface. In this example, the application is coded in PL/SQL, and all of the application resides together in the Oracle RDBMS.

Figure 3.4. Single-tier architecture

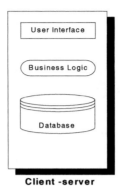

Client -server

Figure 3.5. Two-tier architecture

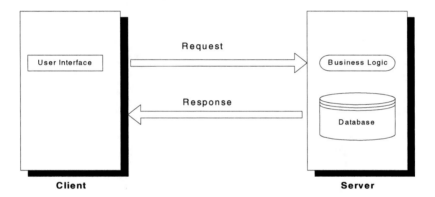

Two-Tier Architecture

Two-tier architecture of the client-server technology is modeled as shown in Figure 3.5 where UI is separated. In this architecture, both business logic and database systems are at server end. Client makes a request for a service such as file transfer or transaction processing. Server lookup for the service requested processes the requests and responds back to the client. This type of architecture burdens the server.

Two-tier architecture is normally adopted for a system with a low user base, typically used in small environments (less than 50 users). A common approach in the client-server environment is to prototype the application in a small, two-tier environment, and then scale up by simply adding more users to the server. This approach will usually result in an ineffective application system, due to the overloading of the server. To properly scale up to hundreds or thousands of users, it is usually necessary to move to three-tier architecture.

Figure 3.6. Three-tier architecture

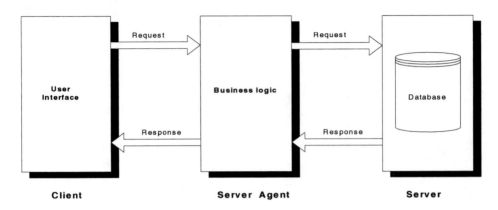

First generation client-server systems were on two-tier architectures. In this architecture, the client using a Personal Computer (PC) or a workstation interacts with the RDBMS through a client program. Similarly, many first generation Web-based systems were also two-tiered. Here also, the Web server connects to an RDBMS, and the code on the Web server executes queries, updates, and database manipulation functions with RDBMS.

Three-Tier Architecture

Three-tier architecture isolates server from processing the business logic as shown in Figure 3.6. Business logic is present at server agent. A server agent acts like a server as well as a client and interacts both with the client and server. A middleware situated between client and server. Server manages the database system.

The role of server agent is many and varied. Some of its important functions are:

- Providing translation services (as in adapting a legacy application on a mainframe to a client-server environment);

- Metering services (acting as a transaction monitor to limit the number of simultaneous requests to a given server); and

- Providing intelligent agent services (mapping a request to a number of different servers, collating the results, and returning a single response to the client).

Finally, large scale Web sites and internal applications are moving to a three-tiered architecture. In this architecture, the Web server or client program makes requests to a server that executes the application logic (often referred to as "business logic"). The

Figure 3.7. Web-based thin client

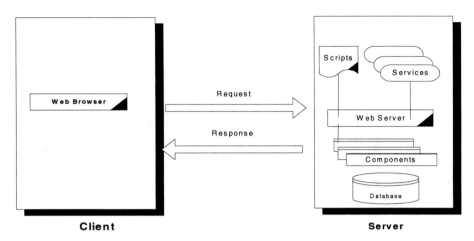

intermediate server executes operations like queries, inserts, deletes associated with the database. Using an application server allows a developer to concentrate on the "business logic" rather than all of the housekeeping details involved in that intermediate server.

Web-Based Thin Client

This architecture is very similar to the two-tier architecture of client-server technology. The basic Web architecture shown in Figure 3.7 is characterized by a Web client that displays information content and a Web server that transfers information to the client. Here all the processing is carried out at server end, and a thin client application performs data presentation task for the user over an HTTP connection via a universal interface: the Web browser.

The application itself resides and is executed on a Web server. The application code contains all the business logic including any code used to access databases. Hence, a Web-based thin client application works without having to install any new software on a client machine.

Web-Based Thick Client

This model is an extended version of the thin client model where clients were exempted from processing any task. However, in this model, processing can be done locally on the client with scripts (Jscript and/or VB Script) to relieve the server of the most mundane tasks such as data validation and to avoid wasting bandwidth. In Figure 3.8, both client and server support scripts, which help to distribute the execution of components. Client processing should only occur after verifying that the client indeed has the capability to perform such tasks.

Three-Tiered Web-Based System

This basic Web architecture is fast evolving to serve a wider variety of needs beyond static document access and browsing. The Common Gateway Interface (CGI) extends the architecture to three tiers (http://www2003.org/cdrom/papers/poster/p274/p274-iijima.html) by adding a back-end server that provides services to the Web server on behalf of the Web client, permitting dynamic composition of Web pages. It may be seen in Figure 3.9, that the business logic is processed separately whereas data required for business processing are stored independently. This data are accessed through database connectivity drivers like Java Database Connectivity (JDBC) in case of Java technology or Open Database Connectivity (ODBC) in case of Microsoft technologies.

Advantages of Multi-Tier Architecture

The multi-tiered approach has several advantages. To begin with, the client application is smaller. This is due to the fact that most of the application resides on the application server. Secondly, because the application is located on the server, code changes can be made once on the server side rather than several times on the client's side. Thirdly, it provides better database security since the client does not directly communicate with the database.

Scalability

In a single-tiered application, RDBMS server processes the business logic. The server memory or the capacity needs an increase with the growing complexity of the application logic, even if the number of actual database operations does not grow. In a two-tiered application, more of the processing can, no doubt, be pushed out to the client machines but they have no facility to share the information. Also updating the Software on all the client machines is a difficult and tedious task.

Separation of Functionality

The three-tiered model allows the data access logic (talking to the database) to be distinct from the business logic. The presentation logic, which interacts with the user, is also independent of the first two functions. This allows for splitting the project across multiple groups. Thus, proper separation of functions will enable reducing the risk of making changes to the code. In a one- or two-tiered application, changing the "presentation logic" (the part that formats data for the user and interacts with the user) runs the risk of breaking the core components because the presentation logic and the application logic are interwoven. This is obviated in the three-tier system.

Figure 3.8. Web-based thick client

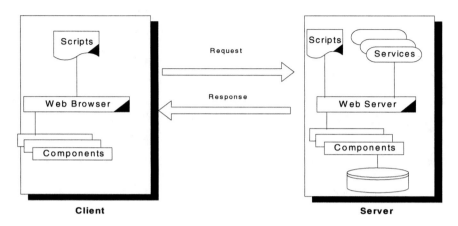

Figure 3.9. Three-tier Web architecture

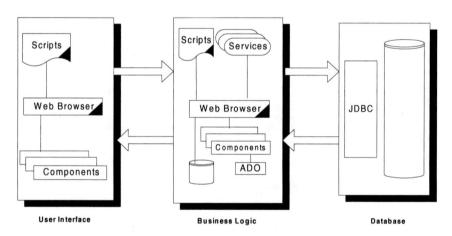

Security

From the angles of security, it is not advisable to connect the Web server directly to the database. Placing an application logic server in between them adds a security dimension to the architecture. Designing an API to the application logic properly (narrow range of functions, without passing SQL code through the API) and placing each tier onto its own network separated by firewalls ensures an architecture protecting layers from invalid access.

Flexibility

It is possible to develop multiple clients for the application logic. One could be a GUI interface for internal users, another the Web-based interface, and a third could be applications that do automated tasks. Having multiple interfaces establishes more independent functioning of the system.

Lower Development and Maintenance Costs

Building three-tier applications reduces the overall costs, as it enables reuse of components from one application to another. As business rules are scripted and stored separately within frequent updating resulting in lower incidence of maintenance cost.

Better Quality and Reusability

As the discreet units form the basic building blocks of a three-tier system, it is easy to test the individual components. In addition, the architecture of this system provides for reusability of the objects, thereby enhancing its applicability.

Scripting Languages for Web-Based Applications

There are many scripting languages available for Web applications akin to procedural languages available for development of software. Needless to add, the ineffective use of these languages have a profound impact on the performance of the systems.

Basic Web Page Development Languages

World Wide Web Consortium (W3C) is an organization with a mandate to set standards for Web development. W3C recommends Hyper Text Markup Language (HTML), Extensible Markup Language (XML), Extensible Hypertext Markup Language (XHTML), and Cascading Style Sheets (CSS) languages for Web page development. However, these languages are not standardized by the browsers.

Hyper Text Markup Language (HTML)

HTML (see HyperText Markup Language (HTML), 2004) is a Web page development language which mainly focuses on how the data look and how they should be displayed in a browser. An HTML file is a text file containing small markup tags which tell the browser how to display the page. An HTML file must have an htm or html file extension and can be created using a simple text editor.

Extensible Markup Language (XML)

XML (see Extensible Markup Language (XML), 2004) is another Web page development language which focuses on what the data are and deals with the description of the data. This language is much like HTML, but not a replacement for HTML. XML can be integrated with HTML for developing quality Web pages. XML was designed to describe data, and XML tags are not predefined. It allows users to define their own tags. XML uses a Document Type Definition (DTD) or an XML Schema to describe the data, and the data are designed to be self descriptive.

Extensible Hypertext Markup Language (XHTML)

XHTML (see XHTML™2.0 W3C, 2004) is a reformulation of HTML in XML. XHTML is a replacement for HTML and is almost identical to HTML 4.01. This language is a stricter and cleaner version of HTML. XHTML is HTML defined as an XML application.

Cascading Style Sheets (CSS)

CSS (see Cascading Style Sheets, 2004) defines how to display HTML elements, and this information is normally stored in Style Sheets. Styles were added to HTML 4.0 and above to solve a problem of layout and display pattern of the data. External Style Sheets can save a lot of work, and these are stored in CSS files. Multiple style definitions will cascade into one for effective presentation of Web information.

Python

Python (see *What is Python?*, 2004) is a Web page development language which comes with a standard library which handles protocols such as HTTP, FTP, SMTP, XML RPC, POP, IMAP, CGI Programming, and operating interfaces such as system calls, TCP/IP sockets, file systems. Python is an interpreted language, which can save considerable time during program development as it demands no compilation and linking procedures.

Virtual Reality Modeling Language (VRML)

VRML (see *VRML History – Introduction*, 2004) is another Web page development language which focuses on describing and displaying three dimensional (3D) pictures. This language is quite helpful to design 3D pictures and provides easy navigation for the user through the browser. VRML pages can be displayed on a special VRML browser which is a plugin for Netscape Navigator and Internet Explorer.

Common Gateway Interface (CGI)

CGI (see *Common gateway interface an overview*, 2004) applications are server executed programs used to dynamically create HTML documents. Many World Wide Web sites use CGI applications for dynamic Web page creation, for parsing forms, and for providing a Web-based interface to other applications, such as databases. Application of CGI calls for addressing many issues like:

- Languages used to create the CGI applications;
- Whether the applications should be compiled or interpreted;
- The performance of the CGI applications and their impact on the server;
- The portability of the applications, should a new server or operating system be chosen for the site.

Writing the Web pages according to Web standards will improve the quality of the Web site. Some of the best practices followed are:

- Using XHTML for Web page development allows cleaner presentation of the information and flexible developing environment.
- Using cascading style sheets, all the information about the style of Web contents can be stored in a single file. Using CSS will improve the quality of the Web site and reduce development cost.
- Using Web validator will check the Web page against Web standard. The validator will throw errors if any nonstandardized information or the style is used in Web pages. Validating the Web page before publishing is always better from a performance point of view.
- Using Web Accessibility Initiative (WAI) guidelines of W3C, the quality of the Web site can be improved and can make the information available to a greater number of users.

CGI applications are critical and must be quality conscious.

Client Side Scripting

Browser level script execution will reduce the number of interactions with the server and enable faster response time to the Web user. These scripts are integrated with static Web development languages to make the Web pages dynamic and more interactive. Client side scripting are the lightweight languages which could be directly embedded into static HTML pages. These are the lines of executable codes, which are handled at client side to eliminate the computational stress and load on the server.

JavaScript

JavaScript (see JavaScript Tutorial, 2004) is used to add interactivity to static pages, improve the design, and validate forms of Web pages. JavaScript was developed by Netscape and is the most popular scripting language on the Internet. It works on all major browsers like Netscape and Internet Explorer.

Jscript

Jscript (see Jscript, 2004) is the Microsoft version of JavaScript. This client side scripting language is embedded in static HTML pages for user input validation and browser level layout designing. It is a lightweight object oriented programming language with sophisticated syntax of high level programming languages.

Visual Basic (VB) Script

Visual Basic script (see VBScript Tutorial, 2004) from Microsoft technology works on Microsoft's IE Web browser. VBScript is a client side scripting language and is a light version of Microsoft's programming language Visual Basic. When a VBScript is inserted into an HTML document, the Internet browser will read the HTML and interpret the VBScript. This technology is quite useful for user input validation.

Server Side Scripting

For the development of a static Web site, only HTML programming could be used. However, for the dynamic and interactive Web sites, some server side technologies need to be embedded with HTML. Server side technologies enable the client to receive dynamic responses. With these server technologies, it has become easier to maintain Web pages, especially on a large and complex site.

Java Server Pages (JSP)

JSP (see Java Server Pages Technology, 2004) is developed by Sun Microsystems where Java is extensively used. Java is a very powerful, object oriented language. Many platform dependency issues have been ironed out with the advent of Java. Thus, Java programs for, say Unix, can be made to run on Windows or the Mac system with little or no effort. Much development is taking place on the Java front with new arrivals like Java Beans, Extended Java Beans, and Java applications for various databases and XML. Using the Java Server, one can also develop dynamic Java Server Pages.

Active Server Pages (ASP)

ASP is promoted by Microsoft technology (see Active Server Pages, 2003). The ASP utilizes some special tags, which can be embedded in the HTML code to generate dynamic Web pages. ASP scripts run on the server, typically, the IIS on Windows NT. ASP pages carry the .asp extension that differentiates them from plain HTML pages and instructs the Web server to pass the pages through the ASP interpreter. It is possible to use VBScript, Java script/Jscript or a combination of the two to write ASP pages. The great advantage in using ASP is the ease of maintenance of the Web site. However, the disadvantage is that the user becomes too dependent on Microsoft technologies.

Microsoft .NET

Microsoft's Dotnet (.NET) (McMullan, 2004) is a new environment for developing and running software applications, featuring ease of development of Web-based services, rich standard run time services available to components written in a variety of programming languages, and interlanguage and intermachine operability. .NET depends on four Internet standards, namely, Hyper Text Transfer Protocol (HTTP), Extensible Markup Language (XML), Simple Object Access Protocol (SOAP), and Universal Description Discovery and Integration (UDDI). Microsoft views this new technology as revolutionary, enabling Internet users to do things that were never before possible, such as integrate fax, e-mail, and phone services; centralize data storage; and synchronize all user computing devices to be automatically updated.

Hypertext Preprocessor (PHP)

PHP (see Hypertext Preprocessor, 2004) was created sometime in 1994 by Rasmus Lerdorf. During mid-1997, PHP development entered the hands of other contributors. Two of them, Zeev Suraski and Andi Gutmans, rewrote the parser from scratch to create PHP version 3 (PHP3). PHP is an open source technology. A PHP page will either have .php or .php3 (depending on how the server has been configured) extension. This is used in open source programmers compared to ASP from Microsoft. PHP not only carries all the goodness of ASP but is also more secure and handles databases more easily. It is a known fact that PHP on Apache Web server runs faster than ASP. PHP code is embedded inside the HTML page and can link to databases to generate dynamic HTML content.

Table 3.1. Server side technologies

Server Technology	Characteristics
Active Server Pages	• Microsoft technology • Embedded with HTML and have .asp extension
Hypertext Preprocessor	• Open source technology • Embedded with HTML and have .php or .php3 extension • More secure and easier handling of database connectivity
Java Server Pages	• Java based technology from Sun Microsystems • Embedded with HTML and have .jsp extension • Platform independent

Server Side Includes (SSI)

SSI (see Server Side Includes (SSI), 2004) involves the embedding of small code snippets inside the HTML page. An SSI page has .shtml as its extension.

Technologies described in Table 3.1 enable an addition of programming code inside the HTML page. This code is passed to the appropriate interpreter which processes these instructions and generates the final HTML displayed by the browser. The embedded code is thus not visible to the client. For instance, a request sent for a PHP page from a client is passed to the PHP interpreter by the server along with various program variables. The interpreter then processes the PHP code and generates a dynamic HTML output. This is sent to the server, which in turn redirects it to the client. The browser is not aware of the functioning of the server. The Web client (browser) just receives the HTML code, parses and formats the content appropriately, and displays on the computer.

Meeting the Challenges

Chapter 3 prepares the reader to qualify to understand the next chapters. Readers must know the basic concept of PT and various views on PT. Also, distinction between various types of PT is also discussed with examples in these chapters. Without understanding the technology, working on PT is not possible. Hence, the topic on reference technology will help readers understand and appreciate the PT discussed in later chapters. This chapter also discusses various issues like network performance, technology, and user's perception on performance.

Summary

Before involving PT activities, one should understand the basic concepts of different technologies, particularly client server and Web technology. Addressing performance issues in both technologies is different. In both technologies, understanding different tiered architectures provides in-depth knowledge on how the system works and what challenges need to be faced during PT. Technology alone does not help, but various languages used for developing systems also make an impact on the performance. Hence, understanding tiered technology and languages is of paramount importance before one gets into addressing the performance of any system.

References

Active Server Pages. (2003). Retrieved December 16, 2003, from http://msdn.microsoft.com/library/default.asp?url=/library/en-s/

An alternate three-tiered architecture for improving interoperability for software components. (2003). Curtin University of Technology. Retrieved September 30, 2004, from http://www2003.org/cdrom/papers/poster/p274/p274-iijima.html

Apache: The number one web server. (2005). Retrieved May 17, 2005, from http://media.wiley.com/product_data/excerpt/12/07645482/0764548212.pdf

Application Server Matrix. (2004). Retrieved December 16, 2004, from http://www.theserverside.com/reviews/matrix.tss

BEA Weblogic platform. (2004). Retrieved December 17, 2004, from http://www.bea.com/framework.jsp?CNT=index.htm&FP=/content/products/platform

Cascading Style Sheets (2004). Retrieved September 12, 2004, from http://www.w3.org/Style/CSS/

Client/server software architectures — An overview. (2004). Carnegie Mellon University. Retrieved September 30, 2004, from http://www.sei.cmu.edu/str/descriptions/clientserver_body.html

Common gateway interface an overview. (2004). Retrieved September 15, 2004, from http://hoohoo.ncsa.uiuc.edu/cgi/intro.html

CORBA® BASICS. (2003). Retrieved December 16, 2004, from http://www.omg.org/gettingstarted/corbafaq.htm

DB2 product family. (2004). Retrieved January 16, 2004, from http://www-306.ibm.com/software/data/db2/

Extensible Markup Language (XML). (2004). Retrieved August 20, 2004, from http://www.w3.org/XML/

Hypertext Preprocessor. (2004). Retrieved December 16, 2004, from http://www.php.net/

HyperText Markup Language (HTML). (2004). Retrieved August 20, 2004, from http://www.w3.org/MarkUp/

IBM WebSphere. (2004). Retrieved December 17, 2004, from http://www-306.ibm.com/software/Websphere/

Information Server Overview and Architecture. (2005). Retrieved May 17, 2005, from http://www.windowsitlibrary.com/Content/141/01/2.html?Ad=1&

Internet Information Services. (2004). Retrieved December 17, 2004, from http://www.microsoft.com/WindowsServer2003/iis/default.mspx

Java Server Pages Techonology. (2004). Retrieved December 16, 2004, from http://java.sun.com/products/jsp/

JavaScript Tutorial. (2004). Retrieved November 11, 2004, from http://www.w3schools.com/js/default.asp

Jscript. (2004). Retrieved November 11, 2004, from http://msdn.microsoft.com/library/default.asp?url=/library/en-us/script56/html/js56jsoriJScript.asp

Marshall, D. (2004). *Remote Procedure Calls (RPC)*. Retrieved September 22, 2004, from http://www.cs.cf.ac.uk/Dave/C/node33.html

McMullan, A. (2004). *.NET framework FAQ*. Retrieved September 17, 2004, from http://www.andymcm.com/dotnetfaq.htm#1.1

Oracle. (2003). Retrieved December 16, 2003, from http://www.oracle.com/index.html

Oracle Application Server. (2004). Retrieved December 16, 2004, from http://www.oracle.com/appserver/index.html

Orion Application Server. (2005). Retrieved January 21, 2005, from http://www.orionserver.com/

Server Side Includes (SSI). (2004). Retrieved September 15, 2004, from http://hoohoo.ncsa.uiuc.edu/docs/tutorials/includes.html

Smith, D. (2004). *Multi tiered architectures and applications servers*. Retrieved September 15, 2004, from http://www.tokyopc.org/newsletter/2003/01/arch_n_app_servers.html

SQL Server. (2004). Retrieved January 16, 2004, from http://www.microsoft.com/sql/default.mspx

SQL *PLUS Quick Reference. (2003). Retrieved September 22, 2004, from http://www.csee.umbc.edu/help/oracle8/server.815/a66735.pdf

Sun ONE Application Framework. (2004). Retrieved December 17, 2004, from http://www.sun.com/software/products/application_framework/home_app_framework.xml

SyBase. (2003). Retrieved December 17, 2004, from http://www.sybase.com/

Tomcat site. (2004). Retrieved December 17, 2004, from http://jakarta.apache.org/tomcat/

What is Python? (2004). Retrieved September 21, 2004, from Executive Summary at http://www.python.org/doc/essays/blurb.html

VBScript Tutorial. (2004). Retrieved November 11, 2004, from http://www.w3schools.com/vbscript/default.asp

VRML History — Introduction. (2004). Retrieved November 11, 2004, from http://www-winfo.uni-siegen.de/vrmlHistory/docs/partVH/introduction.html

XHTML™2.0 W3C. (2004). Working Draft 22 July 2004. Retrieved August 20, 2004, from http://www.w3.org/TR/2004/WD-xhtml2-20040722/

Additional Sources

Orfali, R., Harkey, D., & Edwards, J. (2002). Client/server software architectures.

Sadoski, D. (2004). Client/server survival guide (3rd ed.).

Chapter 4

Test Preparation Phase I:
Test Definition

The core theme of the previous chapters is that a methodical and structured approach to PT is rather necessary right from the early phases of the development cycle. This will ensure predictability and controllability of application performance in practice. The preparatory activities associated with PT (Figure 4.1) are of great importance and are distributed over the life cycle phases of requirement elicitation and analysis, High Level Design (HLD), Detail Level Design (DLD), and several sets of system builds. These activities help define and provide continuity between the high level requirements for application performance, strategies for testing, a framework for designing the tests (see Barber, 2004), and artifacts used to plan and carry out tests. This chapter contains a detailed consideration of the definition phase while Chapters 5 and 6 highlight issues related to the design and build phases associated with the preparatory activities as shown in Figure 4.1.

Need for Test Definition Phase

Customarily, designers address performance issues close to the end of the project life cycle, when the system is available for testing in its entirety or in significantly large modular chunks. This, however, poses a difficult problem, since it exposes the project to a potentially large risk related to the effort involved in both identifying as well as rectifying possible problems in the system at a very late stage in the life cycle. (Refer to

Figure 4.1. Prepartory phases of performance testing

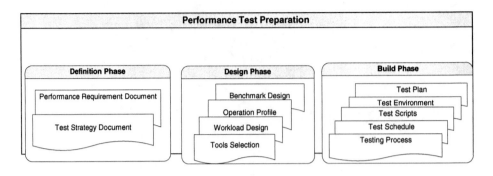

Chapter 1 and Chapter 2 on the problems of debugging.) A more balanced approach would tend to distribute such risks by addressing these issues at different levels of abstraction (intended to result in increased clarity with time), multiple times (leading to greater effectiveness and comprehensiveness in testing application performance), and at different stages during the life cycle. The very first component of activities related to preparation for such testing is in collecting and analyzing requirements related to the performance of the system alongside those related to its features and functions. Hence, this activity would have to take place during the requirement study of business functions and is termed the test definition phase. The main objectives of this phase are to:

- Define goals of PT;
- Remove ambiguities in performance goals;
- Determine the complexity involved in PT;
- Define performance metrics to measure the performance;
- List risk factors involved in PT;
- Define the strategy for PT.

Although most of these activities are carried out during the requirement study phase, some of these have to be revisited for further tuning and clarification during the design phase.

While requirements for modeling business functions and those for performance complement each other, their gathering, as well as analysis, need to be treated as different activities. The performance requirements must be well defined before the design phase, as shown in Figure 4.2, so as to facilitate a more precise design of tests of critical performance parameters.

Collection of performance requirements is a difficult and complex task due to a variety of reasons. It is often easier to elicit requirements associated with business functionality

Figure 4.2. Preparing a performance requirement document

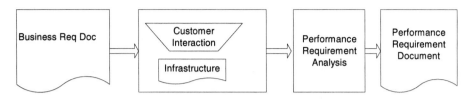

than those related to performance of a system developed to cater to the functionality. In addition, performance parameters are influenced by multiple factors such as:

- The business background and objectives of the organization;
- Information related to current operations of the organization;
- Business growth strategies of the organization;
- User or customer base associated with the organization;
- Operational and deployment logistics as envisaged by the organization;
- Existing and prospective technical infrastructure for the automated system;
- Network environment, hardware and software systems required to run the business.

Typically, most of these factors are not directly available for analysis during the initial stages and/or are implicit and therefore need to be derived from other information. In the following sections, a detailed description and approach is provided to understand the various activities related to performance requirement elicitation, analysis, structuring, and documentation. Figure 4.2 provides the process flow to generate a performance requirement document wherein business requirements, customer interaction, and information on infrastructure are the main inputs.

Performance Requirements and Their Importance

Performance is one of the nonfunctional requirements and has a severe impact on the success of the project. Since designers are not bothered about the performance during the requirements gathering, the real impact will be known only when it fails to meet the users' expectations. If the system fails during its live operation, rectification is a very expensive activity, which may lead to loss of customers. To avoid such implications, treat the performance elicitation activity much in the same way as functional requirements. Broadly, the activities in this phase can be divided into three categories, as related to:

- Business functions related performance requirement;

- Infrastructure and network environment;

- Explicitly specified requirements for performance.

In each category, intensive performance requirement elicitation must be carried out as discussed in the following sections.

Business Functions Related Performance Requirement

Functional requirements gathering is the first step in SDLC. This process is well understood. However, nonfunctional requirements like performance may not be collected during the requirements study due to uncertainties of the expectations on performance. However, it is possible to collect performance requirements based on many business related functions like:

- Business context;

- Business events;

- Business operations;

- Business objectives of the system;

- Logistics of the operations;

- User base.

These functions are explained in the following sections:

Business Context

Many of the detailed plans and processes employed by organizations to achieve business goals can have a significant impact on performance. The business context diagram normally available with the organization provides the in-depth details.

The following questionnaire will help to collect information related to a business context.

- **What is the uniqueness in the business as relevant to the performance?**

  The idea is to find out how the business uniqueness impacts the performance of the system. To illustrate, providing mobile commerce (m-commerce) for the customers of a bank is unique compared to other banks but requires the system to be performance conscious.

- **What are the business functions that are critical for a company's survival?**

  Some of the business functions are critical and must be given top priority while handling the performance. These functions are important to the company's survival in order to stay ahead of their competitors. Identify those functions critical to performance with no scope for compromise.

- **What is the organizational structure?**

  Organizational structure always helps to determine the stakeholders of the performance results. Different groups at different levels in the organization will demand different types of performance results.

- **What are the business goals? List the business goals per the organizational structure.**

  Knowing the organizational structure helps in formulating the performance goals to suit the different levels. For instance, in any organization, senior managers may have different goals compared to marketing or information system (IS) groups. Senior managers may be looking at the growth projection, in terms of increase in number of users, for the next five years whereas the marketing and information system (IS) groups may be working on how efficiently services can be offered to existing customers. In the former, the user base increases whereas the latter addresses the response time of various activities. However, both of them will have an impact on the performance of the system.

- **What is the overall structure of the system?**

  Knowing the structure of the overall system helps in planning the performance. Part of the system may be used internally, and performance may not be the criterion for its function. For instance, executing batch processing could be done during nonprime time so that the impact on the performance is reduced.

Business Events

Many business operations are triggered by various events. These events may originate within the system or driven by the external system. The dependency of operation on an event definitely affects the performance. Events may be triggered manually or automatically. These events are categorized as follows:

External Events

These events are triggered by external entities, which depend on many factors like communications, infrastructure, and people. For instance, fund transfer in a banking system is allowed through a customer's mobile phone. To complete the transaction, the event depends on the health of the mobile phone, features enabled on the mobile phone, and the service provider. The banking system does not have any control over these external events. The performance of the complete transaction depends on the performance of these external entities.

Temporal Events

On occasion, some of the business events are triggered in real time. To illustrate, the purchase order for a specific material is triggered only during the first week of every month. In such cases, there will be an additional load on the system during the specified period, which must be accounted for by measuring the performance of the system.

Business Operations

Different groups within the organization manage business operations, and typically, the objectives of each group are different from one group to another. In some cases, the organizational structure and business operation group may be the same. The intention of making groups according to the business operations is to ensure that the stakeholders, involved in appreciating performance results, will define the performance requirements correctly. To illustrate, in the banking industry, the groups may be categorized broadly into:

- Senior management to plan the business growth of the bank;
- Customer division to manage the customers efficiently and build customer confidence;
- Middle management to strategize the business of the bank for efficient operation and building more profit;
- Information system groups to maintain and monitor the various automated systems.

The objectives and operations of each group must be known so that the performance analyst can assess the impact on performance of the system due to the groups operations. This helps to define the performance objectives at the group level.

Another significant impact on the performance is altering the existing system by:

Introducing the New Business Operation

Based on the business growth and plan, demand may arise to start a new business operation. Depending on the complexity of the new operation, the performance of the system may vary. In-depth study and investigation on new operations must be carried out during this phase. For instance, the service of fund transfer through a mobile phone, if introduced to bank customers at a later stage, will impact the performance of the system.

Table 4.0. Checklist for business operation

Activity	Output of the activity
Identify different working groups within the organization	A list of stakeholders
List the operations of each working group. Determine the complexity of each operation.	A list of operations
Determine how each operations impacts their business growth	Scalability information
Identify any business process in place.	Nil
Determine the critical operations, if any, of the group.	Identify possible bottlenecks for performance.

Enhancing the Existing Operation

The existing business operation may not always be effective and requires modifications that include enhancements. Such modifications may impact the performance of the system.

To illustrate, a money withdrawal facility is available through ATM in a banking system. The authentication procedure used to withdraw money is the ATM card PIN. However, due to business compulsion, management decided to enhance the authentication procedure by introducing the voice recognition of the card holder. This requires upgrading the system using emerging technology and implementing the speech synthesis technique within the system.

Table 4.0 provides the proposed checklist, which highlights various activities involved to carry the business operation and the corresponding outputs for each activity.

Each operation helps in capturing performance requirements.

Business Objectives of the System

Though the overall business objectives of the system are listed as part of the business context, it is necessary to define operation-wise business goals. Many of the business functions are known during the systems requirements study phase. However, those functional requirements (see Robertson, 2005) that impact performance must be revisited and defined properly. Business plans must be explored properly from the angles of scalability testing. Proposed guidelines that may help in obtaining information on business objectives would be:

- List the objectives of the system and categorize them according to business operations.

- What are the business plans for next Y years? Quantify, if possible.

- What are the growth projections for the coming years? Quantify, if possible.

- Identify the parameters that impact growth projections of the organization.

- Are there any specific performance based goals defined by management? If so, list all the goals.

Logistics of Operations

If the business activities are distributed at many places, modeling the logistics of operation is of paramount importance. This is because performance of the system depends on the bandwidth available at the place of operation and vicinity of ISP providers. Volume and type of transactions also vary from place to place which impacts performance. The following guidelines provide an overview on logistics of operations.

- List different places of operations.
- List the complete set of business operations at different places.
- Identify type and volume of transactions at each place.
- Identify the topology of networking and ISP providers place-wise.
- Determine the expectations at each place of operation.
- If you think the priority of objectives changes at different places, list them properly.

User Base

User-wise information on the user base at different locations of operation and type of operations are required. The user base may be broadly categorized into user groups, and each user group can be identified with a set of operations. There may be different groups such as internal and external users. Internal users may be employees. If their base is

Figure 4.3. Typical user base for a bank

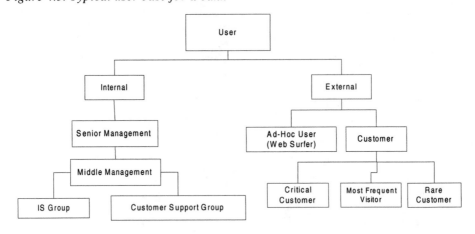

considerably high, create subgroups based on their activities. Similarly, external users may be customers who undertake different activities with the Web site. They may just surf the Web site as a Web surfer, or some customers may transact through the Web site. Activities vary with customers' requirement, and the number of customer visiting the Web site varies with time.

Proposed guidelines to be used to collect information on user bases would be:

- Identify the user base and its growth potential;
- Differentiate internal and external users;
- Determine different groups based on operations;
- Determine different groups based on logistics;
- Prioritize the user group based on their requirements;
- Frequency of accessing the Web site by each user group.

Figure 4.3 provides a possible user base for a typical industry. Observe that internal users are also contributing to performance requirements like external users are. Subsequent categorization depends on the specific industry. User groups will help in planning reload on the system during PT.

Infrastructure and Network Environment

Infrastructure available for the proposed system must be studied exhaustively. Infrastructure mainly involves the computer hardware and software systems. If the proposed system is to be developed from the ground up, the infrastructure recommended for the system must be accounted for in the study. If the proposed system is a reengineered system, existing and new infrastructure must be accounted for in the study. Infrastructure requirements are divided into (1) network environment and (2) hardware/software system.

Network Environment

Evaluate the network environment in terms of Local Area Network (LAN) and Wide Area Network (WAN). If the organization is using LAN, it may be composed of several servers working in a C/S environment connected by fast Ethernet using the 100 BaseT standard (see *Guide to using fast enthernet*, 2005) and rated at 100 Mbps. If the performance result identifies LAN as the bottleneck, the speed of the LAN could be increased to gigabit per second using gigabit Ethernet. Also, T1 lines may be shared between the Web and telephone traffic.

Figure 4.4. Typical computer network (WAN)

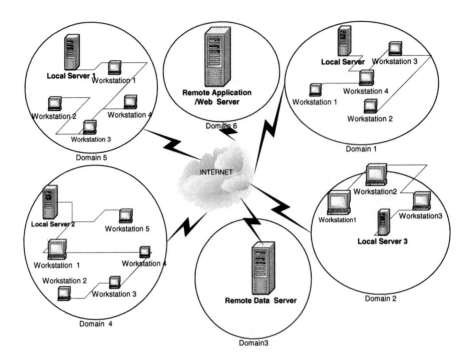

If the organization is using WAN, different offices might be connected through dedicated T1 lines. To illustrate, a typical networking environment for the banking project could be as shown in Figure 4.4.

The system will operate in a client-server network as well as be supported by Web. There will be a cluster of LAN situated at different places. Some of the clusters may have their own Web server and remote data server. All clusters are linked to the headquarters by a WAN. The client-server network will include approximately 2,000 users, with one client workstation per user. A complete topology of the network environment is available with the IS department of the bank.

Hardware/Software System

The proposed/existing application system requires proper hardware/software infra-structures to work efficiently. The organization may procure the relevant ones or may also be in excess. These resources may be utilized exclusively for the proposed system or in addition to the system; they may be used for other activities. In such cases, careful examination is required, as other systems will be considered noises during PT. Table 4.1 provides the checklist for the basic infrastructure required for a typical Web system.

Table 4.1. Checklist for basic infrastructure

Sl. No.	Hardware/Software Types	Descriptions
1	Web Servers	Web servers (see Brain, 2004) are connected to routers, which in turn connected to the Internet through multiple T1 lines. If there are host of web servers, load balancers are used to balance. The load on these load balancers impacts the performance. Web servers may have its own databases but not all data are available in the local database.
2	Application Servers	Application servers may be installed on a single machine along with the web servers or may be in different machine also. Application server is connected to a web server.
3	Database Servers	The database servers may be centralized or distributed. If it is distributed, list all the servers and its profiles. If database servers used for mirroring, it must be described separately. Taking backup during peak hours should be avoided as it will be a background process effecting the other process and hence degrading the performance.
4	Print Servers	Print servers are connected to the LAN and used by many users. Description of each print server is required as it may impact on the performance.
5	Voice Telephone Servers	These servers are used to service and coordinate incoming calls with customers' profiles. The voice telephone service will be supported by call center software. The software will reside on voice response server. The voice service is handled by the same set of T1 lines, which is used for web services.
6	Modems	Modems are part of the network accessories. Users may access the Web site through modems. Specification of each modem available on the network must be known.
7	External Interfaces	Routers and Bridges are few important components that impacts on the performance. Their structures must be known.
8	Platforms	Platforms like Java or Microsoft will also impacts on the performance of the system.
9	Software	List is endless but those software that are useful to Internet applications.

Though the hardware/software is used for the proposed system, there may be other applications running on the system. These applications impact performance by unnecessarily loading the system and network. If these applications are required to run along with the proposed system, the implication of these applications on the performance must be studied.

Other important issues to be noted are the people issues. Management may not be knowledgeable enough to understand the performance issues. The IS department may be very stringent on certain issues related to performance results requirements. All users may not have full knowledge about the expectations on performance of the Web site they are going to use. All these issues must be carefully handled during the performance requirement study.

Explicitly Specified Requirements
for Performance

Performance specific requirements are based on the behavior of the proposed system, shown in Figure 4.5, and are viewed in two ways:

1.   Implementation of the business function and representing the functionality of the system
2.   Ensuring performance of the proposed business functions

The business functions are mapped to a set of use cases, which will be used to model the functional behavior of the system. However, while modeling the functional behavior, much emphasis will not be given on performance of the system during the functional design. Even though performance issues are addressed during functional design, they will be on a low key only. Hence, performance requirement elicitation needs to be carried out separately and comprehensively.

Business functions of the proposed system are captured at the requirements gathering stage of the software engineering life cycle. This phase is well defined, and many processes are available to capture the requirements of the system. Based on the requirements, the architectural plan is proposed, and the design starts from there. The user understands the proposed system through an acceptance test, which will be deployed later.

Interfacing System (If Any)

Some of the organizations want to interconnect their system with the external system through a proper channel. This needs a study of the details of linking with the other

Figure 4.5. Proposed system behavior

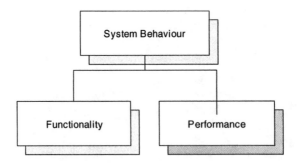

Table 4.2. Template for operation profile

User Group	Identify the user group thru a name. If necessary, list the sub user groups also.
Priority of user groups	The importance of each user/sub user groups must be specified. Use your own scale to specify the priority
Feature/Business Functions	Describe the set of transactions/activities performed in the planned system. If necessary, describe the sub activity also.
Frequency of utilization	List in number of transactions per hour/sec utilization of those transactions selected earlier. Consider different time intervals like peak, normal, etc.
Set Priority	Set the priority of each type of transaction in your own scale.

systems. For instance, a typical banking system wants to interact with another banking system to transfer funds across banks. The performance of interbanking funds transfer depends on the performance of the target bank also.

Responsibilities

Proper teams must be identified for testing, and responsibilities must be assigned appropriately. The main responsibilities include testing the performance of the new system for response time, throughput, scalability, and ability to handle peak loads. The team's immediate requirement may be to prepare a high level strategy document to describe these tasks.

The requirement for better performance is multifaceted. Studying the usage pattern of the system brings out much information and will help in PT. Therefore, the operation profile, in general, must be developed for every system before the beginning of PT.

Operation Profile

The operation profile provides the usage pattern of the proposed system. It tries to list the major demands or the likely demands of the system actually occurring in live operation. It is also known as the usage model of the system, as the dynamic behavior of the system is addressed. The dynamic behavior depends on the types of transaction the system supports. Once the types of transaction are identified, the system's usage and behavior are also known. The behavior means the system's operations and interactions with other transactions, complexity, and usefulness. The usage means frequency of utilization at different intervals like peak or normal hours and criticality of the transaction. The frequency of utilization can be expressed in terms of transactions per hour/second. The operation profile normally does not include overheads and background transactions, if any.

How to Prepare an Operation Profile

System developers may not be interested in preparing an operation profile for performance testers. In such cases, there is a risk of avoiding the real environment. Though the preparation of an operation profile may consume time and might be difficult, as the live operation may not be known at this stage, it is still a worthwhile proposition. Even if it is difficult to collect the data, there should be a serious effort to "guestimate" and verify the same with knowledgeable professionals.

Prepare a good operation profile requires complete knowledge of the proposed system. The system's behavior at different time intervals, different days and months, must be known. User groups must be defined and prioritized properly. A user group is a set of users who operates on similar transactions. To illustrate, the IS group is a valid user group who operates on system related transactions. It may not be of much importance for performance when considering priority. In such cases, the IS group will be valued at a lower rate compared to other groups. Table 4.2 will help in preparing the operation profile.

The frequency of utilization can be determined by many ways and requires knowledge of the business domain. The time intervals must be properly defined. However, the main issue lies in deciding the span of the time intervals and number of transactions within each interval. For instance, if the peak time is defined as two hours every business day, the pattern of distribution of transactions within two hours will not be uniform. It is not correct to take the worst case scenario, as there may be a surge which may not reflect the real distribution. Therefore, selection of the distribution as well as the time interval is difficult. The time interval is important because it is not proper to consider the entire two hours as peak time load test during PT. This is not economical, either.

An operation profile of the typical banking application is given in a case study (Appendix D).

The main features of the system are highlighted in the business requirements document. The frequency of utilization for each group is listed in Table 4.3. For instance, on average, there are 9,300 transactions (main page access) per hour on Monday. Similarly, 700 transactions/hour related to deposit reported on Wednesday.

Service Level Agreements (SLA)

A service level agreement is a document signed by both consultant and client of the proposed system, which depicts the formal agreement on the performance of the proposed system. It is the binding document between the two parties, which means that both parties have agreed to the performance requirements of the systems and expected results during PT. Sometimes, if the project is large, a separate SLA has to be developed for each operational group, and the agreement has to be signed separately by each manager of those groups.

Table 4.3. Operation profile of business functions for one week during peak hours

User Group	Transactions Type / Days	Mon	Tue	Wed	Thu	Fri	Sat	Sun	Priority
Customer Group	Main Page access	9300	8300	8800	8500	8200	8000	7000	High
	Deposit Amount	900	800	700	800	700	500	300	High
	Withdraw Amount	950	850	800	850	850	850	800	High
	Request for new A/Cs	350	250	200	350	350	0	0	Low
	Bill Payment	200	100	75	100	250	212	200	Medium
Administrative Group	Daily Report Generation	6	8	2	3	5	6	2	Medium
	Fund Transfer	450	350	400	300	350	300	250	Medium
	Creation of new A/Cs	50	25	32	28	30	0	0	Low
	Deletion of A/Cs	10	30	20	22	18	0	0	Low
Senior Management Group	Banking features query	620	740	743	851	723	613	541	High
	Ad-hoc query	25	32	23	20	23	0	0	Medium

Note:

- *Frequency of utilization is expressed in terms of transactions per hour.*
- *Normal load is obtained during the routine business hours of transaction observed over a week.*
- *A peak hour of transaction represents the expected load during the worst case hour in a typical week.*
- *The operation profile does not include overhead and background transactions, if any.*

Miscellaneous

Occasionally, organizations would like to know what happens if a new change has to be introduced on the proposed system. This is because taking a risk may not be conducive to the interests of the development of the system, but they would like to know the impact. For instance, top management would like to know the impact on performance if the Web site generates dynamic content.

Management Conditions and Constraints

Sometimes, management will put forth a lot of constraints in terms of resources, budget, and duration of the project. Probably, the resources are not matching the expected performance requirements. The duration of the completion of the project may be too short to implement all the requirements. The organization may insist on conducting the performance test at the customer place itself, or the IS team of the organization may conduct the test.

Performance requirement is a new grey area where no process or methodology is available. The conventional requirements gathering process will not capture the entire performance requirement. Therefore, for a project that is performance sensitive, the performance requirements must be collected separately and analyzed before the system design so that any bottleneck could be addressed before deployment. Once the performance requirements are gathered, a proper test strategy must be developed, which helps during the performance test.

Developing Performance Test Strategy Document

An exhaustive elicitation and recording of requirements would be a precondition for the satisfactory conduction of performance tests. Yet, in practice, it must be appreciated that it is not possible to begin testing for performance until the application in whole, or a number of critical modules, are available in an executable form at various points in the developmental cycle. Furthermore, budgetary, time, and other resource allocations in a project scenario may in turn constrain the quantum of requirements tested, the duration, environment, and locations available for testing. Therefore, to obtain optimal results, it is necessary to develop a strategy that will help designers as well as test executors to unambiguously understand, plan, schedule, and conduct PT within the constraints of time and budget. Accordingly, the strategy would address the relevant choices to be made, given these constraints, on the methodology used, test cases to be identified, time allocated for testing and analysis, target user numbers, locations, and profiles. The corresponding risk factors (Bach, 2004) related to the choices made would also be highlighted in the PT strategy document.

Performance Testing Objectives

The primary goal of the testing activity is to provide sufficient information to the development team about the likelihood that the system will perform adequately in actual operation. The development team always concentrates on functional aspects of the system and ignores the performance requirements. The first step toward performance testing is to determine the objectives that will benefit both the development and performance test team. These include information about the capability of the system to handle the following:

a.   Daily business workloads as anticipated by the organization. Business workloads could be classified into critical, routine, and exceptional. The critical workloads address the success of the system whereas routine workload gives the performance requirements to handle day-to-day business.

b.   Daily, weekly, or monthly periods of peak demand of the system. These demands are required to know the system's capability to manage the business at all times. The peak demand helps in load testing as well as stress testing. These requirements will address resource sufficiency also.

c.   Specialized needs such as those related to batch processing of volumes of interbanking transactions, documents transfer, fund transfer, exceptional reports generation, and so forth.

d.   Ad hoc demands like burst loads in an unexpected situation. An example could be withdrawal of money from the bank due to unfavorable political interference suddenly.

e.   Likely future growth anticipated over a specified period of time. This is important because, as the user base increases, the load on the system also increases, and the performance testing process must analyze the impact on the system.

Some of the questions that typically arise during objective setting are:

- Is the response time acceptable when the system is operating under a realistic load? The acceptable response time varies and depends on the load also. It could be the range with minimum and maximum acceptable response time. Normally, acceptable response time will be elaborated more in the Service Level Agreement.

- Is the system capable of handling peak load? If so, what is the response time during the peak load? The response time at the peak load is critical because most of the users expect their queries to be answered immediately.

- Is the system reliable when accessed simultaneously by multiple users? The system should not envisage any errors related to business functions, database optimization, resource contention, and transaction priorities.

- Is the system scalable at all times? Scalability is referred to as the architecture and capability to handle peak load as the user base increases.

- Does the system provide consistency in performance? Performance consistency helps in assuring the users the same response for repeated action on a specific transaction.

- Is the system reliable? Reliability is addressed both in functional and performance testing.

- Is the system available? Performance testing must ensure the availability of the system on a 24X7 basis.

- Is the entire system tuned optimally? Optimal tuning must be defined properly. It is not just getting the better response time but other factors like throughput, availability, and reliability must also be considered and balanced.

- Does the system degrade gracefully or fail abruptly when the load is pushed beyond its limit?

These questions, once debated with the designers and customers, will remove many confusions and will help in creating proper PT objectives. However, PT objectives differ based on stakeholders.

Stakeholders

Once the performance test is conducted, the results must be compiled and presented to stakeholders. The stakeholders differ within the organization itself. Each one of them expects a different kind of results. For instance, the IS department may require performance results for their day to day running of the system whereas top management needs to know the results for the projection of their business in the future. Some stakeholders like team members of an IS department of the bank and accounts department of the bank may require similar reports. The strategy must be to satisfy all groups.

To illustrate, the following groups in a typical banking project are crucial for the success of the project.

- Senior managers of the bank are the major stakeholders.

- The customer group needs to have sufficient confidence that the system will be able to support the load of their department.

- The IS group within the bank needs information about the levels of compliance with the SLA, which are likely to be achievable in live system operation.

- The clients expect the bank to be performance conscious and have a robust system.

Freezing Project Scope

While working out a strategy, one must be clear about the scope of PT. Normally, the scope includes load, stress, spike, and endurance testing. The PT team may have to analyze the results and suggest solutions if there is a bottleneck in fulfilling the SLA. Test environments must be defined in the scope itself. A test environment may be a production environment or an isolated test lab.

Functional testing and related problems will not be part of the scope. This is because it is assumed that the system is functionally correct before getting handed over to the performance test team. Activities, which are outside the scope of PT, must be elaborated explicitly.

System Acceptance Criteria

The Service Level Agreement (SLA) has to be met first, in all respects. SLAs may not be defined properly during the performance requirements study whereas they will be fine tuned during developing the strategy. The main areas in which the system acceptance criteria must be addressed are:

- Type of test that has to be performed like load, stress, endurance, or spike test. Which test produces results that satisfy most, if not all, of the performance requirements? The strategy that needs to be followed must be described explicitly. All types of tests may not be possible to complete due to resources and time. Each type of test may have to be run multiple times, which may or may not produce the required results. A strategy document must explore these aspects explicitly.

- Measurement criteria and parameters must be finalized. Performance parameters help to evaluate the performance objectives whereas measurement criteria quantify whether objectives are met per the requirements.

- Measuring all the parameters may not be feasible and may be time consuming. Identifying the right parameters is of paramount importance.

- How many virtual users must be simulated? Here, the number of virtual users may be fixed or variable.

- How many times must each test be executed? Since the investment on the environment and resources are greater, each test run costs more, and it is necessary to limit the test run time.

The system acceptance criteria provide a direction to the testers to prepare a detailed plan for performance test execution.

Early Component Level Performance Testing

Most of the large scale applications use various components developed by a third party or in-house. Usage of these components reduces the development time and increases the efficiency, as these are tested and proved at the production environment. Every component used in the system will be tested early before actual PT of the system begins. To test such components, a similar performance study must be carried out. These components must be tuned for optimal performance.

Performance Measurements

Performance measurements, as indicated in the SLA, must be defined explicitly. Performance is measured based on many performance parameters. Some parameters are simple to understand by users, and other parameters are used to achieve the higher level measurement criteria. In most of the projects, the following performance measurement data are collected to study the performance of the application:

- Response time of transactions per the workloads defined in the design. This data at transaction level provide information on which business function takes more time to process and respond to the user query. The response time for each transaction must be measured in seconds.

- Consistency of responses must be maintained. When the same test is executed multiple times, each test run may provide different response times. The difference in response time should not be too variant, and consistency must be maintained. This means, for different test runs, the measured responses for the same load must be consistent.

- Throughput of the system is measured in transactions per second at the server end.

- Resource utilization during testing must be measured such as:

  ➢ Server and client processor utilization;
  ➢ Memory utilization (RAM and disks);
  ➢ Network utilization (LAN and T1 lines);
  ➢ Thread utilization (number of concurrent users of critical hardware and software components).

- Availability of the Web site, on a 24X7 basis, is measured by conducting the load test for long hours. Mainly memory leaks are measured here.

- Ability to access the system resources such as databases, printers, and the Internet while the system is running.

- Bottleneck related measurements are:

  ➢ High resource consumption by each software and hardware component during testing;
  ➢ Network collision rates;
  ➢ Page in page out rates;
  ➢ Number of hits blocked (blocking the Web site visitors);
  ➢ Number of threads blocked;
  ➢ Buffer and queue length overflows.

These measurement parameters (see IDEMA Standards, 2004) may vary depending on the project requirements and ability to measure by using the tool.

Test Execution Methodology

The main objective here is to ensure smooth conduct of the test runs and provide customer based reports within the stipulated time. The customer always expects the test execution to complete with minimum time and effort. In order to ensure this, a proper test strategy must be evolved. As a first step, one has to work out a plan to ensure the following:

- Skilled resources are available to conduct the test;
- Mechanism to ensure the functional correctness of the application;
- The proper environment at the right time;
- Developing and monitoring a proper test schedule;
- Process to maintain the configuration control during the test run;
- Availability of proper automated tools during the test.

Once the basic work plan is ready, develop a test execution process to implement the plan. The test execution process for a testing project could be defined as a strategy. To illustrate, the strategy is to have two different teams:

1.   Functional testing team, which conducts testing and interacts with the development team and conforms to the correctness of business functions of the system.
2.   Performance testing team, which plans and conducts the PT in cooperation with the functional testing team. However, there may be a few members overlapping in both teams.

Each team will use their own test plans and strategies to conduct the test. A separate environment is created for both teams. If it is too expensive, the environment could be the same with additional hardware/software support for the performance testing.

Test Loads Considering Transaction Volumes and Variety

In order that the transactions chosen for testing in the simulated environment are as close as possible to those in the field, an appropriate choice of volumes and mix of transactions (workload) needs to be arrived at. This in turn would provide performance characteristics proximal to that of the application in a real production environment. The load used for measuring the performance is based on:

- Typical daily average business workloads, measured over a period of time;
- Daily peak demand of the business requirements, measured over a period of time;
- Weekly and monthly peak demands, measured over a period of time;
- Ad hoc demands, if any;
- Future demands determined from the projected growth over a defined number of years (this could be arrived based on daily, weekly, and monthly business workload collected already);

- Quarterly, half yearly, and yearly demands;

- Spike test demands, if any (This load depends on what type of spike is expected. This requires business domain knowledge and experience);

- Self created workloads to test the system for a specific purpose. An example could be to create a workload which tests the capability of the architecture.

The accuracy of the load depends on the customer who provides the data. The whole test results depend on the accuracy of the data collected.

Test Environment

An isolated and dedicated test environment is most useful for PT. One should have the availability of the network, servers, flexibility to set up the bandwidth, firewalls, and minimal external noises. However, setting up a separate environment involves additional cost. To minimize the cost, the production environment may be used, but the results may not be accurate.

Several issues (see Subraya, 2004) must be addressed while creating the test environment. Some of them are:

- What if the exact operation environment is not matching the simulated environment?

- What if the operation environment uses 12 processor systems whereas only dual processors are used in the simulated environment?

- What if the operation environment uses a different operating system than the simulated environment?

- What if the firewall used in the operation environment is not used in the test environment?

- What if the operation environment uses a different load balancer compared to the simulated environment?

- What if the size of the database available at the operation environment is not available in the simulated environment?

These issues are critical and must be addressed in the strategy document before the beginning of the test.

Test Data Sources/Test Data Bed

Though a good environment with a good mix of transaction is available, the test may not be effective because the test data available may not be sufficient. If the production data are available, use them; otherwise, creating a test bed may require an enormous amount of effort. Data generator tools may help to generate a good test bed.

User Think Time

Performance of an application in an Internet environment mainly based on the number of concurrent users mapped on to a particular transaction at any instant, for instance, stock trading through a Web site. The number of concurrent users may vary at different time intervals. However, the number of concurrent users depends on the session time. The session time depends on many factors. One such factor is the user think time. This is the time that a person takes to respond to a system while handling a particular situation. For instance, when a user is entering into an order entry form, the user may think for a while and enter a specific entry. This can have a significant impact on its performance. Therefore, how much think time must be used needs to be ascertained in the strategy document.

Stress and Endurance Testing

After the load testing, a final stress (see Wilkinson, 2004) and endurance test will be executed. In order to execute a stress and endurance test, a different workload may have to be selected. The test might be run for more than 24 hours or weeks depending on the project. Response time, throughput, and resource utilization will be measured continually during the test. The strategy should be to reduce the time and resources without diluting the performance test results.

Project Activities and Schedule

The strategy document must explicitly address the various project activities, which includes the project schedule. A proper time plan with team description and responsibility must be described elaborately. Various constraints, if any, must be explicitly described. A proper monitoring process of the project activities must be included in the document.

Project Risks

Project risks are a major concern for the smooth running of test scenarios. Risk must be elaborated, and the mitigation process must also be highlighted. Risks may be from the customer side or may be from the designers. For instance, a typical performance based project may face the following identified risks before completion:

•   Unavailability of the proper testing tools during the test;

- Unavailability of the skill set required for testing and analyzing results;
- Cost involved in setting up of the testing environment;
- Untimely submission of the final product for PT;
- Unavailability of database network administrators during the proper test.

Apart from the above risks, there may be many unforeseen risks that may arise during the execution of the test.

Defining a proper performance strategy is one of the major activities of test designers. Though the strategy is comprehensive, senior management may not be interested in microscopic details of the strategy but only brief information. In such cases, an abstract report may have to be prepared. The strategy document in PT plays a dominant role, as the success of testing in an optimized fashion depends on the strategy.

Summary

Performance requirements elicitation is an important task in the PT life cycle. This phase of activity must be carried out along with the functional requirement phase. Once the requirements are gathered, a detailed operation profile is prepared. The operation profile provides the transactional behavior of the business system. Based on the operation profile, workloads are designed. Once the workload is known, test strategies are studied that help the test analyst prepare for test plan and estimation. Without performance requirements elicitation, jumping into PT does not yield good results.

The performance test strategy must be carefully planned because performance strategy impacts the resources and time required for PT. Project risks are identified in advance, and suitable mitigation plans need to be worked out proactively.

References

Bach, J. (2004). *Risk and requirements-based testing*. Retrieved June 12, 2004, from http://www.satisfice.com/articles/requirements_based_testing.pdf

Barber, S. (2004). *Designing performance tests to accurately predict true user experience*. Retrieved June 15, 2004, from www.perftestplus.com/presentations/Perf_Design.pdf

Brain, M. (2004). *How Web servers work*. Retrieved June 20, 2004, from http://computer.howstuffworks.com/web-server3.htm

Guide to using fast enthernet. (2005). Retrieved January 21, 2005, from http://www.lantronix.com/learning/net-tutor-fastetnt.html

IDEMA Standards. (2004). Retrieved December 21, 2004, from http://www.idema.org/ _smartsite/modules/local/data_file/show_fileRajaram, A., & Desai, A. (2004). *End-to-end performance in Web applications*. Retrieved July 21, 2004, from http:// www.stickyminds.com/sitewide.asp?ObjectId=6221&Function=DETAILBROWSE &ObjectType=ART

Robertson, S. (2005). *Requirements testing - Creating an effective feedback loop*. Retrieved from January 12, 2005, from http://www.systemsguild.com/GuildSite/ SQR/testingloop.html

Subraya, B. M. (2004). *Web PT & issues*. Retrieved May 15, 2004, from http://www.soft.com/ QualWeek/QW2002/papers/W3.html

Wilkinson, C. (2004). *Stress testing Web services: Some tips and guidelines for testers*. Retrieved April 10, 2004, from http://www-106.ibm.com/developerworks/ webservices/library/ws-tip-strstest.html

Additional Sources

Emmerich, W. (n.d.). *Communications software engineering*. Retrieved June 20, 2004, from http://www.cs.ucl.ac.uk/staff/W.Emmerich/lectures/Z01-99-00/z01_day1.pdf

Skinne, N. (n.d.). *Avoiding performance downtime and system outages through goals-based testing*. Retrieved January 16, 2005, from http://www.embarcadero.com/ resources/tech_papers/Goals_Based_Testing.pdf

Subraya, B. M., & Subramanya, S. V. (n.d.). *Web testing and performance issues*. In F. Marinescu (Ed.), *Tips on performance testing and optimization*. Retrieved December 24, 2004, from http://www.theserverside.com/articles/article.tss?l=Tips-On-Performance-Testing-And-Optimization

Validation of BEA WebLogic server in the hp-ux 11i virtual server environment. (n.d.). Retrieved January 16, 2004, from http://www.hp.com/products1/unix/operating/ docs/wlm.weblogic.validation.pdf

Chapter 5

Test Preparation Phase II: Test Design

The focus of Chapter 4 was on the planning and definition phase of PT while this chapter provides an in-depth view of the test design phase. All the necessary inputs for PT are captured under the test definition phase. These inputs are the building blocks for the design phase of PT.

Importance of Test Design Phase

The complete performance requirement document depicts the user's expectations and underlines the need for such expectations. Using these expectations, testing the system directly without a proper design becomes a layman's job, and the results from such an activity will lead to disaster. Therefore, the design phase is an important activity for PT. The first activity in the design phase is benchmark design (see *The benchmark handbook*, 2003), which is the backbone for designing the workload.

Benchmark Design

Real performance test runs depend on how accurately the testers simulate the production environment. To simulate such behavior of the Web site accurately, benchmarks are used. The benchmark is a standard representation of an application's expected behavior

Table 5.0. Basic attributes of a good benchmark

Attribute type	Description of the attribute
Realistic	Must be meaningful within the target domain. It should be close to the real environment; otherwise the results will not be meaningful.
Understandable	Should be easy to understand.
Good metric(s)	Should be linear and orthogonal.
Scalable	Applicable to a broad spectrum of hardware/architecture.
Coverage	Does not oversimplify the typical environment.
Acceptance	Vendors and users must accept it.
Manageable	Possible to conduct the test.

or likely real world working conditions. Benchmark is a distillation of the essential attributes of a workload, which will be used for the test run. It is essential to know how the users are using the Web sites and what the users are doing for conducting a performance test. The behavior of the Web site varies with time, peak or normal, and hence the benchmarks also vary. This means there is no single metric possible. The benchmark should not be too general as it may not be useful in particular. The accuracy of the benchmark drives the effectiveness of the PT. Benchmark is domain specific. There is no point in comparing the benchmarks of one domain to another. To design benchmarks, one should have specific domain knowledge apart from knowing the application.

What Are the Desirable Attributes of a Benchmark?

Any benchmark considered must be defined formally. A benchmark defined formally will have a set of attributes. These attributes, once collated properly, help the designer in understanding the benchmark. Table 5.0 provides the basic attributes of a good benchmark.

These attributes may vary from one to another benchmark. Those transactions which are considered for benchmarks must be relevant to the performance of the system.

How to Design a Good Benchmark

To design a good benchmark, performance testers need to understand the behavior of the proposed system under different conditions. The conditions may be the load on the system at different times like peak, normal, and average. The benchmarks may be different at different times and need not be the same at all times. It is not sufficient to test just under average conditions but at different times. In any conditions, it is highly desirable to determine the duration in which the benchmark has to be developed. For instance, the peak time may span from 30 minutes to 2 hours. It does not mean one has to consider either 30 minutes or 2 hours duration to decide the kind of mix of transactions. It may be different at different time intervals. A good realistic mix of transactions determines the better benchmark. The mix of transactions may vary at different time intervals. Therefore, it is of paramount importance to study the planned behavior of the system including the frequency of operations before designing the benchmark. The systems behavior depends on the behavior of the transactions associated with the system. Different types of transactions may produce different types of behavior.

Some transactions generate more threads; some may be more concurrent; some may be involved in computation and hidden transaction where less user interaction is required. These types of transaction behavior help to design a proper benchmark for PT.

To illustrate, Table D4.1 in Appendix D4 provides a typical transaction behavior of a banking system. The frequency of operation will be known by the operation profile.

Benchmark Requirements

A benchmark must be precise and accurate. In order to design a good benchmark, proper requirements must be captured accurately, and the designer must be equipped with the following tools:

Operation Profile

The operation profile is another input to the benchmark design discussed in Chapter 4. The operation profile lists all transactions required and addresses the behavior of the system. It simulates different types of user activities and indicates the priorities of each activity. Some of the activities may not be relevant to performance but part of the business functions. The operation profile represents the entire behavior of the system. This has to be fine tuned, and a planned behavior of the system for the performance must be generated.

Planned Behavior of the System

The designer must know the expected overall projected behavior of the system. The behavior is derived from the set of activities. The activities are composed of many transactions as shown in Figure 5.1. Thus, the behavior of the system is determined by the set of transactions. The behavior may be complex, and all behavioral components may not be useful while conducting the performance as represented in the operation profile. Certain behavior may be important from the business point of view but may not be relevant to address the performance issues. These activities must be eliminated from the operation profile. On the other hand, certain behaviors may not be part of the business but impact the performance. These activities must be added to the operation profile. The planned behavior must address those components that determine the performance more realistically and are useful in PT. The following tips could be used to generate the planned behavior:

Figure 5.1. Planned behavior of the system

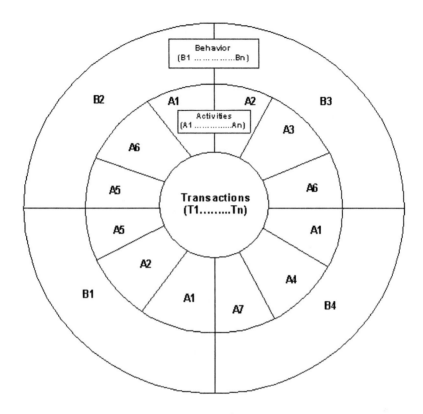

- Define the activity at the user level which impacts the behavior of the system. Initially, list all the activities with the operation profile.

- Identify those activities which are not business specific but participate during the execution of the system. An example could be sending an e-mail during the execution of the system.

- Eliminate those activities that will not impact the performance. Proper judgment and domain expertise help to eliminate unwanted activities from the operation profile.

- Then for each activity, conduct the survey to capture the transactions per hour during different times of operation as stipulated by the designer. The time period may be peak time, slack time, or normal hours.

- Analyze the transactions and determine whether the fine tuned operation profile represents the expected behavior that will impact the performance of the system.

The categorization of behavior provides a structured way of thinking about the overall behavior of the system. These structured behaviors provide direction to plan the proper operation profile that helps to determine the performance of the system. The proper operation profile must have a mix of different types of transactions.

Types of Transactions

As described in the previous section, transactions determine the behavior of the system. There are different types of transactions that determine the different behaviors of the system. Some of these transactions may not participate in the main business functions of the system.

Transactions with More Concurrency

Performance of the system is mostly impacted by many concurrent users simultaneously expecting a response for a similar kind of activity. All those transactions which are processed concurrently impact resources, throughput, and response time. These transactions are critical for performance testing.

Transactions with More Interactions

Most of the transactions that interact with the user interfaces require more time to complete the processing. These transactions not only interact with the user interfaces but may interact with other types of transactions. For instance, while logging into secured Web sites, the system expects multiple answers from the user through interactions.

Transactions with More Computational Activity

Some of the business applications may be involved in number crunching and computations. In such cases, the processor is engaged most of the time. Such transactions consume more time of the processor than the I/O devices. Most of the scientific analysis falls under this category.

Transactions with More Resource Hunger

Those transactions that always depend on resources to complete their processing fall under this category. These transactions always wait for the resource to be available to complete their processing. The wait time will impact performance, provided the required resource is not available at the right time. Typical data entry in a batch processing always requires I/O devices. If transactions are more computation related, it always waits for the processor to be released by the operating system in the multiprocessor environment.

Transactions with More Read/Write

Transactions involved in disk read/write fall under this category. Since disk I/O is slow compared to processor speed, I/O based transactions adversely impact the performance of the system. For instance, a Web user files a query which in turn requires multiple I/O operations on databases in a database server.

Transactions which Generate More Threads

These transactions create subprocesses to speed up the processing thereby helping to improve the performance of the system. A thread is a process inherited by its parent process. If more threads are generated, then managing these threads becomes an overhead which impacts performance. Thus, proper balancing is required to achieve optimum balance.

Transactions which Exhibits Noises

In most of the performance testing, we forget to simulate those transactions which are not part of the system's execution but run during the execution in an isolated fashion. A printer process is active when a Web system is running. This printer process has nothing to do with the Web application. A firewall used in all major corporate sectors is a security monitor applications, also called a daemon (background) process, which affects the performance while surfing the Internet. This may be considered as one of the noise factors while conducting PT. These transactions are called noises and impact the performance of the system.

Guidelines for Designing a Benchmark

Standard benchmarks are available in the market. Most of the benchmarks available in the market address the vendor's product with a set of predefined transactions. This will not help in determining the benchmarks where the system is new and not standard. Hence, a new set of guidelines needs to be derived, which will be useful if one desires to design a business benchmark for a typical project. Some of the tips to derive a proper benchmark are:

*   More than one benchmark is required for presenting better performance results. This will help the analyst to determine the performance of the system from different

perspectives. Also, one can compare and correlate the performance for its effectiveness.

- Identify the demands of the system in the form of transactions and transaction mixes. The demands could be many and different for different stakeholders. These demands are derived from transactions. Sometimes, transaction mixes help to derive proper demands of the system.

- Design a simple to complex benchmark. The complexity depends on the size of the benchmark.

- Determine all types of transactions and transaction mix at different time intervals. The time interval could be days, weeks, and even months. All types of transaction data must be collected at different time intervals.

- Identify critical transactions and prioritize them. Prioritization helps in identifying the critical business and, hence, in designing critical workloads.

- While selecting transactions:
  - Select transactions with more concurrency;
  - Select transactions with more interactions;
  - Select transactions with more computational activity;
  - Select transactions with read/write on the database;
  - Select transactions that generate more threads;
  - Select transactions that are more resource hungry;
  - Select transactions that generate noises.

- Plan transactions based on time zones if the system caters to multiple time zones. If the system caters to different time zones, the priority of transactions may vary depending on the organization's business plans. Identify probable day, week, and month for planned activity. Segregate the time interval as peak, normal, and average. Define time intervals properly. This is necessary to study the performance behavior of the system at different time intervals.

- Plan user groups and map transactions to each user group. Based on the transaction mix and usage planned, identify the probable user groups and tag these user groups with transactions. User groups decide the planned usage patterns of the proposed Web site.

The above guidelines could be supplemented with the project experience of the person who is involved in benchmark design.

How Many Benchmarks Are Required?

Separate benchmarks are required for each significant and distinct workload. Though the number of benchmarks depends on the planned activities of the system, a typical project may employ the following five benchmarks:

- Routine business demands;
- Routine peak demands;
- Specialized requirements, if any;
- Top management's special demands, if any;
- System growth based on demands.

These five benchmarks are just guidelines, but based on the performance requirements and complexity of the project, the number of benchmarks could vary.

A Sample Benchmark

To illustrate, consider the banking system and sample activities highlighting the transactions survey taken on a typical week. The result of the survey result is shown in Table 5.1. This table represents the operations as perceived by the user on a typical day.

There are 50 accounts per hour created on Monday whereas no operations take place on Saturday and Sunday.

Table 5.1 represents the behavior of the entire system. Some of the activities may not affect the performance of the system. If one considers these nonrequired transactions, overheads on the testing activity will be greater. Thus, the operation profile, as shown in Table 5.1, needs to be fine tuned.

Fine Tune the Operation Profile

Though the operation profile is described during requirements gathering (see Chapter 4: Explicitly Specified Requirements for Performance), it has to be fine tuned during the design phase. Some of the attributes like frequency of utilization may vary. The user groups may be added or deleted based on relevance. The importance of each user group will be defined properly; that is, the priority of each user group will be defined at this stage. Some of the functions, which are collected during the requirements stage, will be fine tuned here. Again, some functions, if found irrelevant, may be deleted.

A sample fine tuned operation profile is shown in Table 5.2, which is derived from the Table 5.1. Observe that in Table 5.2, the transaction, Request for new A/Cs, is deleted because it is irrelevant and will not impact performance.

Table 5.1. Operation profile of business functions for one week during peak hours

User Group	Transactions Type / Days	Mon	Tue	Wed	Thu	Fri	Sat	Sun	Priority
Customer Group	Main Page Access	9300	8300	8800	8500	8200	8000	7000	High
	Deposit Amount	900	800	700	800	700	500	300	High
	Withdraw Amount	950	850	800	850	850	850	800	High
	Request for New A/Cs	350	250	200	350	350	0	0	Low
	Bill Payment	200	100	75	100	250	212	200	Medium
Administrative Group	Daily Report Generation	6	8	2	3	5	6	2	Medium
	Fund Transfer	450	350	400	300	350	300	250	Medium
	Creation of Accounts	50	25	32	28	30	0	0	Low
	Deletion of Accounts	10	30	20	22	18	0	0	Low
Senior Management Group	Banking Features Query	620	740	743	851	723	613	541	High
	Ad-hoc Query	25	32	23	20	23	0	0	Medium

Table 5.2. Fine tuned operation profile

User Group	Transactions Type / Days	Mon	Tue	Wed	Thu	Fri	Sat	Sun	Priority
Customer Group	Main Page Access	9300	8300	8800	8500	8200	8000	7000	High
	Deposit Amount	900	800	700	800	700	500	300	High
	Withdraw Amount	950	850	800	850	850	850	800	High
	Bill Payment	200	100	75	100	250	212	200	Medium
	Customer Queries	400	300	400	350	400	290	300	Medium
Administrative Group	Fund Transfer	450	350	400	300	350	300	250	Medium
	Creation of New A/Cs	50	25	32	28	30	0	0	Low
	Deletion of Accounts	10	30	20	22	18	0	0	Low
Senior Management Group	Ad-hoc Query	700	650	645	625	590	450	550	Medium
	Banking Features Query	6200	7400	7430	8510	72300	6130	5410	High

Developing a Workload

Workload (see *Application Workload Load Testing (simulation)*, 2003) is an instrument simulating the real world environment. It is an integrated part of the test execution process. Once the benchmark and the operation profile are known, a detailed workload can be planned. The workload provides indepth knowledge of the behavior of the proposed system. It explains how typical users will use the system once it is deployed. In addition, the workload helps in understanding the requirements in a structured way. Because the system performance capability is viewed from different perspectives, like meeting the goals set by the users, impact on the architecture, and growth potential of the system and so on, the workload could be designed in many ways as shown in Figure 5.2.

Goal Oriented

Every system, when developed, will have definite goals; performance based requirements are driven by them. These goals are used to design the workload for PT. A goal oriented workload is derived from the goals set for the whole system.

To illustrate, the broad goals of a banking system could be:

- The system must be available on a 24X7 basis for the customer

- The response time must be less than 8 seconds for any query

- The existing architecture must be scalable for the growth projections as envisaged

- No failure of transaction during peak hours or very minimal down time

- Graceful transition to backup/mirrors in case of failures at any time

In the above example, the goals are defined from a user perspective and requirement points of view. These goals must be analyzed and converted into possible inputs to design a workload.

Figure 5.2. Design of workload

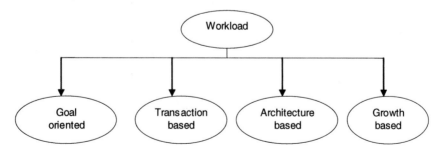

Consider the goal, "No failure of transaction during peak hours or very minimal down time."

First, it is necessary to analyze the probable cause for the failure. The failure could be due to:

- Functional errors which might have escaped during functionality testing;
- Lack of hardware resources and incorrect configuration of the software;
- Network failure during execution of the system;
- Bandwidth soaked during peak hours of operation;
- Unexpected errors during executions.

Most of the causes are not related to the system performance except the following:

- Lack of hardware resources and incorrect configuration of the software;
- Bandwidth soaked during peak hours of operation.

The problem of resource crunch could be identified during PT by selecting proper transactions in the workload which impact various resources like CPU, memory, disk, and so forth. These transactions may be either normal business transactions or any other computation based transactions. Some of the transactions considered may not be relevant to the user. Similarly, to test the bandwidth, simple transactions that create multiple requests and increase the traffic on the network should be considered during workload design.

In the above example, two different goals are identified with probable causes. To test such requirements, it is necessary to design two different workloads which are goal specific.

Transaction Oriented

The objective of PT in a transaction oriented workload is to examine the performance of the system for all business transactions that are relevant to day-to-day business. All identified transactions must be used while designing the workload. The performance goal for these transactions must be to verify the resource efficiency for an acceptable response and throughput.

Transactions are categorized into different types based on business and usage. There are some transactions that are critical from a business perspective. The performance of these transactions is of paramount importance. A separate workload must be defined to assess the performance behavior of these transactions. The usage pattern must be studied for these transactions before designing the workload.

To illustrate, withdrawal and deposit are two critical transactions (refer to case study in Appendix D) from the business perspective of the banking system. These transactions may activate internally with many other transactions. Since these transactions predominantly impact business and hence performance, the workload needs to be developed surrounding these two transactions.

Architecture Oriented

The system architecture needs to be carefully considered when designing the workload. The trends in business and technology that will affect the architecture need to be considered. The architecture might have to be scaled up or may be scaled down depending upon the change in future requirements. The architecture has to be consistent and reliable in the event of any changes. Serious thoughts should be given to check if there are any bottlenecks in the architecture or if there are any redundancies that can be done away with. The workload needs to be designed keeping in mind these factors that are very much part of the real world scenario.

As an illustration, most of the complex queries in the banking system will impact the architecture. Because complex queries always need more resources, as most of the time they involve many SQL joins on different tables, which certainly needs better resources to perform efficiently, this is an uncertainty of the capability of the architecture to handle concurrent users. The workload must be developed surrounding these complexities to test the architecture properly.

Growth Oriented

Once the business grows, the system requires changes in its complexion on functionality, performance, and reliability. If the system is not developed keeping the growth in view, modifications become more costly and time consuming. As the business grows, the performance of the system also changes. The changes in performance must be gauged properly; otherwise customer dissatisfaction may increase. The growth projection is normally carried out during the requirement study. The customer provides the overall growth projections for the next set of years. Based on the projected requirements, the performance expectations are worked out. Once the projected performance growth plan is known, a detailed workload will be designed to verify the system's performance claims. To design such a workload, the following parameters must be considered.

- Transactions that impact the growth must be identified. Growth of resource usage (like memory) with increased transactions must be formulated properly. After identifying the required transactions, the growth profile must be worked out by using the following parameters:

> ➢   Determine users growth based on the transactions;

> ➢   Logistics for the growth recorded;

> ➢   Pattern of growth analyzed.

- Transactions that impact the architecture also need to be identified. To illustrate, most of the operations at peak hours in a typical banking system impact performance of the system for more concurrent users. Growth of the business depends on these operation capabilities to handle more concurrent users.

It is obvious that one could get carried away and lose focus; hence, there should be a well planned review process in place. The review should be done periodically and by domain experts keeping in mind the typical real world scenarios. A good workload can be designed when it is oriented to all these points and is attributed to having an exhaustive consideration of them all.

What Are the Characteristics of a Workload?

The essence of the workload is to study the performance behavior of the proposed system before deployment. Hence, the behavior of the proposed system must be expressed as accurately as possible compared to the real world environment. However, it is difficult to express the real world environment before deployment, as the intricacies of the system, once deployed, are complex. In order to consider the behavior of the system completely and comprehensively, care must be taken to select the type of transactions and assign them to a proper user group. One should consider a good mix of transactions which impact concurrency, resources, and so forth. Characteristics for the requirement of a good workload are explained below.

Categorization of Transactions

Performance related transactions must be identified carefully. Some transactions may be defined in functional requirements, and some may not be defined but are needed for the test. Careful identification and classification will help in designing the workloads (see Types of Transactions earlier in this chapter).

Business Domain Specific

Identify routine and critical transactions based on the use cases. Use cases are derived during the functional design of the system. These use cases help in identifying business related transactions.

These transactions are used to study the behavior of the system under routine business operation. A typical business benchmark will provide this information. Business domain specific workload helps to build confidence with the users because the performance testing conducted under this workload provides the daily pattern of performance.

To illustrate, some of the typical business transactions in the banking system are:

- Deposit amount in the bank;
- Withdraw money from the bank;
- Enquiring about the features of the bank;
- Requesting a new account.

This will meet the daily user requirements of the banking system.

Resource Hungry

Identify those transactions that require more system resources like memory, processor, and so on. Computation of complex transactions will require more processor time and memory. Sometimes, batch processing jobs also require significant system resources.

For instance, some of the resource hungry transactions are:

- Preparing the annual balance sheet of a bank;
- Fund transfer from one bank to another;
- Generating monthly reports at a bank.

Concurrency

Identify those transactions that concurrently access the same record in a database. This will test the effective implementation of the database locks and impact the performance of the system. To illustrate, two or more users attempt to access the same record to update at the same time will be associated with a database lock. In a banking application, consider a scenario where a bank manager is crediting the interest amount to a particular account. During this time, the account holder withdraws the money from the same account.

Interacting

Identifying those transactions that put more load on common resources like printer, network (sending mail by many users), telephone lines, VOIP, and so forth. Most of the testers ignore these types of transactions during PT. As an illustration, a bank might have

80% of its customers subscribed for mobile alerts and e-mail alerts for transactions that happen on their account.

Infrastructure Related

Identify those transactions that affect the bandwidth, connection at the server, browser dependency, and so on.

In any Web-based system, accessing the home page by all users will impact the available bandwidth of the system. If some of the transaction types are not derived from the selected benchmarks, it is necessary to revisit the benchmark design to select appropriate transactions to cover all types. In this way, all possible types of transactions that impact the transactions are addressed.

How to Develop a Workload

Workload development starts with the selection of proper user groups and follows the process shown in Figure 5.3. For each group, set of transactions are mapped so that each group's behavior is defined properly which is close to the reality. If there is more than one group representing the overall behavior of the system, priority of each group must be defined by assigning weights to each group. Similarly, if there is more than one transaction with in the group, priority of each transaction must be defined by assigning weights to each transaction. Figure 5.3 defines the overall process to be followed during development of the workload.

Selection of User Groups

In a real world scenario, different users will access the Web site with different purposes; this means several transactions are initiated simultaneously by different users. To simulate such an environment, one needs to create different sets of user groups. A user group is a collection of users that executes a similar task and generates the same basic workload. The size of the user group may be fixed or variable.

To illustrate, three different user groups with a set of activities are considered for the bank system. They are:

1.   Customer Group
    •   Deposit money
    •   Withdraw money
    •   Enquiring about the features of the bank

Figure 5.3. Process to develop a workload

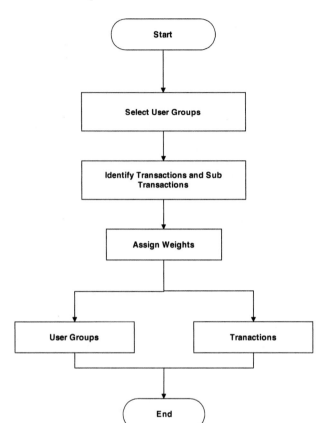

2.   Administrative Group
    •   Preparing the annual balance sheet of a bank
    •   Daily online status report
    •   Generating monthly reports at a bank
3.   Senior Management Group
    •   Ad-hoc query
    •   Daily online status report

A specific transaction, namely, "Daily online status report", is overlapping under two user groups. This means each group may have different types of transactions, and the same transaction may overlap different user groups.

Assigning Weights

Once the user groups and transaction types within the user group are identified, the number of users initiating each type of transaction must be mapped to each group. This is done by assigning weights to transactions. A weight represents the activation level of a particular transaction type. A transaction having a weight of 70% means that, out of 100 users, 70 users are accessing the transaction concurrently. There are two ways in which weights can be assigned, namely, weights to user groups and weights to transaction type.

Weights to User Groups

Before assigning weights to transactions and if there is more than one group, weights must be assigned first to the user groups. These weights are based on the usage profile derived from the benchmark. The number of users simulated group-wide during the test is proportional to the weights mapped to each user group.

In the above three user groups, we assign the following weights:

1.	Customer Group	60%
2.	Administrative Group	20%
3.	Senior Management Group	20%

If there are 100 concurrent users accessing the banking Web site, 60 users are mapped to the customer group, 30 users to the administrative group, and 10 users to senior management group. Because of the assignment of weights to a user group as percentage, the workload is scalable dynamically. It can also be expressed in terms of fixed number of users assign to each user group, provided distributions of users are known in advance.

Weights to Transaction Type

Within the user group, weights must be assigned to each transaction type similarly to the user groups. During simulation, the number of users initiating each type of transaction will be proportional to the weights assigned to it.

Out of three user groups, consider any one of the user groups, say customer group with weight of 60%. This group has three different types of transactions, and each type may have different weights.

1. Customer Group 60%

•	Deposit money	40%
•	Withdraw money	40%
•	Enquiring about features of the bank	20%

Here different types of transactions are initiated based on the weights assigned to each. If 60 concurrent users were mapped on the customer group (40% of 60), 24 users will deposit money, 24 users will withdraw money, and 12 users will enquire about the features of the bank, all simultaneously. Here also fixed weights can be assigned provided they are known in advance.

Sample Workload

Based on the process defined above, a typical workload for a banking system for a specific behavior is defined as shown in Figure 5.4.

Sequencing Transactions

Once the user groups are identified along with the functions or transactions within the group, sequencing of these transactions within the group is important. In a real world environment, all users may initiate the transactions at once or at various points of time. Some transactions may take more time to execute compared to others, though started simultaneously. Some transactions may begin after an event is completed. Such scenarios have to be expressed while designing the workload. Broadly, four different types of sequencing transactions can be considered as explained below.

Consider the above three types of transactions in the customer group. All the three types of transactions either start in sequence as they appear or in random. However, if one considers one type of transaction, say, "Deposit money", there will be many concurrent users who will execute it repeatedly in a fixed interval. The pattern of dynamic flow of these transactions may be characterized as follows:

Continuous

Out of 60 concurrent users in the customer group, 24 users will execute the transaction "Deposit Money". All of them (u1, u2...u24) will start simultaneously at T_0 but finish at different times due to resource availability. In the next run, each user will start at a different time as shown in Figure 5.5. Transactions U1 will start the next run at T_6 whereas U3 starts at T_7. This process continues until the end of the time interval as decided in the run schedule.

In Figure 5.5, the transaction initiated by the user U2 starts at T_0 and ends at time T_5. In the second run, T_5 becomes the start of the transaction. Similarly, other transactions end at different times.

Figure 5.4. Sample workload

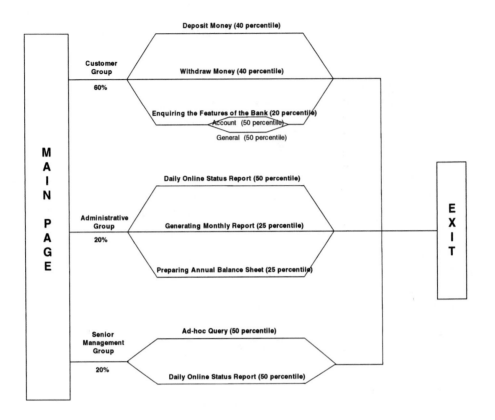

Wait Until All Complete

Though some of the users complete the job earlier, they have to wait until the remaining users complete their jobs. The new run will start simultaneously at T_4 as shown in Figure 5.6. Here some of the users may have to wait for a long time before their next run begins. The average response time may be long compare to the previous one. There may be a starvation because even if one transaction takes a long time to complete, all other transactions have to unnecessarily wait.

Figure 5.5. Timing diagram: Continuous transaction

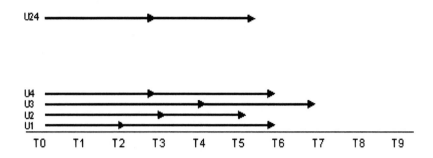

Figure 5.6. Timing diagram: synchronous transaction

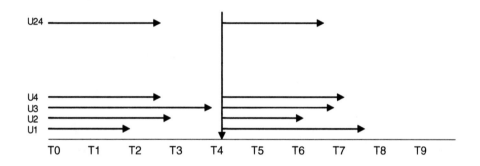

Wait for Min or Max Time before Next Iteration

Though a user completes the first execution at a different time, all of them will not start at the same time in the next run. Transactions wait for a fixed minimum or maximum time interval, during which, if synchronization of transactions is not possible, those transactions that have finished execution will enter into the next cycle. Compared to the previous one, all users may not start the next run simultaneously. Some of the users may start the next run at T_4 after waiting a minimum time interval, known as wait time. Some more users may start at different times but not later than T_6 which is the maximum wait time as shown in Figure 5.7.

To illustrate, transactions U2 and U24 (Figure 5.7) complete early and wait for other transactions to complete before T_4, which is the minimum wait time. Since more transac-

Figure 5.7. Timing diagram: asynchronous transaction

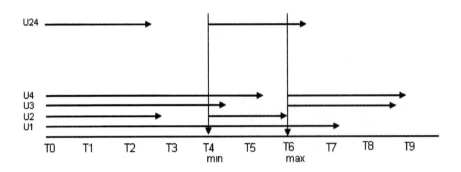

tions still need to complete, these transactions start the next run at T_4. Remaining transactions wait till T_6, which is the maximum wait time before starting the next run. This process continues and provides flexibility for synchronization. The minimum and maximum time can be configured to study the performance behavior of the system more precisely.

Here the average response time is improved compared to the previous one, and starvation is avoided.

Wait for an Event

Though all the transactions started at the same time, these transactions may have to wait for an external event to trigger before completion. The external event may take its own time to respond, and until then, the transaction has to wait. In Figure 5.6, an event may happen at T_4 for the next run. This event could happen any time. For instance, during fund transfer between two banks, the receiving bank, which is an external event, must respond to the request. The successful completion of the transaction depends on the receiving bank to respond and act per the transaction requirement. Hence, the response time may vary.

Selection of Tools

The tools should meet the general requirements. First, they should have clear descriptive documentation, an online tutorial, and an extensive online help facility. Second, they should have good vendor technical support. Third, they should be provided with good performance at a reasonable price. Fourth, they should be hardware/software platform independent (granted, no tool really fills this requirement as yet) (see *Selecting an automated client-server testing tool suite*, 2003). Appendix B elaborates general guidelines for selecting a tool.

Summary

The design of various benchmarks is an important task before conducting PT. Benchmarks are abstracts of real world scenarios. These benchmarks are further elaborated with more intricate details by designing and understanding workloads. A workload provides a detailed view of the test environment. Having clearly understood the blueprint of the PT to be done, in the next chapters, we look at creating a plan, the environment, and also the processes and schedules. The next phase is test build.

References

Application workload load testing (simulation). (2003). Retrieved April 23, 2003, from http://www.perftuning.com/workload_testing.html

The benchmark handbook. (2003). Retrieved April 12, 2003, from http://www.benchmarkresources.com/handbook/1-8.asp

Selecting an automated client-server testing tool suite. (2003). Retrieved November 23, 2003, from http://www.csst-technologies.com/Chapter11.htm

Additional Sources

Customer transaction behavior on the Internet: An empirical study. (2003). Retrieved April 14, 2003, from http://is-2.stern.nyu.edu/~wise98/pdf/five_a.pdf

Geretz, J. (2002). *Scalable architectural guidelines: Designing for flexibility*. Retrieved April 19, 2003, from http://www.devx.com/vb2themax/Article/19885

Mixed workload verification program can maximize consolidation efficiency. (2003). Retrieved April 23, 2003, from http://www.veritest.com/solutions/consolidation/workload.asp

Mosley, D. J., & Posey, B. A. (2002, June). *Just enough software test automation*.

Chapter 6

Test Preparation Phase III: Test Build

The next phase, that is, the build phase, commences after the completion of the design phase. Design provides the guidelines, but the build phase really implements the design so that execution of the test can be carried out later. The first activity in the build phase is to plan the various activities for testing. However, building a comprehensive test plan is as important as executing the test itself. Apart from the test plan, testing the build phase also focuses on setting up a proper test environment, test schedule, and testing processes.

Developing the Performance Test Plan

The test plan is an integral part of any testing activity, either functional or performance. The test plan provides insight on PT. It provides information like details of the system to be tested, objectives of PT, testing processes, and details on workloads. A comprehensive test plan is an instrument for the designer to enforce the direction in which the test is to be conducted. The project manager can use the test plan as a tool for completing and monitoring the testing life cycle. The testers can refer to the test plan as a guide and monitor throughout the testing activity.

The test designers develop test plans. They must be involved in the performance requirement analysis phase wherein the test objectives are defined properly. Typically, the test plan is developed during the design phase of the life cycle.

What Are the Contents of a Typical Performance Test Plan Document?

Though the test plan varies from project to project, the checklists shown in Table 6.0 identify the requirements to prepare a typical performance test plan. The test plan prepared for PT is different from the functional test plan. Test plan objectives must be clearly specified. This includes the intended audience, type of workload model used, expected test outputs, and resource utilization. The set of objectives will directly affect the environment and hence also the estimation. The plan must highlight the usage model in detail. Each usage model depends on the type and number of workloads designed for the proposed test.

Though the checklist provides the guidelines, the actual test plan may not follow the exact sequence and details. A test plan should give a complete picture about the test requirements, testing processes, respective constraints, and above all, it should give details of expected results. A thorough test plan is the work product of the test definition and design phases of test preparation.

A sample test plan template is given in Appendix C2.

Table 6.0. Checklist to prepare a typical performance test plan

Sl No	Requirements of the plan	Descriptions
1	Test Plan Profile	• Plan name, ID# and version number • Date of test plan version • Target audience for the plan • System Name, ID# Author(s) of the plan and how to contact them
2	System Description	• Description of the system under test • Project acceptance criteria • Identification & analysis of risks
3	Performance Test Objectives	• Classify intended audience (clients,users,marketers,other interested parties in the test results) • Define and classify expectations according to audience Group • Highlight success criteria of the project
4	Expected Outputs	• Test log file containing various test runs • Test results in table as well as graph formats • OS monitoring logs, if required • Results Analysis Report
5	Performance Measurements Matrix	• Response Time • Throughput including page views, number of hits, user sessions • Resource utilization both server (CPU, Memory, Disk) and Network (bandwidth, throughput) • Reliability measurements

Table 6.0. cont.

SI No	Requirements of the plan	Descriptions
6	Usage Model	• Identify user groups of the system under test • Determine the operation profile (set of user action) for each user group • Identify test Scenarios for each operations • Develop required workloads based on user group and test Scenarios. • Develop data pools and test cases based on the requirement for each workload • Identify background noises
7	Test Environment	• Describe the operational Environment • Describe the Test Environment • List the major differences
8	Configuration Management	• Identify the storage locations and organization of the test artifacts • Proper naming conventions for all artifacts to be decided. • Explain the versioning conventions and plan • Explain the monitoring and maintenance of test scripts, workloads and the results • Explain the backup plan
9	Interface with third party system	• List any external link to be included during the test • List all third party components that are interfaced with the system • Identify third party system, if any, that drives the inputs to the system under test
10	Prerequisite	• The system under test must be functionally error free • The system development must be completed totally
11	Test Schedule	• Prepare the test schedule and resource requirement for running the tests
12	Testing Process	• Customize the testing process
13	Exit Criteria	• The number of runs planned • In each run, once a specified duration reaches • When it reaches the required number of virtual users • When the performance measurement matrix is satisfied
14	Assumptions	• If the input data is generated from external system, specify it. • If driver and stubs to be written, specify the same
15	Constraints	• If functional test is not completed, specify those modules • If required data is not available, elaborate under what constraint test has to be conducted • Limitation on entry criteria • Date of system release • Exit criteria/stopping rule • Budget constraints
16	Risk Factors	• Evaluate the risk factor if the operational and test environment are different • Analyze the risk while extrapolating the results • People resources availability • Time deadlines

Working with the Proper Testing Environment

Setting a test environment for PT is an important aspect of the build phase. Establishing a proper environment to conduct PT requires a lot of planning and coordination. Planning is required in identifying the hardware and software resources, setting up the network, identifying people, and scheduling the test. Any performance test requires a lot of coordination among the system developers, testers, network and database administrators, and performance analysts. Proper tools must be available and configured for the environment. Availability of proper licenses for the testing tools also needs to be planned.

Operational Environment

Real life problems will be known only when the system is deployed in its operational environment, that is, when the system is in the habitat it was designed to be in. The best place to address performance issues accurately is in the system's habitat. Here the system is operational and working correctly but might not satisfy performance expectations. In this case, either system might not have been tested for performance before launching, or the system needs tuning to improve performance. Since real data are used as inputs, results obtained are quite accurate. However, testing in this environment has its own intrinsic problems.

Some of the problems of testing in the operational environment are:

- Availability of the environment is difficult as it may be in an active state and could be vulnerable;

- Likelihood of damaging other legacy systems or applications running in that environment which are not in the scope of PT;

- Some functionality of the application might get affected due to performance tuning measures that need to be adopted;

Figure 6.1. Typical simulated test environment

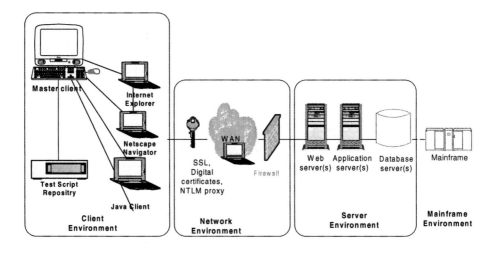

- Conducting a performance test when the system is operational will make the response slow for potential users;
- A lot of monitoring is required to test the system in its operational environment.

Therefore, a dedicated simulated environment similar to operation environment is suggested for effective performance testing.

Simulated Environment

An ideal choice for PT is the operational environment wherein tests could be done in a realistic manner. However, availability and usage of such an environment is very difficult or next to impossible. An alternative choice is to go for a simulated environment. A simulating test environment requires investment on hardware and software. If the system has to be deployed in a complex environment, such an environment might be too expensive and cannot be reused once the testing is complete. A simulated environment is normally an isolated network with its own security and servers. Though it may not be possible to simulate the operational environment, a sincere attempt must be made to come as close as possible to the operational environment. A typical simulated environment for PT is shown in Figure 6.1. This simulation environment consists of an underlying network environment, a server environment, a client environment, and may be a mainframe environment. A server environment may have clusters of servers like Web servers, application servers, and database servers. The client environment consists of multiple clients with different browsers and a repository to store test scripts. The network environment is associated with firewalls, WAN, and proper authentication. The simulated environment could be centralized or distributed.

If a test lab already exists, then the information about the operational environment has to be gathered. Set up and configure the computers to match the configuration of the operational environment. If a dedicated test lab is not present for testing, then start identifying a location where the environment can be simulated. Start assessing hardware and software requirements; make sure to document them in the test plan.

Hardware and Software Requirements

Replicating the real world operational environment requires meticulous planning and perseverance. Simulating the system's habitat is as important as conducting the test. To illustrate, workstation response time measured right next to the server may not be the same as the response time of a remotely located workstation somewhere on the network. This means that an important early step in planning a performance test is to understand specifically what equipment, networks, and software comprise the operational environments.

If multiple environments are to be simulated, then the configurations need to be carefully handled for multiple environments. The domain architecture, services, business applications, and administrative expectations have to be carefully studied to simulate the security model, application deployment, and server storage methods.

The general hardware and software requirements of a typical test environment can be divided into four subdivisions as shown in Figure 6.1. They are client, server, network, and mainframe environment. Some of them may have to be hired from vendors, as setting up them may not be economically feasible.

Requirements to Set Up the Client Environment

The client environment must be as close as possible to the user environment so that all user actions can be simulated. Simulation at the client side is normally done by test scripts wherein actions are captured and replayed during the test. These test scripts must be stored in one place and controlled by a client known as master client (Figure 6.1). Master client is responsible for creating the required number of virtual users and managing the entire test execution. Master client also controls the remaining clients used for the execution. The client environment must also provide facilities to simulate different roles of users based on the user community. To illustrate, a Web site requires several thousands of users to log in with five different roles. This means that five test cases are required to simulate five roles, say, correct log in action and a few more roles to handle invalid logins and related activities. These actions, in the form of test scripts, must be stored in the repository controlled by the master client.

To illustrate, in a typical banking application, the tester has to initiate the roles of the customer, administration, and senior management groups. The tester should follow the test cases written for all the three user communities. The scripts generated are stored in the test script repository, and they are distributed among the client machines. Each user community may have several users according to the distribution represented in the workload. Accordingly, the tester is going to generate virtual users of a specified community. Similarly, many issues have to be addressed while setting up the client environment. Some of the challenges to be addressed during the environment setup are:

- Multiple browsers at different client machines to simulate heterogeneous clients;
- Different hardware configurations (memory, processor, etc.) for different clients;
- Managing cache at each client;
- Managing multiple platforms;
- Configuring protocols at each client;
- Distribution of test scripts across all clients;
- Limitation of simulating the number of virtual users at different clients;
- Monitoring the user actions during the test execution.

Apart from this, some of the clients may have to be used to manage the tools requirement like a dedicated controller and storage of test scripts. Addressing these issues is a challenge for the testers.

Testing with Different Browsers

Client machines can be set up with different browsers to map the operating environment (Figure 6.1). To illustrate, if the load has to be tested for 2,000 users, then 1,000 users browsing through Internet Explorer, 500 users with Netscape Navigator, and 500 Java clients can be simulated. The application should be previewed with different versions too since different versions of the browsers display the screen differently. Not just the browser, client machines can be set up with a mix of hardware and software components. It is difficult to predict the client environment for Web applications. Users of Web applications are unknown and can access from different geographical locations with different hardware and software setups. Therefore, setting up an environment with a thorough mix of clients is advisable.

Testing with Different Operating Systems

Configuring clients across different platforms such as Windows 2000, Windows NT, Windows 98, Linux, and others are needed for a typical test environment. These operating systems contain the TCP/IP stack and the information required to communicate with the Internet. Each operating system implements the stack differently.

Client Caching

Caching the pages at client side allows the pages to be loaded quicker the next time when the same page is loaded. Caching graphics and other Internet medias should be incorporated in some of the client machines.

Different Protocol Setups

TCP/IP is the basic protocol needed for communicating with the Internet. It is a point to point protocol, which allows client to communicate across the Internet to different types of systems and computers. SMTP (Simple Mail Transfer Protocol) (http://www.freesoft.org/CIE/Topics/94.htm) and POP (Post Office Protocol) can be used to send and receive mail in some clients. The rest can be set with IMAP (Internet Mail Access Protocol) for remote mail access activities. It is probable that due to budget limitations, these multiple environments have to be set up with the same networks and platforms. Some of the ways of maintaining the multiple configurations are to have mirrored hard disks or replaceable zip drives that are bootable.

Requirements to Set Up Server Environment

Server environment includes mainly setting up of Web servers, application servers, and database servers (Figure 6.1). The type of servers needed varies from project to project. Some projects may require an additional proxy server to be set up; another may require a file server to be set up; yet another may require a transaction server to be set up and installed. The disk space, memory space, processor type and speed, and caching ability should be studied carefully to create a realistic server environment. Server drivers used or planned to be used should be the same as the servers in the operational environment. Remote access protocols like Serial Line Internet Protocol (SLIP), Point to Point Protocol (PPP), and Point to Point Tunneling Protocol (PPTP) (see Protocols, 2004) must be set up, which allow remote servers to connect to the Internet. Server caching can also be incorporated. Proxy caching is typically performed on a corporate LAN.

Requirements to Set Up Network Environment

To set up the network for the test environment, the initial information that one would require is the network architecture that will be used in the system's habitat. Once the architecture is understood, then the same has to be simulated for the test scenario. In case of a distributed network, the same has to be replicated with simulated network delays and various network equipment. Network connection at the server end as well as client end impacts PT.

In a typical Web based application scenario, the server side network architecture can be simulated, but the client side simulation is not as easy. One of the reasons is that it is difficult to predict the client's environment and also the number of clients. The application should be tested with various connections like dialup modem, DSL (Digital Subscriber Line), cable modem, ISDN, T1, and optical fibers. Bandwidth available per user depends on the type of connection at the client site. It may not be possible to simulate all the connections in the test environment. It is observed that the majority of Web users connect through Internet Service Providers (ISPs) via a modem connection. Therefore, generally, a modem of 56 Kb/s is used in the test environment to connect the client and server setups.

Firewalls are required to manage security issues. One needs to consider configuring of the network to handle other features such as caching and access control. Network sniffers (Mitchell, 2004) can be used to probe and diagnose the flow of data on the network.

If the test environment is connected to a WAN, routers are used for testing the network latency and testing domain controller. A multiple environment can be set up to study the network latency across WAN. A secondary environment can be placed at different geographical locations for more realistic PT.

Requirements to Set Up Mainframe Environment

Mainframes used to be defined by their large size and support of thousands of users. Mainframes are best defined by their operating systems: UNIX and Linux, and IBM's z/OS, OS/390, MVS, VM, and VSE (see Operating Systems, 2004). Mainframes provide huge disks for storage and management of the bulk of data.

Since mainframes often allow for "graceful degradation" and service while the system is running, performance issues do not occur. Mainframes cost millions of dollars, and they can occupy a room. But now a mainframe can also run on a laptop and support multiple users. A huge investment is required to set up a mainframe environment. The above simulated environment, once set up, must be close to the operational environment.

Mapping the Simulated Environment to the Operational Environment

Testing the system for performance in a simulated environment before deploying in the operational environment reduces the risk of performance problems and minimizes downtime of the operational site. The simulated environment could be created by one of the following techniques:

- Simulated environment is exactly equal to operational environment.
- Simulated environment is less equipped than operational environment.
- Simulated environment is more equipped than operational environment.

The real test bed can be used in the test environment if the testing is done after the deployment of the project. However, for predeployment scenarios, as it is difficult to obtain real data, expected data can be simulated to make the test environment equivalent or close to the operational environment.

Though the servers, network, and legacy systems can be simulated according to the operational environment, the client environment is not known in the case of Web applications. Hence, it may not be possible to simulate the diversity of the client environment in the following cases.

Simulated Environment is Exactly Equal to Operational Environment

When one says the simulation environment is exactly equal to operational environment, it means equivalent in every respect. The environments should be equal in terms of servers, network, legacy systems, as well as test bed.

Servers: The number of servers present in an operational environment should be maintained at the simulated test environment too. To illustrate, if the operational site is equipped with three Web servers, one application server, and one database server, then the same number of servers is used for testing in the simulated environment. In addition, if any proxy server or file server or any other type of server is present at the operational site, it should also be available at the test environment.

Not just the number of systems, even the make, model, memory capacity, disk capacity, and processor speed of the servers should be configured in a simulated environment. To illustrate, if the operational site has IIS 4.0 as the Web application server, that is, the server which serves as both Web server and as application server, then the test environment must also be configured with the same.

Network: The simulated environment is designed to handle the same type of network adopted in the operational environment such as the layout of the computers, cables, switches, routers, and other components of the network. The network architecture with details of the use of Ethernet, Token bus, Token ring, or Dual bus architecture is also maintained in the test environment.

The simulated environment should be established with the same client side connectivity, such as cable modem, DSL, ISDN, or a T1 or partial T1, as the networks used in operational site. The topology used to set up the network, such as Bus, Ring, Star, or Mesh topology should also be maintained in the simulated test environment.

Legacy Systems: If the system under test is servicing some legacy operations, even that background process is simulated in the test environment. To illustrate, if the system has a mainframe environment to handle huge database operations or if the system is equipped with Storage Area Network (SAN) to handle huge storage, then a similar setup is established at the testing site.

Challenges: If the organization is already equipped with a sophisticated test lab, then the environment can be upgraded to meet the current project needs. Upgrade the servers so that they all have the same amount of memory and disk capacity and use the same processor type and speed as the servers at the operational site or the same as planned to deploy at the operational site if the testing is for a postlaunch project.

If upgrading is not feasible or the test lab does not exist, then a new test environment has to be established. A suitably equipped test lab leads to clear implementations and gives accurate results. Simulating separate environments for each project is difficult, and the associated cost is high.

A possible solution is to share the test environment for several projects. However, to do so, the project should require a similar environment, and the schedule must be compatible. Another possible solution to handle the budget issues is to take the required

Table 6.1. Template for a likely investment on test environment

Hardware/Software components	Name(sample)	Cost/Item	Quantity	Total cost
Web server	Apache			
Application server	IIS			
Database server	Oracle			
Client machine	DELL			
Client machine	COMPAQ			
Mainframe	IBM			
Browser	Netscape Navigator IE 4.0			
Operating system	Windows 98			
Network connection	56.6 Modem			
Automated tool	Rational's Test manager			
Firewall				
Other security Components	128-bit digital key			
Any other				

components for lease from a vendor and return them once the project is over. Another solution could be to purchase a hardware or software component for a specific project that can be used in the operational environment itself.

Overall, the cost of replicating the operational environment exactly with the simulated environment is quite high. However, this cost is lower than costs of fixing problems in the system's habitat or operational environment.

Simulated Environment is Less Equipped Than Operational Environment

An important step to notice in the test environment is to determine whether it is feasible to establish the exact version of the operational environment for testing purposes. If not, then performance must be measured in a smaller or less equipped simulated environment.

Servers: Generally, the simulated environment will compromise the number of servers. If the operational site has a cluster of Web servers and budget constraints do not allow for the same set up in the test environment, then a lesser number of Web servers may be used for testing. Sometimes, we may have the same number of servers as that of the operational environment, but these servers could have less capacity.

Network: As in servers, the testing team may have to compromise load balancer, the number of routers, and the number of switches. To illustrate, if a load balancer is used to manage load on a cluster of Web servers in the operational environment, it may not be seen in the test environment if a single Web server is used.

Legacy Systems: The simulated environment may not include legacy systems, which are present at the operational site. Since legacy systems have comparatively less impact on performance, the simulation of them is often ignored in the test environment.

Challenges: When the simulated environment is less equipped than the operational environment, the results are extrapolated to produce the likely performance in the real environment. It is dangerous to assume equivalence between the operational environment and the test environment while extrapolating results. This extrapolation is not easy and presents surprises when the system fails to deliver the expected performance in the operational environment.

To illustrate, performance experts of Hewlett Packard (see Hewlett-Packard, 2004) conducted a performance test with a configuration of 50 machines and observed adequate performance. They extrapolated the results and deployed the product in an operational environment, which was quite similar to the test environment. In the operational environment, performance of the product degraded drastically with 51 or more machines.

Therefore, one should remember that perception may not be the same as reality. Expectations and perceived performance may give different results in the operational environment. Therefore, PT requires a test environment that can reasonably accurately simulate the real world operating conditions and real world workloads. These are difficult to achieve in a test environment, which has limited capabilities.

Even if the test environment can model the operational environment adequately, there is always a question of predictability. It is important to note the variation between the expected results vis à vis what is obtained from the test environment and with what criteria these results are extrapolated.

Designing a correct benchmark to handle this predictability is a difficult task. Using the wrong benchmark will lead to misleading results. If realistic growth projections are incorporated in the benchmark design, then the extrapolation results based on them can give justifiable results.

Simulated Environment is More Equipped Than Operational Environment

If a permanent test lab already exists, then the problem of establishing a new environment is eliminated. Sometimes, an existing test environment may be more equipped than the operational environment. Then, the results obtained at the test environment have less reliability than the ones true for the operational environment.

A simple solution to adjust the test environment is to scale down the configurations to map the configurations of the operational site. Scaling down the configuration is a major issue, which makes the test environment change for every project. The environment often has to contract and expand to provide acceptable service that is to handle large as well as small networks.

Investment on Environment

Based on the type of environment decided by the test team, one can plan the investment. The likely investment on a test environment is attributed to computing systems as given in Table 6.1. It provides a template to arrive at the total cost.

Table 6.1 can be updated based on the cost matrix needed for the simulated environment. The major share of investment in setting up the environment lies in purchasing automated tools and installing a mainframe.

Challenges in Creating a Simulated Environment

Once the requirements to simulate the environment are known, apart from investment on hardware and software, one needs to address many other challenges before the environment can actually be used for testing.

Identifying Noises

Once the environment is ready and running, there may be many unknown and unwanted tasks that get executed along with the scheduled workload. Such tasks are known as noises. These tasks contribute to poor performance during simulation, provided they are not accounted for in the workload itself. The following tasks could be categorized as noises.

- Operating system processes are running along with the application.

- Some background process that needs to be started before the test.

- Some additional process, like printing a document, needs to be initiated during the test.

- Identify those processes that will be running apart from the SUPT in the operational environment. These processes have to be simulated in the test environment also.

- The network bandwidth might be shared by many applications. To illustrate, the network might also be used for VOIP in the operational environment. The same process has to be simulated during the test run also.

- Taking backups or running virus checks is an important activity in the operational environment. Normally, these activities are missed when the simulated environment is designed.

- Plan for unforeseen activities or worst case scenarios, which may affect the performance and try to simulate the same in the test run.

Some noises are part of the testing process, but others must be simulated properly in order to replicate the operational environment. These noises related processes must be planned in advance to achieve better results.

Scalability Issues

The simplest approach to establish a simulated environment is to handle the scalability extremes, which the system is expected to encounter. But this approach is difficult to implement when scalability expectation is high.

To illustrate, the Bank of New York (see Bank of New York, 2004) tested for database performance with a relatively small test database in the test lab. Later, the system did not give the expected database performance in the operational environment, with a real database much larger than the one which was tested.

A more complex example of scalability issues is the one where the server's capacity is increased simultaneously along with higher loads than scheduled. Also, increase the RAM size; add the number of network interface cards, the number of switches on the network, and so on. In such situations, servers that perform well at lower loads sometimes may not maintain their level of performance at higher user levels, in spite of increasing the capacity of the server. Poor performance will lead to loss from the customer base.

Gradually increasing the load on the system and carefully monitoring the changes in each cycle is important. Scalability can be viewed in two different dimensions.

- Gradually increasing the load, keeping the system resources constant;
- Gradually decreasing the system resources, keeping the load constant.

In the first case, the capacity is checked for the existing resource at maximum load while a sufficiency check on the resource for the required load is the main objective in the second case.

Resource and Budget Limitations

In most cases, simulating the operational environment is impossible, but a likely operational environment can be simulated. This requires extra investment and resources. Sometimes, a hired testing environment could be used for a specified duration. There are many organizations that will provide such facilities, but they are expensive. Some of them are given in Table 6.2.

These organizations provides necessary infrastructure to conduct PT. This list is not exhaustive, and readers are requested to explore further, based on their requirements.

Table 6.2. Sample outsourcing organization for test environment

Test outsourcers	Location
Benchmark Labs	Edina,MN (www.benchlabs.com) (Accessed on 15th - Dec – 2003)
Berlitz Translation services	New york,Dublin (www.berlitz.com) (Accessed on 20th – Feb – 2004)
National Software Testing L	NTSL,Conshocken,PA(www.nstl.com) (Accessed on 18th – Dec – 2003)
ProSoft Engineering Inc	Pleasonton,CA (http://www.prosofteng.com/) (Accessed on 14th –Feb – 2004)
QALabs	Vancouver,BC (www.qalabs.com) (Accessed on 16th – Dec – 2003)
ReVision Labs	Redmond,WA (www.nwhtweb.com/sic.php?sic=8734) (Accessed on 14th _Feb – 2004) (Requires subscription)
AC Labs	Burlington,MA (www.sqp.com) (Accessed on 17th –Sep – 2004)
ST Labs(Software Testing	Seattle,WA (www.stlabs.com) (Accessed on 17th – sep – 2004)
Testware associates	Piscataway,NJ (www.testware-assoc.com) (Accessed on 16th – Dec – 2004)
VeriTest	Santa Monica,CA (www.veritest.com) (Accessed on 17th – Sep – 2004)

Isolated Environment

A test environment could be isolated from the corporate network of the organization. An isolated environment is situated at a single site. All the resources are dedicated to the environment. The environment is equipped with network infrastructure, server setup, and client computers. Creating an isolated environment depends on the size of the budget and availability of physical space. If a connection is needed to generate background noise, a thorough plan to regulate and control the connection is an overhead. Make sure to terminate the connection, which is used to generate noise as quickly as possible to protect the system under test.

The physical hardware device used to connect to the Internet will not be the same for all users. Different users may use different types of hardware. It may be a desktop computer, a laptop, a Web access device such as Web TV, a cellular phone, or any other handheld device which is designed to access the Internet. Using all hardware devices for testing is not possible due to budget limitations and availability problems.

Developing Test Scripts

Test scripts are the replication of transactions identified for developing a workload but represented in a language. Different tools represent the test script in different formats. Test scripts can be generated in two ways: manual scripting and automated scripting.

Test scripts generated manually are cumbersome, time consuming, and expensive.

However, automatically generated scripts may not be ready for test execution due to interfacing dynamic data within the script. These scripts have to be edited to include additional requirements that are not generated automatically.

Guidelines to Develop Test Scripts

Most test script development follows normal coding standards. Every tool provides its own language to develop test scripts. If the language is known, test scripts could be developed manually also. Otherwise, a record and play facility should be used to develop the test scripts. The following checklist provides the guidelines for writing scripts:

- Once the workload is defined, identify the set of transactions or test scenarios to write the scripts.

- Verify whether the system under test is working or not with those transactions identified for scripting.

- Install the tool and configure with the operating system of the client.

- Using the tool in record and play mode, capture the test script by playing as if the user is using the system and complete the activity for which the script needs to be captured.

- Play back the script and verify the correctness of the script.

- Edit the test script for:

  - ➢ Modifying think time, if necessary;
  - ➢ Handling dynamic sessions, if required;
  - ➢ Accessing the data pool, if required;
  - ➢ Any other items relevant to the recorded script.

The above guidelines are general in nature; each tool provides different facilities to capture the test scripts. Refer to the tool documentation for further explanation.

Issues in Recorded Scripts

In most of the cases, the scripts generated by using the tools need to be modified to customize to a particular environment.

- If the application generates the dynamic data during the execution, the script will not run subsequently. The recorded script will have hard coded data. When the script runs for the second time, the application will generate new data and scripts

Table 6.4. Activity template for a test schedule

Sl No.	Date	Duration to complete the activity	Activity in test schedule	Sub Activities
1	TBD (To Be Decided)	Project dependent	Requirements	• Validate Requirements • Validate usage models • Validate Test strategy • Validate workload designs
2	TBD	Project dependent	Test Environment	• Determine Test environment • Determine dates and locations of testing • Install and configure test environment • Validate connectivity
3	TBD	Project dependent	Tools& Training	• Skill set development on tools • Installation and configuration of automated tools.
4	TBD	Project dependent	Development	• Develop a workload using the tool from the designs • Develop test scripts for the workload
5	TBD	Project dependent	Maintenance of Scripts	• Edit scripts to include data pool • Edit scripts include think time • Validate edited scripts • Map the generated scripts to scenarios • Execute the test
6	TBD	Project dependent	Test Execution	• Capture results of the test • Check for pass/fail criteria • Repeat the test run number of times as specified in the Strategy document • Repeat from serial#4 to serial#6 with different workload till all the designed workloads are implemented
7	TBD	Project dependent	Test Analysis	• Analyze the results, identify for which workload test cycle has failed • Modify the workload, repeat from serial#4 to serial #6 • Analyze results, if results are not according to the acceptance criteria or any bottleneck is identified, follow tuning guidelines and act accordingly • Analyze the test results obtained after performance tuning. • If acceptance criteria are met, present results to the client.

fail. This could be rectified by editing the script and adding new clauses provided by the tool.

• Some of the tools may have problems in handling data in XML format. All servers typically accept the data in a specific format. However, each client or load generator will create its own XML format and send the data to the server and vice versa. In order for the server to a handle common format, the script must be edited.

- If applications use applets, the script generated may not work during the testing. To run the script effectively, all the applet clauses must be installed at the client machines.

- If a data pool is used during the test, the scripts must be appropriately edited to accommodate the data files.

- An important issue to be addressed in any of the script is to handle repeated login/ logout. The recorded script creates new login/logout sessions for every thread, and if every thread runs multiple times, a similar number of sessions will be created. These sessions will become overheads on the server. To solve such problems, most of the tools support INIT and TERMINATE options wherein one can specify it as a one-time activity.

- Often when a new tool is used for the first time on a testing program, more time is spent on automated test scripts than on actual testing. Test engineers may be eager to automate elaborate scripts, but may lose sight of the real goal, which is to test the application.

Most of the tools provide record and play methods to capture the scripts. However, each script generated must be suitably edited to accommodate the necessary changes required to run the test.

Preparing the Test Schedule

The main objective of preparing a complete test schedule is to plan a comprehensive utilization of all types of resources, which could be ensured at an appropriate time. To plan such a schedule, we need to know the type of activities and duration required to handle the activities as well as the resources used during these activities. Table 6.4 provides a template which covers the activities that need to be scheduled and the projected duration. The duration of each activity depends on the complexity of the project. The test team normally prepares the test schedule. While preparing the schedule, the availability of resources must be ensured, particularly relating to those used in the operational environment. If the testing is scheduled in a simulated environment, make sure that resources are dedicated and not getting shared by other applications.

The template shown in Table 6.4 provides guidelines for test engineers to plan the test schedule properly.

Defining the Testing Process

For any project to be successful, a formal testing process must be defined. In the case of PT, the testing process is defined in three phases: planning; design and implement;

Figure 6.2. Testing process

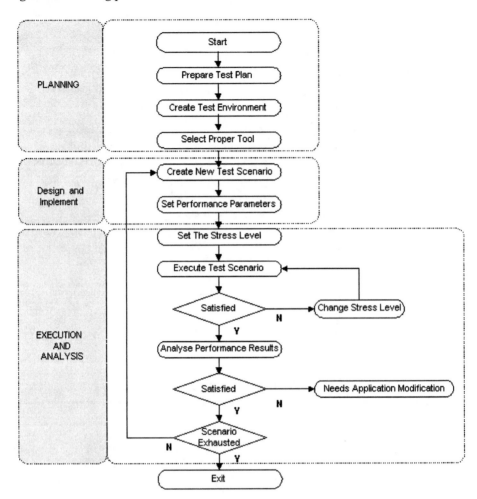

and execution and analysis. Each phase, as shown in Figure 6.2, describes various activities that need to be addressed before moving to the next phase.

In the planning phase, preparing the test plan, setting up the test environment, and selection of tools are addressed. The design and implement phase involves developing workloads, generating test scripts using automation tools, setting performance parameters, verifying those parameters, and related activities. Performance parameters must be defined at the operating system level and must be application specific. The final phase, namely, execution and analysis phase (Figure 6.2), defines the process involved in executing the test as well as presenting and analyzing the test results. Before starting execution of the test, the stress level must be set. The stress level could be in terms of number of concurrent users or fixing the resource constraints for a definite number of concurrent users. For each stress level, a set of scenarios is executed until satisfactory results are reached. Likewise, all sets of scenarios are tested for satisfactory results.

Analysis of Risk Factors

Since PT is a high investment and a skilled activity, the testing team must be ready to face uncertainties and risks. The risks come at any stage of the test execution. They could be functional defects noticed during the test or involvement of unskilled testers or architectural problems or managerial aspects of the entire testing project itself. The probable risks could be classified as follows:

Testing Started before a System Architecture Studied

It is advisable to test a new tool upgrade in an isolated environment to verify its compatibility with the currently existing system architecture, before rolling out any new tool upgrade on a project. For most of the project, the architecture is studied and implemented from the functional aspect whereas the same may not be studied from the performance point of view. Some of the tools may not work with the architecture or may require some add-on utilities. A mainframe system supports a few testing tools. In such situations, realizing the nonfunctioning of the tool at a late project life cycle may cost the project expensively.

Lack of Test Development Guidelines

If the test team has several test engineers, each using a different style for creating test scripts, maintaining such scripts is a nightmare. Test engineers are advised to follow guidelines used for development projects to increase the readability and maintainability of developed test scripts. Every test script development must follow normal coding standards like followed in development of programs. Proper training must be given before the development of test scripts.

Integration Problems with Various Tools in SDLC and STLC

If different tools are used for each phase of the testing life cycle, they may not integrate due to the protocol they conformed to. For metrics purposes and to enforce consistency among the elements and tractability between phases, output of one tool should be an input of another tool. To illustrate, output of the performance requirements capturing tool can be an input of the design tool. Output of the design tool can be an input of the testing tool and so on. If the tools are from different vendors, they do not integrate easily. Trying to consider them as a challenge and making them integrate may require a separate plugin, and this is a time consuming task. Even if one goes for elaborate programming techniques and generates a code to integrate, the tools may not be reusable later. This is not an efficient approach. Purchasing tools that are already integrated into a unified suite may be a better solution. A cost/benefit analysis has to be carried out before buying an integrated suite.

Redundant Information Kept in Multiple Repositories

Proper configuration management tools and policies have to be in place to ensure that information is managed effectively. In several instances, the implementation of more tools can result in less productivity. One should be careful about choosing tools. Requirement management tools and test management tools exhibit the same functionality. If any management tool already exists, we can use it for other purposes too. To illustrate, if the requirements management tool is already purchased, then buying a tool for test management is not necessary. Using many tools with the same functionalities results in duplicate information kept in multiple repositories, and this is difficult to maintain.

The Cumbersome Process of Generating Automated Test Scripts

It is important that all the members of the team should understand that test script automation does not happen automatically, no matter what the vendor claims. In a project, test engineers with experience in manual testing will be involved in creating the automated scripts. Though tool vendors claim the operation of a tool is easy, the test engineers may complain that the creation of automated scripts took longer than expected and that too many workaround solutions had to be found. It is important to understand that tools are not necessarily as easy to use as the vendors claim. It is also beneficial to include one person on the testing personnel who has programming knowledge and appropriate tool training.

Lack of Knowledge on Testing Tools

Sometimes, tool training is initiated too late in the project, resulting in tools not getting used correctly. Often, only the capture/playback portion of the testing tool is used, and scripts had to be repeatedly recreated, causing frustration. When introducing an automated tool, it is important that tool training be a part of the test schedule. Since PT activities need to be involved throughout the project life cycle, tool training should happen early in the life cycle for it to be useful and to ensure that tool issues can be brought up and resolved early. Proper budget allocation must be done at the beginning of the project.

Late Introduction of Testing Tools

Sometimes, test management introduces a new testing tool in the hopes of speeding up the testing effort. If no test automation expert is on the test team, automated tools should not be introduced late in the life cycle. The tool's learning curve may not have allowed the gain of any benefits from incorporating it late in the testing life cycle. Project management must ensure that adequate tool experts are available before the usage of the tools in the project.

Early Expectations of Payback

Often when a new tool is introduced to a project, the expectations for the return on investment are very high. Project members anticipate that the tool will immediately narrow down the testing scope, meaning reduced cost and schedule. An automated testing tool does not replace manual testing completely, nor does it replace the test engineer. Initially, the testing effort in automation will increase, but when automation is done correctly, it will decrease in subsequent stages.

Tool's Problem in Recognizing Third Party Controls

Another aspect of managing expectations is to understand tools' capabilities. In some projects, the test engineers were surprised to find out that a specific tool could not be used for some parts of the application. During evaluation of a tool, it is important to verify whether third party controls are compatible with the automated testing tool's capabilities.

Usage of Multiple Versions of a Tool

If one project has multitool licenses, numerous versions of the tool will be in use. This means scripts created in one version of the tool may not be compatible in another version, causing significant compatibility problems and requiring many workaround solutions. Project management must ensure that the proper configuration and version of the tool must be in use throughout the project.

Risk factors in performance testing projects are many. Since it is a late and last activity in the project life cycle, confusion and uncertainties always prevail. Even in the last phase of testing, there could be a requirement modification envisaged by the customer which jeopardizes the entire project management, including the performance testing. In such situations, the testing team must be ready to face uncertainties and strategize to provide optimum solutions.

Summary

Test build is an important activity, and many test analysts have not understood it properly. They ignore intricacies of various aspects of the test build phase. Though they meticulously prepare the test plan, they may fail to maintain the same aggression to create the test environment and test scripts. Several options are available for simulating a test environment, but one needs to be careful about the investments that have to be made. The test environment must be as close as possible to the operation environment. Instead of creating a company-owned testing environment, a hired or leased testing environment could be considered.

Test script generation may be simple by using a tool, but its direct applicability on testing may not always be possible. Test scripts may have to be modified manually. They must be tested with sample runs, and proper coding standards must be followed.

Finally, knowing the risks involved and planning for risk mitigation at all levels of the test build phase will enhance the effectiveness of performance testing.

References

Bank of New York. (2004). Retrieved December 21, 2004, from http://www.bankofny.com/htmlpages/index.htm

Hewlett-Packard. (2004). Retrieved December 21, 2004, from http://www.hp.com/

Mitchell, B. (2004). *Network sniffers*. Retrieved October 10, 2004, from http://compnetworking.about.com/od/networksecurityprivacy/g/bldef_sniffer.htm

Operating systems. (2004). Retrieved October 10, 2004, from http://www.knowledgehound.com/topics/OSs.htm

Protocols. (2004). *Protocols*. Retrieved December 21, 2004, from http://www.protocols.com/

SMTP overview. (2003). Retrieved September 14, 2003, from http://www.freesoft.org/CIE/Topics/94.htm

Additional Sources

Carson, M. (1997). *Application and protocol testing through network emulation*. Internetworking Technologies Group, NIST. Retrieved from June 10, 2004, from http://snad.ncsl.nist.gov/itg/nistnet/slides

Chengie & Cao, P. (n.d.). *Maintaining strong cache consistency for WWW*. Retrieved October 1, 2004, from http://www.cs.wisc.edu/~cao/talks/icache/sld001.htm

Gerrard, P., & O'Brient, A. (1995, November). *Systeme Evolutif Ltd. 7.* London: Hanover Square. Retrieved October 10, 2004, from http://www.evolutif.co.uk/CSPerftest/CSTPAPER.html

Q.A. Labs (n.d.). *Benefits of test planning – A cost-benefits.* White paper. Retrieved February 18, 2003, from www.qalabs.com/resources/articles/testplanningbenefits.pdf

Subraya, B. M. (2002, September 6). Web performance testing & issues. Infosys Technologies. *Internet & Software Quality Week,* San Francisco.

Subraya, B. M., & Subrahmanya, S. V. (2004). *Design for performance using PePPeR model.* Retrieved October 10, 2004, from www.softwaredioxide.com/Channels/Content/Infosys_Design_Performance_PePPeR.pdf

Weyuke, E. J., & Vokolos, F. I. (2000, December). *Experience with performance testing of software systems: Issues, an approach, and case study.* Retrieved October 10, 2004, from http://www.cs.drexel.edu/~filip/TSEperformance.pdf

Chapter 7

Performance Test Execution Phase

The focus of this chapter is toward the factors needing attention while conducting the tests of performance. Chapters 5 and 6 discuss in detail the test plan as well as the test scripts required for conducting the performance tests. The successful execution of PT calls for coordination of a complex set of activities such as management of personnel, scheduling the tests at an appropriate time, configuring tools for various performance parameters, verification of application readiness for the test, and, above all, management of multiple test runs versus cost of resources. Conducting the tests may spread over a number of days, and it may also warrant customization of the operating system. The team responsible for carrying out the tests must be well aware of these factors.

Typical test execution (see *Test execution*, 2004) phases are shown in Figure 7.1. Each phase must be planned carefully. If these phases are followed in sequence, the probability of test execution errors could be reduced. The main reason behind introducing these phases is to reduce the cost. To illustrate, if we directly run tests without passing through initial phases like elaboration test (say) and an error creeps in later, it will result in unnecessary investment of effort on test runs, which is very expensive. Specialized skills are required to run tests. Sometimes, the test environment (including tools) has to be taken on hire during the test runs. All these involve effort and time, which will go to waste if the tests are not executed properly. Each phase is explained in Figure 7.1.

Entry Criteria

Performance testing is the last activity in the performance test life cycle. Before this, the application is subjected to functional and other related testing. If defects are found, they

Figure 7.1. Different phases of test execution

| Identify Entry and Exit Criteria | Elaboration Test | Self Satisfaction Test | Multiple Runs |

are corrected and tested again. This process continues until the application is free of defects. After this process, the application is ready for performance testing. The process takes more time, but in reality, time is limited, and the delivery of the application must be done per the schedule. Therefore, the applications readiness for PT is questioned and requires various conditions that need to be followed before it is ready for the PT.

One of the cardinal principles is to ensure that any application must, before undergoing the test of performance, satisfy all its business and design requirements. Along with the business functions, the test bed required for PT must also be ready. The process to be adhered to before starting the performance test is shown in Figure 7.2.

Freezing of All Major Business Functions

It is not uncommon to find changes in business requirements even at the final stages of system deployment. Minor business requirements may not affect the performance of the system, but great restraint needs to be shown for a change in requirements. If major business requirement changes are not accounted for in the performance expectations, the tests may not give the desired results.

During the design of workloads, we have considered various transactions which are required to conduct PT. Some of them are critical, and others are noncritical. The scope of these critical transactions must have been frozen before the design. Any changes in these transactions may impact the design and coding. Such changes adversely affect the performance of the system. Great restrain must be shown for any changes at the last moment. However, many customers demand changes at the last moment. Care must be taken to maintain proper versioning of the application and corresponding performance test results.

Working of All Major Business Functions and Features

Though the functional tests are conducted correctly, it is necessary to thoroughly test all major business functions before the beginning PT. To illustrate, functional test teams have tested an application through regression testing and certify it. Later, how do we ensure that the testing has been done correctly and all business functions are covered? In view of the delivery deadline, they may skip some of the functions which may not be critical for them but may be critical from the performance point of view. Hence, the

Figure 7.2. Process for entry criteria

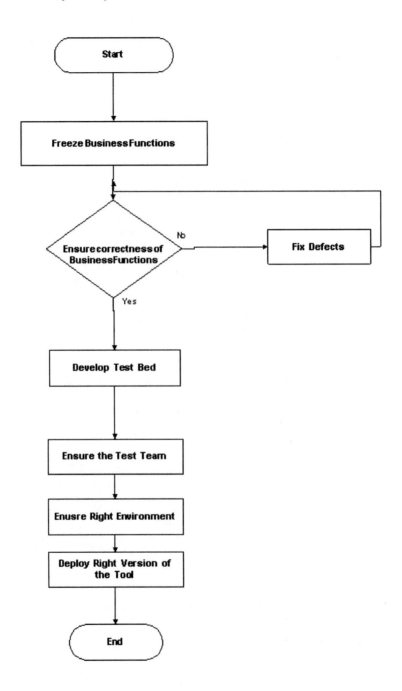

performance test team must have its own process to test, most if not all, critical business functions just before the PT process begins. This is an additional effort but is worth doing to ensure effective PT. Here, the major challenges faced by practitioners are coordination between the functional and performance test teams. It must be ensured that the performance and functional teams deploy the same version of the application to mitigate otherwise avoidable pitfalls.

Fixing and Retesting of All Major Defects

It is a common practice among some developers, although unhealthy, to test the defects but not fix the same on the grounds that they have no impact on the function of the system. It may be true that such defects have no impact on the functions but would greatly undermine the performance of the system. It is a good practice to fix all the defects and recheck the system or application again, after fixing the defects before embarking on the exercise of testing the performance of the system or application.

Availability of Proper Test Bed

It is essential to have a test bed for PT as required for functional testing. The testing can be done either by use of live or simulated data. Care must be taken, in the use of live data, about their location. Remotely connecting to the live database may not produce accurate result. Simulated data, though, provide flexibility but do not reflect the real business scenario.

Some of organizations may provide access to their live test bed which is currently in use. Although operational data is available, for these types of test beds, simulating to a real-time business environment may be difficult to produce correct results as day-to-day interaction of business activity is interfaced during the PT. If the test bed is simulated, the size of the database must be ensured with the operation database. Records complexity must be similar to the complexity of operation data.

Ensure the Availability of the Test Team

A test team comprises test analyst, test script specialist, business domain specialist, network specialist, database administrators, and personnel from various departments involved in the test. Coordination and synchronization of all activities of the team members is the key factor for success of the performance test. The main risk could be if a skilled team member is not available at the time of testing, it would be difficult to reschedule the training because the investment will be high. A proper risk mitigation process must be evolved.

Right Environment for Testing

Performance testing requires the proper environment with proper tools. The hardware and software should be tested after setting up the test environment; this is a prerequisite to ensure that while conducting a PT system, the test should not fail. The application must be executed once before the beginning of the test. Enough disk space must be ensured. A proper network environment (see Joung, 2004) must be available, and it must be tested. Sometimes, network engineers modify the configurations at the last moment, introduce the new plug-in components, and even change the server setup altogether. Hence, evolve a simple testing process to ensure that the correct environment is available for PT.

Right Version of the Tool

Many tools are used for PT. These tools could be related to monitoring, testing, configuration, and project management. Ensure that right versions of the tools are used for PT. Configuration of tools and testing them before PT should be followed as a mandatory procedure. The right plug-in components must be ensured. Some tools do not support all protocols. Care must be taken to test the type of protocols supported. Installation must be done properly. Sometimes, some component of the tool may not be installed at all. If the operating system for client and server are different while installing any tool, a proper agent must be installed at the server end. Otherwise, the tool may behave differently during the testing, impacting the results. All tools must be tested with sample applications and configured accordingly. A tools expert must be available during the testing. Ensure the maintenance contract is active during the testing.

Exit Criteria

In functional testing, the popular question asked by practitioners is when to stop testing. If there is a defect, it needs to be corrected and again subjected to the testing process. If this repeated process takes more time, the application delivery to the customer may be delayed. On the other hand, if the delivery deadline is the criteria for stopping the test, all defects may not be corrected. Hence, it is difficult to set proper conditions for stopping the testing. However, some organization may set its own guidelines for stopping the functional testing. Likewise, similar exit criteria must be defined in performance testing also.

The outcome of the performance testing, in general, is either that the application is exhibiting poor performance or good performance. This is a relative decision and hence adheres to a set of conditions defined in the SLA. These conditions are mapped into response time, throughput, resource utilization, and so on. Though the objective of running the tests is to get the results as defined, multiple runs may have to be made, and each run must satisfy certain conditions. The exit criteria must be set to accommodate the results as well as when to stop the test runs irrespective of the results obtained.

It is worth defining the exit criteria before the beginning of the tests. This includes defining well in advance all parameters and expected results. Initiating the trial runs will help in arriving at the base value of important parameters. Any violation of exit or other conditions must result in the repetition of the test itself.

Successful Completion of Tests Runs

The first condition for any application undergoing performance testing is that the test run should complete successfully. This means that all tests defined in the script must be successfully completed without fail. The system should not crash or enter into a deadlock. Monitoring from the master control must be successful. All system logs and reports for each run must be generated. An application should not crash due to the function defect. In the event of failure, the defects noticed have to be corrected and rerun to be ensured.

Generation of Result Data

The second criterion is that the result data must be generated as envisaged. The results may be useful or not which needs to be decided in the analysis. For instance, log files during the execution are used to verify the healthy states of execution but are rarely useful for analysis. For every test, there are multiple test reports that may be generated. Some may be related systems, logs, and others may be related to application performance. One should have a broad idea about the type of results and its pattern. All test runs must generate the same type of test reports. However, the data could be different.

No Functional Defects during Test Runs

Though the application is successfully tested for functional defects, sometimes the functional defects may arise during performance testing. If functional defects report, the test run must be stopped because the results may not be as expected. The functional defects discovered during the performance test have to be resolved immediately. The functional defects may or may not affect the performance test. However, it is good practice to resolve such defects because they may influence the performance of the system indirectly in spite of the fact that the performance test has been completed successfully.

Setting Performance Parameters

As it has been noticed by several researchers, the design of test suites for PT is radically different from functional testing. In PT, the functional details of the test cases, or the actual values of the inputs, are generally of limited importance. The important concerns are traditionally associated with workloads and physical resources. For instance, the number of users, the frequency of inputs, the duration of tests, the characteristics of the disks, the network bandwidth, and the number and speed of CPUs are the key resources which impact on the performance of any system. These resources could be measured by setting appropriate parameters either at the operating system level or by using performance tools.

Most of the modern testing tools provide a large number of parameters related to the operating system, specific scripting language, browsers, and networks to find the probable impact on performance. Depending on the performance requirements, parameters must be set. These parameters vary from tool to tool and specific operating system. Some of the common parameters needed for every test run are illustrated here.

Response Time

When a user accesses any Web site for a specific purpose, the user expects the system to respond immediately. The system response to any query is measured by the time or duration. The response time is the time interval or period between the time a transaction is submitted and the response of the system to the transaction. It is also known as elapsed time. It is the measure of user productivity. An example could be when a customer performs a query to find out the balance from a bank account and the system takes 3 seconds to respond. The response time is 3 seconds. This will impact the user's feelings while using the application.

Throughput

This is an important parameter and provides the average number of transactions or jobs executed per unit time. The unit time could be seconds or minutes. It is a measure of the capacity of the system used for running the application. This parameter is used by the Web administrator to assess the efficiency of the system.

Utilization

Efficient usage of resources of the system is measured by this parameter. This parameter provides the percentage occupancy of the resources like CPU, disk, network, and memory. A specific value could be set for the exit criteria. If utilization is provisioned for 70%, the basic principle is to achieve 70% utilization of all resources.

The tools may provide multiple parameters to measure the utilization. One should see specific tool details. For each parameter, a specific value should be set for the exit criteria.

Another important set of parameters is in terms of middleware configuration. For instance, the use of J2EE middleware components in the application may require the setting up of the following parameters:

- **Thread Pool Size.** Choosing the right number of threads in the pool helps in utilizing the CPU effectively by the J2EE server. The thread pool size can be computed as a factor of the hardware specification (CPU speed, number of CPUs, etc.) and the number of concurrent processing performed by the server. Most J2EE application servers come with details on how to configure the thread pool size. Increasing the thread pool size beyond the threshold limit of the physical machine may result in poor performance.

- **Database Connection Pool Size.** One of the biggest performance benefits in the J2EE server is obtained by connection pooling. Connection pooling reduces the overhead of connecting/disconnecting to the database on each client request. In a typical production setup, the database is running on a different physical machine and the application server on a different machine. This parameter again is a factor based on the number of concurrent requests the server is expected to handle. Unlike thread pool size, connection pools do not have CPU utilization overhead. So even if the connection pool size is kept slightly higher than the optimal requirement, it may not be a burden for the system. However, the limiting factor here could be the database's own limits on the number of connections.

- **Application Component Cache Size.** Most J2EE application servers use a cache of components in memory in order to remove the overhead of object creation and deletion. In a typical EJB application, entity EJBs are created in memory and kept ready to be populated with requested data. The EJB container manages this transparently. The factors deciding this parameter are physical memory available in the server and the number of concurrent EJB requests that may be required in the system.

- **JVM Heap Size.** Increasing the heap size helps in keeping the overhead of garbage collection low. This parameter is a factor of physical memory available in the system.

- **Message Queue Buffer Size.** Optimization of this parameter helps in increasing the number of concurrent requests that can be handled. Usually an optimal setting is created by the default configuration of most application servers. However, if the available CPU power and physical memory capacity is high on the server, this can be increased to an extent.

When the middleware interacts with the database, performance will differ based on how frequently or rarely the application accesses the database. A given middleware may perform adequately for applications that stress persistence and quite badly for transactions. In some cases, a middleware may perform well or badly for different usage patterns of the same service. Hence, it is necessary to set database related parameters (refer to Appendix A3) before starting the performance test.

In general, the performance of a particular application will be largely dependent on how the middleware primitives are being used to implement the application's functionality.

By setting the exit condition by various methods, one can ensure that the test runs are conducted smoothly and the output is ensured. Further, the test runs should not enter into an indefinite loop and avoid uncertainty.

Once the entry and exit criteria are set, then the application is ready for testing. However, in the entry criteria, the conditions are set and one of the conditions is that all business functions must work correctly. Apart from the business functions, we need to ensure that performance testing also goes smoothly. To ensure some of the performance test related activities like balancing the workload, defining user groups should be done before the real test begins. Without this, if the real test starts and, at the middle of the runs, the system fails due to performance test cases, the investment is high not economical. In order to avoid these issues during the run, it is better to understand how the application behaves by conducting elaboration testing.

Elaboration Testing

The aim of elaboration testing (see *From inception to elaboration*, 2004) is to establish that the system behaves as expected under the performance test. This means that important business functions work correctly, central software architecture is working efficiently, databases are properly set, the platform is configured to suit the system, all performance parameters are set, all user interfaces are working properly to ensure the system is ready for deployment. Elaboration phase testing is important to obtain feedback, adapt, and prove that the core application engine is robust. This phase also helps optimize the cost. The elaboration test helps to:

- Understand the system's behavior when subjected to PT.

  The system need not be tested for all business functions. Only those functions which are critical and decide behavior need to be tested.

- Establish a proof of concept for the PT.

  The proof of concept ideally speaks about the feel of the product. Since PT is expensive and time consuming, the proof of concept is required. The application is subjected to PT for a set of workloads. Each workload will not be tested exhaustively, but systems behavior during the PT is studied. With the proof of concept, the testers will know how the system behaves during PT, and everything needs to be done proactively.

- Improve the confidence level of the testers during the final testing phase

- Partially eliminates the nonperformance related problems early.

  During elaboration testing, if some of the functions do not work, they will be reported early. System and tool configuration issues, wrong parameter settings, correct working of the test bed, network issues, and test script related issues are reported early so that corrective actions could be taken proactively.

- Conduct one-time testing of all business functions used for PT

- Verify the authenticity of the database.

  Selective database queries through workload present the issues in database authenticity early.

- Validate all protocols working correctly or not

- Verify whether the servers are configured properly and working correctly or not

- Verify the capability of handling the maximum number of virtual users.

  This is important because if the stress test is planned for a set of concurrent users and if the tool does not support that number of concurrent users, testers can plan to tackle these situations in advance.

- Understand the complexity of the PT in advance.

  PT is a complex activity, and testers may have to face many uncertainties during the test runs. During the elaboration test, we know in advance various issues and how to address these issues.

In addition to the above, elaboration testing also ensures the correctness of all functions used for PT.

How to Conduct Elaboration Testing

Elaboration testing is conducted for one or two virtual users. The number of virtual users depends on the complexity of the system under PT. If the objective of the elaboration test is to examine the number of maximum concurrent users, then the workload must be simple. The proper test plan for elaboration testing must be available, and the entire test team, as in the final test, must be involved in the testing. Test runs must be conducted per the test plan. It is a normal tendency that testers skip steps in elaboration testing with a presumption that they are not important and the system will be tested anyway in the final test run. Databases must be tuned properly. Tools must be configured, and the workload must be used as in the final test run.

Self Satisfaction Test (SST)

Like the elaboration test, SST is a type of performance test which works on gut feeling. Many times, the experience counts a lot compared to process orientation. Experienced testers rightly identify the test cases and judge whether the test plan is ready for the final test run or not. Experienced test tool experts examine whether the tool is properly configured or not, what the parameters are that must be set as default values, and whether the elaboration test must be conducted or not. If the elaboration test must be conducted, how should one optimize the elaboration test to save effort and time? An experienced domain specialist identifies the common defects and advises the team accordingly. Other major areas where SST helps are:

- Test scripts must be reviewed by experienced testers. Normally, the peer tester reviews the test script. This is not efficient. There are specialized test script reviewers who specialize in specific tools and can review and use their gut feelings and experience to find out whether the test script works or not.

- Conducting elaboration testing by experts who have sufficient experience in the business domain and the testing process.

- In the case of using a testing environment, experts' opinions always help in fine tuning it.

- Before the beginning of the real PT, a business domain expert must be consulted about overall functioning of the system. There are unattended issues in the development phase, which will be scrutinized and audited before the final PT.

SST will also address the presentation style of various results to stakeholders. Experienced testers will help to present the results to different departments. SST is mainly for building more confidence and assessing the system for readiness for final PT.

Multiple Test Runs

When the test runs are conducted, the main question that often arises with everyone is how many times PT must be conducted. What are test cycles and test runs? What is the maximum number of test cycles that must be conducted in a typical test run? Multiple test runs are not the same as regression testing used in functional testing. In regression testing, the same test cases are tested for multiple versions of the application whereas performance test runs are based on workloads. The results in PT are either satisfied or not satisfied. Here there is no pass or fail like in functional testing. The result may be poor response time or satisfied response time.

A test cycle consists of many test runs. A test cycle can have one or many test runs. A test run consists of many workloads, which will be executed one by one. In a typical PT, there must be at least one test cycle. More test cycles provide better results.

A completed test cycle does not mean one can assume that the PT is completed. Based on test results, the test cycle may have to be altered, or a new test cycle may have to be created. The new test cycle may be either modification of the existing test cycle or a newly designed one. The design of a new test cycle is normally based on:

- Change in the existing workload based on the feedback from the first test run;

- The feedback could be that a specific transaction may not impact the performance test results and requires a new type of transaction. It could be that the sequencing of transactions may have to be modified;

- Various performance parameters must have been tuned after the previous test runs, and hence there is a need for a new test cycle;

- Based on the test results, the environment must have changed, which may demand a new test cycle;

- Sometimes, test duration might span to many days or even months. In such situations, the test environment might undergo changes due to many reasons. Accordingly, we have to introduce a new test cycle based on the environment;

- Change in functionality due to the feedback given during the testing.

Though modifications in business functions are not encouraged during PT, it may be necessary with extreme conditions. In such situations, a new test cycle may have to be introduced.

The new test cycle, once subjected to PT, again may undergo changes as discussed above.

A typical test cycle for multiple workloads is given in Table 7.1. It represents a typical test cycle with multiple test runs for each workload. Let W1, W2... be different workloads. Four test runs are considered. To illustrate multiple runs and their impact, consider the following cases with reference to Table 7.1.

Case 1: W1 failed in Test Run #2 of test cycle 1 whereas it has passed in test cycle 2. However, W1 has passed two test runs in test cycle 1, and therefore we assume that the workload W1 has passed. If the exit criteria states that all three runs must pass, then W1 must be run in the second cycle also. In test cycle 2, W1 passed the test run.

Case 2: The workload W2 in test cycle 1 has passed the first three test runs. There is no need to consider Test Run #4. W2 is again considered in test cycle 2 to ensure consistency.

Case 3: Workloads W3 and W4 are considered for all test runs because of more than one failure in test cycle 1.

Case 4: The workload W5 in test cycle 1 failed in all test runs. This means the design of the workload W5 is not correct. It has been modified and called W6 in test cycle 2. W6 passed the test runs and is considered for the final outputs.

Observe that all workloads are considered in both of the test cycles to maintain consistency. Finally, it is the responsibility of the testers to ensure proper test runs, which passed correctly and are considered for outputs.

Table 7.1. Test cycle 1

Workloads	Test Run #1	Test Run #2	Test Run #3	Test Run #4
W1	Pass	Fail	Pass	
W2	Pass	Pass	Pass	
W3	Fail	Fail	Pass	Pass
W4	Pass	Fail	Fail	Pass
W5	Fail	Fail	Fail	Fail

Table 7.2. Test cycle 2 (after tuning and change in workload)

Workloads	Test Run #1	Test Run #2	Test Run #3	Test Run #4
W1	Pass	Pass	Pass	
W2	Pass	Pass	Pass	
W3	Fail	Fail	Pass	Pass
W4	Pass	Fail	Fail	Pass
W6	Pass	Pass	Fail	

Managing the test execution cycle and test runs is a complex job, as it demands maintenance of proper configurations for test cycles. Apart from this, there are many challenges one has to face during test execution.

Challenges in Test Execution

Running performance tests is more complex than functional test runs. Investments on functional testing are less when compared to that of PT. The regression test is most appropriate for functional testing whereas the performance test provides results in which the response time is adequate or inadequate for a preset number of virtual users. The system under the performance test requires 100% bug-free functionality to avoid huge loss on testing time and effort. If the system is not complete in all respects, the following challenges may have to be addressed during performance test execution:

Functional Defects in the Application

Although the application is tested multiple times, defects in the application may still be skipped which will report during PT. Hence, if the system is subjected to a performance test where there is a functional defect and is not addressed properly, the result obtained may not be correct. The defect may impact the performance test itself and the results also. The impacts on the performance test are mainly cost and time. Highest attention must be given to ensure that functional defects are removed before the application is subjected to performance testing.

Problems in Database Connection Pooling

Connection pooling (see Khanine, 2004) problems occur by a "connection leak", a condition where the application does not close its database connections correctly and consistently. Once the connection leak occurs, it remains open until the memory is deallocated. Most of the time, one needs to know whether the application manages to stay within the size of its connection pool or not. If the load does not change but the number of connections constantly creeps even after the initial "warm up" period, the application gets into a connection leak.

Managing Heap Size

During the execution of the application, there may be a possibility of memory shortage, which slows down the execution. This is due to the deallocation process in memory management, which consumes more time. This process affects the performance because server side activity cannot proceed during memory deallocation.

If a large heap size is set, full deallocation becomes slower, but it occurs less frequently. If the heap size is set in accordance with memory needs, full deallocation becomes faster but occurs more frequently. The goal of tuning the heap size is to minimize the time spent in garbage collection (deallocation) while maximizing the number of clients that can be handled at a given time.

Make sure the heap size is not larger than the available free Random Access Memory (RAM) on the system.

Use as large a heap size as possible without causing the system to "swap" pages to disk. The amount of free RAM on the system depends on hardware configuration and the memory requirements of running processes on the machine.

If the system is spending too much time collecting garbage (allocated "virtual" memory is a greater size than RAM can handle), reduce the heap size. Typically, one should ensure 80% of the available RAM (not taken by the operating system or other processes) for the application.

Session Tracking in Test Scripts

Session tracking can be accomplished in several ways, including the following common methods:

- Storing unique session information in a client side cookie;

- Appending a unique session ID to the URL;

- Passing unique session information in a hidden field.

Any of these session tracking methods can be either static or dynamic. Static methods assign the user a single session ID for the entire session, while dynamic methods assign a new session ID with every activity the user performs. Test scripts should be written to handle both static and dynamic sessions.

Since session tracking is critical for most nontrivial Web applications, selecting the right session tracking mechanism is an important decision. Key factors to consider are security, ease of use, and how well the technique melds with the overall system architecture. It is necessary to carefully examine the advantages and disadvantages of each method when building session tracking capability into a Web site. The following are the guidelines observed for session tracking (Kim, 2004):

- Use cookies only for user identification.

- Do not store any data beside a user's identification in cookies.

- Use the HTTP Session tracking mechanism if a servlet (not EJB) implementation is used.

- Save any data that need to be persistent for an indefinite time period to a backend database.

User authorization may be used for simple applications. URL rewriting and hidden form field techniques should be avoided.

Issues in Creating a Test Datapool

A test datapool is a collection of values. It is used by test components as a source of values for the execution of test cases. Datapools can be represented by utility parts or be logically described by constraints. The following precautions must be followed while creating a datapool:

- Ensure that the data in the datapool are correct.

- Ensure that in the datapool section of the script, the variables the tester wants to be read from the datapool are included or excluded per script language (http://www.softpanorama.org/scripting/index.shtml). This is a common mistake normally occurring in the application.

- Ensure enough data or configure the system to consider duplicate data if it is a potential issue. Remember always to check the request or requests before the first identified failure to verify input data.

Test datapools always help to test the system in an automated environment.

Issues with Application Server

Once the application server is running, it should run until the end of the execution. Sometimes, changes in security, application, and OS configuration cause the server to need to be restarted. If two or more applications share an application server (see Alcott, 2003), this can lead to conflicting needs. In addition, all applications on the same application server run under the same OS identity. This has security implications since file permissions associated with the applications on an application server are owned by that OS identity. In this case, the files associated with one application cannot be protected from access by other applications which are running on the same application server. This is because they share the same operating system privileges. If this is not acceptable, separate application servers for each application must be provided in order to provide security protection.

Network May Choke Due to Wrong Configuration

The most commonly encountered host configuration errors to date have been the enabling of the User Datagram Protocol (UDP) services (UDP ports 7, 13, 19, and 37 which correspond to echo, daytime, chargen, and time) (Netcraft Ltd., 2004) especially on routers. Even otherwise well protected networks often have this vulnerability like Cisco routers. The impact is that someone who takes a disliking to a site can use up its bandwidth by sending a packet on a specific port on their router with the source port and source address set to the *echo* port on someone else's router. This will likely cause both routers to loop sending packets to each other and use up a substantial portion of the sites available bandwidth.

Guidelines for Test Execution

Performance test execution is a complex job. Experience and gut feeling play a major role during test execution. Performance test execution is not like functional testing execution. In functional test execution, setting pass/fail criteria is easy. Defects are easy to detect and analyze. In performance testing execution, setting performance parameters and monitoring are complex jobs. Here setting pass/fail criteria is difficult because the defect is the bottleneck for better performance and identifying the bottleneck takes a long time.

Complete test execution must be completed before attempting to identify the bottleneck. Test execution is completed only when all exit criteria are passed. However, a meticulously planned test execution yields more returns than an unplanned test execution. The following guidelines provide direction to plan a proper test execution:

- Define explicitly the testing team, roles and responsibilities starting from planning to execution phase.

- Estimate test execution effort before the beginning of the test.

- Configure the tools properly and check version compatibility.

- Check all additional tools used in testing for version and compatibility.

- Resources from all the different groups (such as network specialist, database specialist, domain specialist, etc.) must be synchronized.

- Run PT more than once with different levels of background activity (noise) to get the true picture.

- Conduct PT with production sized databases for a real life simulation.

- Do not conduct PT in a development environment which leads to inaccurate results.

- Monitor performance counters continuously and take action suitably.

- Monitor test duration continuously and take action suitably.

- Avoid external interference during test execution.

- Monitor the test execution by probing the client to check whether the system under test behaves properly or not.

- Log the results with timings for further analysis.

The above guidelines provide direction for a tester to plan and conduct the test properly. However, each organization may adopt their own methods to test the system effectively. Finally, though test execution is a complex activity, a methodical approach simplifies the job more comprehensively.

Summary

Test execution is an important activity in the PT life cycle and needs the same attention as that of other activities. Normally, testers do not plan the activities of test execution because this results in poor utilization of resources and time. To avoid such problems, it is suggested that meticulous planning is required during test execution.

For any test to be successful, entry and exit criteria must be defined properly. These criteria must be followed strictly during execution. Next, an elaboration test must be conducted to find in advance the various issues that may creep in during the final test execution. The Elaboration test provides indepth information about the complexity of the system under test. Based on the complexity of the system, one can plan the test execution properly to optimize resources and time.

The self satisfaction test provides the rich experience of professionals who have addressed similar projects previously. Their experience on planning, scheduling tests, and analyzing results always helps to complete the performance testing effectively. It also helps in assessing the possible bottlenecks during execution.

PT must be carried out multiple times as one test may not give proper results. To run multiple tests, proper test execution guidelines must be followed. Finally, meticulous planning and skilled resources ensure the success of the performance tests.

References

A slightly skeptical view on scripting languages. (2004). Retrieved November 22, 2004, from http://www.softpanorama.org/Scripting/index.shtml

Alcott, T. (2003). *One or many applications per application server?* Retrieved June 19, 2003, from http://www-106.ibm.com/developerworks/Websphere/techjournal/0211_alcott/alcott.html

From inception to elaboration. (2003). The Metropolitan State College of Denver. Retrieved August 11, 2003, from http://clem.mscd.edu/~hasze/csi3280/notes/Chapter8.html

Incremental testing. (2004). Retrieved June 12, 2004, from http://homepages.nildram.co.uk/~worrelli/cont343.htm

Joung, P. (2004). *General network performance testing methodology.* Retrieved September 21, 2004, from http://www.spirentcom.com/documents/1065.pdf

Khanine, D. (2004). *Tuning up ADO.NET connection pooling in ASP.NET applications.* Retrieved May 6, 2004, from http://www.15seconds.com/issue/040830.htm

Kim, S. (2004). *Safe session tracking.* Retrieved November 2, 2004, from http://www.sdmagazine.com/documents/s=818/sdm0103h/

Netcraft Ltd. (2004). *UDP denial of services.* Retrieved November 21, 2004, from http://www.netcraft.com/presentations/interop/dos.html

Test execution. (2004). Retrieved June 17, 2004, from http://www.donald-firesmith.com/Components/WorkUnits/Tasks/Testing/TestExecution.html

Additional Sources

Adirake, P. (2004, August). *Research on software configuration management in middleware systems.* Retrieved January 17, 2005, from http://www.jaist.ac.jp/library/thesis/is-master-2005/paper/p-adirak/abstract.pdf

Applying eXtreme Programming Techniques to Automated Testing. (2004). Retrieved January 17, 2005, from http://www.bjss.co.uk/press/BJSS_Applying_XP_To_Automated_Testing.pdf

Department of Defense (2003, November). *Testing guide.* Retrieved November 22, 2004, from http://www.eitoolkit.com/tools/implementation/build/testing_guide.doc

Mar, W. (2004). *Performance testing and planning.* Retrieved November 21, 2004, from http://www.wilsonmar.com/perftest.htm

Marick, B. (2004). *Classic testing mistakes.* Retrieved June 19, 2004, from http://www.testing.com/writings/classic/mistakes.pdf

Pauli, K. (2003). *Pattern your way to automated regression testing.* Retrieved January 7, 2003, from http://www.javaworld.com/javaworld/jw-09-2001/jw-0921-test.html

Test guidelines. (n.d.). Retrieved January 17, 2005, from http://www.w3.org/QA/WG/2003/10/TestGL-20031020.html

Chapter 8

Post Test Execution Phase

The phase pertaining to post test execution comprises not only multifaceted activities but is also a tedious task. It is not uncommon to find many testers who normally underestimate the complexity involved in this phase and face an uphill task later, while fine tuning the system for optimum performance. This chapter discusses points arising in the post execution phase by considering:

- Specific test execution scenarios through logs;
- Method/strategy for analysis;
- Results with standard benchmarks;
- Areas for improvement.

Apart from these, the chapter also provides guidelines for performance tuning with a view it will be of help to practitioners who are keen on execution of tests and analyses of results.

The contemporary conventional methodologies overlook the importance of the post execution phase. In the esteemed view of the author, the subject of post execution is as important a phase as any other and demands a skilled person to analyze the results.

Objectives of the Analysis Phase

The importance of the analysis phase is to ensure that the basic criteria of test executions are met. Some of the objectives of the analysis phase are to:

- Check whether all test cycles are executed and conforming according to the test plan.
- Identify script level problems and ensure the script is not a bottleneck for smooth running of the tests.
- Know request/response time of a specific user for a specific query in a normal load.
- Interpret Web server logs, application server logs, and database logs for better understanding of the test runs.
- Identify resource utilization and bottlenecks in resources, if any.
- Isolate excess queue lengths at the server end to assess bottlenecks early.
- Diagnose network traffic, its impact on performance, and find solutions, if required.
- Address code level optimization based on analysis at the end.
- Check whether performance acceptance criteria are met or not by the system.

Setting objectives for the analysis gives proper direction to the test analyst to plan and provide correct solutions on time. The above said objectives could be modified based on the project requirements.

Analysis Process

A well laid out process to validate test results can correctly flush out performance bottlenecks. A well organized analysis helps in justifying the test results and the areas for future performance enhancements. The main outputs of the execution phase are test logs and reports. These are analyzed to isolate bottlenecks based on the strategy and guidelines as shown in Figure 8.1. Test logs play a major role in the analysis. All the test logs must be captured during the execution. Having analyzed test logs, proper strategy must be defined to analyze test results to find bottlenecks and provide solutions. Following proper guidelines helps to analyze faster and arrive at a solution. Various test reports may be required for analysis. Most of the performance test tools provide a large number of test result data. These result data need to be presented properly for better analysis.

Figure 8.1. Test analysis process

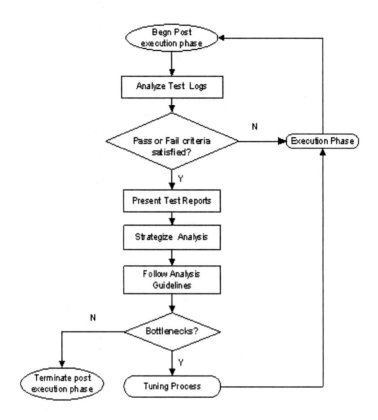

Analyze Test Logs

Test logs are the basic outputs of the execution phase. The test log records all the events during a test script generation. A typical test log is shown in Figure 8.2.

The test log records every virtual test action, unless it is specially turned off by the user. Test logs have record and playback details, complete information about the test cycle, test runs, and result status of all the commands. From this log, one can infer whether test runs are properly executed or not. This ensures the successful completion of a test run. Further data of the test log can be filtered, and results are analyzed using the verification point comparator to determine the reason for test failure at a verification point. Once the test defect is submitted, it will be identified by a defect number for further analysis.

Figure 8.2. A sample test log

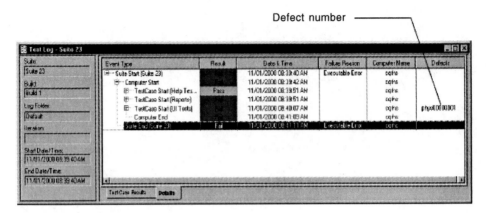

Contents of Test Log

Contents of a typical test log include the details of the log, execution results, log event, configuration, and virtual associated data as shown in Table 8.0. The test log provides the summary of execution results, log event, configuration details, and result related information (Table 8.0).

Need for Test Logs

Test logs are necessary as they not only confirm the correctness of the executed test scripts but also provide an insight into the script failures. The presence of log files helps in isolating the first level of bottlenecks. This is particularly true in the case of reengineering projects where PT is done, but the system is not performing satisfactorily. In such cases, use of test log helps in analyzing the problems. Similarly, in situations wherein the client is requesting guidelines to tune the performance affected areas, the test log reveals the areas affecting performance. The test log also gives a fair idea about the methodology of the test as well as the comparative analysis of the results with respect to the corresponding previous test results. This in turn assists gaining knowledge about the limitations of the previous PT.

Use of Test Logs

Test logs are useful to:

•   View results:

Table 8.0. Contents of a typical test log and details

Contents of Typical Test Log	Description
Log summary	• Test suite name • Build, log folder • Number of iterations • Date and time of start and end of testing
Summary of execution results	• Type of log event • Result status • Date and time of event occurred • Failure reason • Computer name • Associated defects
Summary of log event	• Type of event • Date and time of event started • Date and time of event ended • Result status of event • If failed, failure reason, failure description • Name &line number of failed script • Script verification point name and type • Baseline and actual results file • Additional output defects and information
Summary of configuration	• Memory size and usage • Type, service pack, and version of operating system • Type and number of processor
Virtual tester associated data (if the result is passed)	• Type, status, and protocol of connection • Name of URL and port number • Whether the event is a request or response • Computer name and configuration compatibility • Host name and cookie • Expected and actual HTTP return code • Name and other details of server • Content type and transfer encoding • Date & time of failure • Cookie type if any and status of connection

> ➤ Filter the data to view only the information needed;

> ➤ Sort the events by results or time or failure reasons to make it easy for analysis.

• Submit a defect report for failed log event which will help to correct it in the next test run.

• Preview or print data displayed in the active test log.

• View test logs in multiple windows for better analysis (depends on the features of the tool).

• Diagnose a failure scenario in case of an endurance test and to check the status of the system at the time of failure.

One precaution to be taken note of is to analyze the test logs before starting to look at the test results.

Verifying Pass or Fail Criteria

Verifying the test log for pass or fail criteria reflects the healthiness of test runs, as it builds confidence in test runs and proves useful for future runs. Further, test logs are the starting point for analyzing the correctness of testing. The log files give insight into the real traffic that has occurred or was expected to occur after deployment of software. From the test logs, one can analyze:

- The start and end of test runs;

- Hyper Text Transfer Protocols (HTTP) return codes;

- File contents and size;

- Errors on HTML pages;

- Sequence of command IDs;

- The effects of background activities.

It is essential to analyze the log for such symptoms. Instances have come to notice wherein logs have given false negative results. For instance, the mismatch in HTTP return code may give the result as failed commands. In a record session, the loading of a Web page may be from the Web server, so the HTTP return code is 200 (okay, loaded from server) (see 10 Status code definition, 2004). However, during playback, the loading of the same page may be from cache, and due to this factor, the HTTP code may be 304 (not modified, loaded from cache). The log, due to the mismatch in HTTP return code may exhibit a fail status even though the correct page is loaded in the system. Thus, it is necessary to analyze a test log for such mistakes and reexecute the scripts by adjusting the HTTP return codes.

Another example worth noting, in this regard, is about the case wherein the loading of page contents is proper during record, and the HTTP return code received is also 200 (HTML page with error message), but playback may generate unexpected contents like "Server is down for 4 hours due to maintenance" in spite of the HTTP return code being 200. These sorts of problems need analysis during the post execution phase.

The mismatching file sizes may lead to a possibility of observing the wrong result status. The number of bytes downloaded during recording and the number of bytes downloaded during playback may not match for dynamic HTML pages since the dynamic data can change the file size during playback. Allowing partial responses may minimize the occurrence of such errors.

Another case of a false positive in the log may arise when some Web servers return an HTML page giving details as to why the page requested cannot be serviced. However, the HTTP return code would be 200 (HTML page with error message) in both record and playback sessions instead of 404 (page not found) or 403, giving rise to a pass in the test log.

A thorough analyses of logs can isolate some of the script failure problems such as generation of split scripts wherein ensuring the sequence of command IDs is essential to validate the correct navigation of the virtual user. The presence of a data correlation issue does not make the script pass, even with a single virtual user.

The background activities could make the difference between the record and playback environment, which can lead to wrong results. For instance, if a Word file is created while recoding the script, the same is not created in the playback environment since the file already exists. This can make the log show failure, which has no relation with the application problems.

Though it is true that analysis of some of the data in the log file is possible for their correctness, the bulk of the data in the log would be in assembly language, warranting further processing for converting them into readable format. However, this is not an insurmountable task, as there are quite a number of log analyzers available in the market to serve this purpose. However, the test team should carefully choose an analyzer that best suits their requirement as well as budget.

Test Reports

Presentation of results is the most critical phase of PT. Automated tools generate several results based on different parameters. Results could be presented in many ways. The commonly accepted method is to present the results in terms of tables and graphs. However, this depends on the parameters chosen for the presentation and also the target audience. Hence, it is essential to discuss these factors before proceeding with the methodology of presentation.

Target Audience for the Results

Presentation of results depends on the target audience and a number of parameters. The target audience for the performance test results could be senior management, business managers, performance analysts, or other members of the organization and the team.

The number of parameters to be considered for presentation depends on the interests of the target audience. Performance analysts and other members of the test team always expect a detailed report of the results. Since they are responsible for justifying system performance, they want to make sure that the system is performing according to the specifications. They are interested in knowing of the potential bottlenecks. The results presented to them should include all possible parameters to ensure that all bottlenecks are fixed.

Business managers and senior management would be interested in knowing the end results. They are neither interested in knowing about the identification of bottlenecks nor about the method to fix such bottlenecks. In fact, they are interested in confirming whether the results presented to them validate the acceptance criteria. So the number of parameters considered for presenting results would be comparatively less. If a post-launch project is under test, they may be interested in knowing what made the system go down. They may demand the comparison of results before testing and the results after tuning the system for performance improvement. Performance parameters compared to other competitors might also be required.

Tables and Graphs

Presentation of test results can be in the form of tables and graphs. This format is ideal since, with very little explanation, even stakeholders with little technical background can understand the results. Tables are the most basic form of presentation. These are used when a large amount of parameters has to be compared and organized. Each column in the table represents different parameters, and the columns (parameters) can be inserted depending on the requirements of the target audience.

The graphs can be either simple or complicated. A result in the form of graphs gives a visual evaluation of the test related data. This type of presentation can greatly reduce the time in searching for bottlenecks, which need experience and skill to analyze. By adjusting the parameters, graphs can be modified to flush out the area of the problem. Several permutations and combinations of the parameters help in observing the multi-faceted nature of the results.

Bar Charts

Results can be represented in many ways. Bar chart representation is an effective way of understanding and analyzing results. To illustrate, results obtained for a single user, for 100 users, or for 1,000 users can be captured separately and represented in bar charts. This helps in analyzing the behavior of the system.

Scatter Charts

Scatter charts give an idea about the latency between loading a static page and a dynamic page. To illustrate, in the banking system, the main page is a static page whereas other pages such as facilitating deposit and withdrawing transactions are dynamic pages. The difference in time taken to load a main page and to load other pages can be identified.

The charts are overlaid with resource measurements to determine the bottlenecks occurring at the architecture level. The utilization of memory and CPU at various points

Table 8.1. Types of sample test reports

Reports	Outcome
Performance Report (Figure 8.3)	Response times, Standard Deviation, Mean and Percentiles for each command
Compare Performance Report	Compare the response times of multiple runs with increasing number of concurrent users
Response vs Time (Figure 8.4)	Individual response times and whether the response is passed or failed
Command Status Report (Figure 8.5)	Quick summary of which commands passed or failed
Command Usage Report (Figure 8.6)	Cumulative response time and summary statistics, as well as throughput info for emulation commands
Command Trace Report (Figure 8.7)	Examine failures in detail from the raw data obtained from the test logs

of the system architecture are separately captured and examined for the presence of bottlenecks. Excess queue length at various servers is also identified by setting the resource parameter.

Superimposing the various graphs gives an idea on the location of bottlenecks. Table 8.1 gives a summary of the different types of sample test reports. Each report represents a different type of information, represented in different ways.

These reports are sample ones and generated using the Rational Test Suite; for more information see Rational TestManager User's guide Version: 2002.05.00. Different tools provide their own format to present the results. These reports give an idea for testers on how to present various reports for different stakeholders.

Performance Reports

Performance reports, as shown in Figure 8.3, are the foundation of reporting performance related results in TestManager. They can show whether an application meets the criteria in the test plan or test case. As an example, a performance report can tell you whether 95% of virtual testers received responses from the test system in eight seconds or less, or what percentage of virtual testers did not receive responses from the system in that time.

Performance reports can be used to display the response times recorded during the suite run for selected commands. Performance reports also provide the mean, standard deviation, and percentiles for response times.

Performance reports use the same input data as response vs. time reports, and they sort and filter data accordingly. However, performance reports group the responses with the same command ID.

Performance reports give the following information:

Figure 8.3. Performance report

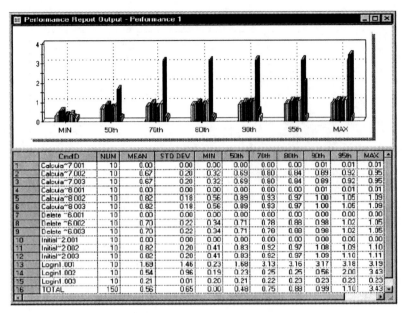

	CmdID	NUM	MEAN	STD DEV	MIN	50th	70th	80th	90th	95th	MAX
1	Calcula~7.001	10	0.00	0.00	0.00	0.00	0.00	0.00	0.01	0.01	0.01
2	Calcula~7.002	10	0.67	0.20	0.32	0.69	0.80	0.84	0.89	0.92	0.95
3	Calcula~7.003	10	0.67	0.20	0.32	0.69	0.80	0.84	0.89	0.92	0.95
4	Calcula~8.001	10	0.00	0.00	0.00	0.00	0.00	0.00	0.00	0.01	0.01
5	Calcula~8.002	10	0.82	0.18	0.56	0.89	0.93	0.97	1.00	1.05	1.09
6	Calcula~8.003	10	0.82	0.18	0.56	0.89	0.93	0.97	1.00	1.05	1.09
7	Delete ~6.001	10	0.00	0.00	0.00	0.00	0.00	0.00	0.00	0.00	0.00
8	Delete ~6.002	10	0.70	0.22	0.34	0.71	0.78	0.88	0.98	1.02	1.05
9	Delete ~6.003	10	0.70	0.22	0.34	0.71	0.78	0.88	0.98	1.02	1.05
10	Initial~2.001	10	0.00	0.00	0.00	0.00	0.00	0.00	0.00	0.00	0.00
11	Initial~2.002	10	0.82	0.20	0.41	0.83	0.92	0.97	1.08	1.09	1.10
12	Initial~2.003	10	0.82	0.20	0.41	0.83	0.92	0.97	1.09	1.10	1.11
13	Login1.001	10	1.69	1.46	0.23	1.68	3.13	3.16	3.17	3.18	3.19
14	Login1.002	10	0.54	0.96	0.19	0.23	0.25	0.25	0.56	2.00	3.43
15	Login1.003	10	0.21	0.01	0.20	0.21	0.22	0.23	0.23	0.23	0.23
16	TOTAL	150	0.56	0.65	0.00	0.48	0.75	0.88	0.99	1.10	3.43

- **Cmd ID** – The command ID associated with the response. A typical command is the scenario captured in a workload.

- **NUM** – The number of responses for each command ID (the number of times each command ID appeared in the test log). In this example, each command ID has 10 responses.

- **MEAN** – The arithmetic mean of the response times of all commands and responses for each command ID.

- **STD DEV** – The standard deviation of the response times of all commands and responses for each command ID.

- **MIN** – The minimum response time for each command ID. In this example, the minimum response times range from 0.00 second (meaning that the command took less than a hundredth of a second to complete) to 1.69 seconds.

- **50th, 70th, 80th, 90th, 95th** – The percentiles of the response times for each command ID.

The percentiles compare the response times of each command ID. As an example, the 50th column shows the 50th percentile of time for each command ID. This means that half of the commands had a shorter response time and half had a longer response time.

In this example, the 50th percentile of Calcula~7.002 is 0.69. This means that 50% of the response times are less than 0.69 seconds. The 95th percentile of Calcula~7.002 is 0.92. This means that 95% of the response times are less than 0.92 seconds.

- **MAX** – The maximum response time of all responses for each command ID. In this example, they range from 0.01 second to 3.43 seconds. The total response time is listed in the table but is not displayed in the graph because, to a casual onlooker, a graph that includes this total might appear skewed. However, one can display the total response time.

Compare Performance Reports

The compare performance report compares response times measured by Performance reports. After generating several performance reports, use a compare performance report to compare the values of a specific field in each of those reports. One can also compare reports that show different numbers of virtual testers or compare reports from runs on different system configurations. Compare performance reports allow one to see how benchmark information differs for various workloads. As an example, one can run the same test with increasing workloads and then compare the performance reports of the test runs to see how performance changes under an ever increasing workload. When the tester runs a compare performance report, the tester should specify the base performance report and up to six other performance reports.

Response vs. Time Reports

Response vs. time reports, shown in Figure 8.4, display individual response times. Response vs. time reports use the same input data as performance reports and sort and filter data similarly. However, response vs. time reports show each command ID individually whereas performance reports group responses with the same command ID. Response vs. time reports are useful to check the trend in the response time. The response vs. time report shows the response time vs. the elapsed time of the suite run.

The response time should be clustered around one point rather than getting progressively longer or shorter. If the trend changes, it has to be checked that the tester has excluded logon and setup time in the results. The worst case is that one might need to change the test design. If the response time is relatively flat except for one or two spikes, one might want to investigate the cause of the spikes. Filtering the data so that they contains only one command ID and then graphing that command ID as a histogram.

The graph shown in Figure 8.4 plots each virtual tester vs. the response time in milliseconds. The graph contains many short lines that resemble dots. The lines indicate that the response times for all the virtual testers are quite short. The longer a line is on the X axis, the longer the response time because the X axis represents the response time.

Figure 8.4. Response vs. time

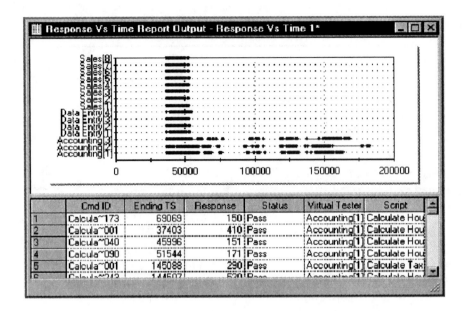

Command Status Reports

The command status report, shown in Figure 8.5, provides the total number of times a command has run, how many times the command has passed, and how many times it has failed. If the response of one received is the same or is expected, TestManager considers the command has passed; otherwise, TestManager considers it has failed.

Command status reports reflect the overall health of a test suite run. They are similar to performance reports, but they focus on the number of commands run in the suite. Command status reports are useful for debugging because one can see which commands fail repeatedly and then examine the related test script.

The graph plots the command number against the number of times the test. Command status reports contain the following information:

- **Cmd ID** – The command ID associated with the response.

- **NUM** – The number of responses corresponding to each command ID. This number is the sum of the numbers in the Passed and Failed columns.

- **Passed** – The number of passed responses for each command ID (that is, those that did not time out).

- **Failed** – The number of failed responses for each command ID that timed out (that is, the expected response was not received).

Figure 8.5. Command status report

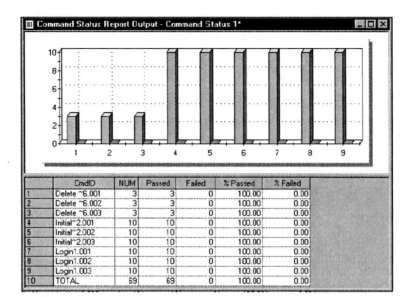

	CmdID	NUM	Passed	Failed	% Passed	% Failed
1	Delete ~6.001	3	3	0	100.00	0.00
2	Delete ~6.002	3	3	0	100.00	0.00
3	Delete ~6.003	3	3	0	100.00	0.00
4	Initial~2.001	10	10	0	100.00	0.00
5	Initial~2.002	10	10	0	100.00	0.00
6	Initial~2.003	10	10	0	100.00	0.00
7	Login1.001	10	10	0	100.00	0.00
8	Login1.002	10	10	0	100.00	0.00
9	Login1.003	10	10	0	100.00	0.00
10	TOTAL	69	69	0	100.00	0.00

- **% Passed** – The percentage of responses that passed for that command ID.
- **% Failed** – The percentage of responses that failed for that command ID.

Command Usage Reports

Command usage reports, shown in Figure 8.6, display data on all emulation commands and responses. The report describes throughput and virtual tester characteristics during the suite run. The summary information in the command usage report gives a high-level view of the division of activity in a test run. The cumulative time spent by virtual testers executing commands, thinking, or waiting for a response can tell quickly where the bottlenecks are. The command usage report can also provide summary information for protocols.

Command usage reports contain a section on cumulative statistics and a section on summary statistics.

Cumulative Statistics

- **Active Time** – It represents the sum of the active time of all virtual testers. The active time of a virtual tester is the time that the virtual tester spent thinking (including

Figure 8.6. Command usage report

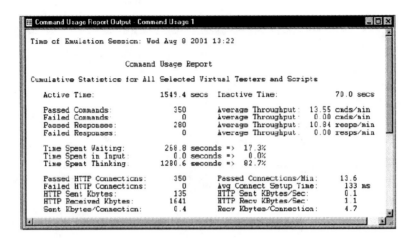

delays after the virtual tester's first recorded command), executing commands, and waiting for responses.

- **Inactive Time** – The sum of the inactive time of all virtual testers and test scripts. The inactive time of a virtual tester is the time before the virtual tester's first emulation command (including the overhead time needed to set up and initialize the run), and possibly interscript delay (the time between the last emulation command of the previous test script and the beginning of the current test script).

- **Passed Commands** – The total number of passed send commands, that is, commands that send virtual tester input to the server.

- **Failed Commands** – The total number of failed send commands, that is, commands that send virtual tester input to the server.

- **Passed Responses** – The total number of responses to send commands that were matched by passing receive commands. This is not the same as the total number of expected receive commands because a response may be matched by an arbitrary number of receive commands. A response is considered expected if all receive commands used to match it have an expected status.

- **Failed Responses** – The total number of responses that were matched by failing receive commands. This is not the same as the total number of unexpected receive commands because a response may be received by an arbitrary number of receive commands. A response is considered unexpected if any receive commands used to match it have an unexpected status because send commands and responses in a test script do not necessarily have a one-to-one correspondence. To illustrate, an HTTP script may issue one send command. The total of passed commands plus failed commands often does not equal the total of passed responses plus failed responses (http_request) and receive multiple responses to the send (http_header_recv and one or more http_nrecv commands).

- **Average Throughput** – Four measurements of average throughput are provided: passed command throughput, failed command throughput, passed response throughput, and failed response throughput. This represents the throughput of an average virtual tester.

- **Time Spent Waiting** – The total time spent waiting for responses, given both in seconds and as a percentage of active time. The time spent waiting is the elapsed time from when the send command is submitted to the server until the server receives the complete response. The time that an http_request spends waiting for a connection to be established is counted as time spent waiting.

- **Time Executing Commands** – The total time spent in executing commands on the agent computer. This measurement is provided both in seconds and as a percentage of active time. The time spent executing VU emulation commands that access an SQL server is defined as the elapsed time from when the SQL statements are submitted to the server until these statements have completed.

- **Time Spent Thinking** – The total time spent thinking, both in seconds and as a percentage of active time. The time spent thinking for a given command is the elapsed time from the end of the preceding command until the current command is submitted to the server. This definition of think time corresponds to that used during the run only if the Test Script Services (TSS) environment variable Think_def in the test script has the default LR (last received), which assumes that think time starts at the last received data time stamp of the previous response. If any VU emulation commands are executed that access an SQL server, the command usage report includes:

- **Rows Received** – Number of rows received by all reported sqlnrecv commands.

- **Received Rows/Sec** – Average number of rows received per second. Derived by dividing the number of rows received by the active time.

- **Average Rows/Response** – Average number of rows in the passed and failed responses. Derived by dividing the number of rows received by the number of passed and failed responses.

- **Average Think Time** – Average think time in seconds for sqlexec and sqlprepare statements only.

- **Avg Execution Time** – Average time in milliseconds to execute an sqlexec or DCOM method call command. Derived by dividing the time spent on sqlexec commands by the number of sqlexec commands.

- **Avg Preparation Time** – Average time in milliseconds to execute an sqlprepare command. Derived by dividing the time spent on sqlprepare commands by the number of sqlprepare commands.

If any HTTP emulation commands are executed that access a Web server, the command usage report includes:

- **Passed HTTP Connections** – Number of successful HTTP connections established by all reported http_request commands.

- **Failed HTTP Connections** – Number of HTTP connection attempts that failed to establish a connection for all reported http_request commands.

- **HTTP Sent Kbytes** – Kilobytes of data sent by reported http_request commands.

- **HTTP Received Kbytes** – Kilobytes of data received by reported http_nrecv and http_recv commands.

- **HTTP Sent Kbytes/Sec** – Kilobytes of data sent per second. Derived by dividing the kilobytes of data sent by all recorded http_request commands by the active time.

- **HTTP Recv Kbytes/Sec** – Kilobytes of data received per second. Derived by dividing the kilobytes of data received by all recorded http_nrecv and http_recv commands by the active time.

Summary Statistics

- **Duration of Run** – Elapsed time from the beginning to the end of the run. The beginning of the run is the time of the first emulation activity among all virtual testers and test scripts, not just the ones filtered for this report. Similarly, the end of the run is the time of the last emulation activity among all virtual testers and test scripts. The elapsed time does not include the process time.

- **Total Throughput** – Four measurements of total throughput are provided: passed command throughput, failed command throughput, passed response throughput, and failed response throughput. The total throughput of passed commands is obtained by dividing the number of passed commands by the run's duration, with the appropriate conversion of seconds into minutes. Thus, it represents the total passed command throughput by all selected virtual testers at the applied workload, as opposed to the throughput of the average virtual tester. The total failed command and the total passed and failed response throughputs are calculated analogously. These throughput measurements, as well as the test script throughput, depend upon the virtual tester and test script selections. The summary throughput measurements are most meaningful when all virtual testers and test scripts are selected. To illustrate, if only three virtual testers from a ten-virtual-tester run are selected, the throughput does not represent the server throughput at a ten-virtual-tester workload, but rather the throughput of three selected virtual testers as part of a ten-virtual-tester workload.

- **Number of Completed Scripts** – Test scripts are considered complete if all associated activities are completed before the run ends.

- **Number of Uncompleted Scripts** – Number of test scripts that have not finished executing when a run is halted. Test scripts can be incomplete if the run is halted or the suite is set to terminate after a certain number of virtual testers or test scripts.

- **Average Number of Scripts Completed per Virtual Tester** – Calculated by dividing the number of completed test scripts by the number of virtual testers.

- **Average Script Duration for Completed Scripts** – Average elapsed time of a completed test script. Calculated by dividing the cumulative active time of all virtual testers and test scripts by the number of completed test scripts.

- **Script Throughput for Completed Scripts** – Number of test scripts per hour completed by the server during the run. Calculated by dividing the number of completed test scripts by the duration of the run, with the conversion of seconds into hours. This value changes if you have filtered virtual testers and test scripts.

If any timers are executed, the command usage report includes:

- **Passed Testcase Commands** – Number of testcase commands that report a passed status.

- **Failed Testcase Commands** – Number of testcase commands that report a failed status.

Command Trace Reports

Command trace reports, shown in Figure 8.7, list the activity of a run and enable a detailed examination. Command trace reports list the activity of a run and enable a detailed examination of unusual or unexpected events. This report formats raw data from the suite run without performing statistical analysis.

Command trace reports display the actual timestamps from the emulation, the counts of data sent and received, and the TSS environment variable settings (if recorded).

Command trace reports contain the following information:

- **Total Number of Virtual Testers Emulated** – The number of virtual testers in the suite run.

- **Number of Virtual Testers in Report** – The number of virtual testers that appear. If filtered virtual testers are present, this number is different from the total number of virtual testers emulated.

- **Time of Suite Run** – The time that the suite started to run.

- **Time of Day Reference for Timestamps** – The time the suite started to run, given as the number of seconds since 00:00:00 GMT, January 1, 1970. To convert these timestamps into time-of-date format, use the UNIX ctime(3) library routine or the Windows localtime() library function.

Figure 8.7. Command trace report

```
Trace of Emulation Session Activity

Total Number of Virtual Testers Emulated: 10
Number of Virtual Testers in Report: 10

Information for Virtual Tester: Accounting[1]
Rational Suite TestStudio Release 8.5

Time of Suite Run: Wed Aug  8 13:22:41 2001
Time of Day Reference for Timestamps:   997291361

Virtual Tester's Environment: Screen = 0, Server_connection = 1, Emulation = NONE,
                  Screen_match = CURSOR_DATA

Login Timestamp:      7069

Virtual Tester: Accounting[1]            Test Script: Login

Beginning timestamp of test script Login:      7069

Src  Cmd                                        First     Last
Line Count Clnt Command      Command ID    Count Timestamp Timestamp Stat
____ _____ ____ _____      _____    _____ _____ _____ ____

  34    1    1 http_request  Login1.001      265      7080     10194
                                                     10194     10194 pass
  49    2    2 http_request  Login1.002      431     10214     10465
                                                     10465     10465 pass

Virtual Tester's Environment: Server_connection = 2 ("Login1.002")

  66    3    2 http_hdr_recv Login1.003      214     10665     10665 pass
  68    4    2 http_nrecv_cache Login1.004     0     10675     10675 pass

Virtual Tester's Environment: Server_connection = 1 ("Login1.001")

  74    5    1 http_hdr_recv Login1.005      163     10784     10784 pass
  76    6    1 http_nrecv    Login1.006      969     10784     10784 pass
```

For each virtual tester, the command trace report lists the following information:

A line showing the virtual tester that is being reported. In this example, the tester is Data_Entry[1] or the first virtual tester in the Data Entry group.

Default TSS environment variable values and environment variable changes taking place on each virtual tester during playback. The changes correspond to environment control commands executed during the suite run.

The command trace report lists the following information:

A test script header, which lists the virtual tester, the release, and the name of the test script.

- **Beginning Timestamp** – The time, in milliseconds (since the beginning of the suite run), at the start of execution of each test script.

- **Login Timestamp** – Recorded for each virtual tester. This corresponds to the time when the virtual tester's logon status changed to ON.

Emulation commands executed during the suite run. A three-line heading appears if any emulation commands are included.

The command trace report gives the following information for each emulation command:

- **Src Line** – The line number of the command in the source file, if available (Java and Visual Basic test scripts do not make this value available; therefore, the command trace report displays N/A).

- **Cmd Count** – A running tally of the number of emulation commands executed in a test script. This tally includes http_request commands that are read from the cache. The report shows 0 for SQABasic timers.

- **Clnt** – The value of the Server_connection environment variable associated with each SQL, HTTP, or socket emulation command. If your test script has multiple connections, this value shows which receive command corresponds to which request. The command trace report leaves this column blank for other commands.

- **Command** – The emulation command that was executed. If an HTTP response was read from cache (rather than from the network), the report shows http_nrecv(c) (rather than http_nrecv).

- **Command ID** – The command ID associated with the command.

- **Count** – These values depend on the type of emulation command. This is the number of bytes of data written to the test log. For SQL emulation commands, this is the number of rows of data written to the test log.

- **First Timestamp** – The time, in milliseconds, the command started executing, relative to the beginning of the suite run.

- **Last Timestamp** – The time, in milliseconds, the command stopped executing, relative to the beginning of the suite run.

- **Stat** – Whether the emulation command passed or failed.

- **Ending Timestamp** – The time, in milliseconds, the test script stopped executing, relative to the beginning of the suite run. This value is reported for each test script. The duration of the test script is also reported.

- **Logout Timestamp** – The time, in milliseconds, the virtual tester's logon status changed from ON to OFF.

Areas of Improvement

In many Web sites, symptoms like No response, Response is low, Download time is high, Availability of Web site is not guaranteed, and so forth are common. These symptoms indicate problems relating to performance. However, in conventional methodologies, these symptoms are taken as those related with database issues. The correctness of this assumption is always open to question. It is likely that a bottleneck may reside at different locations such as the Web server, application server, and security settings and not necessarily at the database. Therefore, without identifying the bottleneck, fine tuning the database may be an exercise in futility in terms of time and resources. Identifying an area of improvement goes hand in hand with performance indicators. In order to do that, it is necessary to define a set of indicators, which provide a good measure of PT and thus the performance behavior of the Web site. One can categorize these indicators from the client and server sides. Though these indicators provide basic information about the performance, they do not provide a true picture of the real environment. Some of the indicators are:

Processor

The processor is an important resource, which affects the performance of the application. It is necessary to measure the amount of time spent in processing the threads by one or many CPUs. If the usage is consistently above 90% for a processor, it indicates that the test is too intense for the hardware. This indicator is applicable only when the system has multiple processors.

Physical Disk

Since the disk is a slow device with more storage capacity, the parameters, like latency and elapsed time, provide information regarding improving performance. Performance of the system depends on disk queue length also. It shows the number of outstanding requests on the disk. Sustained queue length indicates a disk or memory problem.

Memory

Memory in any computer system is an integral part of the hardware system. More memory will speed up the I/O process during execution but burdens the cost parameter. All data and instructions to be executed must be available on the memory comprised on pages. If more pages are available, the faster the execution will be. The observation on number of page faults will give information related to the performance. It is worth considering how many pages are being moved to and from the disk to satisfy virtual memory requirements.

Network Traffic

It is not possible to directly analyze the network traffic on the Internet, as it depends on the bandwidth, type of network connection, and other overheads. However, it is possible to find out the time taken for number of bytes reaching the client from the server. The bandwidth problem will also affect the performance as the type of connections vary from client to client.

Performance indicators provide the basis for performance tuning, and in each category, different types of counters can be set. The values provided by these counters will greatly help in analyzing performance.

Architecture Design and Coding

Improper architecture can cause a heavy penalty for performance like improper design of the database, for example, improper indexing of tables normalization factors. When looking into an object oriented connection, memory management should be considered for maximum extent; for instance, importance should be given to the factors like garbage collection (GC), that is automatic memory management database connectivity drivers, and their usage should be studied. As an example, there are four types of drivers in Java Database Connections (JDBC) to interface Java applets or Java applications with a database. Choose the best of the four methods as per the application.

Tuning Process

Performance tuning is primarily a matter of resource management and correcting resource parameter settings. If the bottleneck observed is not present at the resource level, tuning should be proceeded toward workload design. It is essential to tune for correct workload or else performance will be suboptimum for a higher workload. If the validation of the workload against the user profile is free of bottlenecks, the next level of observation should be toward code. A performance tuning process deals with several stages, as shown in Figure 8.8.

Start Tuning Process

Before commencing the process of start tuning (Figure 8.8), it is worthwhile to bear in mind the goals of performance. As a next step, it is necessary to have the performance reports and correctly analyze them. A difference between the expected results as per goals and the actual results as per the reports forms the baseline for tuning. Before start tuning, one should know the reasons for achieving the performance goals.

Identify the Bottleneck

Before proceeding to know the type of bottlenecks (Figure 8.8) observed during PT of Web applications, it is essential to know the meaning of the term bottleneck. In a typical interpretation, a bottleneck is a narrowing that slows the flow through a channel. In the context of Web architecture, flow refers to the dataflow, and channel refers to the network

Figure 8.8. Tuning process

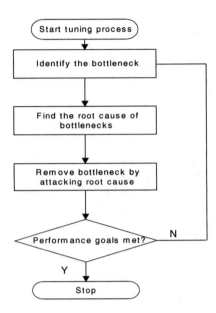

pipe. A bottleneck is a hindrance which slows down or impedes the flow of data due to an obstruction. Bottlenecks are the constriction or squeeze and are the symptoms of performance problems. Often there is confusion between bottlenecks and the causes of bottlenecks.

Bottlenecks

Bottlenecks are the performance problems observed during system operation. The presence of bottlenecks makes system unacceptable. They can be observed by any person who operates the system, that is, the end user or Webmaster. Bottlenecks could be observed at any stage of system operation.

Causes of Bottlenecks

The presence of a bottleneck is an indication that the system is not efficient and unsatisfactory to the users of the system. There are a number of bottlenecks that can occur during PT of Web applications. Some of the bottlenecks are visible to both end user and Webmaster; some of the bottlenecks are visible to Webmasters only, for example, resource intensive bottlenecks.

The most frequently observed bottlenecks during PT are:

- Downloading pages is too slow and takes more time.

The cause of this bottleneck can be due to page/graphic size, server-task prioritization, and incremental page presentation, which are in the hands of the production team. Other important factors can be the modem and type of network.

- Response is too slow for a query.

This could be an issue caused by database design or middleware like Java Database Connectivity (JDBC), Open Database Connectivity (ODBC), or ADO. Poor logic involved, that is, improper usage of SQL, is discussed in Appendix A2.

- Particular page loads slowly
- Unable to connect to Web site
- Erroneous data returned
- Page not available
- Broken pages or error pages
- Response freezes up for quite a long time
- CPU usage is high
- Disk usage is high
- Memory usage is greater
- Number of dynamic pages/second is less
- Lengthy queue for end user requests
- Packet loss during transmission
- Too many open connections between the server and end users
- Memory leaks

A *memory leak* is a program error that consists of repeatedly allocating memory, using it, and then neglecting to free it. A memory leak in a long-running program, such as an interactive application, is a serious problem because it can result in memory fragmentation and the accumulation of large numbers of mostly garbage-filled pages in real memory and page space. Systems have been known to run out of page space because of a memory leak in a single program (see Performance Management Guide, 2005).

- Database deadlocks

This can be because of database server load, which is one of the problems with concurrency. Deadlock occurs when some combination of locking, coding, or transaction management goes wrong. Deadlocks come in two flavors: cycle deadlocks and conversion deadlocks. Both types arise when processes contend for the same resources. Cycle deadlocks arise in contention for data, either a row or a table. Conversion deadlocks occur over contention for lock escalation, where two processes are in competition for exclusivity (see *Avoid database deadlocks with planning*, 2005).

- High network traffic
- Capacity exceeds at low traffic
- Application does not allow too many users to perform a task concurrently
- Application load time at Web server is slow

These bottlenecks vary from system to system. Most of the PT tools provide facilities to identify these bottlenecks.

Find the Root Cause of Bottlenecks

A bottleneck can occur in any segment of the architecture. In a complex architecture, as shown in Figure 8.9, * (star) represents the possible performance bottleneck.

As shown in Figure 8.9, bottlenecks can occur at different tiers such as end user connection points, Internet connection points at ISPs, hardware/software of ISPs, load balancer, Web server farm, application server, server hardware and operating systems, and database server.

By looking into different segments of the architecture, bottlenecks are comprehensively identified as:

Figure 8.9. Areas of bottleneck

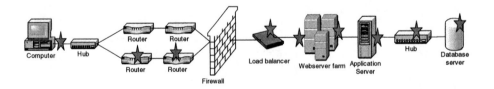

- Database server

- Web server

- Application server

- Network

- Any other external system

Front End Monitoring

Testers can easily detect some of the bottlenecks at the front end (observation made at front end), while others only through the generation of the reports. The following list gives the probable bottlenecks observed by front end monitoring:

- Downloading pages is too slow

- Response is too slow for a query

- Unable to connect to Web site

- Erroneous data returned

- Page not available

- Broken pages

- Response freezes up for quite a long time

These bottlenecks are experienced by users at the front end and easy to locate. Hence, testers can easily monitor these bottlenecks and report to the analyst.

Table 8.2. Type of server counters and location

Type of Server Counters	Location
CPU utilization	Web server, application server, database server
Memory utilization	Web server, application server, database server
Throughput	Web server
Current user connections	Web server
Disk IO	Web server, application server, database server
Formation of queue and queue wait time	Application server
Database connection pool	Application server
Number of table scans	Database server
Table locks	Database server
Cache hit ratio	Web server, application server, database server
Page size	Web server
Page hit ratio	Web server
Database parsing ratio	Application server

Table 8.3. Type of network counters and location

Type of network counters	Location
Number of current user connections	Firewall, load balancer
Number of SSL connections	Firewall
CPU utilization	Firewall, load balancer
Throughput	Firewall, load balancer
Load balancing split	Load balancer

Server Monitoring

Server monitoring is very necessary to capture the performance data with respect to server hardware and software. Server counters are collected by the testing tool which helps in identifying the bottlenecks at the Web server, application server, and database server. Table 8.2 shows some of the generic counters adopted by several industry standard automated tools.

Network Monitoring

Network monitoring reveals the amount of load on the system and the connections. Network details are observed by analyzing the counters at load balancers and firewalls. Table 8.3 shows some of the counters collected by tools at the network level.

Though an experience of several testing projects gives fair knowledge about the common areas of bottlenecks, it is difficult to determine which area is more prone to performance problems. According to the professionals of Mercury Interactive Corp. (see http://www.mercury.com/), database servers are more prone to performance bottlenecks than the network resources, application servers, and Web servers. The causes of bottlenecks as per Mercury Interactive Corp. are given in Figure 8.10.

Alternatively, according to Empirix Inc. (see http://www.empirix.com/), the application server is more prone to bottlenecks than the database server, network resources, and Web server. This is shown in Figure 8.11.

Real bottlenecks will depend on the type of the application and the technology used. Identifying the bottleneck is relatively simple and straight forward. Determining the cause behind that bottleneck is often difficult and time consuming. Causes of bottleneck are identified based on the following factors:

- Type of bottleneck
- Area of bottleneck

Once the type of the bottleneck is identified, the area of bottleneck can be identified by analyzing the performance monitors set by the tool. The data collected in the counters ensure the presence of a bottleneck in a particular area. The next step is to explore the

Figure 8.10. Database servers prone more to performance bottlenecks

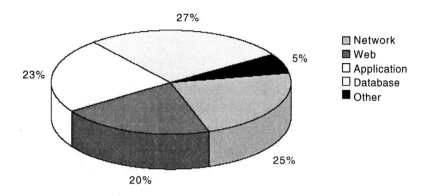

Figure 8.11. Application servers prone more to performance bottlenecks

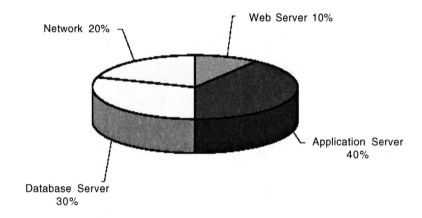

area thoroughly and isolate the root cause of the bottleneck. As explained in the previous sections, areas are broadly divided into Web server, application server, database server, network, and external systems.

Each area is associated with a set of real and logical resources, which can contribute to performance problems quite often. The real resources affecting the performance more often are CPU cycles, memory, I/O bus, various adapters, disk arms, disk space, and network access. Logical resources are generally programming abstractions that are part of real resources. This partitioning is done to share and manage the real resource. Logical resources are less readily identified. Table 8.4 shows the types of real and logical resources.

It is important to be aware of logical resources as well as real resources. Deadlocks can occur due to the lack of logical resources, which are mapped as real resources. Expanding the real resource does not necessarily ensure that additional logical resources are created. Their existence may not be appreciated until a specific performance problem occurs which is related to logical resources.

Based on type of servers and networks, one can identify common causes for bottlenecks for performance. This is highlighted in Table 8.5.

Since servers and networks play a major role in Web application, understanding the type of bottlenecks and their causes is of paramount importance.

Remove Bottleneck by Attacking the Root Cause

A truth of performance tuning is that there is always a possibility of another bottleneck popping up due to the tuning process. Reducing the use of one resource means that another resource is overutilized, which limits throughput and response time. Care must be taken while selecting the candidate for tuning. Major problems, if any, must be addressed first before tackling the minor problems.

Stop Tuning Process

The testing team can improve the performance indefinitely by monitoring and adjusting various parameters. By doing this, performance may be improved drastically. Sometimes, tuning may not produce effective improvement, but the team may not stop the tuning process. In such a situation, when to stop tuning is a question to be addressed carefully. Normally, when all the bottlenecks are successfully fixed, the tuning process is terminated. The efforts and costs of improving performance start to increase considerably as the system becomes more and more optimally tuned, so it is important to know when to stop tuning.

Performance Tuning at Workload Level

If the bottleneck is not identified at the resource level, the cause of the problem should be investigated by examining workloads. To illustrate, if a resource hungry workload is designed, wherein the distribution of resources is CPU: 90%, Disk: 70%, and Memory: 60%, this workload is CPU intensive. If the workload is tuned successfully so that the CPU load is reduced from 90% to 45%, then there might be improvement in performance due to a tuned workload structure like CPU: 45%, Disk: 90%, and Memory: 60%.

Unfortunately, the workload is now I/O intrinsic. The improved CPU utilization allows the programs to submit disk requests sooner, but then the limitation imposed by the disk drive's capacity is overreached. Thus, this performance tuning invokes a new problem.

Care should be taken to tune the system constructively; unstructured performance tuning may result in unexpected system behavior like degraded application performance or a system hang.

Table 8.4. Examples of real resources and the logical resources

Real resource	Logical resource
CPU	• Processor time slice
Memory	• Page frames Virtual-memory segments are partitioned into fixed-size units called *pages*. The default page size is 4096 bytes. Each page in a segment can be in primary memory (RAM), or stored on secondary memory disk until it is needed. Similarly, primary memory is divided into 4096-byte page frames. The role of the VMM is to manage the allocation of real-memory page frames and to resolve references by the program to virtual-memory pages that are not currently in real memory or do not yet exist. From the performance standpoint, the VMM has two, somewhat opposed, objectives: 1. Minimize the overall processor-time and disk-bandwidth cost of the use of virtual memory 2. Minimize the response-time cost of page faults In pursuit of these objectives, the VMM maintains a *free list* of page frames that are available to satisfy a page fault. The VMM uses a page-replacement algorithm to determine which virtual-memory pages currently in memory will have their page frames reassigned to the free list. • Stacks • Buffers • Queues • Tables • Locks and semaphores A Lock is used to maintain exclusive access to a certain resource. Semaphore extends the functionality of a Lock by manipulating an internal integer variable.
Disk Space	• Logical volumes • File systems • Files • Partitions
Network Access	• Sessions • Packets • Channels

Guidelines for Performance Tuning

Performance tuning of an application involves tuning of many components, which participate in the success of the application running. Components like database server, application server, Web server, technology environment, and network are part of the application. Tuning at the component level definitely helps to improve the performance of the application. All components are of different types and from different vendors. Each

Table 8.5. Resources and factors causing performance bottleneck

Resource	Factors Causing Performance Bottleneck
Database Server	• Insufficient Indexing • Large number of temporary tables • Too much of interaction between database server and application server • Fragmented database • Large number of queued requests • Unnecessary triggers • Use of inline SQL code insufficient disk • Insufficient memory • Insufficient cache • Locked tables • Use of ODBC • Poor configuration of server • Out of date statistics
Application Server	• Un optimized code • Insufficient disk • Insufficient memory • Mismanaged cache • Insufficient disk • Memory leaks • Too much of interaction with database • Enough threads are not available to handle requests • Execution of concurrent transactions at a set time • Improper database connection pooling • Mismanaged sessions Queue length and wait time are more
Web Server	• Too much of SSL traffic • Number of requests is more • Page size is more • Source files are stored in disk than in main memory • Too much of file sharing • Unbalanced load on server • Insufficient cache or memory • Insufficient Disk • Poor Web server design • Poorly written DLLs • One or more process consumes too much of processor time
Network	• LAN bandwidth not sufficient • Un segmented networks Poor configuration

vendor provides its own guidelines to tune the component to optimize the performance. An attempt is made to provide general guidelines, which help testers tune each component for better performance.

Application Server

Application server, also called an appserver, a program that handles all application operations between users and an organization's backend business applications or databases. Application servers are typically used for complex transaction-based applications. To support high-end needs, an application server has to have built-in redundancy, monitors for high availability, high performance distributed application services,

Table 8.6. Performance issues and solutions for application server

Performance Issues	Solutions
High CPU usage is observed	• Optimize application code • Tune application server according to manufacturer's specification
Low memory is observed	• Add memory • Check for memory leaks • Introduce cache
Number of dynamic pages/sec is less	• Check for possibility of converting to static pages • Optimize application code • Tune application server according to manufacturer's specification • Make less interaction with database
Response time is high	• Check threading issues in code • Check server set up • Check total number of transactions • Execute several number of concurrent transactions at a time • Check server queue length
Database usage is poor	• Verify connection pooling
High disk usage	• Verify server logging level
Particular page load slowly	• Verify the amount of data accessed from the database

and support for complex database access. Appserver stores business logic and the business model classes of applications, and serves requests for dynamic HTTP Web pages from Web servers. Table 8.6 highlights performance issues and possible solutions for the application server.

We know that any computer can be turned into a Web server by installing server software and connecting the machine to the Internet. There are many Web server software applications, including public domain software from the National Center for Super Computing Applications (NCSA) (see http://www.ncsa.uiuc.edu) and Apache, and commercial packages from Microsoft, Netscape, and others.

Web Server

Once the Web server software is installed on the computer, it renders the Web services or delivers Web pages. Every Web server that is configured has an IP address and possibly a domain name. Since it is like any other computer, the computer or server can have the performance problems as depicted in Table 8.7.

Database Server

A database server is specifically configured to run database software like Oracle and Sybase. Typically, an industry will use a database server combined with other servers

Table 8.7. Performance issues and solutions for Web server

Performance Issues	Solutions
High CPU usage	• Verify whether server is overloaded or not • Add more servers, if feasible • Introduce SSL accelerator to handle SSL traffic
High disk usage	• Verify whether all source files are stored in physical drives than in disk files
High network activity	• Avoid file sharing, store Web files locally • Use Storage Area Network devices for common storage
Page download is slow	• Check overall page sizes

to run a powerful Web application such as e-commerce. Table 8.8 highlights performance issues and possible solutions for the database server.

Network

As we know the computer network is the backbone infrastructure required for communication, the communication may be through modem or T1 lines. Apart from these, there are many other factors which cause performance issues in computer networks. Most common among them is given as a checklist in Table 8.9.

The above tables provide high level guidelines, and practitioners are advised to look into tuning guidelines provided by the manufacturer of each component. Specific tuning parameters and the corresponding solutions for a set of sample components is given in Appendix A1.

Summary

The post execution phase provides the details on representing the test results and how to identify the bottlenecks. Bottleneck correction should be done step by step. A formal approach to identify bottlenecks and address solutions is of paramount importance in PT. Several tools provide various parameters to help in identifying bottlenecks. Care must be taken to choose proper parameters which help in identifying the bottlenecks. Having identified the bottlenecks, the tuning process must be initiated, and the proper resource tuning must be taken up on a priority basis. In general, tuning is an art- and skill-oriented task and requires experience.

Table 8.8. Performance issues and solutions for database server

Performance Issues	Solutions
Large number of queued requests	• Increase the number of connections to handle excess requests • Verify whether the server is tuned to manufacturer's specs
Slow query response	• Optimize query by minimizing sorting • Eliminate unnecessary triggers • Minimize the use of temporary tables • Use parameter based stored procedure • Find and add missing indexes
CPU usage is high	• Minimize the interaction between application server and database server • Use stored procedure instead inline SQL
Disk usage is high	• Store logs, data, and indexes on separate disks • Use RAID configurations • Make sure server has sufficient memory and cache

Table 8.9. Performance issues and solutions for network environment

Network Related Performance Issue	Solution
Packet loss	• Check the configuration network devices • Verify network capacity
Lost connections	• Verify network hardware configuration (firewalls, load balancers, routers, switches etc...) • Verify whether LAN is exceeding rated capacity • Use segmented internal and external networks
Capacity exceeds at low traffic	• Use an intranet for internal traffic
Getting timeout errors or firewall sends errors about no connections	• Verify firewall licensing and configuration • Make sure that number of connections are not exceeding the specified rate
Load balancer is not distributing load properly among Web servers	Verify load balancer configurations

References

10 Status code definition. (2004). Retrieved June 10, 2004, from http://www.w3.org/Protocols/rfc2616/rfc2616-sec10.html

Aikat, K. J., & Donelson Smith, F. (n.d.). Retrieved September 14, 2004, from http://www.cs.unc.edu/~jeffay/papers/ToN-04-Version.pdf

Avoid database deadlocks with planning. (2005). Retrieved May 12, 2005, from http://www.devx.com/getHelpOn/10MinuteSolution/16488/1954?pf=true

Performance management guide. (2005). Retrieved May 12, 2005, from http://publib16.boulder.ibm.com/pseries/en_US/aixbman/prftungd/memperf2.htm#i46342

Additional Sources

Aritt, M. F., & Williamson, C. L. (n.d.). *Internet Web servers: Workload characterization and performance implications.* Retrieved September 14, 2004, from http://www.cc.gatech.edu/classes/AY2005/cs4803enc_fall/papers/InternetWeb Servers.pdf

Barber, S. (n.d.). *Effective performance testing (beyond performance testing).* Retrieved November 27, 2004, from http://www.perftestplus.com/articles/bpt1.pdf

Hava-Muntean, C., McManis, J., Murphy, J., & Murphy, L. (n.d.). *A new dynamic Web server.* Retrieved September 14, 2004, from http://www.eeng.dcu.ie/~murphyj/publ/c19.pdf

HTTP return codes. (n.d.). Retrieved November 21, 2004, from http://www.w3.org/Protocols/rfc2616/rfc2616-sec10.html

Kelly, M. (n.d). *Updated: Using IBM rational robot to run your first performance test.* Software Engineer, QA, Liberty Mutual. Retrieved August 25, 2004, from http://www-128.ibm.com/developerworks/rational/library/5623.html

Killelea, S. (2002, March). *Web performance tuning (2nd ed.). Speeding up the Web.*

Titchkosky, L., Arlitt, M., & Williamson, C. (n.d.). *Performance benchmarking of dynamic Web technologies.* Retrieved September 14, 2004, from http://pages.cpsc.ucalgary.ca/~carey/papers/DynamicContent.pdf

Chapter 9

Performance Test Automation

This chapter delves on the automation aspects connected with performance issues. Adopting a manual method of testing the performance is neither desirable nor feasible. Automating the testing mode is an inevitable necessity. The strategy lies in choosing not only the best of the available tools but also to blend their productivity with human analytical skills. In this regard, it is important to bear in mind that use of tools as such does not amount to automating the entire testing process. This chapter addresses the task of setting up a process for automating the tests and highlights various issues involved in it. It also discusses some of the strategies for success in the automation of performance testing and concludes with a survey on tools currently available for testing in automation mode.

Automation tools do not perform magic, and the deployment of such tools demands not only time but also resources in terms of preparation, planning, and training. This is so because automated testing is a human assisted process. In order to automate testing, the following operations require human interaction.

First of all, one has to analyze the performance requirement specifications, and based on these performance requirement specifications, the performance test objectives have to be set. Then the workload has to be designed based on the operation profile, and the number of workloads for successful test execution has to be decided. The next step would be to design the test cases for each workload, identify and to create the test data bed. The other operations which involve human interaction is to build the traceability matrix (tracing test cases back to the performance requirement specification) and analysis of the test results and identifying bottlenecks.

The various operations in automation mode include setting the parameters per the performance requirements, building the test scripts, executing the test runs, recording and generating test results, and evaluating the results. The automation tools provide a feature to evaluate the results, but if there is an apparent failure, then the reevaluation of the test results has to be done manually. Thus, successful test automation involves both human interaction and the automation process.

This chapter recollects some of the topics discussed already in an earlier chapter for easy understanding of the P.T. automation.

Performance Test Automation Process

Test automation, in general, involves both manual and tool aided activities. Tools will not help without proper inputs for performance testing and exhaustive planning. The complete automation process starts with the preparation phase and ends with the postexecution phase as shown in Figure 9.1.

The preparation phase mainly deals with gathering data related to performance requirements, analysis, and developing a good testing strategy. The planning phase, which is subsequent to the preparation phase, involves development of a workload profile including the hardware and the software environment. The execution phase succeeds the planning phase. The test execution is a complex activity in PT. A proper framework for execution is necessary for smooth conduction of tests. This phase addresses issues like scheduling, correctness of the application, and acceptance criteria. The postexecution phase mainly focuses on identifying the bottlenecks and aspects related to fine tuning the process. A detailed step-by-step process is given in Figure 9.2.

Figure 9.1. Overview of test automation process

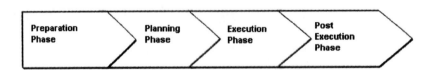

Figure 9.2. Step-by-step process in performance test automation

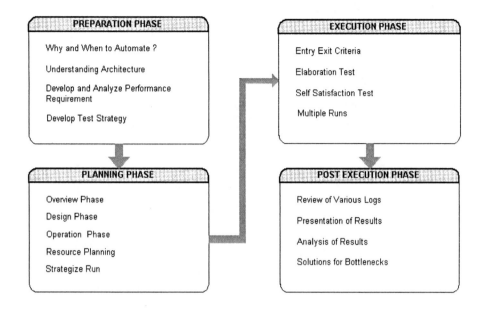

Preparation Phase

Performance test automation is a complex process compared to functional test automation. It involves the understanding of all those elements that have an impact on the performance of the system. Before analyzing these elements, the very purpose of performance test automation must be understood properly. Some of the systems might not be ready for performance test automation. Hence, the first step before starting the process of performance test automation is to check into when would be the appropriate time for performance test automation.

Why and When to Automate

Since test automation involves more cost and time, organizations debate on every step in the automation process. The first step is to appraise the management on the need for automation and when to automate for better results. Some of the salient points to be considered for automation of performance testing are as follows:

It is next to impossible to manually do performance testing. Also, in similar lines of functional regression testing, one has to emphasize the need for regression performance testing so as to ensure the repeatability of testing for better results. It has to be emphasized that automation of performance testing will strengthen the quality process. One has to study and analyze the performance results in multiple permutations and combinations for effective performance testing. The reduction in testing cycle time due to the automation of performance testing is one of the main advantages of automation of performance testing. For a successful automation of performance testing, one has to test multiple workloads with different combinations of transactions. A successful automation of performance testing should provide instant performance results and should reduce human errors by isolating human interventions as much as possible. Also, the performance test should be automated in such a way that it should be possible to run the test by a novice or a less skilled person. One of the other main advantages of automation of performance testing is the possibility of scheduling the tests at nonprime time.

Once the confidence is built up, the next step is to find out whether all systems can be automated or not and, if so, when to automate. The following points would help in finding out as to when one should automate performance testing.

One would look for automating performance testing when stability of the system is required. Also, whenever the scope of the system is fully defined and finalized and when the performance requirement study is complete, one would look for automating performance testing. Whenever the right tool is decided and evaluated and when sufficient test data are available, then one would go for automation of performance testing. Availability of the release version of the software for testing is one of the key points which would indicate the right time for automation of performance testing.

Not all of the above criteria may be effectively addressed for automation by the organization. For instance, the production ready test bed may not be available at the time of testing. In such circumstances, a proper test bed must be generated. For all these, the commitment of management is of paramount importance before automating the testing process. Once management is convinced about the automation, the next step is to understand the architectural setup support for the application.

Understanding Architecture

Web architecture plays a dominant role in Web PT. The Web architecture may be simple or complex, and it needs to be simulated during the testing. The complexity is based on many factors which include the type of the architecture. The complexity of the Web architecture varies based on whether it is a two-tier or three-/multitier architecture. The different types of servers used (like Web server, application server, and database server) and various kinds of browsers (like Internet Explorer, Netscape, AOL) used on the client side add to the complexity of the Web architecture. Further, the various platforms used (which include Mainframe, UNIX, Windows, etc.) and the different types of connectivity used (like dialup, T1/E1, cable, modems) to access the Web application add to the complexity of the Web architecture. Finally, one more dimension is added to the complexity of the Web architecture by the inseparable security requirements and the corresponding protocols like firewalls (Yerxa, 2004), SSL, HTTP, and so forth.

Figure 9.3. Example of complex Web architecture

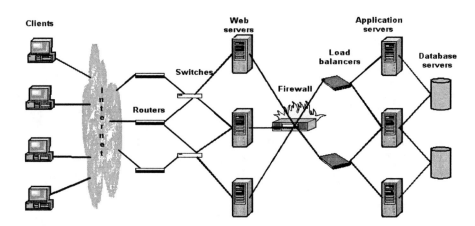

Figure 9.3 provides a schematic representation of a typical Web architecture which needs to be simulated during PT.

The Web architecture consists of various servers such as application servers, database servers, Web servers, load balancers (see Yerxa, 2004), network layer devices such as routers, data link layer devices such as switches, security components like firewalls, and so on. A complete understanding of the entire architecture is necessary to plan for a proper test environment during the period of fine tuning of the Web application.

Some of the issues which need special attention are compatibility issues, which might arise when the architecture is built with multivendor support. These compatibility issues might have an impact on performance if they are not attended to. Also, issues related to performance are dependent upon the configuration of the operating system, databases, Web servers, and on the various applications.

Develop and Analyze Performance Requirements

Similar to functional requirements, performance requirements are also important for the successful completion of PT. Performance requirements are captured during the functional requirement study and are used to model the operation profile and workload. The important step in the performance requirement phase is to develop an unambiguous Performance Requirement Document (PRD). The PRD mainly deals with the following:

Performance Testing Goals

For effective test automation, performance testing goals and objectives must be defined properly. Some of the important aspects which need attention regarding performance testing goals are as follows:

The response time for the application should not be more than t1 seconds, where t1 is defined by the user, and the download time should not be more than t2 seconds, where t2 is defined by the user. Also, the system should service X number of concurrent users at a given time. The system should not crash momentarily when the predicted user level exceeds expectations. Instead, the system should scale down gracefully; that is, there should be a gradual degradation of performance with sudden increase in user level. Also, the performance of the system should not degrade drastically whenever there is a change in the hardware/software, and moreover, the system must be upgradeable to support a specific growth rate determined every year. Many more such goals can be added to the performance testing goals.

Test Objectives and Success Criteria

Explicitly defined requirements of the customer available in the form of goals are transferred into objectives of PT. For instance, the response time can be split into response time of transactions, activities, and subactivities. Response time of a deposit transaction could be an integration of elapsed time for logging in, response time for authentication, response time for upgrading the database, and elapsed time for logout. Here logging in and logging out are the activities. Authenticating and upgrading the database are the subactivities completing the transaction. Some of the objectives derived from the goals are as follows:

The performance test should be able to assess the performance of the current configuration of the system, and it should aim at servicing up to a peak of X customers an hour without losing customers due to performance issues. The performance testing should aim at evolving a system that is stable and fully functional even under stressful conditions. The performance testing should aim at ensuring a proper environment. Note that the test environment cannot be an exact replica of the operational environment, but one needs to take into consideration some points while doing performance automation. To illustrate, if the production environment has three application servers, one database server, and one Web server and the test environment has one application server, one database server, and one Web server, then the issues that occur due to insufficient infrastructure should be analyzed to map to the operational environment. One of the objectives of PT would be to ensure that the system supports a maximum number of concurrent users (with the proposed configurations for acceptable performance). As infinite scalability is not practically feasible, the testers, by using feedback from the owners of the system, must come up with a criteria that will allow them to evaluate and define when the system under test has or has not met the performance expectations. The objectives of performance testing would be to identify the bottlenecks within the application architecture and also to ensure that the software or hardware changes would not crash the system. Once the objectives are finalized, the system must be described comprehensively.

Description of the System to be Tested

Each system subjected to PT needs to be documented. The details of how the system works have to be documented. The description of the system to be tested should also identify the potential users of the system and must specify how the users are distributed across the day/week/month. The activities and transactions carried out by different user groups and the details of external system interaction with the system to be tested have to be described. The description of the system must also include the acceptance rate for the user community, the most system intensive activity/transaction, and must document the complete infrastructure of the system. Some of the data, like acceptance rate, are difficult to collect, but they are required during the analysis.

Constraints on Test Automation

Test automation in a complex job requires attention from all directions. Some of the major constraints in test automation are the budget for automation, time required to complete the test, unavailability of a sophisticated test lab, and unavailability of sufficient infrastructure for realistic testing. Apart from these, there are other aspects to be considered which are project and customer specific.

Scope of the System

Clearly define the scope by determining what needs to be tested during the PT phase. The Performance Requirement Document (PRD) reflects what is to be done and not how it should be done. The "how" part is a complex task, and before addressing it, PRD must be analyzed for its feasibility and for its modeling. The analysis helps in designing and implementation. The analysis of PRD is done based on the following guidelines.

Review the PRD and remove ambiguities, if any. Analyze the document for correct interpretation of the customer's specification and also check for completeness of the document. The document should give complete details of the system under performance testing. Assess whether the document is prepared keeping the architecture in mind and make sure that critical quality factors are addressed with high priority. Further analyze whether the goals specified by the customer and the objectives prepared by the test team synchronize. Ensure that the objectives are realistic and the constraints, if any, are clearly documented. The document should reflect both the immediate performance requirements and the growth performance requirements and also ensure that the scope is properly defined.

Based on the analysis made on the PRD, the operation profile is revisited and fine tuned. The importance and the need for the operation profile is discussed in Chapter 5 of this book.

The operation profile provides a pattern of the business scenario at a particular instance but does not reflect the real user's behavior. Hence, the analysis phase addresses the issues related to modeling the real users.

Model the Real Users

Since the users of a Web application are heterogeneous in many aspects, modeling the users for Web application is the most difficult part of planning. No two users are the same. Their behaviors are different. Their actions with the system are different. Their locations of operation may be different. Therefore, simulation of user actions is a tedious task and requires broad vision and care. While modeling real users, the following points need to be taken into consideration.

Group the users based on the type of actions they do and always address the users with respect to their user community. To illustrate, in a typical banking application, customers, managers, and senior managers form different user groups. Each user group is associated with a set of transactions/activities/subactivities. An example could be that customers carry out typical transactions such as deposit and withdrawal, as well as activities like login and logout whereas managers carry out transactions such as opening an account, closing an account, and so forth, and senior managers carry out transactions such as ad hoc queries, managing monthly reports, and so on.

The users belonging to different groups can do the same set of transactions/activities/ subactivities. For instance, a manager can have an account in the bank for which he works. Then, the customers and managers can carry out the same transactions such as deposit and withdrawal. Also, the duration to accomplish a particular transaction/ activity/subactivity differs from user to user (random simulation of time is advisable) and the input data and quantity differ from activity to activity. For instance, input data may be username and password for login, or account number and deposit amount for a different activity. Also, the input data differ from user to user.

The user possesses a private password and an account number which are unique, and the transaction sequencing differs from user to user. To illustrate, the first time the customer will follow a typical sequencing such as login, opening an account, deposit, and logout whereas a frequently visiting customer need not go for opening an account and can directly login, deposit/withdraw, and logout. Hence, the transaction sequence may vary from user to user.

Noise level management plays a major role in simulating users. Users can run other software in the background while operating the Web application. Some of the other points to be considered while modeling the real users are that all users are not allowed to carry out all activities; users of a Web site think, read, and type at different speeds; and no two users are alike and their actions are also not alike. It is always better to do random simulation of users with different simulated users operating on different browsers and on different platforms. Also, the end users are exposed to different types of security settings, and they have different IP addresses.

Out of the many factors, modeling user "think time" is difficult. This involves user's psychology and actions, which are difficult to model. The user normally thinks and enters input data. The duration of thinking and rate at which the data are entered differ from user to user. Some users may copy and paste the input data; some may recall and input the data; and some users may go to canteen in the middle of the data entry. Therefore, adopting a realistic approach to measure think time is difficult. However, the following points will help the analyst to model the think time of the user.

If the Web site is already deployed, actual user delays are determined by reviewing the log file or extractions from Web traffic monitoring tools. If the log file is not maintained, then metrics and statistics collected from external agencies may have to be referred and assumed as first approximation. If the log file is not present and the metrics collected by other companies are not relevant to the system under test, then simple in-house experiments, like clipboard and stop watch methods, can lead to firsthand approximations about user think time. As a last resort, use intuition or best guess to estimate the range for these delays. Generate random delays (range for the delays, bounded with max and min think time) then static delays. The distribution among this delay range can be set as normal distribution, uniform distribution, and negative exponential distribution.

Assume 500 users access a typical Web site, and their think time varies from one user to another in the range of one second to nine seconds. In such situations, the distribution of the think time vs. number of users can be analyzed as discussed here.

Uniform Distribution of Think Time

Uniform distribution is easier and simpler to model than any other methods. In the illustrated graph shown in Figure 9.4, users are distributed uniformly across the range of think time from one to nine seconds.

About 30 users takes maximum think time (9 seconds) whereas 40 users consume minimum think time (1 second). In this case, one can ignore minimum and maximum think time and consider the average think time for the rest.

Normal Distribution of Think Time

Normal distribution is no doubt accurate but difficult to model. From Figure 9.5, most of the users are accessing the Web site with a think time of 5 to 6 seconds. According to the illustrated graph, 127 users are having a think time of 5 seconds. For simulation purposes, one can consider the average of five and six seconds, as the maximum distribution lies in this range.

Negative Exponential Distribution of Think Time

Negative exponential distribution is rarely needed where all the users have to pass through a set of mandatory activities before switching to other transactions. To

Figure 9.4. Users distributed uniformly with respect to user think time

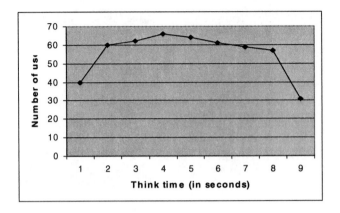

Figure 9.5. Users distributed normally with respect to user think time

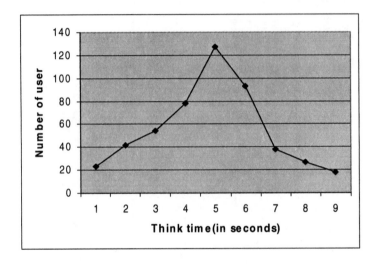

illustrate, in a banking application, before making transactions, users have to login. If the time taken to validate the authentication is one second, then all users will have the same think time for login activity. The think time taken for other activities gets distributed in different fashions as shown in Figure 9.6.

The user may not always enter data correctly. Therefore, it is necessary to simulate wrong data also.

Figure 9.6. Users distributed exponentially negative with respect to user think time

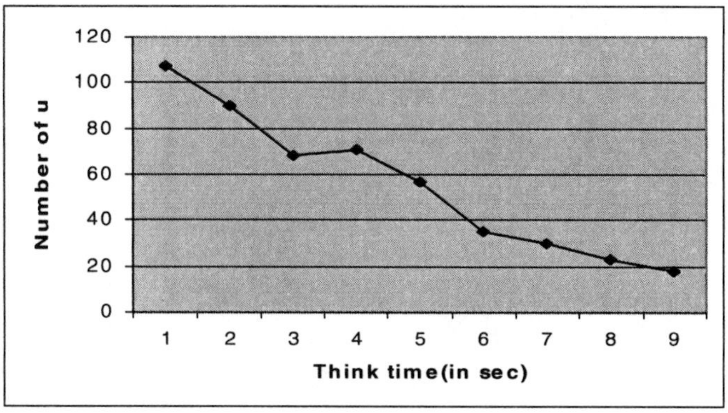

Preparing and finalizing PRD is the first step in performance test automation. Unambiguous and complete PRD increases the accuracy of P.T. automation. Detailed study on performance elicitation is given in Chapter IV. A template of typical PRD is presented in Appendix C1.

Develop Test Strategy

Performance requirements, once captured and analyzed, provide more in-depth information on how to conduct PT. Exhaustive PT may not be possible due to time and cost. Sometimes, it may not be feasible to conduct exhaustive testing. In such circumstances, the need for developing a test strategy is required. The main objectives of the test strategy are to reduce the overall cost of the project, reduce the cycle time of the testing, and to reduce the resource requirement during the project cycle. The test strategy should also look at increasing the accuracy of testing and providing good results. The test strategy should also look at ease in running the test. While developing a good test strategy, the following factors need consideration.

Defining Performance Pass/Fail Criteria

To determine the success of the PT activity, it is of paramount importance to determine pass/fail criteria for each of the key performance goals. This calls for the need to define what constitutes passing the goal and what constitutes falling short of achieving it. The pass/fail criteria should be unambiguous so that they are measurable in absolute terms. Otherwise, the possibility of clients challenging the pass/fail criteria later may not be fully ruled out.

Identifying the Measurement Criteria

Once the performance objectives and pass/fail criteria for each of them are successfully established, the next step is the measurement of each of these criteria. Performance must be measured in absolute terms so that it can be easily compared with the pass/fail criteria. In order to establish proper measurements, it may be necessary to fine tune or reexamine the goal as well as pass/fail criteria. An example might be the following: instead of providing overall response time for an event, it may be required to determine the split response times among various hardware's devices that are associated with the execution of the event.

Selection of Tools

The main objective of this activity is to determine a better automation tool for PT. Since the cost of any performance automation tool is high, more attention must be given before finalizing the tool. One needs to strike a balance between the cost of the tool vs. its efficiency. The following points would help in the selection process of tools.

The tool must support all measurements that have been envisaged. The selected tool must be cost effective, and it must have the ability to use virtual database users. The most significant of this is the database connectivity method or methods, such as ODBC or other RDBMS specific methods like DBLIB, ADO, and so forth. Appendix B2 provides a list of tools available on the market.

Performance Measurements

A performance measurements matrix needs to be finalized before the beginning of the test. While testing, it is proposed to collect the following performance measurement data to get the complete picture of the behavior of the system.

The response time of the transactions per the workloads defined is to be collected. The consistency of responses among different test runs has to be measured, and the throughput (measured in transactions per second) is calculated. Also, the resource utilization during testing and the server and client processor utilization are measured during testing. Some of the other utilization parameters that need to be measured during testing are memory utilization (RAM and disks), network utilization (LAN and T1 lines), and thread utilization (the number of concurrent users of critical hardware and software components). Data regarding the availability of the system, that is, the ability to access the system resources such as databases, printers, and the Internet while the system is running, are also collected during testing. Bottleneck related parameters like high resource consumption by each software and hardware component during the testing, network collision rates, page-in page-out rates, number of hits blocked (blocking the Web site visitors), number of threads blocked, and buffer and queue length overflows are also monitored and measured during testing.

Table 9.0. Performance parameter matrix

Primary Parameters	Secondary Parameters
% CPU Usage	• Percentage of interrupts per second • Number of threads • Percentage of CPU usage by user (loading machine) • Context switches per second
Memory Usage	• Total available bytes in RAM • Disk free space • Cache hits per second • Cache faults per second
Network Usage	• LAN • T1 Lines
Failed and Successful Transactions (Hits)	• Socket errors
Response Time	• Output request queue length for network • Time to first byte/time to last byte • (TTFB/TTLB)
Total Disk Operations (Read/Write)	• Disk read/write bytes per second • Page faults per second • Output disk queue length
Throughput	• Byte per second • Connections per second • Requests per second

A set of performance measurements matrix to be captured during PT is given in Table 9.0.

The above matrix could be expanded to many more parameters. This depends on the type of tool used and the operating system environment.

Virtual Users

Decision on the maximum number of virtual users depends on the anticipated load for the system as specified in the performance requirement document. The growth rate of the system should be studied carefully to make a decision on the number of virtual users. The number of virtual users will have a direct impact on the tool as it requires procurement of an equal number of licenses.

Consider an example where the current Web users for a typical banking system (refer to case study in Appendix D) are around 30,000. According to a growth rate specified by bank management, the user base will increase up to 54,000 users after 5 years. Based on these statistics, even if it is considered that 10% of them are accessing concurrently, it will be 54,000 virtual users. The automated tool should be licensed to facilitate the generation of 54,000 virtual users for load testing. Load testing alone does not complete the PT. As specified earlier, PT includes stress testing also. Therefore, it is advisable to take license for more than 54,000 virtual users, as this facilitates testing the capability of the system to handle the load beyond the specified level.

Acceptance Criteria

Another important strategy plan is to determine the conditions for acceptance of the performance test results. Acceptance criteria provide the essentials to be satisfied for the acceptance of application by the end user. Performance efforts are associated with two sets of acceptance criteria. The first are requirements and objectives; the second are engagement criteria.

Requirements and objectives can be expressed in absolute terms or can be in terms of range, if the requirements are in measurable units. The acceptance criteria, in general, are satisfied if all the requirements, objectives, and engagements are met.

Acceptance criteria can be incorporated as part of the Service Level Agreement (SLA) that can be justified by the performance team. To illustrate, one way of expressing the acceptance criteria for the banking case study can be as given in Table 9.1.

More stringent acceptance criteria could also be defined by the customer.

Test Runs and Test Cycles

As specified earlier, the main objective of adopting a strategy is to reduce the duration of the test cycle. How many test cycles having to be executed to ensure the correctness of results is specified in the strategy document, and this is a question that requires careful analysis.

A test cycle comprises several test runs based on the strategy adopted by the test team. A typical test cycle consists of many test runs for each workload. A test run is a test execution process wherein the test run result is expressed in terms of pass or fail. A pass is one in which the test execution is completed successfully as planned, and results are obtained. A fail criterion is one in which the test execution has failed with no desired results. The failure may be due to many reasons like script failure, functional bugs during the execution, server crash, and so forth. More elaboration on this is given in Chapter 8.

Test Duration

It is mandatory to explicitly state the duration of tests; otherwise, the tests may never stop. The following termination options may be useful in this regard.

Terminated Explicitly Using Stop Option

The test can be controlled explicitly using the stop (interruption) option available with most of the tools. A planned test can be run without specifying the termination timing.

Table 9.1. Sample acceptance criteria for the banking case study

Parameter	Acceptance Criteria
Response time for a query	1.5-2.5 sec
Download time of a page	Not more than 8.5 sec
Availability of the Web site	24X7 basis, 365 days
Memory problems	Nil
Scalability	Scales gracefully as load increases
Load	54,000 Web users (as per the growth rate of 20% every year for the next 5 years)
Response at peak time	Do not exceed 2.5 sec
Resource utilization	Monitored carefully

This is an ad hoc method and needs supervision throughout the execution period. This approach is not advisable for large datasets and for complicated workloads.

Set by Tester Using the Tool

Every automated tool comes with an option to set the duration for testing. It has to be set with a valid time format and executed. The test terminates once the time specified is reached. This approach requires no continuous monitoring throughout the execution period and is best suited for endurance testing.

Set Based on Some Conditions

Duration of the test can also be set based on some specified termination conditions. Test execution terminates on the fulfillment of these specified conditions. This approach also needs no continuous supervision and is best suited for stress and spike testing. However, if the execution has not reached the termination condition, then the test should be controlled manually.

Minimizing Risk Factors

The risks can be minimized to a large extent if PT is conducted based on a proper methodology. The areas of risk and the related help to minimize these risks are mentioned below.

The preparation and planning phase should be handled carefully to avoid early mistakes which can lead to greater problems. The problems that occurred at early stages due to negligence are not easy to fix. The entry (http://www.chambers.com/au/glossary/entrycri.htm) and exit (http://www.chambers.com/au/glossary/exit_cri.htm) criteria for the execution phase are the most neglected areas in PT. A thorough analysis of the entry and exit criteria can cut down the cost and effort involved in testing. An automated tool should be selected by mapping the performance requirements to the features of the tool. Looking at the budget constraints before deciding to buy the tool is also equally important. In order to avoid the risks of scalability, conducting load testing, stress testing, spike testing, and endurance testing are necessary. Also, the lack of guidelines for the testing process can maximize the rate of risks. The risks can be avoided, provided comprehensive guidelines and checklists are available for each critical stage of PT.

Planning Phase

Planning is an important phase for automation of any project. Planning must be carried out immediately after the analysis of performance requirements. The important activities in the planning phase include design of workload, planning operations, and managing resources. The goals must be defined unambiguously in the planning phase.

Overview Phase

The performance test plan must be identified uniquely among all projects. It must start with detailed testing goals, objectives, and success criteria. PT goals are explicit requirements of the customer. These goals are microscopically defined in the form of objectives. These objectives are subsequently addressed in the design phase. The planning document must contain PT goals as discussed in earlier.

Similarly, the test objectives and success criteria (see preparation phase) must also be documented in the planning phase.

Design Phase

The input for the design activity is the clear understanding of the objectives and requirements. The design team first designs the workload, and the automation process uses the design to build the script. There may be more than one workload to be used for a set of performance requirements. The complete discussion is available in Chapter 5 of this book. The salient features of the workload are mentioned below.

The workload represents the user groups and activity types. A benchmark of typical business is required to formulate a workload. There may be several workloads for a project. One has to identify a representative subset of users in these workloads and develop the activities/scripts (test cases). Also, workload has to taken into consideration, specifically, whether any batch jobs need to be started manually in the background. Once the workload is defined, any PT tool can automate it.

Operation Phase

Based on the planning phase, the entire plan has to be implemented in the operation phase. The operation phase is a complex process and involves coordination from many segments. The operation phase mainly deals with the selection of tools, their implementation, resource management, development of workload and test scripts, and test environment management.

The tool is an important aid for automation. Selection of the right tool at the right time is as important as selecting the vendor and vendor's credibility. Since performance tools are expensive, a proper analysis and study of each tool is very important. Some of the general information that needs to be considered while selecting the right kind of tool is as follows.

One has to take into consideration the vendor characteristics, the market share of the tool, and its position in the market to ensure proper support and effectiveness for the tool purchased. The number of virtual users, number of other products, and the quality of customer service is also one of the parameters used while selecting the tool for automating PT. Proactive publication of information about tool bugs and workaround by the vendor are other criteria that can be considered while selecting the right kind of tool. Some of the other points to be taken into consideration while selecting the right kind of tool are the frequency of news releases, sound history of the vendor standing behind these products, financial stability of the vendor and its likelihood of continuing to be in business, geographical proximity of the vendor support personnel to work locations, training and consulting assistance from the vendor, and facilities for the test tool evaluation team. Finally, analyze the standard tools in the market and, if possible, consult the people who are already using these tools for PT to know about their experience while using them for automation.

Tools Analysis and Usage

Many of the performance tools support basic functions required for PT. However, each tool is different in its own way. The differentiation may be in terms of providing additional features, supporting protocols, and the way of measuring the performance parameters, as well as presentation of results.

To illustrate, if a user places a request with the Web site, the request is processed at different levels. It may be at the Web server, application server, or database server. Based on the processing time at each level, the response time is determined. In such circumstances, the response time may have to be measured at each level. Many tools provide different mechanisms to solve this problem.

Mercury's PT tool (see Mercury, 2004) provides a feature to capture response time at each level, that is, at the Web server, application server, and database server level. This feature helps in identifying the location for performance problems due to response time.

Rational's Performance Studio (see IBM Software Quality, 2004) provides a different mechanism to capture the response time. A separate script must be written to capture the response time. Each tool provides a set of features. Some of the points to be considered before purchasing a tool would be to check the characteristics of the tool and to map the characteristics of the tool with the documented performance requirements. Do not make the tool shelfware. Always study the growth stats of the system before selecting a tool and understand the constraints specified by the vendor. Make sure that demos, training, and timely assistance are provided by the vendor. Purchase the add-ins from the same vendor to avoid interoperability problems.

Guidelines for Selecting Tools

Many tools are available on the market. Selecting a good tool requires an indepth study and analysis of the available testing tools. Many tools do not work well or do not work at all on different platforms or in various configurations. Sometimes, the offered features may not be feasible for the project. Some of the points to be considered in these regards are given below.

Always look for the cost of a tool and analyze its needs vs. features. Enquire about the kind of postdelivery service offered and check the platform dependency characteristic of the tool. Also check the protocols supported by the tool and ensure version compatibility of the tool. One of the other important points to be considered is to check for the constraints on number of concurrent users. For detailed characteristics of a good tool, refer to Appendix B1.

Develop Workloads

Once the number of workloads and their structures are known, each workload must be developed using the tool that is already selected. Workload development is split into two parts. One is development of workload structure, that is, user groups, transactions, scenarios, and weightage, and the other is development of test scripts for each scenario.

To develop a good workload, one has to consider the following points.

Identify the various user groups and the scenarios under each user group. Map the test scripts, which are generated/developed and have a mix of test scenarios in a workload. Determine the proper sequence for the scripts and plan properly so as to distribute the scripts across many clients. Also, document all the workloads that are developed.

A snapshot of a workload is given in Figure 9.7. This is developed using Rational Performance Tool. At this stage, no test scripts are available. Test scripts are developed in the build phase; however, testers can sit and develop both in a single session.

Develop or Generate Test Scripts

Based on the structure of various scenarios (Figure 9.7), test scripts are developed. The following guidelines help to develop a good test script.

Develop test scripts for each scenario as described in the workload. Build the test scripts using the play and record method. Ensure the use of different browsers while scripting and edit the scripts based on the requirements. Follow proper coding standards for developing test scripts and execute the script and verify its correctness. Document the

Figure 9.7. Developed workload for a sample banking application

scripts properly and identify common steps and convert them into functions. Provide room for extensibility and also provide the facility to generate proper logs.

Though scripts are developed for workloads designed, separate scripts may have to be developed for specific activity/page. Some of the activities, which require the script by default, are mentioned below.

It is required to have a script to test the pages on the site that gets the most hits (or that is estimated to get the most hits) and also a script to test the home page. Though it may not be one of among the busiest pages, it should be fast. Also, scripts are required to test the most commonly used business transactions on the site (deposit, withdraw, etc.), to test the most critical business functions on the site (ad hoc query by senior manager), and to test pages that developers may suspect to have a bottleneck.

Most of the tools provide a record and play option to generate the test scripts for various scenarios defined in the workload. Different tools follow different formats, but all tools follow the same process.

Set Up Test Environment

As discussed in Chapter 6 of this book, the environment must be ready before the testing. All servers should be configured and set up, as they would be in the production environment. Databases should be loaded with production data or the data that are sized appropriately for production. Some of the important points to be considered for setting up the test environment are as follows:

Figure 9.8. Typical performance test environment

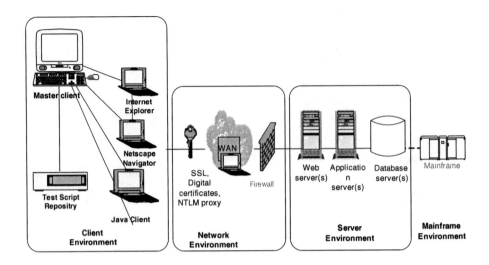

Replicate the operation environment as much as possible, in cases where replication is not feasible or possible; take great care in making assumptions about the scalability of the hardware components. It is not correct to assume that a system with two servers will perform doubly better in comparison to a system with one server. One can generally assume that the system with two servers will perform better, but by how much is really difficult to gauge without benchmarking. Check whether multiple environments are possible; one way is to have two identical architectures with identical software installed but keep the number of servers different. By this multiple environment setup, it is possible to generalize how the number of servers affects performance, provided all other factors remain identical for both environments. Choose the appropriate configuration for PT and avoid a shared environment as much as possible. Ensure optimization of investment on the test environment, and follow a detailed description of the test and operational environments.

Figure 9.8 represents a typical test environment used for PT. Master client in the client environment controls the test run with the available script stored in a test script repository. Multiple clients with different browsers could be simulated. The network environment provides all necessary security features and supports the required protocols. The server environment supports all servers whereas the mainframe environment supports the mainframe database.

Some of the issues that need to be addressed in setting up a test environment are given below.

Hidden costs, if any, must be looked into and links across different testing centers must be managed. Ensure the accuracy of the functionality of the application and the availability of a domain specialist during testing. Check if there are any other applications/services running on the systems to be tested and also evaluate the associated risks with shared environments (if used) like memory, disk I/O, and drive space.

Setting up of the test environment is an important task in performance automation, as it involves cost, resources, and time. Careful planning is always advised.

Resource Planning

After the test environment is ready, the resource issues required for the test are to be addressed. The important resources are test team (Mar, 2004), test bed, and any external resources, if any.

Test Team

Composition of a team for testing is complex. It requires meticulous planning and a suitable strategy before the actual starting of the test. Since PT requires knowledge of the business domain as well as technical domain, identifying a suitable resource person is difficult. PT requires people from multiple disciplines which include networking, databases, domain specialists, and a host of tool specialists. A typical test automation team would consist of:

- **Project manager:** The person who coordinates, motivates, and drives the PT activities. The project manager has the complete responsibility to manage the testing team to carry out their testing activities.

- **Scripter/scheduler:** Scripter must know the tool syntax and knowledge to change the program as and when it is required.

- **Real users:** Sometime, real users help is sought for recording filed level actions to simulate production like actions.

- **Database administrator (DBA):** DBAs main task involves maintaining the user profiles, password management, taking backups, and restoring the system immediately in case the system stops. A database expert is required during the test run to help spot and optimize database performance problems.

- **System administrator:** The system administrator mainly helps in installing products and maintaining the system under test. They help in restore and backup activities also.

- **Network administrator:** A network administrator's task is to manage the network during PT. A network expert can help spot configuration problems at the network level, including problems with firewalls, hubs, switches, routers, load balancers, and SSL accelerators and the network itself.

Plan Test Bed

The test bed must be comprehensive and exhaustive. If live data are available, the test bed would be better, and results will be accurate. While creating a data bed, some of the questions that need to be answered are mentioned below.

How many data are required? Which data are to be considered for testing? How do we generate data? How does one reset data? Is there enough disk space available on the machines?

Several tools are available to generate data used for testing. Care must be taken to ensure all business transactions are represented while generating simulated data.

Strategize Run

Sometimes smartness gives more efficient results than the routine and time consuming process management. The best way to get an optimal result is to plan various strategies to run PT. The main purpose of the strategy is to optimize the time, resources, and utilization of the team during the execution.

The following guidelines would help the planning team to define a good strategy for their system under test:

Run Elaboration Test

Plan to run the elaboration test (refer to Chapter VII) first before actually running the whole system. This helps in finding initial bugs, if any, in the application and also provides knowledge about the smoothness of the test run.

Decide Number of Test Runs Required

How many test runs to be conducted is the main question that always worries the test manager. Since each run accounts for extra costs, more attention must be drawn to decide the number of test runs. In the typical environment, the number of test runs would be three, and out of these, at least two test runs must successfully complete the pass criteria. However, use project experience to decide on duration and number of test runs.

Ensure the Presence of Test Bed and Number of Users

The test bed and the number of virtual users are other issues which worry the test manager. Though the test bed is identified and decided, how many data within the test bed must be used during the test run is a real issue to be addressed. If you use the entire test bed in the first run, the test may fail in between, and the entire effort may go to waste. To avoid such issues, try the test bed with 30%, 70%, and 100% for three runs, respectively. Here, the test bed is gradually increasing to reach the maximum.

Allocate More Time for Critical Workload

Critical workloads must always be tested for their accuracy and result sustenance. More time allocation for such workloads is always recommended.

Select Minimum Set of Parameters

Before the beginning of the performance test, parameters must be set at server end. Depending on the project, parameters must be selected. There may be system specific parameters which need to be set as required by the test goals. Parameters can be categorized as base parameters and optional parameters. The base parameters are mandatory and must be set during PT for all systems whereas optional parameters may be set based on the systems test requirements. All parameters must be set at server end using the tool. Some of the parameters that need to be set are number of requests per second, percentage of memory utilized by servers (application server, Web server, and database server), percentage CPU utilization (application server, Web server, and database server), minimum response time, maximum response time, and average response time. These parameters could vary based on the type of tools used for automation.

Test Scenarios

Last but not least of the activities that are to be performed in the planning phase is to create various test scenarios based on the test design. To create such scenarios, proper tools must be selected. While creating scenarios, the following points need to be observed:

Identify all those activities carried out by the users which are needed for a specific workload, and capture each activity in the form of scripts by the play and record method in the form of scenarios. Ensure that any manual changes made to scripts are reflected back on the test scenario and create larger scenarios by sequencing many transactions created earlier.

Thus, the planning phase plays a dominant role in test automation. The success of test automation depends on how meticulously planning is done and documented.

Execution Phase

Once the plan is ready and the environment is set up, the system is ready for testing. However, before executing the test, some of the preexecution tests must be carried out. In a complex project, though the meticulous planning is done, there may still be chances of slippage in certain areas. There could be an identified functional bug which is not rectified, or a partial system may be ready or not confident to run the test completely in one shot. To avoid such problems, follow the procedures discussed below, which recheck the system for test execution.

Entry/Exit Criteria

Before every cycle of a test run, the system must be verified for entry and exit criteria. For the entry criteria, ensure that the scope of all the major business functions is finalized and all major business functions and features are working properly. Check if all major defects have been fixed and retested. A proper test bed must be available during the test run and also ensure the availability of the test team.

For the exit criteria, ensure that the result data are generated and various test logs are made available. All test runs must be completed successfully, and no functional bugs should be reported during the testing.

More discussion on entry/exit criteria is available in Chapter VII.

Elaboration Test

Building confidence during PT is a difficult task. For instance, running the test for the duration specified and number of virtual users as planned in the first instance, probability of generating the results is difficult and risky. Instead, the alternative is to look for short duration of the test with less number of virtual users and run the elaboration test. This will enable knowing all problems early so that problems, if any, could be corrected, and time can be saved.

The elaboration test is carried out with minimal users before the actual test to build confidence. The elaboration test helps in Proof Of Concept (POC) for PT and builds confidence during final testing. It eliminates nonperformance related problems early and is normally carried out for one or two virtual users. It tests for correctness of all those functions used for PT and verifies the authenticity of the database. The elaboration test validates all protocols to check if they are working correctly; it verifies whether the servers are configured properly and working correctly or not, and it also verifies the capability of handling the maximum number of virtual users.

The elaboration test is an important activity in test automation, and it must be carried out compulsorily. It is a normal tendency to skip the elaboration test to save time. This is an important task as well as milestone for the preexecution phase.

Multiple Runs

When the test execution starts, there may be many uncertainties like how many times each test run must be conducted. What is the guarantee that each test run provides the correct result? What if a particular test run fails? Do we start the same test again or do we accept the fail case as it is? If we have different workloads, how do we sequence each workload during execution?

To answer these questions, we need to define a test cycle and test run. A test cycle is a complete set of test runs with all workloads tested for multiple test runs. A test run is a typical test execution of a specific workload within the test cycle. Tables 9.4 and 9.5 show two test cycles consisting of many test runs for different workloads. The fail/pass in the table represents whether each test has passed or failed. To summarize, a test cycle consists of many test runs, and a test run consists of many workloads which will be executed one by one. The minimum number of test cycles must be one, and the maximum number of test cycles may be one or more. Also, a new test cycle is created which is based on the change in workload, the change in various parameters that must be tuned, change in environment, and change in functionality.

In Table 9.5, a new workload W6 is introduced, as W5 in Table 9.4 failed in all test runs. There may be an error in the design of the workload W5 itself. The fail cases during the test runs are due to many reasons. However, some common errors during the execution are due to functional bugs in the application, problems in database connection pooling, nonavailability of enough heap size, problems in handling dynamic sessions during test execution, problems in creating a data pool, and nonindexing of tables.

The failure in the test runs may be due to the external factors also. Some of the common failures that could attribute during the execution are due to an application server crash,

Table 9.4. Test cycle 1 with multiple test runs

Workload	Test Run#1	Test Run#2	Test Run#3	Test Run#4
W1	Pass	Fail	Pass	
W2	Pass	Pass	Pass	
W3	Fail	Fail	Pass	Pass
W4	Pass	Fail	Fail	Pass
W5	Fail	Fail	Fail	Fail

Table 9.5. Test cycle 2 after tuning and change in workload

Workload	Test Run#1	Test Run#2	Test Run#3	Test Run#4
W1	Pass	**Pass**	Pass	
W2	Pass	Pass	Pass	
W3	Fail	Fail	Pass	Pass
W4	Pass	Fail	Fail	Pass
W6	**Pass**	**Pass**	Fail	

network congestion due to wrong configuration, and OS level errors that may lead to failure. For instance, one processor may fail in a multiprocessor environment.

Performance test execution is a complex job. It has to be monitored from multiple directions. In order to run the test executions effectively, the following points must be considered mandatory during execution:

Run the PT more than once with different levels of background activity (noise) to get the true picture and monitor all performance counters continuously. Also monitor test duration always and avoid external interference. Do monitor the test execution by probing client and log the results with timings.

Most of the tools provide facilities to monitor and manage various performance parameters.

Postexecution Phase

Once the test execution is completed, the next step is to examine the postexecution scenario. This includes review of logs generated and examination of the result data output. Do not analyze the result without analyzing the logs. Logs provide insight into the execution process. The main task that needs to be carried out in postexecution phase is shown in Figure 9.9. Observe that before the analysis of result data for possible bottlenecks, result data must be presented properly, so the analyst could examine correctly and easily. However, the first step in this phase is the review of logs.

Review of Logs

Confidence building is an important activity in performance test execution. Nothing provides more confidence about the successful execution of the test than reviewing the logs. Execution logs provide transparency in test execution and determine how healthy the execution is. Observation of execution logs gives the status on the test script failure during execution, duration of the test runs, OS level failure, if any, and application level failures, if any. Chapter 8 provides more information on this phase of activity.

Presentation of Results

Based on the parameters set during execution, the output would be several hundreds of pages of results. These result data would be available in the form of tables, graphs, and such. The main objective of the result data is to convince the customer of the performance and use it for bottleneck identifications. Sometimes, none of the result data may be useful and would be difficult to study. In these circumstances, presenting the result is itself is a major task. While presenting the results, the following points must be considered:

Identify the target users of the results (business managers, marketers, Sr. management, etc.) and decide the presentation formats based on users (graphs, tables, abstracts, bottlenecks isolation, etc.). Decide the number of parameters to be presented and overlap different results, if necessary, for easy understanding. Always maintain configuration management in all results and show summarized data validating requirements. Also, be prepared to deliver formatted raw data as backup.

Detailed discussion on presentation of results is available in Chapter VIII of this book. Most of the automation tools support different ways of presenting results. Proper presentation of results always helps in analysis.

Analysis of Results

Once the results are presented properly, analysis becomes easier. Analysis of results does not mean identifying the bottlenecks only. It provides a healthy picture of the system. Management may be satisfied with the results but analysis may still be required to understand more on resource utilization for optimal response of the system. Analyzing the results mainly helps in determining resource utilization so that bottlenecks in resources can be found. It would help to identify script level problems, if any, and also to determine script level response time and resource usage. Analysis of the results would further help to isolate excess queue lengths at the server (if any), address code level optimization at the end, and check for script failures like scripts pass.

For a complete discussion on this, refer to Chapter 8 of this book.

Identifying and Fixing Bottlenecks

Bottlenecks exist within the system for a number of reasons such as inadequate server hardware to support the projected system load, inadequate network capacity, poor architectural design decisions, databases that are incorrectly implemented or tuned, developers not being mindful of performance considerations during development, and absence of in-house expertise on system performance. Tight deadlines and changing requirements can also be a cause of bottlenecks.

Figure 9.9. Postexecution process

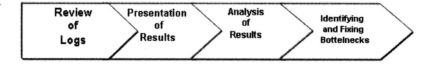

Even the best designed and implemented systems will have some performance problems such as memory leaks, dangling memory references, and array bound errors which are difficult to be identified at the stage of unit testing or by system testing. A well planned PT is the only way to isolate, identify, and resolve those issues before launching the system to potential users.

Bottlenecks can reside at any place within the architecture of the application. There may be one or more bottlenecks in the applications that have not yet been tuned. Since only one bottleneck is identified at a time, it is necessary to iteratively test and fix the bottlenecks. Some of the points to be noted here are mentioned below:

Fix the Bottlenecks at web server, application server level, database server level, and communication links level. Check iteratively whether all bottlenecks are resolved or not and continue tuning until goals are met or until the bottlenecks are deemed to be "unfixable" for the current release. Identify areas for potential improvement in the future that are out of scope currently and also summarize results with the tuning details/settings/configurations, if it adds value. An expert is always required to address the bottlenecks and tune the system during PT.

In postexecution activities, fixing bottlenecks and tuning the system is important, as the whole process of PT culminates at tuning the system for better performance. Tuning is a complex job and requires proper guidelines to be followed for easy and better results.

Guidelines for Performance Tuning

Most Web applications involve many transactions occurring at the same time. With multiple scripts running at the same time, producing multiple hundreds or thousands of transactions and spotting the problematic transaction is very challenging.

Application/System Tuning

There are several ways in which the system could be tuned. Some of the tips to tune to the system are to address code level tuning and to verify the control level statements and optimize them. To illustrate, if there are multiple nested IF-ELSEIF clauses, change them to CASE statements. This is because the last ELSEIF is processed only after all IF clauses are processed. Ensure optimization of the loop constructs by removing the dead codes, reducing the buffers, and so forth. Also optimize the size of server side files by reducing unnecessary spaces (asp, applets, servlets, etc.) and optimize the buffer space declared in the code. Most of the language manuals provide more information on code level tuning.

Infrastructure Level Tuning

Infrastructures are classified into Web servers, application servers, database servers, CPU, and memory. Each server needs tuning based on the testing results and type of bottleneck found. Some of the tuning tips for these systems are given below.

Web Servers

Most of the Web servers, once installed, will have their own memory management systems. Plan proper memory management based on the file size, cache size, and RAM size.

As an example, in the IPLANET Web server, configuration for better performance can be done as follows:

The cache is divided into three regions:

Small: 3KB (default)
Medium: 30Kb
High: 100KB

These memory regions can be tuned to the required size. Further, the Web server has its own storage area within the RAM. Corresponding regions are:

Small: 20MB
Medium: 30MB
High: 30MB

These parameters can also be tuned to the required values. In order to get the optimum performance, do the following:

Organize files into three categories based on the sizes closest to the cache size. If that is not possible, determine the three types of files based on size and use the best fit concept. For instance, assume that there are 1,000 files which need allocation:

Small: 600 files belong to the size between 3KB to 8KB,
Medium: 350 files belongs to the size between 9KB to 50KB, and
High: remaining 50 files come under the 100KB range.

Once analysis is completed, modify the parameters to 8KB, 50KB, and 100KB, which provides the optimal performance. Thus, a simple configuration of cache provides better performance.

CPU

In an ideal situation, CPU utilization must be 90% including all processes (targeted + any other application + OS processes). Sometimes, CPU may be underutilized, say 40%. In such situations, to increase the CPU utilization, the number of threads parameter must be increased. If the number of threads by default is 128, changing it to higher values will increase the CPU utilization and performance of the system as more threads are processed simultaneously.

Application Servers

Normally, when the number of threads at the Web server level is increased, the corresponding parameter at the application server level also must be tuned. In the case of the IPLANET application server, this can be achieved by increasing the JVM (2 JVMs). Sometimes, proper session management must be maintained. Availability of API drivers and application prototypes to drive API must be in test mode. Ensure that the return codes from interfaces are routinely checked by the application, and if the return code has an invalid value such as a null value, the application should be designed to take corrective action.

Database Servers

Tuning database servers provides maximum yield because many queries take more time. One can either optimize query scripts or tune the parameter of the database itself.

Some of tuning tips for the database servers are given below:

Check the use of memory and disk space required by SQL statements, as well as their access time and rate of throughput. To improve performance, increase buffer sizes and use of fast cached memory. Increase the number of access keys and the number of index keys, and update the indexes more often. Use static instead of dynamic queries because dynamic SQL is a lot trickier to program than static SQL and would probably have more bugs. The performance of static query is easier to predict and optimize than a dynamic one because the processing of the static one can be determined at compile time. Joins are easier to predict and may execute faster if performed one at a time in sequence, rather than in one compound multijoin SQL statement. The database performance monitoring tools can be used to understand the working of the queries and updates, the execution time, and the database bottlenecks, if any.

Beware of the performance implications of tools that automatically generate SQL statements. Often, these tools are accurate but inefficient. They generate SQL queries to bring data from the database on the server down to the client PC and perform a join there, rather than joining on the server. This strains both the client and the network bandwidth. These tools can leave the users helpless in dealing with inefficiencies. In heterogeneous database environments, check for compatibility and consistent responses across the different databases. Though database products have been considered as sophisticated backend software, incompatibilities persist. SQL 2 conformed to the ISO standard in 1992 but has not yet been implemented by all DBMS product vendors.

Stabilize the database structure during the testing and keep the data contents under version control to a possible degree and make a note to revise the SQL statements when the database structure changes, and in this case, an overhead of rewriting SQL test cases appears.

Firewalls

Make sure that the total number of current established connections does not exceed the limitations set by the license of the firewall. If the rate of SSL connections is greater than 100/sec/Web server, then the system might be running into SSL bottlenecks, and the system administrator should consider using SSL accelerators. The CPU utilization allows a check to see if the load is actually causing the firewall to reach its maximum capacity rating. Make sure that the throughput required does not exceed the firewall's rating.

Load Balancers

Make sure that total number of current established connections does not exceed the limitations set by the license of the load balancer. Load balancing split verifies that the load balancer is properly spreading the load across all available servers. Check the CPU utilization to see if the load is causing the load balancer to exceed its capacity rating and make sure the throughput does not exceed the load balancer's rating.

External Systems

Make sure there are enough connections to handle the requests to the external systems. Verify that bandwidth to the external system providers is sufficient and make sure that queue wait time is not excessive.

Installation Level Tuning

Uninstall any applications that are no longer needed and restart the OS to completely remove uninstalled applications. Identify the software which conflicts with each other and check and compact the registry and, if necessary, clean the registry. Defragment the hard drives if necessary and check the consistency of device driver interfaces and so forth.

Tuning is an important activity and must be done carefully. Several tools are also available for tuning. In spite of standard guidelines available, it is always recommended to refer to concerned hardware/software manuals for optimal results.

Summary

Automation is a must for any application which undergoes rigorous PT. Before beginning PT, meticulous planning is required. Planning in preparing the workloads, generating scripts, setting up of an environment, creating the resources, preparing the test bed, selecting tools, and executing multiple tests are required. Automation provides flexibility, consistency, and uniformity in executing tests. Though initial investments are high, regression activities could be completed with the same efficiency and robustness. Analysis of results is time consuming but provides more in-depth information on behavior of the system. Several tools can be used for analysis thereby reducing the analysis time. Effort and time must always be properly analyzed before one starts to automate any testing activities.

References

Entry criteria. (2003). Retrieved August 11, 2003, from http://www.chambers.com.au/glossary/entrycri.htm

Exit criteria. (2003). Retrieved August 11, 2003, from http://www.chambers.com.au/glossary/exit_cri.htm

IBM software quality. (2004). Retrieved November 17, 2004, from http://www-306.ibm.com/software/rational/offerings/testing.html

Mar, W. (2004). *Roles in a performance project.* Retrieved November 21, 2004, from http://www.wilsonmar.com/perftest.htm

Mercury. (2004). Retrieved November 17, 2004, from http://www.mercury.com/

Yerxa, G. (2004). *Firewall & load-balancer: Perfect union?* Retrieved November 17, 2004, from http://www.networkcomputing.com/1102/1102ws1.html

Additional Sources

Barber, S. (n.d.). *Beyond performance testing (effective performance testing).* Retrieved November 17, 2004, from http://www.perftestplus.com/articles/bpt1.pdf

Bourke, T. (n.d.). *Load balancers as firewalls.* O'Reilly Media, Inc. Retrieved November 22, 2004, from http://sysadmin.oreilly.com/news/loadbalancing_0801.html

Denaro, G. (n.d.). *Early performance testing of distributed software applications.*

Firesmith, D. (n.d.). *Test execution.* Open Process Framework. Retrieved June 17, 2004, from http://www.donald-firesmith.com/Components/WorkUnits/Tasks/Testing/TestExecution.html

Hava-Muntean, C., McManis, J., Murphy, J., & Murphy, L. (n.d.). *A new dynamic Web server.* Retrieved September 14, 2004, from http://www.eeng.dcu.ie/~murphyj/publ/c19.pdf

Incremental Testing. Retrieved June 12, 2004, from http://homepages.nildram.co.uk/~worrelli/cont343.htm

Jeffay, K., & Donelson Smith, J. (n.d.). Retrieved September 14, 2004, from http://www.cs.unc.edu/~jeffay/papers/ToN-04-Version.pdf

Joung, P. (n.d.). *General network performance testing methodology.* Retrieved September 21, 2004, from http://www.spirentcom.com/documents/1065.pdf

Kelly, M. (n.d.). *Updated: Using IBM Rational Robot to run your first performance test.* Software Engineer, QA, Liberty Mutual. Retrieved August 25, 2004, from http://www-128.ibm.com/developerworks/rational/library/5623.html

Khanine, D. (n.d.). *Tuning up ADO.NET connection pooling in ASP.NET applications.* Retrieved May 6, 2004, from http://www.15seconds.com/issue/040830.htm

Killelea, P. (2002, March). *Web performance tuning* (2nd ed.). Speeding up the Web.

Kim, S. (n.d.). *Safe session tracking.* Retrieved November 22, 2004, from http://www.sdmagazine.com/documents/s=818/sdm0103h/

Le, L., & Aikat, J. (n.d.). *The effects of active queue management on Web performance.*

Mercury Interactive. (n.d.). *Tune IT systems to efficiently meet business objectives.* Retrieved November 27, 2004, from http://www.mercury.com/us/pdf/products/tuningoverview.pdf

Pauli, K. (n.d.). *Pattern your way to automated regression testing.* Retrieved January 7, 2003, from http://www.javaworld.com/javaworld/jw-09-2001/jw-0921-test.html

Polini, A., & Wolfgang, E. (n.d.). Retrieved April 11, 2004, from http://www.cs.ucl.ac.uk/staff/w.emmerich/publications/WOSP04/paper.pdf

Titchkosky, L., & Arlitt, M. (n.d.). *Performance benchmarking of dynamic Web technologies.*

Williamson, C. (n.d.). Retrieved September 14, 2004, from http://pages.cpsc.ucalgary.ca/~carey/papers/DynamicContent.pdf

Chapter 10

Introduction to Performance Monitoring and Tuning:
Java and .NET

For any applications to be performance conscious, its performance must be monitored continuously. Monitoring performance is a necessary part of the preventive maintenance of the application. By monitoring, we obtain performance data which are useful in diagnosing performance problems under operational conditions. Based on data collected through monitoring, one can define a baseline — a range of measurements that represent acceptable performance under typical operating conditions. This baseline provides a reference point that makes it easier to spot problems when they occur. In addition, during troubleshooting system problems, performance data give information about the behavior of system resources at the time the problem occurs, which is useful in pinpointing the cause. In order to monitor the system, the operational environment provides various parameters implemented through counters for collection of performance data.

Applications developed must ultimately be installed and run on a specific operating system. Hence, applications performance also depends on factors that govern the operating system. Each operating system has its own set of performance parameters to monitor and tune for better performance. Performance of applications also depends on the architectural level monitoring and tuning. However, architectural design depends on specific technology. Hence, technology level monitoring and tuning must be addressed for better results. To achieve all these, proper guidelines must be enforced at various stages for monitoring and tuning.

All the previous chapters, together, described the performance testing from concept to reality whereas this chapter highlights aspects of monitoring and tuning to specific technologies. This chapter provides an overview of monitoring and tuning applications with frameworks in Java and Microsoft .NET technologies. Before addressing the technology specific performance issues, we need to know the overall bottlenecks that arise in Web applications.

Areas of Bottlenecks in Web-Based Applications

Web applications are developed in a multi-operating system (OS) environment. Server modules may run in Unix OS whereas client modules may run in Windows OS. The overall design of architecture includes Web server, application server, network environment, firewalls, and so on. When a Web server is installed on the system (Figure 10.1), there are many aspects that need to be addressed which can impact performance of the system by blocking the throughput. Obviously, the network is one of the factors but so are all the other servers that are being accessed. It is important to understand how the Web applications are developed, what optimization flags have been used, how many servers are in place as well as how performance is being measured. Several of the parameters chosen in the Web may cause performance issues. Causes could be because of server resources like CPU, memory, disk I/O, and network bandwidth. As shown in Figure 10.1, there could be performance bottlenecks at server side, introduction of firewall and routers, slowness of load balancers, and could be due to poor performance of database servers. Server configuration can have a serious impact on performance and may need to be reevaluated.

Other possible bottlenecks in a Web application could be in the different application layers like:

• Poor database design during the application development;

• Poor standards followed in table design;

Figure 10.1. Anticipated bottleneck in Web application system

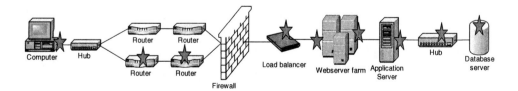

- Poor indexing of databases;

- Poor partitioned data across tables;

- Poor logic used in queries;

- Inappropriate stored procedure.

Other common causes of bottlenecks on the application server or Web server side would be:

- Inefficient session state management;

- Thread contention due to maximum concurrent users.

Chapters 2 and 3 discuss various possible bottlenecks in more detail.

These areas of bottlenecks described previously, in general, vary from one technology to another. However, some of the common bottlenecks could be identified at the OS level itself and can be rectified. In order to determine the bottlenecks, each OS provides various performance counters which need to be monitored during the execution of the system.

Performance Counters in the Operating System

The operating system provides a platform to host Web-based applications wherein servers and various tools are installed. The OS supports its own processes which always run in the background along with the applications. Specific technology platforms (like Java or Microsoft) must be created before running the application. This depends on the application in which it has been developed. When such applications are running, OS provides various parameters which can be set to specific values for optimal performance. Such parameters are monitored and measured by various counters. Knowing those counters that help in tuning OS from a performance point of view is of paramount importance for all test analysts. We mainly discuss important counters related to the Windows 2000 system and the UNIX system as most of the applications are run under these two OSs.

Performance Monitoring and Tuning in UNIX

In UNIX, the major resource types that need to be monitored and tuned are the CPU, memory, disk space, communication lines, I/O time, network time, and application programs.

The UNIX OS maintains several counters which keep track of the system resources and their utilization. Some of these counters are the CPU utilization, buffer usage, disk I/O activity, tape I/O activity, terminal activity, system call activity, context switching activity, file access utilization, queue activity, interprocess communication (IPC), paging activity, free memory and swap space, kernel memory allocation (KMA), and so forth.

UNIX Tools for Monitoring the Performance of the System

UNIX provides various commands and tools to monitor the system performance. These include commands like uptime, sar, ps, vmstat, iostat, netstat, nfsstat, and so on. Some of these commands and their usage is discussed below (Lynch, 2005).

- **Uptime:** The uptime command is one of the most simple commands that can be used to monitor the UNIX system performance. This command tells how long the system has been running. It gives a one-line report which contains the current time, how long the system has been running, how many users are currently logged in, and the system load averages for the past 1, 5, and 15 minutes. One such report provided by the uptime command is given here:

```
$uptime

10:47am  up 37 days, 25 min,  1 user,  load average: 0.00, 0.00, 0.00
```

- **Sar:** The sar command is used to monitor the system utilization over a period of time. The sar command gives a high level report of the system utilization. The sar command, in its simplest form, can also be used to generate a report similar to that of the uptime command; that is, the sar command can be used instead of the uptime command. The sar command provides other advanced reports which provide details of the system utilization and its performance over a specified period of time. There are various options that can be specified with the sar command. Two such examples of the sar command with different options are given below:

> ➤ The sar command with the –q option provides statistics on the average length of the run queue, the percentage of time the run queue is occupied, the average length of the swap queue, and the percentage of time the swap queue is occupied. One such report provided by the sar command using the –q option is given below:

```
$sar –q 3 2

10:08:31 AM  runq-sz  plist-sz  ldavg-1  ldavg-5
10:08:34 AM     0        39       0.00     0.00
10:08:37 AM     0        39       0.00     0.00
Average:        0        39       0.00     0.00
```

The options 3 and 2 in the above example refer to the interval (in seconds) and count. So the above report is generated 2 times each after a time interval of 3 seconds. There are various performance counters which are measured by the sar command when used with the –q option. Some of these performance counters and their description are given in Table 10.0.

The sar command with the –u option provides statistics on the CPU utilization. One such report provided by the sar command using the –u option is given next:

```
$sar –u 3 2

10:32:31 AM  CPU  %user  %nice  %system  %idle
10:32:34 AM  all  0.00   0.00   0.00     100.00
10:32:37 AM  all  0.00   0.00   0.00     100.00
Average:     all  0.00   0.00   0.00     100.00
```

The options 3 and 2 in the above example refer to the time interval and the count. Some of the performance counters measured by the sar command when used with the –u option are given in Table 10.1.

Table 10.0. Performance counters in UNIX: sar –q options

Performance Counter	Description
runq –sz	This is the length of the run queue during the interval.
plist –sz	This is the number of processes in the process list.
ldavg -1 and ldavg -5	These counters give the system load average for the last minute and the past five minutes respectively.
%run occ	This is the percentage of time that the run queue is occupied.
swpq-sz	This is the average length of the swap queue during the interval. It includes processes which are sleeping.
%swpocc	This is the percentage of time that there are swapped jobs or threads.

Table 10.1. Performance counters in UNIX: sar –u options

Performance Counter	Description
%usr	This is the percentage of time the CPU is in user mode.
%sys	This is the percentage of time the CPU is in system mode (kernel mode).
%idle	This is the percentage of time the CPU is idle. If the percentage is high and the system is heavily loaded, there is probably a memory or an I/O problem.
%nice	This is the percentage of CPU utilization that occurred while executing at the user mode with nice priority.
%wio	This is the percentage of time the CPU is waiting on completion of I/O from disk, NFS, or RFS. If the percentage is regularly high, then one has to check the I/O systems for inefficiencies and bottlenecks.

Table 10.2. Additional performance counters in UNIX

Performance Counter	Description
I/O Time and Network Time	The amount of time spent moving data and servicing I/O requests.
Virtual Memory Performance	Includes context switching and swapping.
Time Spent	Time spent running other programs – i.e., when the system is not servicing this application because another application currently has the CPU time.
User-state CPU	The time spent by the CPU executing library calls, excluding time spent in the kernel on its behalf. This value can be greatly affected by the use of optimization at compile time and by writing efficient code.
System-state CPU	The amount of time the CPU spends in the system state on behalf of this program. All I/O routines require kernel services. The programmer can affect this value by the use of blocking for I/O transfers.

There are various other performance counters which could be measured, and some of these important performance counters are provided in Table 10.2.

These performance counters can also be measured using various other commands and tools which UNIX provides. Some of the commonly used such commands and tools are described in Table 10.3 along with a brief description of these commands and tools.

When one takes a structured approach to diagnose the performance issues in a system, then it is definitely possible to rapidly isolate the problem area. Also one has to do this performance monitoring even when the system is healthy and behaving normally as this will help in creating a baseline for future measurements.

Performance bottlenecks in a system could be due to a CPU problem, I/O problem, paging problem, or network problem. These bottlenecks could be because of the processes that are CPU bound or I/O bound. In order to identify these problems and fix them, one has to follow the structured approach as described in Figure 10.2.

First, run the basic commands like iostat, sar, and uptime to find out where exactly the performance bottleneck is. From the reports generated from the above mentioned commands, one can find out if the performance bottleneck is because of CPU bound, I/

Table 10.3. Commonly used commands in UNIX

Tools/Commands	Description
Cron	It is a deamon to execute scheduled commands. It aids in process scheduling.
Nice/renice	Prints/modifies the scheduling priority of a job.
setpri	Sets priorities for the jobs.
netstat	Prints network statistics like network connections, routing tables, etc.
nfsstat	Prints Network File System statistics.
uptime	System load average.
ps	Reports the process statistics.
iostat	Reports the I/O statistics.
vmstat	Reports virtual memory statistics.
gprof	Displays call graph profiling for data.
Prof	Displays process profiling.

O bound, or other problems. One such example is the following: If the percentage utilization of usr + sys > 80%, then there is a good chance the system is CPU constrained. In similar lines, one can figure out other bottlenecks too.

If there is a performance bottleneck because of the CPU, then one can try fixing this (Figure 10.2) by using the other tools and commands like profiling, time, optimization, priority changing, and so forth to fix this bottleneck. Also one can upgrade the CPU so as to get better performance.

If the performance bottleneck is due to I/O, then one can fix this bottleneck as described in Figure 10.2 by monitoring the files using filemon command or by looking at the physical or logical volume using the lspv and lslv commands. One can also fix this bottleneck by increasing the disk space and reorganizing the file systems.

If the bottleneck is due to paging, then one can take corrective measures as shown in Figure 10.2 by using commands like svmon and pstat and also by adding more memory and disk. Note that the syntax for the usage of some of these commands might vary based on the flavor of UNIX system used.

Finally, if the performance bottleneck is due to network congestion, then one could use commands line nfsstat, netstat, and so on to get the report on network utilization and its statistics and can take appropriate corrective measures to overcome this bottleneck as shown in Figure 10.2. Also one can use the trace command to go deep into any of these performance measures and get detailed statistics of the system's performance and its bottlenecks. This would also help in fixing the performance related issues in the system. The workflow of this structured approach is also shown in Figure 10.2.

Figure 10.2. Workflow for the structured approach

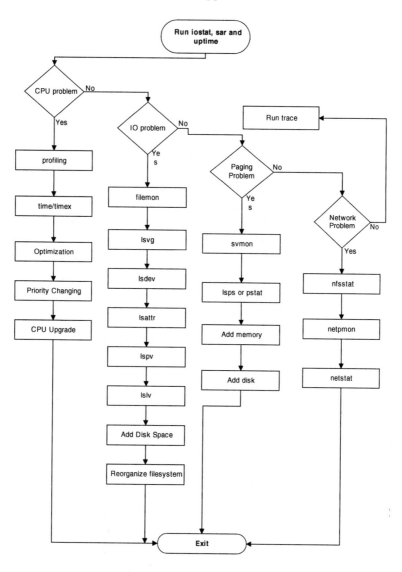

Performance Monitoring and Tuning in Windows 2000

Windows 2000 is a "self-tuning" operating system. This means that in most cases, Windows 2000 automatically adapts to perform optimally depending on the environment in which it is running, assuming the hardware is properly configured. For instance, when

Windows 2000 is deployed as a Web server, other services that are also present but not used are put into a state where they occupy very few system resources such as CPU and memory. However, like many other operating systems, performance depends on many outside factors such as hardware, device drivers, applications, workload, network, and so forth. In addition, there are certain practices and tuning guidelines that can be followed to optimize the performance of Windows 2000 in certain environments.

Windows 2000 defines the performance data it collects in terms of *objects*, *counters*, and *instances*. A *performance object* is any resource, application, or service that can be measured. Using System Monitor and Performance Logs and Alerts, one can select performance objects, counters, and instances to collect and present data about the performance of system components or installed software.

Each object has *performance counters* that are used to measure various aspects of performance such as transfer rates for disks or, for processors, the amount of processor time consumed, total elapsed time consumed, number of page faults in unit seconds, and so on. The object may also have an *instance* that is a unique copy of a particular object type; not all object types support multiple instances.

Each counter is assigned a counter type. The counter type determines how the counter data are calculated, averaged, and displayed. The performance console supports more than 30 counter types, although many of the available counter types are not implemented in the counters installed with Windows 2000. Some of the performance counters are described in Table 10.4 (see http://msdn.microsoft.com). These performance counters are used to monitor the performance of the system and also to tune its performance.

Windows 2000 supports a tool called PERFMON (see http://www.microsoft.com/technet/prodtechnol/Windows2000Pro/reskit/part6/proch27.mspx) which supports all the counters and counter types described in Table 10.4. Using this tool, one can easily monitor various parameters and their values during the test execution.

Most of the applications are developed either in Java or Microsoft technology. Both the technologies require the application architecture to be defined in advance before the development of the application. These technologies support their own frameworks for defining the architecture. However, there are certain architectural similarities between these technologies to define the system. These similarities help us to define common guidelines for monitoring performance counters and tuning applications.

Architectural Similarities between Java and .NET

J2EE and Microsoft's .NET technology share a broad common foundation of standards, and they both have adopted the multitiered architecture approach that typically implements applications in different logical layers, which separate presentation from internal structure (business logic and data management) (see xTier™ Java and .NET Middleware Components Overview, 2005).

Table 10.4. Performance counters in Windows 2000

Counter Name	Counter Type	Description
% Privileged Time	PERF_100NSEC_TIMER	Shows the percentage of elapsed time the process threads have spent executing code in privileged mode.
% Processor Time	PERF_100NSEC_TIMER	Shows the percentage of elapsed time all of the process threads used the processor to execute instructions.
% User Time	PERF_100NSEC_TIMER	Shows the percentage of elapsed time the process threads spent executing code in user mode.
Creating Process ID	PERF_COUNTER_LARGE_RAWCOUNT	Shows the Process ID of the process that created the process. The creating process may have terminated, so this value may no longer identify a running process.
Elapsed Time	PERF_ELAPSED_TIME	Shows the time, in seconds, this process has been running.
Handle Count	PERF_COUNTER_RAWCOUNT	Shows the total number of handles currently open by this process. This is the sum of the handles currently open by each thread in this process.
ID Process	PERF_COUNTER_LARGE_RAWCOUNT	Shows the unique identifier of this process. ID Process numbers are reused, so they only identify a process for the lifetime of that process.
IO Data Bytes/sec	PERF_COUNTER_BULK_COUNT	Shows the rate that the process is reading and writing bytes in I/O operations.
IO Data Operations/sec	PERF_COUNTER_BULK_COUNT	Shows the rate at which the process is issuing read and write I/O operations. This counter counts all I/O activity generated by the process to include file, network, and device I/Os.
IO Other Bytes/sec	PERF_COUNTER_BULK_COUNT	Shows the rate at which the process is issuing bytes to I/O operations that do not involve data such as control operations. It counts all I/O activity generated by the process to include file, network, and device I/Os.
IO Other Operations/sec	PERF_COUNTER_BULK_COUNT	Shows the rate at which the process is issuing I/O operations that are neither read nor write operations. It counts all I/O activity generated by the process to include file, network, and device I/Os.
IO Read Bytes/sec	PERF_COUNTER_BULK_COUNT	Shows the rate at which the process is reading bytes from I/O operations. It counts all I/O activity generated by the process to include file, network, and device I/Os.
IO Read Operations/sec	PERF_COUNTER_BULK_COUNT	Shows the rate at which the process is issuing read I/O operations. It counts all I/O activity generated by the process to include file, network, and device I/Os.
IO Write Bytes/sec	PERF_COUNTER_BULK_COUNT	Shows the rate at which the process is writing bytes to I/O operations. It counts all I/O activity generated by the process to include file, network, and device I/Os.
IO Write Operations/sec	PERF_COUNTER_BULK_COUNT	Shows the rate at which the process is issuing write I/O operations. It counts all I/O activity generated by the process to include file, network, and device I/Os.
Page Faults/sec	PERF_COUNTER_COUNTER	Shows the rate of page faults by the threads executing in this process. A page fault occurs when a thread refers to a virtual memory page that is not in its working set in main memory.

Table 10.4. cont.

Counter Name	Counter Type	Description
Page File Bytes	PERF_COUNTER_LARGE_RAWCOUNT	Shows the current number of bytes this process has used in the paging file(s).
Page File Bytes Peak	PERF_COUNTER_LARGE_RAWCOUNT	Shows the maximum number of bytes this process has used in the paging file(s).
Pool Nonpaged Bytes	PERF_COUNTER_RAWCOUNT	Shows the size, in bytes, in the nonpaged pool, an area of system memory. For objects that cannot be written to disk but must remain in physical memory as long as they are allocated.
Pool Paged Bytes	PERF_COUNTER_RAWCOUNT	Shows the size, in bytes, in the paged pool. Memory/Pool Paged Bytes are calculated differently than Process/Pool Paged Bytes, so it might not equal Process (_Total)/Pool Paged Bytes. This counter displays the last observed value only; it is not an average.
Priority Base	PERF_COUNTER_RAWCOUNT	Shows the current base priority of this process. Threads within a process can raise and lower their own base priority relative to the base priority of the priority.
Private Bytes	PERF_COUNTER_LARGE_RAWCOUNT	Shows the current size, in bytes, this process has allocated that cannot be shared with other processes.
Thread Count	PERF_COUNTER_RAWCOUNT	Shows the number of threads currently active in this process. An instruction is the basic unit of execution in a processor, and a thread is the object that executes instructions. Every running process has at least one thread.
Virtual Bytes	PERF_COUNTER_LARGE_RAWCOUNT	Shows the current size, in bytes, of the virtual address space the process is using. Virtual space is finite, and by using too much, the process can limit its ability to load libraries.
Virtual Bytes Peak	PERF_COUNTER_LARGE_RAWCOUNT	Shows the maximum number of bytes of virtual address space the process has used at any one time.
Working Set	PERF_COUNTER_RAWCOUNT	The set of memory pages touched recently by the threads in the process. Shows the current size, in bytes, in the Working Set of this process.
Working Set Peak	PERF_COUNTER_RAWCOUNT	Shows the maximum size, in bytes, in the Working Set of this process at any point in time.

The most common similarities of the two technologies are given Figure 10.3.

- Both J2EE and .NET architecture models use the Object Oriented (OO) approach for mainstream enterprise computing, with powerful OO frameworks (class libraries) for services such as enterprise components management, object persistence, transactions, Web services, asynchronous communication, loosely coupled event services, messaging, and more.
- The use of virtual machine (VM) architecture is common to J2EE and .NET. Application development tools produce intermediate level code instead of platform-specific binary code, which means the VM interprets that code in real time or performs Just-In-Time (JIT) compilation.

Figure 10.3. Architectural similarities between .NET and Java

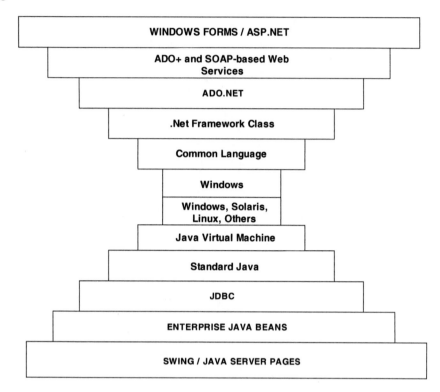

- J2EE and .NET share a broad common foundation that implements the multitiered approach. The high level conceptual architecture models for both platforms look similar to those shown in Figure 10.3.

Once the architectural similarities between two technologies are known, it is easy to define general guidelines for performance monitoring.

General Guidelines for Performance Monitoring

Applications developed either in Java or Microsoft technology must be performance conscious. The performance must be monitored continuously so that tuning becomes easy. In order to ensure better performance monitoring of the system, practitioners need to follow general guidelines.

For routine monitoring, always start by logging activity over 15-minute intervals. If the problem is very specific, then it is to be monitored by varying the interval and by setting frequent update intervals. If the monitoring of the problem itself manifests slowly, such as a memory leak, then use a longer interval.

Consider the overall length of time needed to monitor when choosing this interval. Updating every 20 seconds would be realistic only if it is monitored for less than 4 hours. An interval shorter than 300 seconds is preferred if the system is monitored for 8 hours or more.

Try to balance the number of objects that are monitored and the sampling frequency to keep the log file size within manageable limits.

If the tester prefers to maintain a long update interval when logging, the tester can still view data fluctuations that occur between those intervals (see http://msdn.microsoft.com).

When monitoring computers remotely, the tester has two options to collect data.

- Log performance data on the administrator's computer by collecting data continuously from each remote computer.

- The tester can initiate a service on each remote computer to collect data at regular intervals. Later, the tester can run a batch program to transfer data from remote computers to the administrator's computer for analysis and arching.

Collection on a local computer from remote computers that are monitored is simple to implement because only one logging service would be running. Data can be collected from multiple systems into a single log file. However, it causes additional network traffic and might be restricted by available memory on the administrator's computer. Select appropriate counters when the data are collected centrally.

Data collection that occurs on remote computers that are monitored does not incur the memory and network traffic problems of centralized collection. However, it does result in delayed availability of the data, requiring the collected data to be transferred to the administrator's computer for review. For a distributed data collection, use computer management on a local computer to select a remote computer from which to collect the data.

When monitoring remote computers, note that the remote computer will only allow access to user accounts that have permission to access it.

Testing the application requires choosing the parameters that will monitor the most worthwhile activity of the application. The best parameters for the purposes of this project — performance analysis — should retrieve the most valuable data for analyzing where bottlenecks may occur. These chosen parameters should reflect the performance related to the server (memory, CPU, disk) and the Web site (application throughput, requests/sec, etc.).

Once the general guidelines are followed for monitoring, the next step would be to monitor various counters on technology like Java or Microsoft technology.

Performance Monitoring and Tuning: Java

Applications developed in Java technology are subjected to performance monitoring during execution. Various performance counters could be used in JVM for monitoring and tuning. Proper coding guidelines need to be followed for better performance. JVM supports various counters to monitor performance of the application.

Performance Counters in JVM

One of the most annoying experiences for users with less than ideal memory configurations is garbage collection (GC) pauses. There are a number of settings that affect the way the JVM allocates memory and the behavior of garbage collection in J2SE 1.4.1.

The main purpose of monitoring GC and hence tuning is to reduce the frequency of major garbage collection events without increasing their accumulating duration. NetBeans as a GUI application produces and accumulates a considerable large number of objects.

In order to measure the performance of the JVM, one has to know the performance metrics which are explained in the following sections.

Time in Seconds Spent in Garbage Collection

This is the total number of seconds that the process spends in doing garbage collection, including:

- Number of GC events during the run;
- Average garbage cycle duration;
- Session duration.

The frequency of the above GC events should be minimized to achieve better performance.

Events Monitoring

The events that can be monitored are:

- Thread synchronization or contention;

- Thread cooperation; this event describes the occurrences of cooperation between threads in Java;

- Process scheduling information;

- Method invocation;

- Object allocation and deallocation.

The above JVM counters help to measure performance as well as monitoring. Java technology provides a good tool known as Jconsole to monitor the performance of the application.

Performance Monitoring Tool: Jconsole

Jconsole (see Using Jconsole, 2005) is a Java management extension (JMX)-compliant monitoring tool. It uses the extensive JMX instrumentation of the Java virtual machine to provide information on performance and resource consumption of applications running on the Java platform.

Figure 10.4. Snapshot of Jconsole monitoring tool

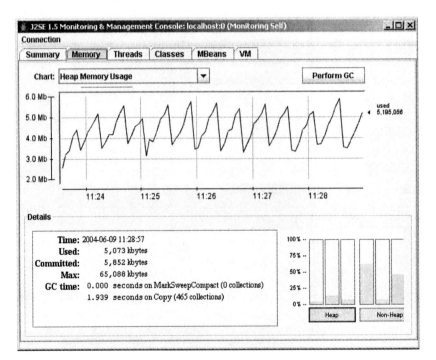

The Jconsole executable is in *JDK_HOME*/bin, where *JDK_HOME* is the directory where the JDK is installed. If this directory is on the system path, one can start the tool by simply typing Jconsole in the command (shell) prompt.

Performance counters that can be monitored using Jconsole are given in Figure 10.4. These counters are:

- Summary

- Threads

- Memory

- MBeans

- VM

- Classes

Summary Tab

This tab gives information regarding the following metrics:

- Uptime: how long the JVM has been running.

- Total compile time: the amount of time spent in just-in-time (JIT) compilation.

- Process CPU time: the total amount of CPU time consumed by the JVM.

Threads Tab

This tab gives information regarding the following metrics:

- Live threads: current number of live daemon threads plus nondaemon threads.
- Peak: highest number of live threads since JVM started.
- Daemon threads: current number of live daemon threads.
- Total started: total number of threads started since JVM started (including daemon, nondaemon, and terminated).

Memory Tab

This tab gives information regarding the following metrics:

- Current heap size: number of Kbytes currently occupied by the heap.

- Committed memory: total amount of memory allocated for use by the heap.

- Maximum heap size: maximum number of Kbytes occupied by the heap.

- Objects pending for finalization: number of objects pending for finalization.

- Garbage collector information: information on GC, including the garbage collector names, number of collections performed, and total time spent performing GC.

The memory pools available depend on the JVM used. For the HotSpot JVM (see Java HotSpot Technology, 2005), the pools are:

- **Eden Space (heap):** pool from which memory is initially allocated for most objects.

- **Survivor Space (heap):** pool containing objects that have survived GC of eden space.

- **Tenured Generation (heap):** pool containing objects that have existed for some time in the survivor space.

- **Permanent Generation (non-heap):** holds all the reflective data of the virtual machine itself, such as class and method objects. With JVMs that use class data sharing, this generation is divided into read-only and read-write areas.

- **Code Cache (non-heap):** HotSpot JVM also includes a "code cache" containing memory used for compilation and storage of native code.

The Details frame shown in Figure 10.4 presents several current memory metrics:

- **Used:** the amount of memory currently used. Memory used includes the memory occupied by all objects including both reachable and unreachable objects.

- **Committed:** the amount of memory guaranteed to be available for use by the JVM. The amount of committed memory may change over time. The Java Virtual Machine may release memory to the system, and committed memory could be less than the amount of memory initially allocated at startup. Committed will always be greater than or equal to used.

- **Max:** the maximum amount of memory that can be used for memory management. Its value may change or be undefined. A memory allocation may fail if the JVM attempts to increase the used memory to be greater than committed memory or even in some cases wherein the amount used is less than or equal to max (for example, when the system is low on virtual memory).

The bar chart at the lower right in Figure 10.4 shows memory consumed by the memory pools in heap and non-heap memory. The bar will turn red when the memory used exceeds the memory usage threshold. One can set the memory usage threshold through an attribute of the MemoryMXBean.

Heap and Non-Heap Memory

The JVM manages two kinds of memory: heap and non-heap memory, both created when it starts.

- **Heap memory** is the runtime data area from which the JVM allocates memory for all class instances and arrays. The heap may be of a fixed or variable size. The garbage collector is an automatic memory management system that reclaims heap memory for objects.

- **Non-heap memory** includes a method area shared among all threads and memory required for the internal processing or optimization for the JVM. It stores per-class structures such as a runtime constant pool, field and method data, and the code for methods and constructors. The method area is logically part of the heap, but depending on implementation, a JVM may not garbage collect or compact it. Like the heap, the method area may be of fixed or variable size. The memory for the method area does not need to be contiguous.

In addition to the method area, a JVM implementation may require memory for internal processing or optimization which also belongs to non-heap memory. An example could be the JIT compiler requires memory for storing the native machine code translated from the JVM code for high performance.

Memory Pools and Memory Managers

Memory pools and memory managers are key aspects of the JVM memory system.

A *memory pool* represents a memory area that the JVM manages. The JVM has at least one memory pool, and it may create or remove memory pools during execution. A memory pool can belong to either heap or non-heap memory.

A *memory manager* manages one or more memory pools. The garbage collector is a type of memory manager responsible for reclaiming memory used by unreachable objects. A JVM may have one or more memory managers. It may add or remove memory managers during execution. A memory pool can be managed by more than one memory manager.

MBean Tab

The MBean tab displays information on all the MBeans registered with the platform MBean server.

The tree on the left shows all the MBeans arranged according to their objectNames. When Bean is selected in the tree, its attributes, operations, notifications, and other information are displayed on the right. The tester can set the value of attributes can be, if they are writeable.

VM Tab

The Virtual Memory (VM) tab provides information on the JVM which includes the following:

- **Uptime:** Total amount of time since the JVM was started.
- **Process CPU Time:** Total amount of CPU time that the JVM has consumed since it was started.
- **Total Compile Time:** Total accumulated time spent in just-in-time (JIT) compilation.

Garbage Collection

Garbage collection is how the JVM frees memory occupied by objects that are no longer referenced. It is common to think of objects that have active references as being "alive" and unreferenced (or unreachable) objects as "dead". Garbage collection is the process of releasing memory used by the dead objects. The algorithms and parameters used by GC can have dramatic effects on performance.

The HotSpot VM garbage collector (see Java HotSpot Technology, 2005) uses *generational garbage collection*. Generational GC divides memory into several *generations* and assigns each a memory pool. When a generation uses up its allotted memory, the VM performs a partial garbage collection (also called a *minor collection*) on that memory pool to reclaim memory used by dead objects. This partial GC is usually much faster than a full GC.

The HotSpot VM defines two generations: the young generation and the old generation. The young generation consists of an "eden space" and two "survivor spaces". The VM initially assigns all objects to the eden space, and most objects die there. When it performs a minor GC, the VM moves any remaining objects from the eden space to one of the survivor spaces. The VM moves objects that live long enough in the survivor spaces to the "tenured" space in the old generation. When the tenured generation fills up, there is a full GC that is often much slower because it involves all live objects. The permanent generation holds all the reflective data of the virtual machine itself, such as class and method objects.

Classes Tab

This tab gives information regarding the following metrics:

- Current classes loaded: number of classes currently loaded into memory.
- Total classes loaded: total number of classes loaded into memory since the JVM started, including those subsequently unloaded.
- Total classes unloaded: number of classes unloaded from memory since the JVM started.

Jconsole is a powerful tool used in the development of Java based applications.

Java Coding Guidelines

Java technology is most commonly used in present day development of Web applications.

Some of the broad guidelines (see HBS2005) are given below:

- Appropriate string manipulation code should be used.
- Choose appropriate database drivers.
- Avoid returning a collection (Vector or Hashtable). It is always better to return a class which hides the real collection and better to return an interface, as this will allow refactoring of the code if performance issues are found.
- A good code is always a small code which has clarity and follows coding standards.
- Follow naming conventions properly.
- Use a logging framework.
- Use a loosely coupled system or process. An example could be to create metadescriptions data storage if there are a lot of layers in the system, or use Web services.

Appendix A4 provides detailed coding guidelines.

Performance Monitoring and Tuning: .NET

Most of the applications developed in Microsoft technology are in the .NET framework. This framework provides a good platform for both development and running of applications. Like in Java, it provides counters to measure and monitor performance of the applications.

Performance Counters

Performance counters are used to monitor the utilization of the processors, the memory, the network, and the I/O devices. Performance counters are organized and grouped into performance counter categories. For instance, the processor category contains all counters related to the operation of the processor such as the processor time, idle time, interrupt time, and so forth.

Windows provides many predefined performance counters that can be retrieved programmatically or displayed using the Performance Monitor. As said earlier, these counters are used to monitor the usage of the operating system resources. In .NET the Common Language Runtime (CLR) exposes its own set of performance counters. These performance counters cover every aspect of the CLR operations ranging from exception processing to security checking.

CLR Performance Counters

The .NETCLR provides nine important performance counter categories to help the tester monitor and tune the application's performance. These counters provide information about security, memory management, networking, compilation, and interactions with other COM objects. This information helps in tuning the application.

Table 10.5 provides a list of these categories along with a brief description.

There are several other categories of counters which are not highlighted here, as they are not important. Along with these counters, .NET provides counters on its framework to monitor performance of the application.

Table 10.5. CLR performance counters

Performance Counter Category	Description
Exceptions	Provide information about the exceptions thrown by the application.
Interop	Provides information about the application's interaction with COM components, COM+ services, and type libraries.
JIT	Provides information about code that has been compiled by the Just In Time compiler.
Loading	Provides information about assemblies, classes, and AppDomains that have been loaded.
Locks and Threads	Provide information about managed locks and threads used by the application.
Memory	Provides information about the garbage collector.
Networking	Provides information about the data sent and received over the network by the application.
Remoting	Provides information about remote objects used by the application.
Security	Gives a description about the security checks the CLR performs on the application.

.NET Framework Performance Counters

Like in JVM, the .NET framework provides a set of performance counters which are described in Table 10.6. Wide range of counters varying from measuring the memory, processor utilization, time taken for waiting, execution of various requests can be monitored. For instance, the counter %Processor time gives an indicator of the total processor utilization in the system. The value range must be lower than 80-85% for optimal results.

Table 10.6. Important .NET framework performance counters

Performance Counter	Description	Comments
Processor (_Total)/% Processor Time	Gives an indicator of the total processor utilization in the machine.	80-85% is acceptable; the lower the better
.NETCLR Exception/# of Excep Thrown/sec (_Global_)	This is the number of managed code exceptions thrown per second.	This has to be 0 under normal circumstances
.NETCLR Loading/Current Assemblies (_Global_)	Indicates and records the number of assemblies that are loaded in the process.	None
.NETCLR Loading/Rate of Assemblies	Rate at which assemblies are loaded into the memory per second.	None
.NETCLR Loading/Bytes in Loader Heap	Indicates the number of bytes committed by the class loader across all AppDomain.	This counter has to be in a steady state, or else large fluctuations in this counter would indicate that there are too many assemblies loaded per AppDomain
.NETCLR Memory/# Bytes in all Heaps	This counter indicates the current memory allocated for the Garbage Collector heap. While using large data sets in memory, excess cache entries, using reg-ex and string parsing, excess view-state or excessive session objects contribute to the heavy memory requirement. Hence, this counter is used to start the diagnostic.	This has to be less than the Process\Private Bytes counter
.NETCLR Memory/% Time in GC	This indicates the percentage of time spent performing the last GC. If there are any spikes in this counter, then those are accepted. Allocating large strings to cache, heavy string operations, etc. leave a lot of memory spaces the GC has to clean up.	Lower value, in the range of 5-10%, is an acceptable value
.NETData Provider for SQLServer/NumberOfActiveConnections	Number of active connections in the pool in-use presently.	None
ASP.NET/Request Execution Time	Time in milliseconds to execute the last request.	None
ASP.NET/Request Wait Time	Time in milliseconds to wait before the request got executed.	None
ASP.NET/Requests Current	Indicates the total number of requests handled by the ASP.NETISAPI. Beyond this, the requests are rejected.	This counter needs to be lesser than the requestQueueLimit defined at the process Model configuration

Table 10.6. cont.

Performance Counter	Description	Comments
ASP.NET Applications/Cache Total Hit Ratio	This is the total hit-to-miss ratio of all cache requests .	This needs to be as high as possible
ASP.NET Applications/Errors during Execution	The total number of run-time errors.	This needs to be as low as possible
ASP.NET Applications/Requests/sec	This is the total number of requests executed per second	None
Process/% Processor Time (aspnet_wp and inetinfo)	The percentage of time the threads of these processes spend using the processor.	This has to less than 70%; this counter allows us to eliminate the effect of OS requirement and other external factors
Process/Handle Count (aspnet_wp and inetinfo)	This is the total number of handles open by these processes. This has to be on an acceptable value.	A value less than 10,000 and more than 2,000 is acceptable; a value very high can mean there are large request hits being made
Process/Virtual Bytes	Virtual Bytes is the current size in bytes of the virtual address space the process is using.	None
Memory/Available Mbytes	The amount of physical RAM available in the system.	This has to be at least 10-15% of the physical RAM available

The suggested value in Table 10.6 is an indicator, and practitioners can use their experience and judgment to arrive at a proper value. Only important counters are listed here, and testers are advised to refer to the MSDN manual for more details.

Once the performance counters and their possible values are known, the system is now ready for tuning. This technology provides a tool known as PERFMON which will be used for monitoring as well as tuning the framework.

Performance Monitoring Tool: PERFMON

The performance monitor, PERFMON, is a system performance viewer that comes with Windows NT, Windows 2000, Windows 2003, and Windows XP. PERFMON allows the user to select counters from a list of available performance counter categories and display them either in graph, histogram, or report format. The tool provides a provision to collect data from a remote computer. It also provides selection of the required performance object. The performance object could be any resources like processor, memory, or any other objects related to the framework. The procedure to execute and monitor usage of PERFMON is given in Appendix A6.

Table 10.7. Important performance counters used to identify CLR bottlenecks

Area	Counter	Description
Memory	Large Object Heap Size	This counter displays the current size of the Large Object Heap in bytes. Objects greater than 20 KBytes are treated as large objects by the Garbage Collector and are directly allocated in a special heap; they are not promoted through the generations. This counter is updated at the end of a GC; it is not updated on every allocation.
	% Time in GC	Time in GC is the percentage of elapsed time that was spent in performing a garbage collection (GC) since the last GC cycle. This counter is usually an indicator of the work done by the Garbage Collector on behalf of the application to collect and compact memory. This counter is updated only at the end of every GC, and the counter value reflects the last observed value; it is not an average.
	# Bytes in all Heaps	This counter is the sum of four other counters; Gen 0 Heap Size; Gen 1 Heap Size; Gen 2 Heap Size; and the Large Object Heap Size. This counter indicates the current memory allocated in bytes on the GC heaps.
	# Gen 0 Collections	The youngest, most recently allocated are garbage collected (Gen 0 GC) since the start of the application. Gen 0 GC occurs when the available memory in generation 0 is not sufficient to satisfy an allocation request. This counter is incremented at the end of a Gen 0 GC. Higher generation GCs include all lower generation GCs. This counter is explicitly incremented when a higher generation (Gen 1 or Gen 2) GC occurs. _Global_ counter value is not accurate and should be ignored. This counter displays the last observed value.
	# Gen 1 Collections	This counter displays the number of times the generation 1 objects are garbage collected since the start of the application. The counter is incremented at the end of a Gen 1 GC. Higher generation GCs include all lower generation GCs. This counter is explicitly incremented when a higher generation (Gen 2) GC occurs. _Global_ counter value is not accurate and should be ignored. This counter displays the last observed value.
	# Gen 2 Collections	This counter displays the number of times the generation 2 objects (older) are garbage collected since the start of the application. The counter is incremented at the end of a Gen 2 GC (also called full GC). _Global_ counter value is not accurate and should be ignored. This counter displays the last observed value.
	# of Pinned Objects	This counter displays the number of pinned objects encountered in the last GC. This counter tracks the pinned objects only in the heaps that were garbage collected; e.g., a Gen 0 GC would cause enumeration of pinned objects in the generation 0 heap only. A pinned object is one that the Garbage Collector cannot move in memory.

Table 10.7. cont.

Area	Counter	Description
Exceptions	# of Exceps Thrown/Sec	This counter displays the number of exceptions thrown per second. These include both .NET exceptions and unmanaged exceptions that get converted into .NET exceptions; e.g., null pointer reference exception in unmanaged code would get rethrown in managed code as a .NET System.NullReferenceException; this counter includes both handled and unhandled exceptions. Exceptions should only occur in rare situations and not in the normal control flow of the program; this counter was designed as an indicator of potential performance problems due to large (>100s) rate of exceptions thrown. This counter is not an average over time; it displays the difference between the values observed in the last two samples divided by the duration of the sample interval.
	Throw to Catch Depth/Sec	This counter displays the number of stack frames traversed from the frame that threw the .NET exception to the frame that handled the exception per second. This counter resets to 0 when an exception handler is entered; so nested exceptions would show the handler to handler stack depth. This counter is not an average over time; it displays the difference between the values observed in the last two samples divided by the duration of the sample interval.
Locking and Threading	Contention Rate/Sec	Rate at which threads in the runtime attempt to acquire a managed lock unsuccessfully. Managed locks can be acquired in many ways: by the "lock" statement in C# or by calling *System.Monitor.Enter* or by using *MethodImplOptions.Synchronized* custom attribute.
	# of Current Logical Threads	This counter displays the number of current .NET thread objects in the application. A .NET thread object is created either by new *System.Threading.Thread* or when an unmanaged thread enters the managed environment. This counter maintains the count of both running and stopped threads. This counter is not an average over time; it just displays the last observed value.
	# of Current Physical Threads	This counter displays the number of native OS threads created and owned by the CLR to act as underlying threads for .NET thread objects. This counter's value does not include the threads used by the CLR in its internal operations; it is a subset of the threads in the OS process.
	# of Current Recognized Threads	This counter displays the number of threads currently recognized by the CLR; they have a corresponding .NET thread object associated with them. These threads are not created by the CLR; they are created outside the CLR but have since run inside the CLR at least once. Only unique threads are tracked; threads with the same thread ID reentering the CLR or recreated after thread exit are not counted twice.

Table 10.7. cont.

Area	Counter	Description
	# of Total Recognized Threads	This counter displays the total number of threads recognized by the CLR since the start of this application; these threads have a corresponding .NETthread object associated with them. These threads are not created by the CLR; they are created outside the CLR but have since run inside the CLR at least once. Only unique threads are tracked; threads with the same thread ID reentering the CLR or recreated after thread exit are not counted twice.
Security	Total Runtime Checks	This counter displays the percentage of elapsed time spent in performing runtime Code Access Security (CAS) checks since the last such check. CAS allows code to be trusted to varying degrees and enforces these varying levels of trust depending on code identity. This counter is updated at the end of a runtime security check; it represents the last observed value; it is not an average.
	Stack Walk Depth	This counter displays the depth of the stack during that last runtime Code Access Security check. The Runtime Code Access Security check is performed by crawling the stack. This counter is not an average; it just displays the last observed value.

.NET Framework Tuning

After monitoring various performance counters, the .NET framework is ready for tuning. First, it is required to tune the CLR. Tuning CLR affects all managed code regardless of the implementation technology. Then, other technology like ASP.NET applications or Web services and ADO.NET code needs to be tuned.

CLR Tuning

CLR tuning is mostly achieved by class designing and then optimizing the code. To enable the CLR to perform its tasks efficiently, the design needs to enable efficient garbage collection. The main CLR related bottlenecks are because of the contention for resources, inefficient resource cleanup, misuse of the thread pool, and resource leaks.

The few important performance counters shown in Table 10.7 would give an idea of how to identify CLR bottlenecks. Counters can be added to monitor and analyze using PERFMON depending on the requirements.

CLR counters provide first level indication for possible bottlenecks. The system counters also provide next level bottlenecks which are described.

Bottlenecks Identified Using System Counters

Some of the common bottlenecks that occur in applications developed using managed code are identified using system counters as given in Table 10.8.

An increase in the contention rate or a significant increase in the total number of contentions is a strong indication that an application is encountering thread contention. To resolve this issue, one has to identify code that accesses shared resources or uses synchronization mechanisms.

The next set of tuning activities must be considered with ASP.NET tuning.

ASP.NET Application: Identifying Bottlenecks and Tuning

ASP.NET is a technology from Microsoft for building Web applications and XML Web services. ASP.NET pages employ a compiled, event-driven programming model that enables the separation of application logic and user interface. ASP.NET pages and ASP.NETXML Web services files contain server side logic. During the process of Web application development, developers normally get performance issues that need to be addressed.

Table 10.8. Common bottlenecks identified using system counters

Bottlenecks	Counter	Comments
Excessive memory consumption	Process/Private Bytes .NETCLR Memory/# Bytes in All Heaps Process/Working Set .NETCLR Memory/Large Object Heap Size	An increase in Private Bytes while the # of Bytes in all heaps counter remains the same indicates unmanaged memory consumption. An increase in both counters indicates managed memory consumption.
Large working set size	Process/Working Set	The working set is the set of memory pages currently loaded in RAM. A high value might indicate that a number of assemblies are loaded.
Fragmented large object heap	.NETCLR Memory/Large Object Heap Size	Objects greater than 83 KB in size are allocated in the large object heap, which is measured by High CPU utilization.
High CPU utilization	% Time in GC .NETCLR Exceptions/# of Exception Thrown/Sec Thread\Context Switches/Sec	None
Thread contention	.NETCLR LocksAndThreads/Contention Rate/Sec .NETCLR LocksAndThreads/Total # of Contentions	None

The following sections highlight different areas that are causing the bottleneck and how to tune them optimally.

ASP.NET Performance Counters

First, we need to identify the counters that are required in the ASP.NET application to detect the bottleneck. The performance counters shown in Table 10.9 help to identify ASP.NET bottlenecks.

ASP.NET Application Bottlenecks

The following list describes several common bottlenecks that occur in ASP.NET applications and explains how to identify them using the system counters listed in Table 10.9.

- **Thread pool starvation.** Thread pool bottlenecks can occur when ASP.NET runs out of worker and I/O threads to process incoming requests or perform I/O work.

  To identify this symptom, observe the following performance counters:

  - ➢ ASP.NET/Requests Queued
  - ➢ Process/% Processor Time (aspnet_wp.exe or w3wp.exe)

  If requests are being queued with low processor utilization levels, this is a strong indication that ASP.NET is performing non-CPU bound work. If the application makes calls to remote or local Web services, then the thread pool can be tuned to resolve the issue.

  As an alternative, custom performance counters could be used to monitor the thread pool to investigate the available I/O and worker threads further.

- **Thread contention.** Thread contention occurs when multiple threads try to gain access to a shared resource.

- **Memory bottlenecks.** These can result from memory leaks, fragmentation issues, inefficient resource cleanup, or simply allocating too much or too little memory for the worker process.

  To identify this symptom, the following performance counters are observed in addition to the system level memory related counters.

  - ➢ Process/Private Bytes (aspnet_wp.exe or w3wp.exe)
  - ➢ Process/Virtual Bytes (aspnet_wp.exe or w3wp.exe)
  - ➢ .NETCLR Memory/# Bytes in all Heaps (aspnet_wp.exe or w3wp.exe)

Table 10.9. Performance counters used to identify ASP.NET bottlenecks

Area	Performance Object	Performance Counter	Description
Worker Process	ASP.NET	Worker Process Restarts	Number of times a worker process has restarted on the machine.
Throughput	ASP.NET Applications	Requests Timed Out	The number of requests that timed out.
	ASP.NET Applications	Requests/Sec	The number of requests executed per second.
	Web Service	ISAPI Extension Requests/Sec	The rate of ISAPI Extension requests that are simultaneously being processed by the Web service.
	ASP.NET	Requests Current	The current number of requests, including those that are queued, currently executing, or waiting to be written to the client. Under the ASP.NET process model, when this counter exceeds the requestQueueLimit defined in the processModel configuration section, ASP.NET will begin rejecting requests.
	ASP.NET Applications	Requests Executing	The number of requests currently executing.
Response Time/Latency	ASP.NET	Request Execution Time	The number of milliseconds it took to execute the most recent request.
Cache	ASP.NET Applications	Cache Total Entries	Total number of entries within the cache (both internal and user added).
	ASP.NET Applications	Cache Total Hit Ratio	Ratio of hits from all cache calls.
	ASP.NET Applications	Cache Total Turnover Rate	Number of additions and removals to the total cache per second.
	ASP.NET Applications	Cache API Hit Ratio	Ratio of hits called from user code.
	ASP.NET Applications	Cache API Turnover Rate	Number of additions and removals to the API cache per second.
	ASP.NET Applications	Output Cache Entries	Current number of entries in the output cache.
	ASP.NET Applications	Output Cache Hit Ratio	Ratio of hits to requests for output cacheable requests.
	ASP.NET Applications	Output Cache Turnover Rate	Number of additions and removals to the output cache per second.

- **Worker Process Restarts.** Restarting the ASP.NET worker process takes time and consumes resources. The following factors can contribute to recycling causing performance bottlenecks.

- Changes to a configuration file (Note that these changes are not logged to the Application Log)

- Deadlocks

- Exceeding memory limits (<processModel memory Limit=/>)

- Request and timeout limits specified in Machine.config

ASP.NET Application Performance Tuning

When tuning the performance of an ASP.NET application, the factors required to be considered are:

- The client's interaction with ASP.NET
- The worker process itself (i.e., aspnet_wp.exe)
- Remote or local Web service calls from ASP.NET

Most ASP.NET tuning is performed by modifying the configuration parameters in the system-wide Machine.config file and the application.

There are a number of options for tuning ASP.NET applications, most of which involve tuning the settings in Machine.config file. This configuration file has many sections, but the following sections are most critical from the performance point of view (see Marquardt, 2005).

- \<httpRuntime>

The \<httpRuntime> element configures the ASP.NET runtime settings. One can specify these at the machine, site, application, and subdirectory levels. The default settings from Machine.config are

```
<httpRuntime executionTimeout="90" maxRequestLength="4096"
useFullyQualifiedRedirectUrl="false" minFreeThreads="8"
minLocalRequestFreeThreads="4" appRequestQueueLimit="100"
enableVersionHeader="true"/>
```

For a detailed description of each attribute, see "\<httpRuntime> Element" in the .NET Framework documentation (see .NET framework general reference, 2005).

- \<process Model>

The attributes on the \<processModel> element apply to the ASP.NET worker process (aspnet_wp.exe) and to all applications hosted in the worker process on an IIS 5 or 6 Web server. Many of the settings are tuned by default and do not require further changes. The default settings are as follows:

```
<processModel enable="true" timeout="Infinite" idleTimeout="Infinite"
shutdownTimeout="0:00:05" requestLimit="Infinite"
requestQueueLimit="5000" restartQueueLimit="10" memoryLimit="60"
WebGarden="false" cpuMask="0xffffffff" userName="machine"
password="AutoGenerate" logLevel="Errors"
clientConnectedCheck="0:00:05" comAuthenticationLevel="Connect"
comImpersonationLevel="Impersonate" responseDeadlockInterval="00:03:00"
MaxWorkerThreads="20"  maxIoThreads="20"/>
```

Table 10.10. Key attributes in <processModel> and <httpRuntime>

Attributes	Description	Comments
Maxconnection	If an application makes calls to a remote a Web service and the requests are waiting for the call to complete, one can increase the CPU utilization and the application performance by changing the maxconnection attribute on the <ConnectionManagement> element in Machine.config.	Increasing maxconnection also can lead to an increase in CPU utilization. This increase in CPU utilization is caused by the fact that more incoming requests can be processed by ASP.NET instead of having the incoming requests wait for their turn to call the Web service. The tester needs to balance the maxconnection with the other attributes discussed in this list and the actual CPU utilization.
maxWorkerThreads and maxIOThreads	These attributes define the maximum number of worker and I/O threads the ASP.NET worker process is allowed to create. These values do not reflect the actual number of threads created by the worker process	The maximum value for these attributes is 100 per processor.
maxconnection and minFreeThreads	This attribute defines the number of threads that can be used for work other than processing incoming requests to the worker process. This attribute prevents the ASP.NET process from using a thread from the thread pool to handle a new HTTP request if this would mean that the free thread count drops below this limit.	The attribute is specified on the <httpRuntime> element and has a default value of 8.
minFreeThreads	One can use this attribute to help prevent deadlocks by ensuring that a thread is available to handle callbacks from pending asynchronous requests. A deadlock can occur if all of the threads in the thread pool are currently in use handling incoming HTTP requests, and one or more of those requests are waiting for asynchronous callbacks. In this situation, there are no available threads to service the callback.	One can set minFreeThreads to ensure that some free threads are available to process the callbacks.

Table 10.10. cont.

Attributes	Description	Comments
minLocalRequestFree Threads	Increasing minFreeThreads means that one can reserve more threads to make remote calls.	In all cases, one should ensure that maxWorkerThreads – minFreeThreads >=12. Twelve is the optimum number of threads that should be made available to the ASP.NET worker process to service requests. This value means that ASP.NET cannot execute more than twelve requests concurrently. This limit is based on a series of performance tests, which demonstrate that normally the worker process uses four of these threads. If the processor is fully utilized (greater than 95% utilization) and the application makes long running calls, the worker process is likely to use all twelve threads.

For a detailed description of each attribute, see "<processModel> Element" in the .NET Framework documentation (see http://msdn.microsoft.com/library/default.asp?url=/library/en-us/cpgenref/html/gngrfProcessmodelSection.asp).

• Thread Pool Attributes

Throughput can be improved by making effective use of threads. Tune the thread pool to reduce connections and to avoid blocking threads because blocking threads reduces the number of available worker threads.

Table 10.10 describes the key attributes (in <processModel> and <httpRuntime>) in the Machine.config file related to ASP.NET ThreadPool.

Once the key attributes of <processModel> and <httpRuntime> in Machine.config file are tuned to appropriate values, the system is ready for tuning the ASP.NET thread pool.

Tuning the Thread Pool in the ASP.NET Application

Tune the thread pool using the formula for reducing contention. The formula for reducing contention can give a good empirical start for tuning the ASP.NET thread pool. Microsoft's recommended settings (see Bromberg, 2005) are shown in Table 10.11.

The above section shows how to identify the most commonly faced bottlenecks while developing ASP.NET Web applications and the steps that need to be taken to avoid and overcome performance issues so that one can build good ASP.NET.

Table 10.11. Microsoft's recommended threading settings for reducing contention

Configuration setting	Default (.NET1.1)	Recommended value	Purpose
Maxconnection	2	12 * #CPUs	This setting controls the maximum number of outgoing HTTP connections allowed by the client.
maxIOThreads	20	100	Controls the maximum number of I/O threads in the CLR thread pool.
maxWorkerThreads	20	100	Controls the maximum number of worker threads in the CLR thread pool. This number is automatically multiplied by the number of CPUs by the worker processor.
minFreeThreads	8	88 * #CPUs	Used by the worker process to queue all of the incoming requests if the number of available threads in the thread pool falls below the value for this setting.
minLocalRequestFreeThreads	4	76 * #CPUs	Used by the worker process to queue requests from *localhost* if the number of available threads in the thread pool falls below this number. This setting is similar to minFreeThreads, but it only applies to requests originating on the local server.

Coding Guidelines

The concept of Object Oriented Programming using C# in the .NET framework calls for a different environment programming. The CLR provides many features such as automatic memory management, type safety, and exception handling as part of the framework. Apart from this, there could be some coding pitfalls like any other programming languages. Necessary coding guidelines for the following implementation need to be followed in order to achieve better performance.

- Garbage Collection
- Finalize and Dispose Method
- Asynchronous Execution
- Locking and Synchronization
- Exception Management
- Iterating and Looping
- String Operations

- Arrays and Collections
- Reflection and Late Binding
- Data Access

Along with implementation of the above, care should be taken while designing both application as well as class design. For more details on coding guidelines, see Appendix A5.

Summary

Web-based applications require a proper operating environment to run efficiently. The operating environment includes a specific operating system, hardware/software required, and technology specific resources. The operating system plays a major role in managing the performance of the system. In order to manage efficiently, each operating system provides a mechanism to monitor and measure the performance parameters. The values of these parameters will help tune the system for optimal performance at the operating system level.

Applications have to be developed specific to a technology like Java or .NET. The architecture design also depends on these technologies. While designing the architecture, care must be taken to improve the performance. For this, the designers must follow general guidelines so that the implementation of the application is better and performance may improve.

Finally, technology specific aspects must be addressed to improve the performance. Both Java and .NET provides various parameters at different levels to monitor and tune performances. These parameters are measured through various counters. Monitoring these counters provides performance related data which can be used to tune the system. Finally, practitioners need to follow various guidelines for monitoring and tuning the system, in general.

References

Bromberg, P. A. (2005). *IIS 6.0 tuning for performance*. Retrieved October 14, 2005, from http://www.eggheadcafe.com/articles/20050613.asp

Lynch, J. (2005). *UNIX and Web performance*. Retrieved May 14, 2005, from http://www.circle4.com/jaqui/papers/Webunuk.html

Marquardt, T. (2005). *ASP.NET performance monitoring, and when to alert administrators*. Retrieved May 18, 2005, from at http://msdn.microsoft.com/library/en-us/dnaspp/html/monitor_perf.asp

.NET framework general reference. (2005). Retrieved May 18, 2005, from http://msdn.microsoft.com/library/en-us/cpgenref/html/gngrfHttp RuntimeSection.asp

Java HotSpot Technology. (2005). Retrieved March 5, 2005, from http://java.sun.com/products/hotspot/

Java language coding guidelines (2005). Retrieved May 17, 2005, from http://www.horstmann.com/bigj/style.html

Using Jconsole. (2005). Retrieved May 26, 2005, from http://java.sun.com/j2se/1.5.0/docs/guide/management/jconsole.html

xTier™Java and .NETMiddleware components overview. (2005). Technical whitepaper. Retrieved May 17, 2005, from http://www.fitechlabs.com/articles/xtier_overview_article.pdf

Additional Sources

(2005). Retrieved May 17, 2005, from http://www.microsoft.com/resources/documentation/windows/2000/professional/reskit/en-us/part6/proch27.mspx

(2005). Retrieved May 17, 2005, from http://msdn.microsoft.com/library/en-us/cpgenref/html/gngrfProcessmodelSection.asp

(2005). MSDN Home Page. Retrieved May 25, 2005, from http://msdn.microsoft.com/

At your service: Performance considerations for making Web service calls from ASPX pages (n.d.). Retrieved May 13, 2005, from http://msdn.microsoft.com/library/en-us/dnservice/html/service07222003.asp

Burk, R., & Horvath, D. B. (n.d.). *UNIX Unuleashed, system administrator's edition. The main pages in the UNIX system trouble-shooting and diagnostic guide.* Retrieved May 18, 2005, from http://java.sun.com/j2se/1.5/pdf/jdk50_ts_guide.pdf

FIX: SetMinThreads and GetMinThreads API Added to Common Language Runtime ThreadPool Class. Retrieved May 11, 2005, from http://support.microsoft.com/default.aspx?scid=kb;en-us;810259

Microsoft Windows 2000 Professional Resource Kit- Overview of Performance Monitoring. (n.d.). Retrieved May 14, 2005, from http://www.microsoft.com/resources/documentation/windows/2000/professional/reskit/en-us/part6/proch27.mspx

Microsoft Support WebCast. Microsoft ASP.NET Threading. Retrieved May 20, 2005, from http://support.microsoft.com/default.aspx?scid=%2f servicedesks%2f Webcasts%2fen%2ftranscripts%2fwct060503.asp

PRB: Contention, poor performance, and deadlocks when you make Web service requests from ASP.NET applications. (2005). Retrieved May 13, 2005, from http://support.microsoft.com/default.aspx?scid=kb;en-us;821268

PRB: Sudden Requirement for a Larger Number of Threads from the ThreadPool Class May Result in Slow Computer Response Time. Retrieved May 20, 2005, from http://support.microsoft.com/default.aspx?scid=kb;en-us;827419

Appendix Section

Appendix A:
Performance Tuning Guidelines

Performance tuning guidelines for a Web server (Apache), a database (Oracle), and an object oriented technology (Java) are presented here. The guidelines are not standards in themselves, but care has been taken to make it a reliable set of guidelines.

A.1. Apache Web Server

Concerns with Hardware and Operating Systems

One of the major issues affecting Web server performance is Random Access Memory (RAM). A Web server should never have to swap, as swapping increases the latency of each request. This causes users to hit refresh, which further increases the load. It is necessary to control the maximum number of clients so that your server does not spawn many child processes. This can be done by determining the size of average process list and dividing this into the total available memory, leaving some room for other processes. Next get CPU, a network card, and the disks, where the speed of each has to be determined by experimentation.

Tuning Apache http(s) d.conf

Once compilation and installation of Apache is behind us, the tuning of the server is done via the file httpd.conf (or httpsd.conf if you have included SSL).

Parameter	Description
MaxClients	When Apache starts up, it creates a number of HTTPD processes to handle requests for Web pages. The creation and deletion of these are controlled by the root httpd process and are dependent on the load on the Web server and other parameters in httpd.conf. MaxClients sets the limit on the number of httpd processes that a machine can create. This is to stop a heavily loaded Web server from taking up more and more resources from the host machine. The MaxClients directive sets the limit on the number of simultaneous requests that can be supported; no more than this number of child server processes will be created. To configure more than 256 clients, the HARD_SERVER_LIMIT entry must be edited in httpd.h and recompiled.
MaxRequestsPerChild	When there are more requests than processes, the server will spawn new child processes to handle the requests (assuming, of course the hard limit of MaxClients has not been reached). After MaxRequestsPerChild requests, the child process will die. If MaxRequestsPerChild is 0, then the process will never expire. Setting MaxRequestsPerChild to a non-zero limit has beneficial effects; it limits the amount of memory that the process can consume by memory leakage and by giving processes a finite lifetime, it helps reduce the number of processes when the server load reduces.
MinSpareServers	The MinSpareServers set the minimum number of idle child server processes. An idle process is one which is not handling a request. If there are fewer than MinSpareServers idle, then the parent process creates new children at a maximum rate of 1 per second. Tuning of this parameter should only be necessary on very active sites. Setting this parameter to a very large number is almost always a bad idea. This directive has no effect on Microsoft Windows.
StartServers	The StartServers set the number of child processes on the server which are created at startup. As the number of processes is dynamically controlled depending on the load, there is usually little reason to adjust this parameter. When running under Microsoft Windows, this directive has no effect. There is always one child which handles all requests. Within the child, requests are handled by separate threads. The ThreadsPerChild (the maximum number of connections the server can handle at once) controls the maximum number of child threads handling requests, which will have a similar effect on the setting of StartServers on UNIX.
MaxKeepAliveRequests	The MaxKeepAliveRequests limits the number of requests allowed per connection when KeepAlive (enables HTTP persistent connections) is on. If it is set to 0, unlimited requests will be allowed. It is recommended that this setting be kept to a high value for best server performance (Liam Holohan).

Additional Sources

Dean Gaudet of apache software foundation. Retrieved October 15, 2004, from httpd.apache.org/docs/misc/perf-tuning.html

Liam Holohan. Retrieved October 12, 2004, from http://www.smartframeworks.com/qt-apache-perf.html

A2. Structured Query Language (SQL)

The purpose of this document is to provide valuable tips pertaining to writing SQL queries and to make them work more efficiently and enhance performance. This is applicable to all commonly available databases.

Structure of Tables Used in this Document

The two tables that have been used to prepare this document are:

Table 1. dwtable1 (This table contains 2, 00,000 rows as test data)

Field Name	Data Type
IDNO	NUMBER(6)
IDNAME	VARCHAR2(20)
PARTNUM	VARCHAR2(10)
SPECNUM	VARCHAR2(10)

Table 2. dwtable2 (This table contains 1,00,000 rows as test data)

Name	Data Type
EMPNO	NUMBER(6)
ENAME	VARCHAR2(10)
SAL	NUMBER(6)
LOC	VARCHAR2(10)

Hardware Specifications

The configuration of the Oracle Server is:

Processor Type: P4 (1.6 GHz)

Operating System: Microsoft Windows 2000

RAM: 256MB

SQL Tuning Examples

The following examples have been executed using Oracle 8i. The term "Elapsed" in the examples below indicate the time taken by the query to execute and is displayed in the clock format (Hours: Minutes: Seconds). The time taken by the query to execute is dependent on many factors like query complexity, table structure, system load, database used, and so forth.

1.   **Concatenation of Different Data Types**

An SQL query involving concatenation of different datatypes takes more time to execute.

Example:

SELECT * FROM dwtable2 WHERE empno||ename='1234name1234';

Elapsed: 00:00:00.66

The same query can be effectively written as:

SELECT * FROM dwtable2 WHERE empno=1234 AND ename='name1234';

Elapsed: 00:00:00.19

2.   Usage of "WHERE" Instead of "HAVING"

Using a "where" clause in place of "having" is often effective, in group by statements. The where clause is applied before selecting the data, whereas the having clause is applied after data retrieval.

Example:

SELECT count(*) FROM dwtable2 GROUP BY empno HAVING empno=7890;

Elapsed: 00:00:01.59

The same query can be effectively written as:

SELECT count(*) FROM dwtable2 WHERE empno=7890 GROUP BY empno;

Elapsed: 00:00:00.03

3.   Position of Table with Fewer Rows in the "SELECT...FROM" Query

It is advisable to put the table that returns the fewest rows at the end of the from list.

Example:

SELECT count(*) FROM dwtable2,dwtable1 WHERE rownum<=10

Elapsed: 00:00:04.53

The same query can be effectively written as:

SELECT count(*) FROM dwtable1,dwtable2 WHERE rownum<=10;

Elapsed: 00:00:01.81

4.   Usage of "BETWEEN" in Place of Comparison Operators

If a query involves a range of values to be searched on, then usage of "between" is advisable over the comparison operators.

Example:

SELECT * FROM dwtable1 WHERE idno >= 200 AND idno<=300

101 rows selected.
Elapsed: 00:00:01.84

The same query could be more effectively written as:

SELECT * from dwtable1 WHERE idno BETWEEN 200 AND 300;

101 rows selected.
Elapsed: 00:00:01.10

5.   Usage of Table Aliases

If more than one table is used in a query, then it is advisable to use table aliases, as they would enhance the speed of the parse phase of the query.

Example:

SELECT idno, empno FROM dwtable1,dwtable2 WHERE table1.idno = dwtable2.empno AND dwtable2.empno<=100;

99 rows selected.
Elapsed: 00:00:01.62

The same query can be written more efficiently as:

```
SELECT idno,empno FROM dwtable1 dt, dwtable2 ds WHERE dt.idno=ds.empno AND ds.empno<=100;
```

99 rows selected.

Elapsed: 00:00:01.18

6.   Usage of NOT or != Operators

Unless it is absolutely necessary, one should avoid the usage of != or NOT operators in SQL queries.

Whenever these operators are used, a FTS (Full Table Scan) is done.

7.   Usage of Index or Indexes

Index enables faster retrieval of data, but is an overhead when insertion, updating, and deletion processes are involved.

The index is a separate structure attached to a table. This structure holds the indexed column value and a pointer to the physical data.

Hence, any query which involves searching based on indexes would first access the index structure and then would retrieve the data from the respective table.

But if the table contains more than 4 to 5 indexes, then the performance comes down.

The selectivity for index is determined by the ratio of unique values in a given column to the total number of values.

If the value is nearer to 0, then usage of index is not advisable.

If the value is nearer to 1, then usage of index would enhance the performance of the system.

8.   Materialized Views

A view is a window to the table. The view does not store data.

Whenever an operation involving a view is performed, two queries would be executed.

The first query would be the query involving the view, and the second one is the query contained in the view.

Example:

```
CREATE view view1 AS  SELECT  * FROM dwtable1;
```

View Created.

SELECT * FROM view1;

The above query, when executed, would further execute the query "select * from dwtable1" contained in the view.

Views are not meant for performance, as they degrade performance.

Hence, for performance, it is advisable to use Materialized Views.

9.   Usage of NULL

Null values are never stored in index structure.

Any query using the clause "IS NULL", does not make use of index and does a FTS (Full Table Scan), thereby taking more time to execute.

10.   Queries Using OR Clause

If two or more expressions use OR, put the least restrictive (which returns the most rows) expression first.

Oracle follows short circuit mode of evaluation in the case of conditional expressions.

In case of queries with the OR clause, if the first condition is satisfied, then it does not check the second condition.

11.   Resource Intensive Operations

Avoid using resource intensive operations like UNION, MINUS, DISTINCT, INTER-SECT, ORDER BY, and GROUP BY. DISTINCT uses one sort whereas other operators use two sorts or more.

12.   Usage of "ORDER BY"

Avoid "ORDER BY" wherever possible as it works on output of the query and hence involves double processing. The exception is if any of the columns to be sorted in DESC order are wanted.

13.   Usage of "EXISTS" and "NOT EXISTS" Clauses

Wherever it is possible,"EXISTS" or "NOT EXISTS" should be used. Using the "EXISTS" clause may eliminate unnecessary table accesses.

14.   Usage of Functions

Using functions in the where clause suppresses the use of indexes.

Example:

SELECT * FROM dwtable2 WHERE to_number(empno)=783;

Elapsed: 00:00:00.15 This query could be written more efficiently as:

SELECT * FROM dwtable2 WHERE empno=783;

Elapsed: 00:00:00.01

References

Guidelines and Good Practice Guide for Developing SQL by Tina London.

A3. Performance Tuning Parameters for Oracle DBA

The Oracle database is commonly used in most of the application. The following table provides tuning guidelines for various parameters. The guidelines also provide suggested values for certain parameters, which help the designer during testing.

Parameter	Default Value	Range	Description	Significance	Suggested value
DB_BLOCK_BUFFER /DB_CACHE_SIZE	48M	OS Dependent	Size of the buffer cache in the System Global Area (SGA)	Make sure cache-miss ratio is low	Typical values are in the range of 20 to 50 per user session. More often, this value is set too high than too low. Having an insufficient number of block buffers results in higher than normal I/O rates and possibly an I/O bottleneck
				The ratio of PHYSICAL READS to DB BLOCK GETS and CONSISTENT GETS is the cache-miss ratio	
DB_BLOCK_SIZE	2048	2048 to 32768	Specifies the size (in bytes) of Oracle database blocks	As OLTP transactions are small in nature and simultaneous 2k is sufficient	4
DB_FILE_MULTIBLO CK_READ_COUNT	8	OS Dependent	It specifies the maximum number of blocks read in one I/O operation during a sequential scan	Used to minimize I/O during table scans	4 to 16
DISK_ASYNCH_IO	TRUE	True/False	These parameters enable or disable the operating system's asynchronous I/O facility	It allows query server processes to overlap I/O requests with processing when performing table scans	TRUE
DB_WRITER_PROCE SSES (see PBM2004)	1	1 to 10	It specifies the initial number of database writer processes for an instance	It is useful for systems that modify data heavily	The value should be set to high for applications that require frequent and heavy updates to database
DML_LOCKS	(4 * TRANSACTIONS)	20 to unlimited; a setting of 0 disables enqueues	DML_LOCKS specifies the maximum number of DML locks	One for each table modified in a transaction	For the value of 0, enqueues are disabled and performance is slightly increased

Parameter	Default Value	Range	Description	Significance	Suggested value
ENQUEUE_RESOUR CES	Derived from SESSIONS parameter	10 to unlimited	This one sets the number of resources that can be concurrently locked by the lock manager		If sessions <= 3
					Database files + 20
					If Sessions <> 4 to10
					Database files + ((SESSIONS - 3) * 5) + 20
					If sessions > 10
					Database files + ((SESSIONS - 10) * 2) + 55
DISTRIBUTED_TRAN SACTIONS	0.25 * TRANSACTIONS	0 to the value of the TRANSACTIONS parameter	It specifies the maximum number of distributed transactions in which this database can participate at one time	The value of this parameter	Cannot exceed the value of the parameter TRANSACTIONS
Parameter	**Default Value**	**Range**	**Description**	**Significance**	**Suggested value**
MAX_DUMP_FILE_SI ZE (see LLA2004))	UNLIMITED	0 to unlimited, or UNLIMITED	Specifies the maximum size of trace files (excluding alert files)	The dump files could be as large as OS permits	Change this limit if trace files use too much space
OPEN_CURSORS	50	1 to 4294967295 (4 GB -1)	It specifies the maximum number of open cursors a session can have at once	Can use this parameter to prevent a session from opening an excessive number of cursors. Application dependent	Set the value of OPEN_CURSORS high enough
OPTIMIZER_MODE	choose	Rule/choose/ first_rows_n/ first_rows/ all_rows	It establishes the default behavior for choosing an optimization approach for the instance		
PARALLEL_ADAPTIV E_MULTI_USER	Derived from the value of PARALLEL_AUTO MATIC_TUNING	True/False	When set to true, enables an adaptive algorithm designed to improve performance in multiuser environments that use parallel execution	The algorithm automatically reduces the requested degree of parallelism based on the system load at query startup time. The effective degree of parallelism is based on the default degree of parallelism, or the degree from the table or hints, divided by a reduction factor	TRUE

Parameter	Default Value	Range	Description	Significance	Suggested value
PARALLEL_BROADC AST_ENABLED	FALSE	TRUE/FALSE	PARALLEL_BROADC AST_ENABLED lets improve performance of hash and merge join operations		Set it to True for Joins
PARALLEL_MAX_SE RVERS	Derived from the values of CPU_COUNT, PARALLEL_AUTO MATIC_TUNING, and PARALLEL_ADAP TIVE_MULTI_USE R	0 to 3599	It specifies the maximum number of parallel execution processes and parallel recovery processes for an instance	As demand increases, Oracle increases the number of processes from the number created at instance startup up to this value	If set, this parameter is set to very low value; some queries may not have a parallel execution process available to them during query processing. If set to a very high value, memory resource shortages may occur during peak periods, which can degrade performance
PARALLEL_MIN_SE RVERS (see CUE2004)	0	0 to value of PARALLEL_MAX_ SERVERS	It specifies the minimum number of parallel execution processes for the instance	This value is the number of parallel execution processes Oracle creates when the instance is started	Recommended value is 0
PARTITION_VIEW_E NABLED (see OBO2004)	FALSE	True/False	Specifies whether the optimizer uses partition views or not	If set to True, the Optimizer skips unnecessary table access in a partition view	

Parameter	Default Value	Range	Description	Significance	Suggested value
PROCESSES (see CUD2004)	Derived from PARALLEL_MAX_SERVERS	6 to OS Dependent	It specifies the maximum number of operating system user processes that can simultaneously connect to Oracle	Depending Parameters	Application requirement
				Sessions	
				Transactions	
SESSIONS (see CUO2004)	(1.1 * PROCESSES) + 5	1 to 231	It specifies the maximum number of sessions that can be created in the system	Depending Parameters: ENQUEUE_RESOURCES and TRANSACTIONS	Set this parameter explicitly to a value equivalent to the estimated maximum number of concurrent users, plus the number of background processes, plus approximately 10% for recursive sessions
SHARED_POOL_SIZE (see CUS2004)	For 64-bit platform, 64 MB, 32-bit platform, 8MB	300 KB to OS Dependent	It contains shared cursors, stored procedures, control structures, and other structures	When "Misses Ratio" is greater than 1% or "Hit Ratio" is less than 99% or Dictionary cache "Ratio" is greater than 10%, increase this value	Larger values improve performance in multiuser systems. Smaller values use less memory.
SORT_AREA_SIZE	65536	6 Database blocks to OS dependent	Specifies in bytes the maximum amount of memory Oracle will use for a sort	Increasing SORT_AREA_SIZE Size improves the efficiency of large sorts	Application dependent
Parameter	Default Value	Range	Description	Significance	Suggested value
TRANSACTIONS_PER_ROLLBACK_SEGMENT (see CID2004)	5	1 to OS Dependant	It specifies the number of concurrent transactions that each rollback segment to have to handle	Check for Rollback contention by observing V$WAITSTAT table	Can acquire more rollback segments by naming them in the parameter ROLLBACK_SEGMENTS
			Segment to have handle		
				Adjust this value accordingly	
STAR_TRANSFORMATION_ENABLED (see CSU2004)	FALSE	TEMP_DISABLE/TRUE/FALSE	It determines whether a cost-based query transformation will be applied to star queries	If value is True, the optimizer will consider performing a cost-based query transformation on the star query	

PGA_AGGREGATE_TARGET (see CHD2004)	0	10 MB to 4096 GB -1	It specifies the target aggregate PGA memory available to all server processes attached to the instance	Increasing the value of this parameter, indirectly increases the memory allotted to work areas	While setting this parameter, examine the total memory of the system that is available to the Oracle instance and subtract the SGA. Then assign the remaining memory to PGA_AGGREGATE_TARGET
				Consequently, more memory-intensive operations are able to run fully in memory and less will work their way over to disk	
PARALLEL_AUTOMATIC_TUNING (see CFD2004)	FALSE	FALSE/TRUE	When set to TRUE, Oracle determines the default values for parameters that control parallel execution	In addition to setting this parameter, specify the PARALLEL clause for the target tables in the system	

Parameter	Default Value	Range	Description	Significance	Suggested value
CURSOR_SPACE_F OR_TIME	FALSE	FALSE/TRUE	Allows usage of more space for cursors in order to save time	Able to access the shared SQL areas faster	When the shared pool is large enough to hold all open cursors simultaneously, set this value to TRUE
				It affects both the shared SQL area and the client's private SQL area	
ROLLBACK_SEGME NTS	Public rollback segments	Any rollback segment names listed in DBA_ROLLBACK_ SEGS except SYSTEM	While setting this parameter, the instance acquires all of the rollback segments named in this parameter, even if the number of rollback segments exceeds the minimum number required by the instance	Cannot change the value of this parameter dynamically, but can change its value and then restart the instance	
				When UNDO_MANAGEME NT is set to AUTO, ROLLBACK_SEGME NTS is ignored	
MAX_ROLLBACK_SE GMENTS (see CEE2004)	MAX(30, TRANSACTIONS/T RANSACTIONS_P ER_ROLLBACK_S EGMENT)	2 to 65535	MAX_ROLLBACK_SE GMENTS specifies the maximum size of the rollback segment cache in the SGA	The number specified signifies the maximum number of rollback segments that can be kept online (that is, status of ONLINE) simultaneously by one instance	Keep it high
LOG_SMALL_ENT RY_MAX_SIZE (see PIO2004)	80		LOG_SMALL_ENT RY_MAX_SIZE specifies the size in bytes of the largest copy to the log buffers that can occur under the REDO allocation latch.	Look for the ratio of MISSES to GETS in V$LATCH.	If miss ratio is high, minimize the value of this parameter

UNDO_MANAGEME NT	MANUAL	MANUAL/AUTO	UNDO_MANAGEMENT specifies which undo space management mode the system should use	When set to AUTO, the instance starts in automatic undo management mode. In manual undo management mode, undo space is allocated externally as rollback segments.	AUTO
UNDO_RETENTION (see CSL2004)	900Seconds	0 to 232-1 (max value represented by 32 bits)	It specifies (in seconds) the amount of committed undo information to retain in the database	Use UNDO_RETENTIO N to satisfy queries that require old undo information to rollback changes to produce older images of data blocks	Set it to the duration of the longest running query
					Allocate sufficient space for the Undo tablespace
CURSOR_SHARING	EXACT	FORCE/SIMILA R/EXACT	It determines what kind of SQL statements can share the same cursors	For large applications that do not use bind variables, cursor sharing can be enforced by setting the initialization parameter CURSOR_SHARIN G=FORCE	FORCE

References

(CEE2004). Retrieved December 17, 2004, from http://www.cise.ufl.edu/help/database/ oracle-docs/server.920/a96536/ch1111.htm

(CFD2004). Retrieved December 17, 2004, from http://www.cise.ufl.edu/help/database/ oracle-docs/server.920/a96536/ch1150.htm

(CHD2004). Retrieved December 17, 2004, from http://www.cise.ufl.edu/help/database/ oracle-docs/server.920/a96536/ch1158.htm

(CID2004). Retrieved December 17, 2004, from http://www.cise.ufl.edu/help/database/ oracle-docs/server.920/a96536/ch1214.htm

(CSL2004). Retrieved December 17, 2004, from http://www.cise.ufl.edu/help/database/ oracle-docs/server.920/a96536/ch1216.htm

(CSU2004). Retrieved December 17, 2004, from http://www.cise.ufl.edu/help/database/ oracle-docs/server.920/a96536/ch1204.htm

(CUD2004). Retrieved December 17, 2004, from http://www.cise.ufl.edu/help/database/ oracle-docs/server.920/a96536/ch1158.htm

(CUE2004). Retrieved December 17, 2004, from http://www.csee.umbc.edu/help/oracle8/ server.815/a67775/ch24_pex.htm#43059

(CUO2004). Retrieved December 17, 2004, from http://www.cise.ufl.edu/help/database/ oracle-docs/server.920/a96536/ch1189.htm

(CUS2004). Retrieved December 17, 2004, from http://www.cise.ufl.edu/help/database/ oracle-docs/server.920/a96536/ch1194.htm

(LLA2004). Retrieved December 17, 2004, from http://www.lc.leidenuniv.nl/awcourse/ oracle/server.920/a96536/ch1109.htm

(OBO2004). Retrieved December 17, 2004, from http://oracle.basisconsultant.com/ oracle_tuning_parameters.htm

(PBM2004). Retrieved December 17, 2004, from http://publib.boulder.ibm.com/tividd/td/ tec/SC32-1233-00/en_US/HTML/ecoimst96.html

(PIO2004). Retrieved December 17, 2004, from http://www.performance-insight.com/ html/ora3/back/REDOlog_14.html

A4. Java Technology

Java Technology is most commonly used in present day development of Web applications. Here an attempt has been made to provide a set of guidelines while writing Java code during development.

A4.1. Guidelines for Writing Java Code

1. Wherever possible, use local variables in preference to class variables.

2. Recycling of objects is one of the best ways to improve the performance (Object Pooling).

3. While performing arithmetic operations in Java,

    a. Compound assignment operators such as n += 4; these are faster than n = n + 4 because fewer bytecodes are generated. But this will be at the cost of readability.

    b. Multiplication is faster than exponential calculation.

4. Avoid premature flushing of buffers as it reduces performance.

5. Usage of StringBuffer is better when dealing with changing strings, especially when there are string concatenations. Always initialize the StringBuffer with proper size.

6. Performance is reduced if there is any premature object creation, so create the required object as and when required.

7. Thread usage should try to match the resources available to the system. One CPU-intensive thread per CPU is probably optimal (non-CPU intensive threads do not count in this scenario).

8. Four types of drivers that are supported by JDBC are:

    Type 1: JDBC-ODBC Bridge

    Type 2: Native-API/partly Java driver

    Type 3: Net-protocol/all-Java driver

    Type 4: Native-protocol/all-Java driver

    Type 2 and Type 4 Drivers are most used for software development because of their performance.

9. Usage of JDBC Connection Pool in J2EE applications is a must. When connection pooling is used, a set of connections are kept open by the server for the application to use, which in turn increases the performance.

10. Must close the connection once the usage is complete or else connections that are not closed can lead to multiple unused connections (Connection leak) to the database server and will reduce the performance.

11. When it comes to performance issues concerning JDBC programming, there are two major factors to consider: performance of the database structure and the SQL statements used against it.

12. For relative efficiency of the different methods, one can use the JDBC interfaces to manipulate a database.

13. By default, JDBC's auto-commit feature is set on; a small performance increase can be achieved by turning off auto-commit. This way one can ensure that the commit occurs after all the transactions are complete, instead of doing it after every statement.

14. Use prepared statements.

15. A prepared statement object has to verify its metadata against the database once, while a statement has to do it every time. The fact is that statement takes about 65 iterations of a prepared statement before its total time for execution catches up with a statement. This will have performance implications for the application. Hence, using a Prepared Statement object is advisable as it is faster than using a Statement object.

16. SQL is always sent to the database server as a character string, for example, "{call getempNumber (5467)}". In this case, even though the application programmer might assume that the only argument to getempNumber is an integer, the argument is actually passed inside a character string to the server. The database server would parse the SQL query, consult database metadata to determine the parameter contract of the procedure, isolate the single argument value 12345, then convert the string '5467' into an integer value before finally executing the procedure as an SQL language event.

17. Use stored procedures.

18. Cache data to avoid repeated queries.

A4.2. Performance Guidelines for EJB and Servlet Based Application Development

1. Using large objects will produce large serialization overhead. For instance, we should not store large object graphs in javax.servlet.http.HttpSession. Servlets may need to serialize and deserialize HttpSession objects for persistent sessions.

2. Use the tag "<%@ page session="false"%>" to avoid creating HttpSessions in JSPs.

3. Synchronization in Servlets should be minimal; this is to avoid multiple execution threads becoming effectively single-threaded.

4. Avoid the use of javax.servlet.SingleThreadModel if the intended users are many. The Web server servlet engine handles the servlet's reentrance problem by creating separate servlet instances for each user. This causes a great amount of system overhead and hence SingleThreadModel should be avoided. Developers typically use javax.servlet.SingleThreadModel (deprecated in latest API) to protect updateable servlet instances in a multithreaded environment. A much better approach would be to avoid using servlet instance variables that are updated from the servlet service method.

5. Use the HttpServlet's init method to perform expensive operations that have to be done only once.

6. Access entity beans from session beans, not from client or servlet code.

7. Use Read-Only methods where appropriate in entity-beans to avoid unnecessary invocations to store.

8. The EJB "remote programming" model always assumes EJB calls are remote, even where this is not so. Where calls are actually local to the same JVM, try to use calling mechanisms that avoid the remote call.

9. Remove stateful session beans (and any other unneeded objects) when finished to avoid extra overhead in case the container needs to be passivated.

10. Beans.instantiate() incurs a file system check to create new bean instances. Use "new" to avoid this overhead.

Additional Sources

Harvey W. Gunther. Retrieved October 15, 2004, from http://www.javaperformancetuning.com/tips/j2ee.shtml

Patrik. Retrieved October 15, 2004, from http://patrick.net/jpt

Performance Guidelines while using Java Database Connectivity (JDBC). Retrieved November 15, 2004, from http:// www .oreilly .com/ catalog/jorajdbc/chapter/ch19.html

A5: .NET Coding Guidelines

The concept of Object Oriented Programming using C# in the .NET framework calls for a different environment programming. The CLR provides many features such as automatic memory management, type safety, and exception handling as part of the framework. Apart from this, there could be some coding pitfalls like any other programming languages. Some of these are addressed in the following sections with possible coding guidelines for the same.

Guidelines for Garbage Collection

Garbage collection (GC) is how the Common Language Runtime (CLR) frees memory occupied by objects that are no longer referenced. It is common to think of objects that have active references as being "alive" and unreferenced (or unreachable) objects as "dead." Garbage collection is the process of releasing memory used by the dead objects. This section provides recommendations to help improve garbage collection (see DJG2005) performance.

- **Identify and Analyze the Application's Allocation Profile**

  Object size, number of objects, and object lifetime are all factors that impact the application's allocation profile.

  To identify when allocations occur and which generations they occur in, application's allocation patterns are to be observed by using an allocation profiler such as the CLR Profiler.

- **Avoid Calling GC.Collect**

  The default GC.Collect method causes a full collection of all generations. Full collections are expensive because literally every live object in the system must be visited to ensure complete collection. As a result, do not call GC.Collect directly and let the garbage collector determine when it needs to run.

  The garbage collector is designed to be self-tuning. Programmatically forcing collection can hinder tuning and operation of the garbage collector.

  If GC.Collect is to be called at all, it is called in the following way:

  Call GC.WaitForPendingFinalizers after GC.Collect is called. This ensures that the current thread waits until finalizers for all objects are called.

  After the finalizers run, there are more dead objects (those that were just finalized) that need to be collected. One more call to GC.Collect collects the remaining dead objects.

- **Using Weak References**

  Use weak references mostly for objects that are not small in size because the weak referencing itself involves some overhead. They are suitable for medium to large sized objects stored in a collection.

  Consider using weak references when there is a need to work with cached data, so that cached objects can be reused again easily if needed or released by garbage collection when there is memory pressure.

- **Prevent the Promotion of Short Lived Objects**

  Objects that are allocated and collected before leaving Gen 0 are referred as *short lived objects*.

  The following principles help ensure that short lived objects are not promoted:

  ➤ Do not reference short lived objects from long lived objects

  Example: Assigning a local object to a class level object reference.

  ➤ Avoid implementing a Finalize method

  The garbage collector must promote finalizable objects to older generations to facilitate finalization, which makes them long lived objects.

> ➢ Avoid having finalizable objects refer to anything

This can cause the referenced object(s) to become long-lived.

- **Set Unneeded Member Variables to Null before Making Long Running Calls**

> ➢ If there is no need for a static variable in a class, or some other class, set it to null.
> ➢ If there are any objects that could be disposed before the long running call, set those to null.
> ➢ Do not set local variables to null (C#) because the JIT compiler can statically determine that the variable is no longer referenced and there is no need to explicitly set it to null. The following code shows an example using local variables.

```
void func(  )
{
String str1;
str1=abc;
// Avoid this
str1=null;
}
```

- **Minimize Hidden Allocations**

  Memory allocation is extremely quick because it involves only a pointer relocation to create space for the new object. However, the memory has to be garbage collected at some point and that can affect the performance.

- **Avoid or Minimize Complex Object Graphs**

  Avoid using complex data structures or objects that contain a lot of references to other objects. These can be expensive to allocate and create additional work for the garbage collector. A common mistake is to make the graphs too general.

- **Avoid Preallocating and Chunking Memory**

  If memory is preallocated, it may cause more allocations than needed; this could result in unnecessary garbage collections (see MMS2005).

Guidelines for Finalize and Dispose

Finalization is a service used to clean the processing by the GC. This is often used for releasing unmanaged resources like filehandles, database connections, and COM interfaces. Finalize is a method used to implement the finalization service.

The dispose method is used for types that contain references to external resources like bitmap or databases that need to be explicitly freed by the calling code.

This section suggests recommendations in usage of Finalize and Dispose.

- **Call Close or Dispose on Classes that Support It**

  If the managed class uses Close or Dispose, then one of these methods is called as soon as it is finished with the object.

Some of the common disposable resources for the corresponding classes are given in Table A5.1.

Table A5.1. Classes and disposable resources

Classes	Disposable Resources
Database related	Connection, Data Reader, and Transaction.
File based	FileStream and BinaryWriter.
Stream based	StreamReader, TextReader, TextWriter, BinaryReader, and TextWriter.
Network based	Socket, UdpClient, and TcpClient.

- **The Using Statement in C#**

  The using statement in C# automatically generates a try and finally block at compile time that calls Dispose on the object allocated inside the using block.

- **Do Not Implement Finalize Unless Required**

  Implementing a finalizer on classes that do not require it adds to the finalizer thread and the garbage collector. Avoid implementing a finalizer or destructor unless finalization is required.

- **Implement Finalize Only If there Is Unmanaged Resources across Client Calls**

  Use a finalizer only on objects that hold unmanaged resources across client calls.

  For instance, if an object has only one method named GetData, that opens a connection, fetches data from an unmanaged resource, closes the connection, and returns data; there is no need to implement a finalizer.

- **Move the Finalization Burden to the Leaves of Object Graphs**

  If an object graph with an object referencing other objects (leaves) holds unmanaged resources, finalizers should be implemented in the leaf objects instead of in the root object.

  Moving the finalization burden to leaf objects results in the promotion of only the relevant ones to the finalization queue, which helps in optimizing the finalization process.

  IDisposable should be implemented if the finalizer is implemented. In this way, the calling code has an explicit way to free resources by calling the Dispose method.

The finalizer should be implemented along with the Dispose because one cannot assume that the calling code always calls Dispose. Although costly, the finalizer implementation ensures that resources are released.

- **Suppress Finalization in Dispose Method**

  The purpose of providing a Dispose method is to allow the calling code to release unmanaged resources as soon as possible and to prevent two cycles being taken for the object's cleanup.

- **Allow Dispose to Be Called Multiple Times**

  Calling code should be able to safely call Dispose multiple times without causing exceptions.

- **Call Dispose on Base Classes and on IDisposable Members**

  If the class inherits from a disposable class, then make sure that it calls the base class's Dispose.

- **Provide Thread Safe Cleanup Code Only if User Type is Thread Safe**

  If user type is thread safe, make sure user cleanup code is also thread safe. One must be ensured to synchronize threads calling Close and Dispose simultaneously.

Guidelines for Asynchronous Execution

Asynchronous calls provide a mechanism for increasing the concurrency of the application. Asynchronous calls are nonblocking and occur when a method is called asynchronously. This section suggests guidelines for optimized performance during asynchronous execution.

- **Consider Client Side Asynchronous Calls for UI Responsiveness**

  Asynchronous calls can be used to increase the responsiveness of client applications. Because asynchronous calls introduce additional programming complexity and hence require careful synchronization logic to be added to the application's graphical interface code.

- **Use Asynchronous Methods on the Server for I/O Bound Operations**

  Performance of the application is increased by executing multiple operations at the same time whenever the operations are not dependent on each other.

- **Avoid Asynchronous Calls That Do Not Add Parallelism**

  Since the calling code blocks while waiting for the Web service call to complete, avoid asynchronous calls that do not add parallelism.

Guidelines for Locking and Synchronization

Locking and synchronization provide a method to grant exclusive access to data or code to avoid concurrent execution. This section provides guidelines to consider when developing multithreaded code that requires locks and synchronization:

- **Acquire Locks Late and Release Them Early**

  Acquire a lock on the resource just before it is needed to access it and release the lock immediately after one is finished with it.

- **Avoid Locking and Synchronization Unless Required**

  Synchronization requires extra processing by the CLR to grant exclusive access to resources. If there is no multithreaded access to data or require thread synchronization, do not implement it.

- **Use Granular Locks to Reduce Contention**

  When used properly and at the appropriate level of granularity, locks provide greater concurrency by reducing contention.

- **Avoid Excessive Fine Grained Locks**

  Fine grained locks protect either a small amount of data or a small amount of code. When used properly, they provide greater concurrency by reducing lock contention. Used improperly, they can add to the complexity of the application and may also decrease the performance and concurrency.

- **Avoid Making Thread Safety the Default for User Type**

  When a specific class is designed, the proper level of atomicity may not be known to the class designer, especially for lower level classes. Thread safety is required at the higher layer of the software architecture and not always at an individual class level.

Guidelines for Exception Management

This section provides recommendations which aid in the usage of Exception Management for performance. Exceptions add significant overhead to an application. If the application does not handle an exception, it propagates up the stack. If it is an ASP.NET application exception, it will be handled by the ASP.NET exception handler. When handling exception, consider the following:

- **Do Not Use Exceptions to Control Application Flow**

  Throwing exceptions is expensive. Do not use exceptions to control application flow. If one can reasonably expect a sequence of events to happen in the normal course of running code, then one probably should not throw any exceptions in that scenario.

- **Use Validation Code to Reduce Unnecessary Exceptions**

  If it is known that a specific avoidable condition can happen, proactively write code to avoid it.

- **Use the Finally Block to Ensure Resources are Released**

  For both correctness and performance reasons, it is good practice to make sure all expensive resources are released in a suitable finally block. The reason for this is a performance issue as well as a correctness issue as timely release of expensive resources is often critical to meet performance objectives.

- **Do Not Catch Exceptions That Cannot Be Handled**

  Exceptions are not caught unless they are specifically required to record and log the exception details.

- **Be Aware That Rethrowing is Expensive**

  The cost of using throw to rethrow an existing exception is approximately the same as throwing a new exception.

Guidelines for Iterating and Looping

Iteration and Looping, if not used properly or not optimized, there would be increased memory consumption resulting in exhausting CPU. The following guidelines give an idea to utilize the looping statement and iterative constructs for better performance.

- **Avoid Repetitive Field or Property Access**

  If one uses the data that is static for the duration of the loop, it should be obtained before the loop instead of repeatedly accessing a field or property.

- **Optimize or Avoid Expensive Operations within Loops**

  Identify operations in the loop code that can be optimized. Look for code that causes boxing or allocations as a side effect.

- **Copy Frequently Called Code into the Loop**

  Instead of repeating the code at several points in the program, put it in the loop and execute. This is normally used in database applications.

- **Consider Replacing Recursion with Looping**

  Recursion may impact the stack overflow and hence the program may crash. Therefore, replace recursion with looping which has a definite end point for execution.

- **Use "for" Instead of "for each" in Performance Critical Code Paths**

    Tuning Guidelines for String Operations

This section summarizes recommendations to help improve the usage of string and string functions.

- **Avoid Inefficient String Concatenation**

  - ➤ Excessive string concatenation results in many allocation and deallocation operations because each time an operation is performed to change the string, a new one is created and the old one is subsequently collected by the garbage collector

  - ➤ Concatenation of nonliteral strings is done by the CLR at run time. So using the + operator creates multiple strings objects in the managed heap

  - ➤ Note that concatenation of string literals is done by compiler at compile time

  - ➤ Use StringBuilder for complex string manipulations and when it is needed to concatenate strings multiple times

  - ➤ Use + When the Number of Appends Is Known

  - ➤ Do Not use + on strings inside a loop or for multiple iterations. Use StringBuilder instead

  - ➤ Treat StringBuilder as an Accumulator

  - ➤ Use the Overloaded Compare Method for case insensitive string Comparisons

  - ➤ Avoid using ToLower because one could end up creating temporary string objects. The String.Compare method uses the info in the CultureInfo.Compare Info property to compare culture sensitive strings

Arrays and Collection Performance Guidelines

This section provides recommendations to help improve the usage of Arrays and Collections.

- **Prefer Arrays to Collections Unless Needed for Functionality**

  Arrays perform faster than collections, and Arrays also avoid the boxing and unboxing overhead.

- **Use Strongly Typed Arrays**

  Avoid using object arrays to store types; instead use strongly typed arrays for maximum extent, which results in avoiding type conversion or boxing, depending upon the type stored in the array.

- **Use Jagged Arrays Instead of Multidimensional Arrays**

  - ➤ A jagged array is a single dimensional array of arrays. The elements of a jagged array can be of different dimensions and sizes. Use jagged arrays instead of multidimensional arrays to benefit from Microsoft Intermediate Language (MSIL) performance optimizations.

- **While sorting the collection, the following are to be considered:**

  - ➤ Use ArrayList to bind the read only sorted data to a data grid as a data source. This is better than using a SortedList if it is required to bind read-only data using the indexes in the ArrayList. The data are retrieved in an ArrayList and sorted for display.

  - ➤ Use SortedList for sorting data that is mostly static and needs to be updated only infrequently.

  - ➤ Use NameValueCollection for sorting strings.

  - ➤ SortedList presorts the data while constructing the collection. This results in a comparatively expensive creation process for the sorted list, but all updates to the existing data and any small additions to the list are automatically and efficiently reported as the changes are made. Sortedlist is suitable for mostly static data with minor updates.

  - ➤ If it is required to search the collection, do the following:

    - ○ Use Hashtable if the search is on collection randomly based on a key/value pair

    - ○ Use StringDictionary for random searches on string data

    - ○ Use ListDictionary for sizes less than 10

  - ➤ If it is needed to access each element by index, do the following:

    - ○ Use ArrayList and StringCollection for zero based index access to the data

  - ➤ Use Hashtable, SortedList, ListDictionary, and StringDictionary to access elements by specifying the name of the key.

  - ➤ Use NameValueCollection to access elements, either by using a zero-based index or specifying the key of the element.

While developing a user defined (custom) collection, the following guidelines are followed:

  - ➤ Since all standard collections are passed by value, it is better to develop user defined (custom) collection in order to marshal (pack and send) by reference

  - ➤ Create a strongly typed collection for user defined custom object to avoid the costs of upcasting or downcasting, or both (custom collections are needed, if one requires a read only collection. One can have it as a separate point)

➢ Strongly typed collection should have custom serializing behavior

➢ Cost of enumeration is to be reduced

- **Initialize Collections to the Right Size Whenever Possible**

➢ Initialize collections to the right size if it is known exactly, or even approximately, how many items needed to store in the collection; most collection types allow specification of the size with the constructor

➢ Even if the collection is able to be dynamically resized, it is more efficient to allocate the collection with the correct or approximate initial capacity

- **Consider "for" Instead of "foreach"**

➢ Use for instead of foreach (C#) to iterate the contents of arrays or collections in performance critical code, particularly if there is no need to have the protections offered by foreach

➢ foreach, in C#, uses an enumerator to provide enhanced navigation through arrays and collections

➢ If one can use the for statement to iterate over the collection, consider doing so in performance sensitive code to avoid that overhead

- **Implement Strongly Typed Collections to Prevent Casting Overhead**

➢ Implement strongly typed collections to prevent upcasting or downcasting overhead

➢ StringCollection and StringDictionary are examples of strongly typed collections for strings

Reflection and Late Binding

Reflection provides the ability to examine and compare types, enumerate methods and fields, and dynamically create and execute types at runtime. Even though all reflection costs are high, some reflection operations cost much more than others. The first (comparing types) is the least expensive, while the last (dynamically creating and executing) is the most expensive. This is accomplished by examining the metadata contained in assemblies. Many reflection APIs need to search and parse the metadata. This requires extra processing that should be avoided in performance critical code.

The late binding technique uses reflection internally and is an expensive operation that should be avoided in performance critical code.

This section provides recommendations to minimize the performance impact of reflection or late binding code.

- **Prefer Early Binding and Explicit Types Rather Than Reflection**

  In C#, reflection is used explicitly. Avoid reflection wherever possible by using early binding and declaring types explicitly.

The following operations are some examples that are performed when reflection in C# are used explicitly:

- ➤ Type comparisons using **TypeOf**, **GetType**, and **IsInstanceOfType**
- ➤ Late bound enumeration using **Type.GetFields**
- ➤ Late bound execution using **Type.InvokeMember**

- **Avoid Late Binding**

  Early binding allows the compiler to identify the specific type required and perform optimizations that are used at runtime. Late binding defers the type identification process until runtime and requires extra processing instructions to allow type identification and initialization. The following code loads a type at runtime.

```
Assembly asm = System.Reflection.Assembly.LoadFrom("C:\\myAssembly.dll");
Type myType = asm.GetType("myAssembly.MyTypeName");
Object myinstance = Activator.CreateInstance(myType);
The above code can be modified as:
MyTypeName myinstance = new MyTypeName();
```

In some cases, it is required to have dynamic execution of types, but when performance is critical, avoid late binding.

Data Access

The following are to be considered during the database related project.

Connections are used efficiently by following the below guidelines:

- Open and close the connection within the method
- Explicitly close connections using a finally or using block
- When using DataReaders, specify *CommandBehavior.CloseConnection*

- If using Fill or Update with a DataSet, do not explicitly open the connection. The Fill and Update methods automatically open and close the connection
- Creating database connections is expensive. It is reduced by pooling the database connections
- Pooling the connections are done by connecting to a database as a single identity rather than flowing the identity of original caller to the database. Flowing the caller's identity results in a separate connection pool for each user
- Changing the connection string even by adding an empty space creates a separate pool for that connection string
- To ensure that connection is promptly returned to the pool, Close or Dispose method should be called
- Ensure the pool size is set appropriately.

  ➤ It is important to optimize the maximum and minimum levels of the pool size to maximize the throughput for the application. If it is set to the maximum levels to values that are too high, it may end up creating deadlocks and heavy resource utilization on the database. If too low values are used, then there would be a risk of underutilizing the database and queuing up the requests
  ➤ Determine appropriate maximum and minimum values for the pool during performance testing and performance tuning

- Make sure that the code uses the correct data provider.

  ➤ Each database has a specific provider which is optimized for a particular database as shown in the Table A5.2

Table A5.2. Database provider with specific database

Database Provider	Database
System.Data.SqlClient	SQL Server 7.0 and later
System.Data.OleDb	SQL Server 6.5 or OLE DB providers
System.Data.ODBC	ODBC data sources
System.Data.Oracle.Client	Oracle
SQLXML managed classes	XML data and SQL Server 2000

Even though the database can be linked using compatible providers, it should be chosen appropriately depending on the database used in an application for better performance.

Design Considerations

One key factor affecting application performance is the application architecture and design. This section describes some design aspects of .NET applications for better performance.

General Design Considerations

This section describes the major design considerations to be considered when one designs managed code solutions.

- Design for Efficient Resource Management
- Avoid allocating objects and the resources they encapsulate before they are needed, and ensure they are released when the processing is complete.
- This is applicable to all resource types including database connections, data readers, files, streams, network connections, and COM objects.
- Use finally blocks or using statements to ensure resources are closed or released in a timely fashion, even in the event of an exception.
- The C# using statement is used only for resources that implement IDisposable; whereas finally blocks can be used for any type of cleanup operation.
- Reduce Boundary Crossings

  Plan to reduce the number of method calls that cross remoting boundaries as this introduces marshaling and potential thread switching overheads.

  With managed code, boundaries to be considered are:

  - *Cross application domain:* This is the most efficient boundary to cross because it is within the context of a single process.
  - *Cross process:* Crossing a process boundary significantly impacts performance. It should be done only when it is absolutely necessary.
  - *Cross machine:* Crossing a machine boundary is the most expensive boundary to cross, due to network latency and marshaling overheads

- Before introducing a remote server into one's design, it is required to consider the relative tradeoffs, including performance, security, and administration.

  - *Unmanaged code:* Calls to unmanaged code can introduce marshaling and potential thread switching overheads.
  - *The Platform Invoke (P/Invoke) and COM:* These interop layers of the CLR are very efficient, but performance can vary considerably depending on the

type and size of data that need to be marshaled between the managed and unmanaged code.

- Prefer Single Large Assemblies Rather Than Multiple Smaller Assemblies: To help reduce the application's working set, it is preferred to have single large assemblies rather than multiple smaller assemblies. If there are several assemblies that are always loaded together, they should be combined to create a single assembly. The overhead associated with having multiple smaller assemblies is:

  ➢ The cost of loading metadata for smaller assemblies
  ➢ Touching various memory pages in precompiled images in the CLR in order to load the assembly (if it is precompiled with Ngen.exe)
  ➢ JIT compiler time
  ➢ Security checks

- Factor Code by Logical Layers: When code is well factored, it becomes easier to tune to improve performance, maintain, and add new functionality. However, there needs to be a balance between functionality and performance. While clearly factored code can improve maintainability, simple designs can be effective and efficient.

  ➢ *Treat Threads as a Shared Resource:*
     Do not create threads on a per-request basis because this can severely impact scalability.
     Creating new threads is also a fairly expensive operation that should be minimized
     Treat threads as a shared resource and use the optimized .NET thread pool
  ➢ *Design for Efficient Exception Management:*
     The performance cost of throwing an exception is significant
     Although structured exception handling is the recommended way of handling error conditions, avoid usage of exceptions for regular control flow

Class Design Considerations

Class design choices can affect system performance and scalability. This section summarizes guidelines for designing managed classes:

- **Do Not Make Classes Thread Safe by Default**

  - Careful consideration is needed to make an individual class thread safe
  - Thread control is needed at a higher level
  - The overhead from the thread-safety features that the class offers remains even though features are not required
  - The collection class likely had a more complex design in the first place to offer those thread-safety services, which would be expensive whenever the class is used
  - In contrast to regular classes, static classes should be thread safe by default. Static classes have only global state and generally offer services to initialize and manage that shared state for a whole process. This requires proper thread safety

- **Consider Using the Sealed Keyword**

  - Utilize sealed keyword at the class and method level
  - If it is not required to extend the base classes by other developers, it should be marked with the sealed keyword
  - Before using the sealed keyword at the class level, extensibility requirements should be carefully looked upon

- **Consider the Tradeoffs of Virtual Members**

  - Use virtual members to provide extensibility
  - If there is no need to extend class design, virtual members need to be avoided because they are more expensive to call due to a virtual table lookup, and they defeat certain runtime performance optimizations

- **Consider Overriding the Equals Method for Value Types**

  Override the Equals method for value types to improve performance of the Equals method. However, the overhead associated with the conversions and reflections can easily be greater than the cost of the actual comparison that needs to be performed. As a result, an Equals method that is specific to the value type can do the required comparison significantly more cheaply.

- **Know the Cost of Accessing a Property**

  - The use of properties represents good object-oriented programming practice because it allows to encapsulate validation and security checks and to ensure they are executed when the property is accessed, but their field-like appearance can cause them to be misused

➤ Be aware that if a property is accessed, additional code, such as validation logic, might be executed

➤ This means that accessing a property might be slower than directly accessing a field. However, the additional code is generally there for good reason, to ensure that only valid data are accepted

➤ For simple properties, there is no performance difference compared to accessing a public field because the compiler can inline the property code

➤ If the object is designed for remote access, it should use methods with multiple parameters instead of requiring the client to set multiple properties or fields. This reduces round trips

➤ Do not use properties to hide complex business rules or other costly operations because there is a strong expectation by callers that properties are inexpensive

- **Limit the Use of Volatile Fields**

➤ Limit the use of the volatile keyword because volatile fields restrict the way the compiler reads and writes the contents of the field

➤ Accessing volatile fields is slower than nonvolatile ones because the system is forced to use memory addresses rather than registers

In spite of following the above guidelines, designers should adhere to the company coding standards. The class designer has to balance the above guidelines and coding standards to achieve better performance.

References

(DJG2005). Garbage Collection in the Java HotSpot Virtual Machine. Retrieved May 18, 2005, from http://www.devx.com/Java/Article/2197

(MMS2005). Improving Managed Code Performance. Retrieved May 15, 2005, from http://msdn.microsoft.com/library/default.asp?url=/library/en-us/dnpag/html/scalenetchapt05.asp

A6: Performance Monitoring Tool: PERFMON

1. To launch PERFMON, type *perfmon* on the command prompt and click ENTER. The application is displayed as shown in Figure A6.1.

Figure A6.1. Perfmon screenshot

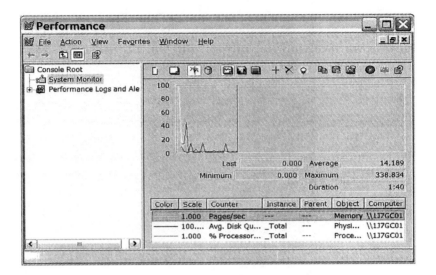

2.   To add a counter to the Performance Monitor, right click the mouse anywhere within
      the right pane. A context menu will display with the *Add Counters...* menu item.

3.   Selecting *Add Counters...* will display the Add Counters dialog.

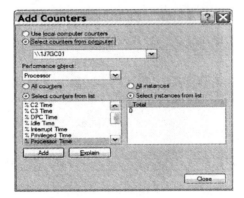

4.   In this dialog, the computer from which performance data are to be captured is specified. This can be the local machine or a machine on the network. Note that to capture the performance data for a machine in the network, it is necessary for the server process to be running on the remote machine.

5.   The desired counters for measurements are categorized based on the performance object and are displayed as shown in the figure above.

6.   Select the specific instances of the performance object to monitor. One can choose all instances or select from a list of available instances.

     Note: Some performance objects can have, at most, one instance associated with them while others may have multiple instances. Selecting counter from list and then clicking on Explain button will give a description for that counter.

     .NET uses the term *category* while the Performance Monitor uses the term *performance object*.

8.   Select a package of .NET Framework SDK and select the required performance counter for that package and run it by selecting the .NET CLR Memory performance counter category.

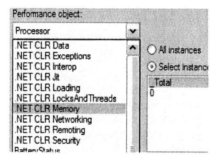

After the counters are added by clicking the Add button and closing the Add Counters dialog box, one gets the Performance Monitor as shown in the figure below.

9.   The performance monitor will now begin capturing the selected performance counter information.

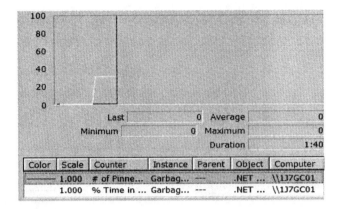

10. Start to monitor the state of the CLR, for example, using the predefined performance counters.

Additional features: With Performance logs and alerts, one can collect performance data automatically from the local or the remote computers. One can view logged counter data using System Monitor or export the data to spreadsheet programs or databases for analysis and report generation (see MTP2005).

References

(MTP2005). Microsoft Tech Net. Retrieved May 18, 2005, from http://www.microsoft.com/ technet/prodtechnol/windowsserver2003/library/ServerHelp/b3d458a8-7d62-4f2a-80bb-c16e75994b1d.mspx

B: Testing Tools

Characteristics of a good performance testing tool and a comparative study of various tools are presented in this appendix.

B1. Desirable Characteristics of a Good Performance Testing Tool

The following characteristics would be desirable when selecting a tool for PT:

1.   Supports standard database software such as DB, Sybase, and Oracle

2.   Supports standard protocols such as HTTP, IIOP, and SOAP

3.   Supports distributed technologies such as DCOM, RMI, and CORBA

4.   Supports Automated Cookie/Dynamic Cookie

5.   Has high-level, easy-to-use test scripting language

6.   Incorporates a powerful, easy-to-use recording capability

7.   Allows sophisticated users to directly access, read, modify, and control the automated test scripts

8.   Allows writing high-level test scripts early, and then later adding more detailed test cases for those scripts, as the application design evolves and stabilizes

9.   Provides features to easily edit and convert the raw script as captured into a reusable test case or a template for future test cases

10. Facilitates generation of multiple test cases

11. Allows test data to be stored separately from test scripts for easier maintenance and reuse

12. Allows all test suites to be recorded and executed stand-alone and also to be coordinated in intra- and intertest libraries

13. Provides compiled test cases or interpreted test cases or the choice of either

14. Provides the ability to quickly execute "dry runs" in order to check out whether the tests have been constructed correctly

15. Provides test script debuggers

16. Has capabilities to organize a library of test cases

17. Provides a useful novice-level help facility and effective online tutorials

18. Provides built-in templates of test scripts and test cases

19. Comes with usable documentation

20. Installs easily on the tester's workstations and in the test lab environment

21. Allows simultaneous, multiworkstation capture of test cases

22. Allows dependencies among test cases to be captured, maintained, and reviewed

23. Concatenates test components and provides steps to create multistep test cases

24. Allows test cases to be executed randomly or in predefined sequence

25. Provides tutorials and demos to show how to develop automated test cases

26. Provides enough functionality to keep the automated test repository up to date with changes to the application under test

27. Provides an interface for test cases written in C, Perl, Visual Basic, or any other language of choice

28. Provides the facility to easily browse and navigate around the repository of test cases

29. Has the ability to make changes to groups of test cases

30. Provides the capability to update old expected results by the new actual test results

31. Provides facilities to migrate tests across platforms

32. Maintains consistency of related test cases while migrating across platforms

33. Develops test cases that can rerun without modification, after migrating across platforms

34. Provides a version control capability on test cases and related test data

35. Enables test cases to be selectively activated and deactivated

36. Allows test cases to be added easily to test suites, or inherited, modified or replicated

37. Provides the capability to add multiple tags for a test case so that it can easily be selected in a subset of all test cases which share a common characteristic

B2. Web Performance Testing Tools

Tool name	Vendor name	Supported protocols	Characteristics
Loadrunner (Free Trial)	**Mercury** www.mercuryinteractive.com /products/	SNMP, HTTP/HTTPS, SOAP, WAP	Web load testing capabilities such as a "Web Transaction Breakdown Monitor" to isolate performance problems more efficiently, a "Data Wizard", XML support, "AutoLoad" technology for predefining tests.
Astra Loadtest (Free Trial)	**Mercury** www.mercuryinteractive.com	HTTP/HTTPS, SNMP	Web load/stress testing tool; can support Broadvision, ColdFusion, SilverStream, WebLogic, and IBM WebSphere; includes record/playback capabilities; allows breakpoints for debugging; functional and content verification checkpoints; integrated spreadsheet parameterizes recorded input to exercise application with a wide variety of data. Creates unique IP address for each virtual user; "Scenario Builder" visually combines virtual users and host machines for tests representing real user traffic. "Content Check" checks for failures under heavy load; supports various security features.
TestManager	**Rational** www.rational.com	HTTP, HTTPS, IIOP	Runs on Windows 95, 98, or NT workstations. Executes multiple test types at once. Links test cases to requirements. Generates meaningful reports.

Tool name	Vendor name	Supported protocols	Characteristics
NetPressure	**Synthetic Networks** www.syntheticnets.com	HTTP, FTP, NNTP, POP3, SMTP, SSL, DHCP, PPPOE	Unlimited scalability; GUI-driven management station; no scripting; open API. Errors isolated and identified in real-time; traffic monitored at every step in a protocol exchange (such as time of DNS lookup, time to logon to server, etc.). All transactions logged, and detailed reporting available.
WAPT **(Free Trial)**	**Novosoft Inc** www.loadtestingtool.com	HTTPS/SSL	Web load and stress testing tool. Handles dynamic content; easy to use; support for redirects and all types of proxies; clear reports and graphs.
Microsoft Application Center Test	**Microsoft** www.msdn.microsoft.com/library	SSL	Tool for stressing Web servers and analyzing performance and scalability; problems including ASP, and the components they use. Supports several authentication schemes. The programmable dynamic tests can also be used for functional testing. Visual Studio .NET Edition.
SiteStress	**WebmasterSolutions** www.Webmastersolutions.com	HTTPS(SSL)	Remote load test and consulting service where hundreds or thousands of virtual users are generated to simulate interaction with a site generated from global server network. Service includes recommendations to boost performance and reduce failure rates.
e-Load Expert	**Empirix** www.empirix.com	HTTP, HTTPS(SSL)	Virtual Users have small memory footprints and make efficient use of CPU resources, thus facilitating large load tests with minimal hardware. Accurately emulates multi-threaded browser requests and automatically validates server. responses and page content for accurate test results that closely correlate with real user load. Virtual users can be simulated by a single server or distributed among multiple servers located anywhere on a LAN or WAN. Windows NT, Windows 2000, and Unix platforms can be used to generate load.
WebServer Stress Tool	**Paessler GmbH,** www.paessler.com	HTTP,HTTPS	Web stress test tool handles proxies, passwords, user agents, cookies and ASP-session IDs. Shareware. For Windows.
WebSpray	**CAI Networks,** www.redhillnetworks.com	HTTP	Low-cost load testing tool includes link testing capabilities; can simulate up to 1,000 clients from a single IP address; also supports multiple IP addresses with or without aliases. For Win 98/2000/NT

Tool name	Vendor name	Supported protocols	Characteristics
eValid	**Software Research Inc**, www.soft.com	HTTP,HTTPS	Web test tool that uses a 'Test Enabled Web Browser' test engine that provides browser based 100% client side quality checking, dynamic testing, content validation, page performance tuning, and Web server loading and capacity analysis.
WebPerformanc e Trainer **(Free Trial)**	www.Webperformanceinc.co m	HTTPS(SSL)	Load test tool emphasizing ease-of-use. Supports all browsers and Web servers; simulates up to 400 users per playback machine at various connection speeds; records and allows viewing of exact bytes flowing between browser and server; no scripting required. Modem simulation allows each virtual user to be bandwidth limited. Can automatically handle variations in session-specific items such as cookies, usernames, passwords, and any other parameter to simulate multiple virtual users. For NT, Linux, Solaris, most UNIX variants.
e-Load	**Empirix**, www.empirix.com	HTTPS,SSL	Load test tool for use in conjunction with test scripts from their e-Tester functional test tool. Allows on-the-fly changes and has real-time reporting capabilities.
QALoad	**Compuware**, www.compuware.com/produ cts/qacenter/	HTTP,SSL,IIOP, FTP	Load/stress testing of database, Web, and char-based systems. Integration with EcoTOOLS test tool provides an in-depth view by monitoring its operating system, database and network components, as well as the application itself. Works with a variety of databases, middleware, ERP.
Microsoft WCAT load test tool **(Free download)**	**Microsoft**, www.support.microsoft.com	SSL	Web load test tool for load testing of MS IIS on NT; other MS stress tools also listed.
SilkPerformer	**Segue**, www.segue.com	HTTP	Load and performance testing component of testing toolset. Can work with their SilkTest functional testing product.
Radview's WebLOAD **(Evaluation copy)**	**Radview Software**, www.radview.com	WAP,HTTP,SNM P,	Web load testing tool .Capabilities includes over 75 Performance Metrics, can incorporate any data from Windows NT Performance Monitor or UNIX RSTATD directly into the test metrics; can view global or detailed account of transaction successes and failures on an individual Virtual Client level, assisting in capturing intermittent errors; allows comparing of running test vs. past test metrics.

Tool name	Vendor name	Supported protocols	Characteristics
QuotiumPro (Free Trial)	**Quotium Technologies**, www.quotium.com	HTTP,HTTPS	Cookies managed natively, making the script modeling phase shorter; HTML and XML parser, allowing display and retrieval of any element from a HTML page or an XML flux in test scripts; option of developing custom monitors using supplied APIs; more.
smartest	**interNetwork Inc**, www.inw.com	HTTP,HTTPS(SSL/TLS), FTP,NNTP,POP 3,SMTP, RSTP,DHCP	Creates real traffic across OSI layer's 2-7 to identify application/device weakness, assesses scalability limits
EasyWebLoad (Free Trial)	**PrimeMail Inc**, www.easyWebload.com	HTTP, Does not support HTTPS(SSL)	Easy-to-use Web site load testing tool For Windows.

C: Templates

Templates for capturing the performance requirements and for test plans are presented here. These templates provide basic guidelines to prepare performance requirements and test plan documents.

C1. Template for Performance Requirement Document

1   Introduction

   <Brief details of the system>

2   Business related

   2.1 Business background

   <Objective and goals>

   2.2   Business operations

   <Organization structure>

   2.3   Business objectives of the system

   <The overall business goals of the system >

   <And specific business objectives for the new proposed system if it is a new system>

3   Logistics of operations

   <Distribution of operation of organization>

4   User base

   4.1   Internal users

4.2 External users

<Like customers, vendors, and/or partners>

5   Business growth projections

<Growth rate projection of the system in next **n** years>

6 Infrastructure

6.1 Network environment

<Complete details of N/W Topology ISP and all technical specification with respect to network>

6.2 The backend servers

<Backend servers (DB servers) and their functional details>

6.3 The Web servers

<Backend servers (DB servers) and their functional details>

6.4 Software

<Software like OS and other related application details>

7   Proposed functions of the system

<The major proposed functions of the organization>

8   Interfacing system (if any)

<External Sources, if any, which are dependent on current system or vice versa>

9   Responsibilities

<Prepare high-level strategy document to describe main responsibilities including testing the performance of the new system for response time, throughput, scalability, and ability to handle peak loads>

10   Performance test objectives

<List all the objectives of the performance test>

11   User profile

<Tabulate the frequency of utilization of the system with priority>

12   Testing methodology

12.1 Identify team

12.2 Automated testing facilities

<Identify the tool used to test performance>

12.2.1 Service level agreements (SLA)

<Prepare SLA as per specification given by customer>

12.2.2 Miscellaneous

<Other customized requirements to be added>

12.2.3 Management conditions and constraints

<Conditions and constraints as expressed by management>

C2. Template for Performance Test Plan

1. Plan Identification

   \<Test plan name, ID# with version number, name, system details, date, intended audience(s) for this document, author(s) of this test plan, and how to contact them>

2. System Description

   \<Brief description, project *acceptance criteria,* identification and analysis of performance-related risks>

3. Goals of the System

   \<Customer expectations, marketing requirements>

4. Performance Test Objectives

   4.1 Target audience

   \<Users/clients, marketers interested in performance test results>

   4.2 Expected end products of testing

   \<Test environment doc, Test logs, Abstract test results, detailed test results, Test schedule,   Evaluation of test data: Presentation of results, analyze data and verify whether the performance goals have been met or not>

   4.3 Success criteria

   - Measure responses of Activity, Subactivity, Transactions (SQL, HTTP, Tux calls, ODBC, JDBC, etc.)
   - Identify and record acceptable response time in percentiles

5. Test Constraints

   \<Identify people resources availability, test facilities availability, Time deadlines, Entry criteria (readiness for testing), and budget constraint, Constraints on test completion, Criteria for Pass/fail, and suspension/resumption criteria>

   6. Performance Measurements

   \<Response time, Throughput, Resource utilization (CPU, memory, disk, etc.)>

   \<Operation profiles: Workload(s), user groups, source of the operational profile>

7. Test Environment

   \<Test hardware/software, networks, Tools, OS with proper configurations, Creating concurrent workload during testing (background noise), etc.>

8. Test Schedule

   \<Specify the detailed time schedule for the following>

   - Learning the tool
   - Creating and validating test scripts

- Collecting the test data
- Executing each scenario
- Problem resolution
- Meeting schedule for both pre- and postexecution of test

9.   Test Execution Process

<Sequencing of tests based on criticality, duration of the test, parameter setting during the testing, and monitoring the tests>

10.   Plan Test Bed

<Determine how much data required. Which data to be considered for testing. How to generate and store it>

11.   Plan Team

<Identify team and responsibility and tabulate as follows>

SI No.	Member of Team	Responsibility
1	Project manager	Problem resolution
2	Real users for recording	
3	Scripter/Scheduler	Should be technical with the ability to change a program
4	DBA should be available	Need passwords Restore/backup
5	System Administrator	Install products Restore/backup Monitor the execution of application
6	Network Administrator	Monitoring and troubleshooting the network

12.   Develop Test Scripts

<Develop test scripts by following the below guidelines>

Identify Test Scenarios Using Various Transactions

- Build Test Scripts using Play and Record method
- Use different browsers while scripting
- Edit the scripts based on the requirements
- Follow proper coding standards for test scripts
- Execute the script and verify for its correctness
- Document the scripts properly
- Identify common steps and convert them into functions
- Provide room for extensibility
- Facilitate to generate proper logs
- Independence of selective execution
- Clean exit on abrupt termination

- Self-sufficiency in individual test cases
- Inclusion of dynamism
- Incorporating user-friendliness
- Provision for efficient error recovery during execution

13. Develop Workload

    <Based on the operation profile, build the workload structure>

14. Entry Criteria

    <Give preconditions for testing>

15. Exit Criteria

    <Give accepted results which could be measurable>

D: Case Study

D1. Business Function Requirments Document

INFYNITY BANKING CORPORATION (IBC) is a global banking organization that provides standard banking services to its customers spread across the globe. The vision of the bank is anywhere, anytime banking. The head office is located in Chicago with several hundred centers situated outside of the United States. The aim of this proposed banking system is to create a paperless bank. The bank employees as well as the account holders will use the proposed system through the Web-based interface. The bank has several branches in different cities; each branch is identified by a unique code.

Business requirements are described as follows:

Types of Accounts:

1. The bank provides multiple types of accounts to its customer for managing cash, savings, and loans.

2. The bank internally maintains office accounts using a double book entry system of accounting.

3. Interbank and foreign bank accounts are maintained by the bank to facilitate clearing of bills/checks of different banks, countries, and currencies.

Creating an Account:

1. Account Number should be generated by the system in ascending order and must be unique.

2. The system must record the name and address of the account holder.

3. The minimum opening balance of an account is $500.

4. Each user gets a user name and password that the user can use to login from the Web.

Operating an Account:

Deposits:

1. The minimum deposit amount is $100.

2. Any amount greater than or equal to $100 is valid.

3. Whenever a deposit is made, the final balance should be made known to the account holder.

4. The account may be operated using a Web interface.

5. Fund transfers, demand draft requests, password changes, account statements, request for checks/bill books may be obtained using the Web interface.

Withdrawals:

1. The minimum withdrawal limit is $100.

2. Account balance should never be less than $100.

3. Whenever a withdrawal is made, the final balance should be made known to the account holder.

4. Withdrawals may be made from any of the branches or through ATM outlets as designated by the bank.

5. Using ATMs should be possible, irrespective of a centralized or distributed database.

6. The ATMs must be immune to link failures and should be able to operate in both online and off-line modes.

Loans:

1. Bank provides loans to its account holders, charging a higher rate of interest in comparison to the interest provided by the bank on saving and current account.

2. Loans that are not cleared per the schedule are subjected to penalty.

Deleting an Account:

1. The account holder information will be deleted permanently from the bank database on closure of the account.

2. All accounts that have not been operated within 10 years and above are considered dormant accounts.

Other Details:

1. It should not be possible to modify the account number at any stage.

2. An enquiry option should be provided, so those users (bank employees) can see the account number, name, and balance sorted either by account number or by account holder's name.

The proposed banking system is divided into four modules:

1. **Account Maintenance:** This module is used to perform the operations on accounts such as opening an account, closing of an existing account, and navigation through accounts. Some of the characteristics of this module are:

• The user interface for this module is account maintenance Web form
• When the form is loaded, it displays the first account number and its details
• Four navigational buttons are used to move across accounts

   ➢ MoveFirst: Navigates to the first record
   ➢ MovePrevious: Navigates to the previous record
   ➢ MoveNext: Navigates to the next record
   ➢ MoveLast: Navigates to the last record

• Insert and Commit: Allows the user to insert a new account in the Accounts table. It clears all the text fields on the screen except the Account Number text box which is generated automatically by the system. The user has to fill up all the remaining fields legibly and click commit to insert the record
• Delete: Allows the user to delete the current record. Upon selection of Delete the system confirms the same by displaying a message box "Are you sure you want to delete?" If the user selects "Yes", it will delete the record or else it will undo the operation

Validations:

• The initial deposit amount should not be less than $500. Otherwise, error message "Invalid Amount Enter Number Greater Than or Equal To $500" is displayed
• The date should be a valid date; otherwise it will display an error message "Invalid Date"

2. **Transactions Maintenance:** This module provides facilities to perform different transactions on accounts such as deposits, withdrawals, bill payments, fund transfers, and so forth.

- New: Allows a choice for a new transaction
- Commit: Allows saving the transaction
- Offers choice of either withdraw or deposit in the transaction

Validations:

- If the withdrawal transaction results in a balance amount less than $100, then the system will prompt the message "Balance less than $100"
- If the user enters any non-numeric data or number less than 100 for amount, then the system will prompt an error message "Amount should not be less than $100"
- If the date given is not a valid date, then there will be an error message "Invalid Date"
- If the user clicks Commit without selecting any transaction, then the system will prompt an error message "Select type of Transaction (deposit/withdraw)"

3. **Accounts Enquiry Details:** This module helps in enquiring about the account details (account number, account holder's name, address, and balance) sorted either by account number or by account holder's name.

- If a user selects sorting by account number, the user has to select the Account Number radio button. The user may choose an account number prefixed with 1001. In that case, details of all accounts whose account number has the starting digits 1001 will be displayed in the ascending order of account numbers on a separate page.
- Similarly, the user may choose a listing of details sorted by name by selecting the Name radio button. If the name field is populated with "Ra" (say), the system displays all the records sorted by name in the ascending order whose name has the characters "Ra". If the name field is not populated, a listing of all account holders is displayed in the ascending order by names.

4. **Transaction Enquiry Details:** This module facilitates the customer to generate the reports and statements of a particular account in the specified range of dates.

- By default, the system displays the screen with all existing account numbers using combo box. The user has to select one Account Number, the type of transaction (withdraw or deposit), and the range of dates between which the transactions are committed. After clicking Retrieve, it will display all the transactions of the specified account.

Validations:

- The user has to select either Deposit or Withdraw or both. If user selects neither of them, then the error message "Select type of Transaction (Deposit/Withdraw)" will be displayed

- The user has to enter the start date in such a way that it should be a valid date. The valid date must be greater than the date of accounts creation. If it fails to show the proper date, an error message "Invalid Date" will appear. The same message will appear if the user selects the end date that is greater than the current date or less than the accounts open date.

NOTE: A brief functional requirements document is prepared. The main objective is to use the document to highlight the performance testing rather than the business problem. Hence, more emphasis has been given to performance than business function in the case study.

D2. Performance Requirements Document for IBC

IBC is a global banking organization that provides standard banking services to its customers spread across the globe. The vision of the bank is anywhere, anytime banking. The head office is located in Chicago with several hundred centers situated outside of the United States. The proposed system supports both Client/Server and Web platforms. A detailed specification on business functions is available in a separate document (see business requirements documentation). In this document, we capture the details required for performance testing.

Requirements are gathered in three different categories, namely:

A.   Business related
B.   Proposed system related
C.   Performance test related, if any

A.   *Business Related*
1.   Business contents and events

To create a unique banking system through automation of all its services like customer service, managerial operations, and interbanking transactions at more competitive prices, IBC is in the process of building a comprehensive new information system. It added a new feature to provide fund transfers with all standard banks across the globe.

2.   Business operations
IBC is organized into four main groups:

a.   Senior Management to plan business growth

b.   Customer Group to manage customers efficiently

c.   Administration Group to strategize the business of the bank

d.   The Information System Groups to maintain and monitor the various automated systems

The function of each group is not highlighted in this document. Each group has its own team to manage its functions.

3.   Business objectives of the system

The overall business objectives of the system are as follows:

a.   Grow business at the rate of 20% every year

b.   Improve profitability

c.   Increase customer satisfaction

The specific business objectives for the new proposed system are as follows:

a.   Fulfill all requirements listed in the requirements document

b.   Improve the productivity in the customer service by 30%

c.   Maintain the highest level of security for all accounts

d.   Ensure the system performance from the customer perspective

e.   Ensure 100% uptime for the system

The customer is not in a position to give more accurate than the stated objectives.

4.   Logistics of operations

The operations of the bank are distributed across the globe since senior management believes in the anywhere banking concept. However, the major business activities are concentrated in and around the US with the headquarters located in Chicago. Most of the customer oriented business is carried out through the Internet which in turn depends on ISP providers and the quality of connection to the system at the customer place. A set of in-house operations are carried out in a C/S environment.

5.   User base

The user base is split into two categories:

a.   Internal users: Most of the administrative functions are performed by internal users (employees of the bank) in a C/S environment. The current internal user base is around 2,000 which will grow at the rate of 20% every year.

b.   Customers: Customers are not only the account holders but also the prospective customers who want to start business with the bank in due course. All customers are Web clients who will be using the system via Internet. The current Web client base is around 30,000, and the growth projection is given in the following section.

6.   Business growth projections

The system must be scalable to support the growth rate of 20% per year for the next 5 years. The growth depends on providing Internet based banking and percentage of change over from traditional banking to Internet banking. The traditional banking is carried out in a C/S environment. The growth rate depends on customer satisfaction, which is of paramount importance to the business. One such illustration for customer satisfaction is the quick response time for any query. The change over from traditional banking to Internet banking is proposed in Table D2.1.

7.   Infrastructure

The infrastructure proposed/available for IBC is outlined below:

Network Environment:

The system operates in a traditional C/S network as well as accessed from the Internet. There will be a cluster of LAN situated at different places. Some of the clusters may have their own Web server. All clusters are linked to the headquarters by a Wide Area Network (WAN) situated in India. The C/S network will include approximately 2,000 users, with one client workstation per user. A complete topology of the network environment is available with the IS Department of the bank.

The Backend Servers:

The system will have centralized database servers situated at the head office. There will be a set of database servers, which are used for database mirroring. In other words, all updates will be made concurrently to all of the copies of the databases, and these updates will be periodically monitored by the database management system (DBMS).

A complete backup copy of the database will be taken in certain intervals. The process takes approximately 30 minutes. During this time, the user response time may be slow. No guarantee will be given to the user about the amount of slowness, that is, worst-case performance of the system. However, the managers would like to know the complete details, which is within the scope of the performance objectives.

The Web Servers:

There will be a host of Web servers connected to routers, which in turn connect to the Internet through multiple T1 lines. Each T1 line has sufficient capacity to accommodate required sessions using 56 Kbps modems. Firewalls are provided on the Web servers, which may slow down the overall performance.

Though the Web servers will have their own databases, they will not contain all the data needed to answer queries or process the requests, as they need to access the database servers.

Software:

Standard software like Windows 2000, MS Access, and Apache software are used.

B. Proposed System Related

Based on the business process and requirements, the proposed system is viewed from two perspectives:

i.   Business functionality
ii. Performance of the system

The business functions are mapped to a set of use cases, which are used to design the system. While modeling the system, performance issues are also considered. The following sections provide information on both functionality and performance issues.

8.   Proposed functions of the system

The major functions of the banking system are:

a.   Creation and maintenance of accounts
b.   Providing fast queries
c.   Routine banking transactions
d.   Faster transactions through ATMs
e.   Overall maintenance of the system

The proposed system must comply with the W3C standards. The detailed functions are available in the business requirements document.

9.   Interfacing system, if any

IBC is planning to connect with other global banking systems for interbanking transactions. It is proposed to automate all interbanking transactions in the coming days.

C. *Performance Test Related*

In order to ensure the performance of the system, it is necessary to conduct performance testing in an isolated environment with automated tools. To use the automated tools, we need to define the objectives and responsibilities before starting the performance testing. The following sections provide brief information on requirements for conducting performance testing.

10. Responsibilities

The main responsibilities include testing the performance of the new system for response time, throughput, scalability, and ability to handle peak loads. The immediate requirement is to prepare a high-level strategy to describe the above task.

11. Performance test objectives

a. Working out a satisfactory response time of the system under a realistic load. Response time consistency has to be worked out in consultation with the IS team (say 25%). This means, if the average response time for a transaction is expected to be 2 seconds, then 90% or more of the measured response time should fall within the range of 1.5 and 2.5 seconds.

b. Reliability of the system (checking memory leaks, etc.)

c. Capability of handling peak load

d. Understanding of the system's capability to handle load beyond its planned capacity

e. Scalability

12. Operation profile

The features of the system are highlighted in the business requirements document. Based on the business operation, we have identified the set of transactions which are active during the business hours. These transactions are tabulated, and their frequency of operations are also collected in two phases under normal and peak business hours over a period of one week.

Table D2.2 provides the frequency of utilization of various transactions for normal hours. To illustrate, on Monday, an average 6,000 transactions per hour are active during access of the main page. Similarly, about 350 concurrent users withdraw money in an hour on Wednesday. This is a high priority transaction as the impact is more on the performance.

Similarly, the Table D2.3 provides active transactions distribution over a period of one week for peak hours. The peak hour is defined based on the inputs received from management. The peak could vary from one day to another day. Observe that most of the frequency utilization in Table D2.3 is more than the normal hours shown in Table D2.2. The data are collected for each day during peak hours. The duration of the peak hours could be different for each day. The average is calculated per hour based on these data for each transaction.

We have considered two operation profiles for this case study.

13.   Testing methodology

It is proposed to have two different teams:

a.   Functional testing team, which interacts with the development team and conforms to the correctness of business functions of the system.

b.   Performance testing team, which plans and conducts the performance testing in cooperation with the functional testing team. Each team will use its own test plans and strategies.

14.   Automated testing facilities

The team will use appropriate testing tools for functional and performance testing. They will use Rational Robot for functional and WAS (from Microsoft) for performance testing.

15.   Service Level Agreement (SLA)

A separate SLA has been developed for each operational group, and the agreement has been signed by the manager of the bank and the IS Department.

16.   Miscellaneous

Senior management would like to know the impact on performance if the Web site generates dynamic contents.

17.   Management conditions and constraints

There is no deadline on the schedule. However, once the strategy document is prepared and presented, cost and deadline will be determined. In case of testing tools, the management has recommended to use only freeware tools available in the market.

D3. Test Strategy Document for IBC

This document provides high-level strategies for the smooth conduction of performance testing of the proposed banking system before deployment. The exhaustive list of strategies to achieve optimal results will not be presented to senior management, but it has been prepared as a necessary document before taking their approval to proceed with the project.

1.   Identifying the Performance Testing Objectives

The primary goal of this system is to provide adequate information to the senior managers about the likelihood that the system will perform adequately in actual operation. This includes information about the capability of the system to handle: (a) typical daily business loads of IBC; (b) daily and weekly peak demand; (c) specialized needs such as the need to generate volumes of interbanking transactions, fund transfers, and so forth; (d) ad hoc demands like bursting loads unexpectedly; and (e) likely future growth over the next 5 years.

2.   Defining Performance Pass/Fail Criteria

We need to define what constitutes passing the goal and what constitutes falling short of achieving it. The pass/fail criteria should be unambiguous so that they are measurable in absolute terms. Otherwise, the clients may challenge the pass/fail criteria later. The strategy for IBC is to achieve step by step the goals set.

Step 1: Derive benchmark for: (i). Routine business demands, (ii) Routine peak demands (iii) Specialized requirement to handle unforeseen circumstances (data must be provided by IBC), and (iv) Top management's special demands, if any.

Step 2: Design workloads for each category of Step 1.

Step 3: Define Entry/Exit criteria for each workload separately.

Step 4: Define proper measurement criteria for each workload.

Step 5: Set the pass/fail criteria for each test run with each workload.

Performance parameters and pass/fail criteria may overlap for a set of workloads.

3.   Identifying the Measurement Criteria

Once the performance objectives and pass/fail criteria for each of them is successfully established, then we can start determining how each will be measured. Performance must be measured in absolute terms so that it can be easily compared with the pass/fail criteria. In order to establish proper measurements, it may be necessary to fine tune or reexamine the goal as well as pass/fail criteria. Broadly, it is decided to measure the response time, throughput, memory leaks, if any, and availability. Since the IBC system is developed in ASP, performance monitors related to ASP objects, OS related objects, and resource related objects are also considered for the measurement matrix.

4.   Stakeholders

Expectations on performance among many groups within the organization are different, and it is difficult to satisfy all. For instance, senior management may expect the results at the abstract level whereas middle management wants more microscopic level details. The stakeholders considered for IBC are:

•   Customer group needs to have sufficient confidence the system will be able to support the workload of their department.

Table D2.1. Transformation from traditional to Internet banking

Time frame	Percentage of Banking	
	By Traditional Banking	By Internet Banking
Current Year	90 %	10 %
2 years ahead	40 %	60 %
4 years ahead	70 %	30 %
5 years ahead	10 %	90 %

- The Administrator group of IBC needs information about the levels of compliance with the SLAs which are likely to be achievable in live system operation.
- Customers who expect the system to be performance conscious and robust.

5.   Project Scope

The scope of performance testing will include load, stress, spike, and endurance testing in client server and Web environments. The performance testing team must also analyze the results and suggest solutions to bottlenecks (if any) in fulfilling the SLA.

Note: Functional testing and related problems will not be part of the scope. It is assumed that the system is functionally correct before handing it over to the performance test team.

6.   Benchmarking

Based on the requirements document and discussion with the customer group, the following business benchmark is finalized for the proposed performance testing:

- Features query

    ➢   Display the home page
    ➢   Enter features page and read all the information available
    ➢   Enter a request for a new account using the request Web page

- Money transaction

    ➢   Deposit

- ○   Log in through the home page
- ○   Deposit the money through the deposit page
- ○   Log out and exit

> ➤   Withdraw

- ○   Log in through the home page
- ○   Enquire of the balance
- ○   Withdraw the money through the withdraw page
- ○   Log out and exit

- •   Administration

> ➤   Account creation

- ○   Log in as Administrator
- ○   Check the request for the new account
- ○   Check whether the required criteria are satisfied or not
- ○   Create a new account
- ○   Inform the account holder about the new account
- ○   Log out

The above benchmarks may vary as we go along with the design and execution of the test.

7.   Identifying the Key Transactions

This activity is aimed at gaining more indepth understanding of the system and how it is expected to be used in real-world operations. This is another key area that is critical to the success of client server and Web applications. Identify the applications' real life use and capture this information in operational scenarios. There may be different sets of customers, each with its own distinct operational scenarios. Once the operational scenarios have been clearly identified, then we can determine the key transactions or the mixture of transactions generated by each operational scenario. This activity helps in understanding the technical details of the product's design when each operational scenario is executed, such as objects invoked, interaction with outside object, calling ODBC/SQL drivers, and so forth. These operational scenarios represent business transactions of some kind, not necessarily SQL transactions processed on the server's database.

Table D2.2. Operation profile of business functions for one week during normal hours

User Group	Transactions Type Days	Mon	Tue	Wed	Thu	Fri	Sat	Sun	Priority
Customer Group	Main Page Access	6000	5300	5800	6500	5200	5000	4500	High
	Deposit Amount	400	350	300	350	250	200	150	High
	Withdraw Amount	250	400	350	450	500	400	350	High
	Request for New A/Cs	30	25	0	35	10	0	0	Low
	Bill Payment	100	50	40	45	15	100	75	Medium
Administrative Group	Daily Report Generation	3	4	2	3	5	6	0	Medium
	Fund Transfer	150	100	200	125	200	100	50	Medium
	Creation of New A/Cs	10	5	0	10	10	0	0	Low
	Deletion of A/Cs	5	10	0	7	10	0	0	Low
Senior Management Group	Banking Features Query	400	340	350	451	347	332	273	High
	Ad-Hoc Query	10	15	13	11	17	0	0	Medium

It is essential to identify the proper operational scenarios that generate the correct percentage of transactions and the correct mixture for each operational scenario. For instance, the baseline for a performance goal on the IBC banking system could be 10 concurrent connections doing simultaneous database synchronization, each with unique object instances, broken down as follows:

- 2 clients creating new customer accounts (20% of the transaction mix)
- 3 clients creating new deposits incident objects (30% of the transaction mix)
- 3 clients creating new withdraw incident objects (30% of the transaction mix)
- 2 clients creating new customer queries (20% of the transaction mix)

If the next performance measurement was scaling from 10 to 20 concurrent connections, the new test cases would reflect:

- 4 clients creating new customer accounts (20% of the transaction mix)
- 6 clients creating new deposits incident objects (30% of the transaction mix)
- 6 clients creating new debit incident objects (30% of the transaction mix)
- 4 clients creating new customer queries (20% of the transaction mix)

Table D2.3. Operation profile of business functions for one week during peak hours

User Group	Transactions Type Days	Mon	Tue	Wed	Thu	Fri	Sat	Sun	Priority
Customer Group	Main Page Access	9300	8300	8800	8500	8200	8000	7000	High
	Deposit Amount	900	800	700	800	700	500	300	High
	Withdraw Amount	950	850	800	850	850	850	800	High
	Request for New A/Cs	350	250	200	350	350	0	0	Low
	Bill Payment	200	100	75	100	250	212	200	Medium
Administrative Group	Daily Report Generation	6	8	2	3	5	6	2	Medium
	Fund Transfer	450	350	400	300	350	300	250	Medium
	Creation of New A/Cs	50	25	32	28	30	0	0	Low
	Deletion of A/Cs	10	30	20	22	18	0	0	Low
Senior Management Group	Banking Features Query	620	740	743	851	723	613	541	High
	Ad-Hoc Query	25	32	23	20	23	0	0	Medium

Note: Frequency of utilization is expressed in terms of transactions/hour.

This must be the pattern for any number of concurrent users for the given key transactions and transaction mix. These transaction mixes may vary based on the benchmarks and final workloads.

8.   System Acceptance Criteria

The Service Level Agreement (SLA) has to be met in all respects.

9.   Early Component-Level Performance Testing

No third party component is used in the application.

10.   Performance Measurements

While testing, it is proposed to collect the following performance measurement data to get the complete picture:

- Response times of transactions per the workloads defined
- Consistency of responses
- Throughput (measured in transactions per second)
- Resource utilization during testing

> ➤   Server and client processor utilization
> ➤   Memory utilization (RAM and Disks)
> ➤   Network utilization (LAN and T1 lines)
> ➤   Thread utilization (the number of concurrent users of critical hardware and software components)

- Bottleneck related

> ➤   High resource consumption by each software and hardware component during the testing
> ➤   Network collision rates
> ➤   Page-in page-out rates
> ➤   Number of hits blocked (blocking the Web site visitors)
> ➤   Number of threads blocked
> ➤   Buffer and queue length overflows

The above measurements may marginally vary during the testing because they depend on the type of tool used for the test.

11.   Test Load – Volume and Mix

The load used for measuring the performance is based on:

- Typical daily business workloads
- Daily peak demand
- Weekly peak demand
- Ad hoc demands, if any

We have considered only one test load which is weekly peak demand in this case study.

12.   Test Environment

The real environment is ideal to conduct load testing but difficult to obtain. In such circumstances, the better option is to have a subset of the real environment. We have considered a two-tier architecture which is explained in design document (see Appendix D4).

13.   Selection of Proper Test Automation Tool

The main objective of this activity is to determine a better automation tool for performance testing. Since the cost of any performance automation tool is high, more attention must be given before finalizing the tool. For simplicity and cost effectiveness, we have used freeware tool Microsoft Web application stress tool (WAS) (http://Webtool.rte.microsoft.com) for performance testing.

14.   Test Data Sources

The main database will be updated with the real environment database. The test scripts captured in functional testing will be modified and used for performance testing. A test data generator will be used to create test data wherever necessary.

15.   User Think Time

The strategy is to use a few customers and ask them to use the system with all possible transactions considered in the workload.

16.   Project Activities and Schedule

A detailed schedule will be prepared in consultation with the administrator group. The approximate duration for the entire test is 4 weeks.

17.   Project Risks

The major risks identified in this project are:

- Unavailability of the proper testing tools which may result in having to use the freeware tool
- Proper skill set required for testing and analyzing results
- Timely availability of functionally correct application for the performance testing
- Unavailability of database network administrators on time

18.   Conclusion

Since senior management is not interested in microscopic details of the strategy, only brief details have been highlighted. A detailed comprehensive document based on this report and feedback from the management may have to be prepared.

D4. Test Design Document for IBC

This document describes the analysis and design of the IBC Web application. It begins with a description of benchmark and operation profile of the system tested. The application is kept simple so that the focus of the project is on performance testing. The design document mainly focuses on benchmark design to arrive at an accurate workload.

Architecture

Two implementations of the application were developed. The first implementation was two-tier architecture and the second was three-tier architecture.

The main difference between the two implementations was the database subsystem. The two-tier implementation used Microsoft Access, and the three-tier architecture was implemented by developing some of the commonly identified COM components.

The application is divided into client and server components as shown in Figure D4.1. The client has a Web browser (Internet Explorer 6.0). The server is running Windows NT® Server, an Active Server Page (ASP) server (Microsoft Internet Information Server), and a database (Microsoft Access).

Benchmark for IBC

For the IBC banking system, a snapshot of transaction behavior is given in Table D4.1. Different types of behavior can be seen in this system. Some examples generate more threads, some may be more concurrent, some may be involved in computation and hidden transactions where less user interaction is required. These types of transaction behavior help to design a proper benchmark for performance testing. Here transaction behavior is studied from the performance point of view. Observe that in Table D4.1, some of the transaction types may repeat with multiple transaction behaviors. For instance, withdrawals and deposits are more concurrent transactions and affect the bandwidth.

Benchmarking the System

Separate benchmarks are required for each significant and distinct workload. Though the number of benchmarks depends on the planned activities of the system, benchmarks considered in the IBC application are:

1.   Routine business demands

2.   Routine peak demands

3.   Specialized requirements, if any

4.   Top management's special demands, if any

These four benchmarks are identified based on the performance requirements and complexity of the project. The number of benchmarks could be varied in other applications.

Sample Benchmarks

Consider the banking system and sample activities highlighting the transactions survey taken on a typical week. The result of the survey result is shown in Table D4.2. This table

Figure D4.1. Application architecture

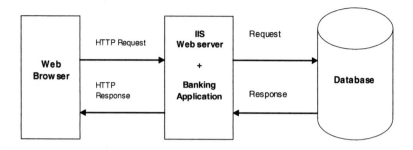

Table D4.1. Transactions identified with respect to transaction behavior for IBC Bank

Transaction Behavior	Transaction Types
More concurrent	Main Page Access Withdrawals Deposits
Applications interacting with each other	Billing Fund transfer Chatting Customer Queries
Involves more computation	Interest Calculation Collections for Relief Fund Fund Transfer
Involves read/write operation	Creation of Account Deletion of Account Database Backup Daily Report File Download
Generating more threads	Ad-hoc Queries Fund Transfer Bill Payment
More interactive with users	Banking Features Query Creation of Accounts Request for New Accounts Ad-hoc Query E-mail Chatting
Less interactive with users	Backup of Database Printing
Transaction affecting bandwidth	Chatting E-mail Withdrawals Deposits

represents the operations as perceived by the user on a typical day. For instance, there are 50 accounts created on Monday whereas no operations on Saturday and Sunday. Some of the nonbusiness activities like e-mail chatting are considered as these transactions impact the performance of the system.

Based on the behavior of the transactions, we are illustrating two benchmarks which will be used for the performance testing. These two benchmarks are related to normal and peak

Table D4.2. Sample benchmarking considering all types of transactions for normal hours

Sl No	Transactions Type / Days	Mon	Tue	Wed	Thu	Fri	Sat	Sun	Priority
1	Main Page Access	6000	5300	5800	6500	5200	4500	4500	High
2	Deposit Amount	400	350	300	350	250	200	150	High
3	Withdraw Amount	250	400	350	450	500	400	350	High
4	Request for New A/Cs	30	25	0	35	10	0	0	Low
5	Bill Payment	100	50	40	45	15	100	75	Medium
6	Ad-hoc Query	10	15	13	11	17	0	0	Medium
7	Fund Transfer	150	100	200	125	200	100	50	Medium
8	Creation of New A/Cs	10	5	0	10	10	0	0	Low
9	Deletion of A/Cs	5	10	0	7	10	0	0	Low
10	Banking Features Query	400	340	350	451	347	332	273	Medium
11	Daily Report Generation	3	4	2	3	5	6	0	Low
12	E-mail	100	125	100	130	251	30	25	Low
13	Downloading Page	75	75	80	60	55	5	2	Low
14	Chatting	75	85	90	105	95	80	85	Low
15	Printing	30	25	20	22	34	30	0	Low
16	Collections for Relief Fund	15	20	25	25	22	15	10	Low
17	Customer Queries	300	200	350	250	350	190	150	Medium

Table D4.3. Distribution of transactions into different categories of benchmarks for normal hours

Planned Activities for Benchmarking	Transaction Types (Sl No. of Table D4.2)
Routine business demands	1,2,3,4,5,8,9,10,11,17
Routine peak demands	1,2,3,5,6,7,8,10,17
Specialized requirements	1,7,3
Top management specialized requirements	1,15,16,6

hours. For each transaction, weekly data are collected on the basis of frequency utilization per hour. The total number of transactions considered for both benchmarks are the same.

Normal Hours

Table D4.2 provides the distribution of all transactions over a week. The data are collected for several weeks and later, the average is computed. To illustrate, there are 250 concurrent users who withdraw amounts on Monday. Similarly, the transaction Main Page access is active 5,200 times simultaneously on Friday. Likewise, all transactions listed in Table D4.1 are considered for deriving the benchmark.

Table D4.4. Fine tuned operation profile for routine business demands for normal hours

User Group	Transactions Type / Days	Mon	Tue	Wed	Thu	Fri	Sat	Sun	Priority
Customer Group	Main Page Access	6000	5300	5800	6500	5200	4500	4500	High
	Deposit Amount	400	350	300	350	250	200	150	High
	Withdraw Amount	250	400	350	450	500	400	350	High
	Bill Payment	100	50	40	45	15	100	75	Medium
	Customer Queries	300	200	350	250	350	190	150	Medium
	Request for New A/Cs	30	25	0	35	10	0	0	Low
Administrative Group	Fund Transfer	150	100	200	125	200	100	100	Medium
	Creation of New A/Cs	10	5	5	10	10	0	0	Low
	Deletion of A/Cs	5	10	5	7	10	0	0	Low
	Daily Report Generation	6	8	2	3	5	6	2	Low
Senior Management Group	Ad-hoc Query	10	15	13	11	17	0	0	Medium
	Banking Features Query	400	340	350	451	347	332	273	Medium

Table D4.5. Fine tuned operation profile for routine peak demands for normal hours

User Group	Transactions Type / Days	Mon	Tue	Wed	Thu	Fri	Sat	Sun	Priority
Customer Group	Main Page Access	6000	5300	5800	6500	5200	4500	4500	High
	Deposit Amount	400	350	300	350	250	200	150	High
	Withdraw Amount	250	400	350	450	500	400	350	High
	Bill Payment	100	50	40	45	15	100	75	Medium
	Customer Queries	300	200	350	250	350	190	150	Medium
Administrative Group	Fund Transfer	150	100	200	125	200	100	100	Medium
	Creation of New A/Cs	10	5	5	10	10	0	0	Low
	Deletion of A/Cs	5	10	5	7	10	0	0	Low
Senior Management Group	Ad-hoc Query	10	15	13	11	17	0	0	Medium
	Banking Features Query	400	340	350	451	347	332	273	Medium

These transactions are categorized into four types of planned activities shown in Table D4.3. These planned activities are derived based on the business domain knowledge and considering the impact on the performance of the system. Some of the transactions may not figure into any of the categories as these transactions may not impact much on the

Table D4.6. Sample benchmarking considering all types of transactions for peak hours

SI No	Transactions Type / Days	Mon	Tue	Wed	Thu	Fri	Sat	Sun	Priority
1	Main Page Access	9300	8300	8800	8500	8200	8000	7000	High
2	Deposit Amount	900	800	700	800	700	600	400	High
3	Withdraw Amount	950	850	800	850	850	850	800	High
4	Request for New A/Cs	350	250	200	350	350	0	0	Low
5	Bill Payment	200	100	75	100	250	212	200	Medium
6	Ad-hoc Query	700	650	645	625	590	450	550	Medium
7	Fund Transfer	450	350	400	300	350	300	250	Medium
8	Creation of New A/Cs	50	25	32	28	30	0	0	Low
9	Deletion of A/Cs	10	30	20	22	18	10	5	Low
10	Banking Features Query	620	740	745	850	730	630	540	Medium
11	Daily Report Generation	25	32	23	20	23	20	0	Low
12	E-mail	200	225	200	230	451	40	45	Low
13	Downloading Page	150	100	120	100	102	10	5	Low
14	Chatting	105	110	120	150	125	130	115	Low
15	Printing	40	35	20	22	44	30	0	Low
16	Collections for Relief Fund	15	20	25	25	22	15	10	Low
17	Customer Queries	400	300	400	350	400	290	300	Medium

Table D4.7. Distribution of transactions into different categories of benchmarks

Planned Activities for Benchmarking	Transaction Types (SI No. of Table D4.6)
Routine business demands	1,2,3,4,5,8,9,10,11,17
Routine peak demands	1,2,3,5,6,7,8,10,17
Specialized requirements	1,7,3
Top management specialized requirements	1,15,16,6

performance. The transaction Chatting in Table D4.2 is totally omitted in any of the categories because it will not impact the performance.

Based on the distribution, the new sets of fine tuned operation profiles are created. Table D4.4 and Table D4.5 represent the fine tuned operation profile for Routine Business Demands and Routine Peak Demand under normal hours. Observe that now there are two operation profiles, and many transactions are overlapping. The process for creating a new set of operation profiles is:

• Create the operation profile consisting of all transactions. These transactions include business function related, noise related, and other transactions which are active during the running of the system. There could be more than one operation profile depending on the test needs.

Table D4.8. Fine tuned operation profile for routine peak demands for peak hours

User Group	Transactions Type / Days	Mon	Tue	Wed	Thu	Fri	Sat	Sun	Priority
Customer Group	Main Page Access	9300	8300	8800	8500	8200	8000	7000	High
	Deposit Amount	900	800	700	800	700	500	300	High
	Withdraw Amount	950	850	800	850	850	850	800	High
	Bill Payment	200	100	75	100	250	212	200	Medium
	Customer Queries	400	300	400	350	400	290	300	Medium
Administrative Group	Fund Transfer	450	350	400	300	350	300	250	Medium
	Creation of New A/Cs	50	25	32	28	30	0	0	Low
	Deletion of A/Cs	10	30	20	22	18	0	0	Low
Senior Management Group	Ad-hoc Query	700	650	645	625	590	450	550	Medium
	Banking Features Query	6200	7400	7430	8510	72300	6130	5410	High

- Considering all transactions, create planned activities by grouping sets of transctions from the operation profile.

- For each planned activity, create a new operation profile which may or may not contain all transactions. This operation profile is known as the fine tuned operation profile.

Peak Hours

Similar to the transaction survey conducted for normal hours, the IBC system is subjected to the peak hour's survey. The behavior of the system during peak hours is different from the normal hours. Table D4.6 provides the survey of transactions conducted over a period of one week.

Four categories of benchmarks are considered for IBC. From Table D4.6, distribute all transactions into these four categories based on the business domain expertise available. These categorized transactions are given in Table D4.7. Based on these categories, now the operation profile needs to be fine tuned.

Out of four categories of benchmarks, we have considered one benchmark, namely, routine peak demands. This has many benchmarked transactions. Using these transactions, the operation profile defined in the performance requirement document (Table D2.3) needs to be fine tuned. Thus, the operation profile undergoes a transformation with more or less transactions compared to the original one. The fine tuned operation profile is given in Table D4.8.

Table D4.9. Workload transactions derived for IBC for routine peak demands in normal hours

User Group	Weights for Group	Transactions Type	Peak (Average) Transactions	Priority	Weight for Transactions
Customer Group	60	Deposit Amount	300	High	20
		Withdraw Amount	380	High	20
		Bill Payment	60	Medium	5
		Customer Queries	250	Medium	15
Administrative Group	20	Fund Transfer	125	Medium	10
		Creation of New A/Cs	5	Low	5
		Deletion of A/Cs	4	Low	5
Senior Management Group	20	Ad-hoc Query	10	Low	10
		Banking Features Query	350	High	10

Design of Workload

The workload pattern model captures the various workloads the system is subjected to. A workload is made up of workload components. A workload component defines the load caused by instances of a transaction requested by initiators of the transaction in an operating window and the growth of the load over a range of time.

The essence of the workload is to study the performance behavior of the proposed system before deployment. One should consider a good mix of transactions which impact concurrency, resources, and so forth.

Workload for Routine Peak Demands for Normal Hours

The workload is derived from the fine tuned operation profile. The average load over a week is considered for transactions with minor variations. Group weights have been calculated based on business requirements and performance goals. The customers group carries the maximum weight as 60 whereas other groups carry equal weights. Similarly, weights for each transaction are also given. For every fine tuned operation profile, there exists a workload. However, we have considered only two workloads.

The final workload is given in Table D4.9. This workload is derived from the fine tuned operation profile described in Table D4.6. Weights are calculated based on priority and business domain experts.

Table D4.10. Workload transactions derived for IBC for routine peak demands in peak hours

User Group	Weights for Group	Transactions Type	Peak (Average) Transactions	Priority	Weight for Transactions
Customer Group	60	Deposit Amount	700	High	20
		Withdraw Amount	800	High	20
		Bill Payment	200	Medium	5
		Customer Queries	349	Medium	15
Administrative Group	20	Fund Transfer	250	Medium	10
		Creation of New A/Cs	24	Low	5
		Deletion of A/Cs	16	Low	5
Senior Management Group	20	Ad-hoc Query	601	Low	10
		Banking Features Query	694	High	10

Note: Main Page is not considered for the workload as it is common to all groups.

Workload for Routine Peak Demands for Peak Hours

The workload shown in Table D4.10 is derived from the fine tuned operation profile shown in Table D4.8.

Tool Selection

The performance-testing tool chosen for the project was Microsoft's Web Application Stress Tool (WAS). It was chosen because of its ability to test ASP products, which is a necessary requirement for testing the application (information about this tool can be found at http://Webtool.rte.microsoft.com).

Test Plan

Testing of the application was to carry out in a black box fashion, as there is little or no knowledge of the actual code or design of the application. Criteria for selecting how to test the application are based upon knowledge of the application behavior and some logical assumptions. For IBC application testing, the following test plan was considered:

Table D4.11. Test team for IBC

SI No.	Member of Team	Responsibility
1	Project manager	Problem resolution
2	Testers and test script writer	For conducting test, tester should be technical with the ability to change a program
3	DBA	Passwords management Restore/backup
4	System Administrator	Install products Restore/backup Monitor the execution of application
6	Network Administrator	Monitoring and troubleshooting the network

Defining Entry and Exit Criteria

Entry Criteria

- Should be functionally correct
- Proper test bed should be present during testing
- Ensuring the availability of the test team given in Table D4.11

Exit Criteria

- All tests runs must be completed successfully
- Result data must be generated
- No functional bug should be reported during testing

Setting Performance Parameters

Performance Monitors

Testing the application requires choosing the parameters that will monitor the most worthwhile activity of the application. The best parameters for the purposes of this project – performance analysis – should retrieve the most valuable data for analyzing where bottlenecks may occur. They should reflect the performance related to the server (memory, CPU, disk) and the Web site (ASP throughput, requests/sec, etc.). The parameters that were chosen are limited to those available by the Microsoft Web Application Stress Tool. Table D4.12 explains the monitors selected and why they were selected.

D5. Analysis of Test Results for IBC

The test is executed in steps by assigning weight per the workload model derived in the design document and by giving valid inputs as mentioned in the business function requirement document. Several results data have been taken for analysis. The following sections highlight the analysis done on the IBC system.

Test Results and Analysis

The bottlenecks of the Web application are found by profiling the Web requests using TTFB data as shown in Figure D5.1. These data indicate the amount of time it took for the user to receive a response to a request. A Web request is considered a bottleneck if it took a significantly longer time than other requests.

Looking at the test using 500 threads as the thread level, we can see that the fifteenth and sixteenth requests become time hogs. These are ASP requests for the Transactions Maintenance page and the Next button of the IBC system.

Other performance problems are encountered for the fourth, fifth, eleventh, twelfth, and fourteenth requests. These are the background image, the Accounts Maintenance page, the Next button, the Last button, and the Delete button.

Repeating this method for other transactions as mentioned in the business function requirement document, bottlenecks of the application and their impact are determined as shown in Figure D5.2.

System Bottlenecks

The other types of bottlenecks that affect the performance of a Web application are those caused by the system. Bottlenecks in the system are often caused by insufficient

Table D4.12. Performance monitors for IBC application testing

Performance Monitors	Description
ASP Objects	The ASP monitors are important for giving an indication of how heavy the ASP pages stress the resources of the computer. They serve little purpose for evaluating a site by itself with only one version and no changes. By looking at the ASP monitors for different implementations of the same site, both hardware and software, there is an indication of whether certain changes have improved or diminished the performance of the site. Since ASP pages are executed on the server side, unlike most Web content, which is processed on the client side by the browser, it should play a significant role in the performance of a Web server. Each ASP counter chosen for this project should be used in any Web application that is implemented with ASP.
Active Server Pages/Request Execution Time	This shows how long it takes for each ASP page to get executed. An average of different ASP pages may give distorted results since one ASP may be a resource hog. The percentiles will indicate how long it takes for a page to get executed in a certain quartile. If there is a large discrepancy between the median and the average, then perhaps one page that gets executed is excessively hogging the resources or one page requires very little resource usage.

Table D4.12. cont.

Performance Monitors	Description
Active Server Pages/Requests Queued	This gives an indication of the ASP throughput. If the queue gets too large, some requests in the back of the queue may time-out. The queue for IIS is limited to a size of 490, so if this monitor reaches that number, the rest of the requests will be rejected. By increasing computing resources or making the ASP pages more efficient, the queue should get smaller. If an excessive amount of errors are received, then perhaps the queue is full and this monitor will be helpful in evaluating that.
Total of Active Server Pages/Requests Succeeded and Active Server Pages/Requests	These monitors make sure that the ASP requests are successful. If the number of successful requests is significantly less than the total number, then there are problems with servicing ASP requests.
Active Server Pages/Requests/Sec	This monitor gives an indication of ASP throughput. It tells how many ASP requests are serviced per second. By increasing computing resources or making the ASP pages more efficient, the throughput should increase.
Memory Related Objects	These objects were selected to show the efficiency of the server's memory system. However, determining the bottleneck within the memory is difficult and requires much more analysis. All of the memory system performance counters for this project, with the exceptions of Read and Write Operations/Sec, were chosen as generic memory counters, and thus are suggested for any type of Web site. If it were expected that the hard drive might be used excessively to modify files on the server, it should be necessary to include specific disk counters like Read and Write Operations/Sec.
Internet Information Services Global/Cache Hits %	This monitor indicates the efficiency of the Web server's caching system. For a small Web site, this should be near perfect, 99.0% or higher, and may not provide much useful information. However, it will eliminate any questions regarding the Web server's efficiency of caching Web objects.
Memory/Cache Faults/sec	Unlike the previous counter, which indicates the caching of objects in the server, this indicates the caching of the whole computer. If there are a lot of faults, then the memory system may be inefficient or there is poor locality of reference.
Memory/Committed Bytes	This is the size of virtual memory that is being used and includes all processes. If the size of committed bytes is larger than RAM and there are many page faults, then the system probably needs more RAM.
Memory/Page Faults/Sec	A Page Fault occurs when a process refers to a virtual memory page that is not in its working set in main memory. A Page Fault will not cause the page to be fetched from disk, if that page is in use by another process, with whom the page is shared. Again, this is helpful for indicating if more RAM is needed.
Memory/Pages/Sec	Pages/sec is the number of pages read from the disk or written to the disk to resolve memory references to pages that were not in memory at the time of the reference. This is the sum of Pages Input/sec and Pages Output/sec. This counter includes paging traffic on behalf of the system Cache to access file data for applications. This value also includes the pages to/from noncached mapped memory files. This is the primary counter to observe if concerns arise about excessive memory pressure (that is, thrashing) and the excessive paging that may result. This may be considered redundant with committed bytes and page faults/sec.

Table D4.12. cont.

Performance Monitors	Description
Physical Disk(_Total)% Disk Read Time, Physical Disk(_Total)/% Disk Time, & Physical Disk(_Total)/% Disk Write Time	These monitors indicate the amount of disk usage. If the % Disk Time was to be considered abnormally high, then it could be contributed to either reading or writing. Excessive use of the physical disk may be due to a poor paging system or inefficient disk operations invoked by a program.
System/File Read Operations/Sec & System/File Write Operations/Sec	These monitors indicate how many disk operations are being serviced by the system. These should be used in conjunction with the % Disk monitors. Together, they can show if an application is making too many Read/Write operations and how much of an effect it has on the overall disk usage. These were selected for this project because it was expected that the MS Access implementation of the server would use the disk heavily while accessing the database.
Miscellaneous System Counters	Each of these serves a specific purpose in validating the results of a test and/or helping find bottlenecks and should be used for any generic Web site.
Server/Bytes Total/Sec	The number of bytes the server has sent to and received from the network. This value provides an overall indication of how busy the server is.
Thread(_Total/_Total)/Context Switches/sec	This indicates how often the processor is switching between threads. If this number gets excessive, around 2,000, the processor may be spending more time switching between threads than executing them.
Processor(0)/% Processor Time	This monitor is both important for the client and the server. If the client machine is consistently above 90%, then more client machines should be added. It also indicates the load on the server's processor.
Web Site and Web Page Objects	These monitors are helpful for understanding how the Web site is working as a whole, from the user's perspective, and can profile pages to see which individual Web page objects are taking the most time to request. These are also generic counters and should be used for any Web site to profile performance characteristics.
Number of Hits	Since all tests are for the same period of time, this statistic, used over different implementations of the same site, indicates how many hits the server received. If the site has become more efficient, this number should increase.
Requests/Sec	This gives an indication of the throughput of the server for all types of requests. Should this number decrease over higher thread levels, then perhaps errors are being encountered or the site is becoming inefficient.
TTLB/TTFB (Time To Last Byte and Time To First Byte)	These statistics are generated for the request of individual Web objects within a Web site, not just pages but also pictures and other media. This can be used to profile the objects requested in a script to see where the bottlenecks are in Web pages.

hardware resources or improper software configuration. For instance, the system can have too little RAM, which is a hardware resource, or the server may be improperly configured, which is a software-related problem.

Hardware Problems

The hardware of an ordinary PC running NT Server has three components: the network, the main system, and the memory. The network should consist of a network card and connection, for instance, a 3COM 10Mbs card running on a T1 connection. The main system should consist of a CPU, like a PIII-450, and the motherboard. The memory consists of all the elements of a virtual memory system (cache, RAM, and the physical disk drive).

Network

The network is costly to replace and while changing it may increase the throughput of the server, it should not be the bottleneck. The network used in the test is an Ethernet-based LAN and should be more than sufficient. If we look at the plot of number of threads vs. server (Figure D5.3), we see that the server, which was erring at a load level of 700 threads, did not maximize the use of the network.

The graph of Figure D5.3 demonstrates that the server erred without reaching more than one-third the transfer rate that it had attained in the earlier test run. This should sufficiently show the network is not the bottleneck.

Figure D5.1. Bottleneck due to Web request

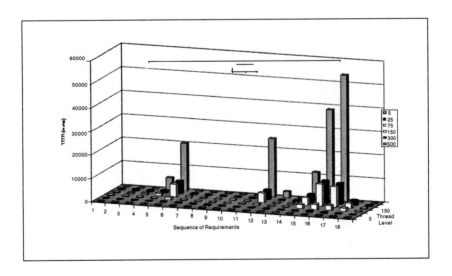

Figure D5.2. Bottleneck determined for IBC

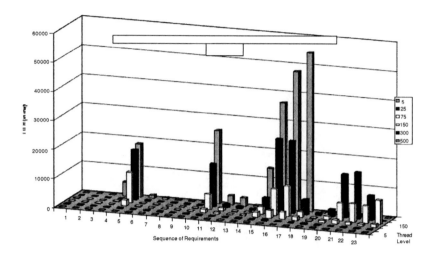

Figure D5.3. Number of threads vs. server bytes/sec

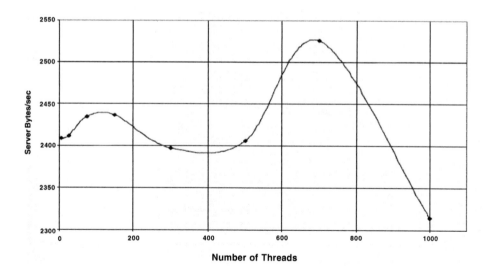

Memory

The virtual memory system in most NT systems has three components: cache, RAM, and physical disk. Since the cache would never realistically be changed, it serves no purpose to analyze this portion of the memory system. So the RAM and the physical disk are analyzed in an attempt to find a bottleneck.

Figure D5.4. Number of threads vs. pages/sec

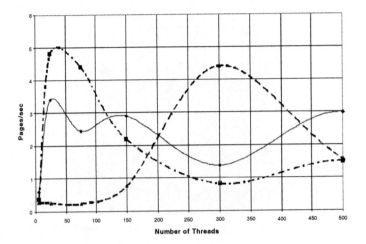

There are also software components that may be considered when determining the bottlenecks of the memory system. This would include the size of the virtual memory, which is a configurable option on Windows NT.

RAM

Pages/sec was the first counter examined to ensure the system had sufficient RAM. This counter would be the most important because there is a concrete number to examine which indicates whether the system needs more physical memory.

The indicator values for this counter are mentioned in an NT server reference book, "Normal rate for this value is less than 5...if the system begins to sustain a value of 10 or greater, the system is thrashing" (see CMK1998). Using this guideline, it is obvious that the system is not in need of more RAM. In the plot of Pages/Sec (Figure D5.4), none of the scripts reached above 5 Pages/Sec, so it can be concluded that the amount of physical memory was more than adequate.

Other Memory Considerations

Although the analysis shows that the physical disk and the main memory should not be the bottleneck, there are some observations to note about the memory system.

Figure D5.5. Number of threads vs. page faults/sec

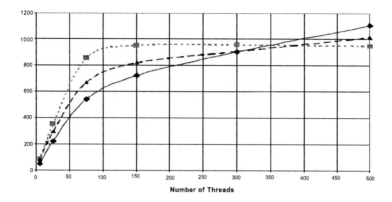

Number of Threads

Page Faults/Sec

In each of the three tests, the Page Faults/Sec reached high levels (Figure D5.5). When a page fault occurs, it can be for one of three reasons: the page does not exist in main memory, the page is on a standby list, or the page is in use by another process. Since we already examined the Pages/Sec (Figure D5.4) and realized that the virtual memory system is not using the physical disk, we know that a page fault cannot be due to a page missing in main memory. Thus, the page faults are due to another process using a given page or the page queuing on a standby list.

Software Configuration

In Windows NT, the size of the virtual memory is configurable through the system properties dialog box. If the virtual memory size was not large enough, the server would have given server side errors indicating that Windows NT was low on memory and applications should be shut down. It also would have been noticeable in several of the logical memory counters, which were not used for this test. Since the regular memory tests gave no indication of poor virtual memory performance, further investigation on the software settings was not done.

CPU

CPU was chosen to look at last. The rationale for looking at the CPU last is that the symptoms of a CPU bottleneck may be caused by a different component of the system. It is very easy to say the CPU is the bottleneck without it being the source of the performance problem.

Figure D5.6. CPU usage of the server (median values)

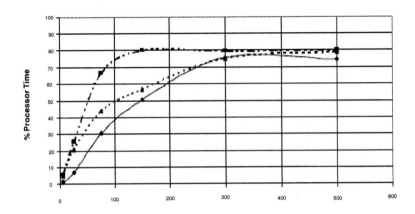

% Processor Time (Server)

The first counter observed for the CPU is % Processor Time. The average % Processor Time may give misleading results regarding consistent CPU usage due to peaks and minimums in the data, so look at the median CPU usage. Should this reach levels above 90%, then it is almost certain that the CPU is the bottleneck.

From the graph of CPU usage (Figure D5.6), it is not possible to immediately determine that the CPU is a hardware bottleneck since the CPU does not reach above 80% usage, but one can tell that the CPU is heavily used.

Context Switches/Sec

The rate of context switches is important in determining how much the CPU has to handle thread switching. A thread switch occurs when a thread asks another for information or the CPU gives control to higher priority threads. A rate of 2,000-3,000 switches/sec is high and may cause the CPU to spend more time switching between threads than running (see WMC2003). Although the CPU is never the source for high rates of context switching and would not alleviate such a problem, it may be the only hardware resource to indirectly improve performance.

Figure D5.7 shows that for all three test executions, once the load level is over 100 threads, the rate of context switching is excessive. This is indicative of a bottleneck. Since the CPU usage is low enough that the CPU could be stressed more, the CPU is not the simple answer for a bottleneck. As shown above, the context-switching rate indicates that the

Figure D5.7. Rate of context switching

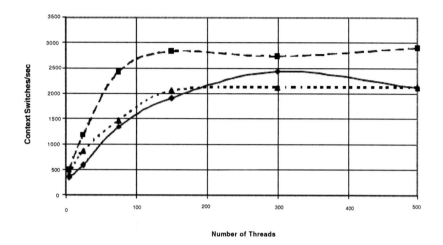

CPU is spending a large amount of time switching threads. Also, previous analysis shows that other hardware components are not the bottleneck, and thus not the cause of the high rate of context switching. Thus, the CPU is the only hardware resource, if improved, that would correlate to better application performance by reducing the overhead of thread switching.

Analysis

From the Web request profiling, it is clear to see what functionality or objects in the application can be improved. Simple fixes include optimizing the speed of execution for the ASP files and reducing the resolution of an image to reduce the image size. However, the analysis of the system hardware resources was less conclusive since the application started failing before a single resource was completely stressed.

Improvements to the network and memory system would provide marginal performance gains, if any, because they were never stressed. A better CPU is the only hardware enhancement that would provide significant improvement in application performance, but this does not solve the real bottleneck. Determining the bottleneck in the tested Web application required more complex analysis than was originally expected.

It was concluded that the bottleneck is in the application and the way it accesses the database. Either the application architecture is not designed to support a large amount of concurrent users or the coding of the application was not meant to support an intensive multithreading environment. A problem with the application architecture may result from the MS Access database not being able to support a large amount of concurrent connections. A problem due to the coding of the application may be due to inefficient use of locks.

Going forward because of the trends observed earlier in both Pages/Sec and Context Switches/Sec, in both graphs, there is a strong correlation in the significant increase between the stress levels of 5 and 150 threads. Since all of the threads should be the same priority, the high rate of context switching is probably due to one thread asking another for information and not thread preemption. Also, the heavy rate of Pages/Sec cannot be contributed to the virtual memory system. As discussed earlier, it is either due to a page used by another process or a page that is on a standby list.

Combining these observation results lead us to believe that a shared resource is locked in memory related to the application and has caused the high rate of page faults and thread switching. This means the application needs to be more efficient with the way it handles shared data. Of course, the only means to improve this would be to change the architecture that supports the handling of shared data or make the code that controls the locks of shared data more efficient.

References

Goncalves, M., & Spencer, K. (CMK 1998). *Windows NT server management and control.* Prentice Hall.

Chang, C. (WMC 2003). *Web application stress test and data analysis.* Unisys electronic document distributed at http://webtool.rte.microsoft.com (Accessed on September 17, 2003.)

Glossary

A

Active Server Pages (ASP) – A Microsoft Technology that helps in producing dynamic HTML Reponses based on the user query. ASP is essentially a program that runs inside the web server of Microsoft Operating systems listening to the Web requests. Based on the request, this program dynamically generates the content and returns the response to the user.

ADO – Microsoft ADO (ActiveX Data Objects) is a Component object model object for accessing data sources. It provides a layer between programming languages and databases, which allows a developer to write programs which access data, without knowing how the database is implemented. No knowledge of SQL is required to access a database when using ADO, although one can use ADO to execute arbitrary SQL commands. The disadvantage of this is that this introduces a dependency upon the database.

ASP.NET – Similar to Microsoft's ASP. ASP.NET is rewritten to fit into a larger .NET framework. Unlike ASP, ASP.NET supports code written in complied languages such as VB, C#, C++, and Perl.

Asynchronous Transfer Mode (ATM) – International standard for cell relay in which multiple service types (such as voice, video, or data) are conveyed in fixed-length (53-byte) cells. Fixed-length cells allow cell processing to occur in hardware, thereby reducing transit delays. ATM is designed to take advantage of high-speed transmission media such as E3, SONET, and T3.

ActiveX – A set of technologies that allows software components to interact with one another in a networked environment, regardless of the language in which the components were created.

Application Server – A server program in a computer within a distributed network that provides the business logic for an application program. The application server is frequently viewed as part of a three-tier application, consisting of a graphical user interface (GUI) server, an application (business logic) server, and a database and transaction server.

Authentication – The process for verifying an entity or object is who or what it claims to be. Examples include confirming the source and integrity of information, such as verifying a digital signature or verifying the identity of a user or computer.

B

Bandwidth – The data transfer capacity of a transmission medium. In digital communications, the transfer capacity expressed in bits per second (bps) or megabits per second (Mbps).

BEA WebLogic – A J2EE application server and also an HTTP Web server by BEA Systems of San Jose, California, for Unix, Linux, Solaris, Microsoft Windows, and other platforms. WebLogic supports Oracle, DB2, Microsoft SQL Server, and other JDBC-compliant databases. WebLogic Server supports WS-Security and is compliant with J2EE 1.3.

Browser – Software that interprets the markup of files in HTML, formats them into Web pages, and displays them to the end user. Some browsers also permit end users to send and receive e-mail, read newsgroups, and play sound or video files embedded in Web documents.

Business-to-Business (B2B) – Is also referred to as Business Automation or e-business. This term is applied to the electronic transaction taking place among the related partners and collaborators in an enterprise scenario.

Business-to-Customer (B2C) – Corresponds to the retailing part of electronic commerce that takes place on the Internet. In B2C, the interchange of services, products, or information takes place between the business and consumer directly.

C

Cable Modem – A device that enables hook up of a PC to a local cable TV line and receive data at about 1.5 Mbps. This data rate far exceeds that of the prevalent 28.8 and 56 Kbps telephone modems and the up to 128 Kbps of Integrated Services Digital Network (ISDN) and is about the same as the data rate available to subscribers of Digital Subscriber Line (DSL) telephone service. A cable modem can be added to or integrated with a set-top box that provides your TV set with channels for Internet access.

Cache – A special memory subsystem in which frequently used data values are duplicated for quick access.

Cascading Style Sheet (CSS) – Set of overlay rules that are read by your HTML browser, which uses these rules for displaying, layout, and formatting of the XML-generated HTML file(s). CSS allows for fast changes in look and feel without having to plunge into the HTML file(s).

Client – The requesting program or user in a client/server relationship. For example, the user of a Web browser is effectively making client requests for pages from servers all over the Web. The browser itself is a client in its relationship with the computer that is getting and returning the requested HTML file.

CLR – The type, metadata, and execution systems provided by the .NET Framework, which supply managed code and data with services such as cross-language integration, code access security, object lifetime management, and debugging and profiling support. By targeting the CLR, compilers and other tools can offer these services to developers.

Common Gateway Interface (CGI) – A standard way of extending Web server functionality by executing programs or scripts on a Web server in response to Web browser requests.

COM – Stands for Component Object Model. It is the component technology that works on Microsoft's operating system.

Connection Leak – Is a situation when connection from the pool was not closed explicitly.

Connection Pooling – A technique used for establishing a pool of resource connections that applications can share on an application server.

Cross Site Scripting – Often attackers will inject JavaScript, VBScript, ActiveX, HTML, or Flash into a vulnerable application to fool a user in order to gather data from users.

D

DataBase Management System (DBMS) – A set of computer programs for organizing the information in a database. A DBMS supports the structuring of the database in a standard format and provides tools for data input, verification, storage, retrieval, query, and manipulation.

DB2 – An RDBMS product suite from IBM. DB2 is available on almost all operating environments.

Deadlock – When two or more transactions conflict in such a way that each is waiting for the other before they proceed. For instance, Transaction A might have a lock on Record 1 while trying to write to Record 2, while Transaction B has a lock on

Record 2 while trying to write to Record 1. The two transactions will wait for each other forever unless the deadlock is somehow resolved.

DSL – Acronym for Digital Subscriber Line which is a family of digital telecommunications protocols designed to allow high speed data communication over the existing copper telephone lines between end-users and telephone companies. (From www.adaptivedigital.com/services/serv_definitions.htm).

E

E-Commerce – (Electronic commerce or EC) is the buying and selling of goods and services on the Internet, especially the World Wide Web. In practice, this term and a newer term, e-business, are often used interchangeably. For online retail selling, the term e-tailing is sometimes used.

Enterprise Java Beans (EJB) – A component as well as specification proposed by Sun Microsystems. These components are deployed on the business tier of application servers. They are responsible for business logic and they often execute the business logic in a secure, reliable, and transaction environment. There are three types of EJBs: Session Bean, Entity Bean, and Message Driven Beans.

Exception – Handling is a programming language mechanism designed to handle runtime errors or other problems (exceptions) inside a computer program.

F

Fat server – In a client/server architecture, a server that performs most of the processing, with the client performing little or no processing.

File Transfer Protocol (FTP) – An Internet tool/software utility which allows the transfering of files between two computers that are connected to the Internet. Anonymous FTP allows connection to remote computers and to transfer publicly available computer files or programs.

Firewall – A security feature in the intranet of a company that ensures a secure environment for the organization. A firewall forms an entry point for the requests coming from the outside environment. Likewise, a firewall acts as the exit point for the requests that are going out of the organization into intranet. A firewall system can be configured to provide security environment at one of these three levels via Packet Filtering, Circuit relay, or Application level Gateway. While packet filtering provides the basic screening of source and destination IP address and/or port along with the protocol, Application Gateway acts as a proxy that controls the requests and responses along with authentication, authorization as well as an access control mechanism.

G

Gateway – A dedicated device that routes network traffic and enables communication between different networking protocols.

GUI – Software designed to make applications easier to use by giving them all the same look and feel, usually involving a mouse to move a pointer on the computer screen, menus to select actions, and a variety of buttons or sliders which can be used to perform tasks or manipulate the screen.

H

HTML – Stands for Hyper Text Markup Language. It is used to design and develop Web pages.

HTTP – HyperText Transfer Protocol. A team led by Dr. Tim Berners-Lee at CERN designed this protocol. This protocol helps in the transport of hypertext across the networks in request-response behavior.

Hub – The master station through which all communications to, from, and between microterminals must flow. In the future, satellites with on-board processing will allow hubs to be eliminated, as MESH networks are able to connect all points in a network together.

Hypertext Preprocessor (PHP) – A scripting language that is available on the Linux systems. PHP helps in the creation of dynamic Web pages similar to Microsoft's ASP or Sun's JSP. The PHP files carry an extension of .php, .php3, or .phtml. When a user requests this page, the contents of the PHP pages are interpreted to generate the dynamic contents to produce the HTML content to the end user.

I

Inter Process Communication (IPC) – A capability supported by some operating systems that allows one process to communicate with another process. The processes can be running on the same computer or on different computers connected through a network.

Internet – Defined as the network of networks that spans the entire globe. No one owns it and controls it. However, it is useful to every individual as well as organizations. The Internet popularized the TCP/IP protocol, and TCP/IP has become the de facto business protocol among enterprise users. The Internet can be credited with the enormous success of B2C businesses. E-mail and IRC, the applications that work on the Internet, have shrunk communication time enormously. In fact, e-mail and IRC can be considered as new communication for individuals as well as businesses. The World Wide Web (WWW) is the most frequently and widely used part of the Internet.

Internet Mail Accessing Protocol (IMAP) – A protocol for retrieving e-mail messages. The latest version, IMAP4, is similar to POP3 but supports some additional features. For example, with IMAP4, users can search through e-mail messages for keywords while the messages are still on the mail server. Users can then choose which messages to download to their machines.

Internet Service Providers (ISP) – A business or organization that offers users access to the Internet and related services. Most telecommunications operators are ISPs. They provide services such as Internet transit, domain name registration and hosting, dialup access, leased line access, and collocation.

Intranet – A private network of various computers within an organization. An Intranet is used to share company information and computing resources among employees. An intranet uses regular Internet protocols and, in general, looks like a private version of the Internet.

IP Address – An identifier for a computer or device on a TCP/IP network. Networks using the TCP/IP protocol route messages based on the IP address of the destination. The format of an IP address is a 32-bit numeric address written as four numbers separated by periods. Each number can be zero to 255. For example, 1.160.10.240 could be an IP address. Within an isolated network, IP addresses can be assigned at random as long as each one is unique. However, connecting a private network to the Internet requires using registered IP addresses (called Internet addresses) to avoid duplicates.

ISDN – (Integrated Services Digital Network) is a set of CCITT/ITU standards for digital transmission over ordinary telephone copper wire as well as over other media. Home and business users who install an ISDN adapter (in place of a telephone modem) receive Web pages at up to 128 Kbps compared with the maximum 56 Kbps rate of a modem connection. ISDN requires adapters at both ends of the transmission, so the access provider also needs an ISDN adapter.

J

J2EE – A platform-independent, Java-centric environment from Sun for developing, building, and deploying Web-based enterprise applications online. The J2EE platform consists of a set of services, APIs, and protocols that provide the functionality for developing multitiered, Web-based applications.

Java – A simple, object oriented, multi-threaded, robust, secure, platform independent programming language created by Sun Microsystems. Java was initially called Oak. Dr. James Gosling created this language sometime in the middle of 1995. Over the years, Java has witnessed tremendous growth in terms of acceptance and applicability in the client/server, distributed and intranet, extranet, and Internet environments. Java is not only thriving on computer systems, but also driving devices such as PDA, mobile phones, set top boxes, buttons, cards, etc.

Java Beans – An object model being developed by SunSoft that is targeted to interoperate with a variety of other object models, including COM and CORBA.

JavaScript – A scripting language developed by Netscape to enable Web authors to design interactive sites. Although it shares many of the features and structures of the full Java language, it was developed independently. JavaScript can interact with HTML source code, enabling Web authors to spice up their sites with dynamic content. JavaScript is endorsed by a number of software companies and is an open language that anyone can use without purchasing a license. It is supported by recent browsers from Netscape and Microsoft, though Internet Explorer supports only a subset, which Microsoft calls Jscript.

Java Server Pages (JSP) – Popularly called JSP, are the presentation components on the Web tier. JSP technology, introduced by Sun Microsystems, allows encoding Java Programming language into the HTML pages. These JSP pages are identified by a .jsp extension.

JIT Complier – In computing, just-in-time compilation (JIT), also known as dynamic translation, is a technique for improving the performance of interpreted programs, by allowing parts of a program to be partially compiled. This represents a kind of hybrid approach between compiled and interpreted languages.

JVM – A crucial component of the Java platform. The availability of JVMs on almost all types of hardware and software platforms enables Java to function both as middleware and a platform in its own right.

K

Kernel – The fundamental part of an operating system. It is a piece of software responsible for providing secure access to the machine's hardware to various computer programs. Since there are many programs, and access to the hardware is limited, the kernel is also responsible for deciding when and how long a program should be able to make use of a piece of hardware, in a technique called multiplexing. Accessing the hardware directly could also be very complex.

L

Legacy Systems – Hardware and software applications in which a company has already invested considerable time and money. Legacy systems have typically performed critical operations in companies for many years even though they may no longer use state-of-the-art technology. Replacing legacy systems can be disruptive and therefore requires careful planning and appropriate migration support from the manufacturer.

Load Balancing – A technique with the help of which incoming request to a system can be evenly distributed among the several systems and system software so that the accessibility of the systems for the users is addressed properly. Load balance can be implemented in software or hardware or a combination of the two. Web servers and application servers of enterprises that are exposed to Internet and intranet usually require load balancing.

Load Testing – The testing of a system that attempts to cause failures involving how the performance of a system varies under normal conditions of utilization (e.g., as the load increases and becomes heavy). Load testing can identify failures involving scalability requirements as well as distribution and load balancing mechanisms in distributed, scalable systems. Contrast with stress testing.

Local Area Network (LAN) – A computer network that spans a relatively small area. Most LANs are confined to a single building or group of buildings. However, one LAN can be connected to other LANs over any distance via telephone lines and radio waves.

M

M-Commerce (mobile commerce) – The buying and selling of goods and services through wireless handheld devices such as cellular telephones and personal digital assistants (PDAs). Known as next-generation e-commerce, m-commerce enables users to access the Internet without needing to find a place to plug in. The emerging technology behind m-commerce is based on the Wireless Application Protocol (WAP), (From http://searchmobilecomputing.techtarget.com/sDefinition/ 0,,sid40_gci214590,00.html).

Managed Code – Code that is executed by the CLR. Managed code provides information (i.e., metadata) to allow the CLR to locate methods encoded in assembly modules, store and retrieve security information, handle exceptions, and walk the program stack. Managed code can access both managed data and unmanaged data.

Memory pool – A private free store from which related memory allocations occur. Memory pools permit memory to be partitioned for different uses. Such partitioning improves locality, which, in turn, reduces swapping. The allocations from a given SmartHeap pool may be fixed size or variable size. SmartHeap permits controlling how much memory is retained in the private free store of a given pool and controlling when such free memory is returned to the operating system for others to use.

Modem –Short for modulator-demodulator device. Modems allow computers to transmit information to one another via an ordinary telephone line.

Multi-Processor – A Central Processing Unit (CPU) which has more than one processor.

Multimedia – Human-computer interaction involving text, graphics, voice, and video. Often also includes concepts from hypertext. This term has come to be almost synonymous with CD-ROM in the personal computer world because the large amounts of data involved are currently best supplied on CD-ROM.

Multithreading – Running several processes in rapid sequence within a single program, regardless of which logical method of multitasking is being used by the operating system.

N

Network Operating System (NOS) – Designed to pass information and communicate between more than one computer. Examples include AppleShare, Novell NetWare, and Windows NT Server.

O

Object Request Broker (ORB) – A component in the CORBA programming model that acts as the middleware between clients and servers. In the CORBA model, a client can request a service without knowing anything about what servers are attached to the network. The various ORBs receive the requests, forward them to the appropriate servers, and then hand the results back to the client.

ODBC – Open DataBase Connectivity, a standard database access method, was developed by the SQL Access group in 1992. The goal of ODBC is to make it possible to access any data from any application, regardless of which database management system (DBMS) is handling the data. ODBC manages this by inserting a middle layer, called a database driver, between an application and the DBMS. The purpose of this layer is to translate the application's data queries into commands that the DBMS understands.

Operating System (OS) – The most important program that runs on a computer. Every general-purpose computer must have an operating system to run other programs. Operating systems perform basic tasks, such as recognizing input from the keyboard, sending output to the display screen, keeping track of files and directories on the disk, and controlling peripheral devices such as disk drives and printers.

Oracle – A relational database management system (RDBMS) developed and copy-righted by the Oracle Corporation.

P

Performance Testing (PT) – In software engineering, performance testing is testing that is performed to determine how fast some aspect of a system performs under a particular workload.

Post Office Protocol (POP) – Used to retrieve e-mail from a mail server. Most e-mail applications (sometimes called an e-mail client) use the POP protocol, although some can use the newer IMAP (Internet Message Access Protocol).

Process – A program that is running. A process is the active element in a computer. Terminals, files, and other I/O devices communicate with each other through processes. Thus, network communications are interprocess communications (that is, communication between processes).

Processor – Also known as the CPU (central processing unit). The CPU is the brains of the computer because it performs most of the calculations to run programs and allows the performance work on the machine. In terms of computing power, the CPU is the most important element of a computer system.

Q

Quality – The totality of features and characteristics of a product or service that bear on its ability to satisfy stated or implied needs.

Queue – A list that allows additions at one end and deletions at the opposite end. Items in a queue are usually processed on the first in, first out (FIFO) principle, in that the first item entered is the first item to be processed.

R

Redundant Array of Independent Disks (RAID) – A data storage method in which data, along with information used for error correction such as parity bits, is distributed among two or more hard disk drives to improve performance and reliability. The hard disk array is governed by array management software and a disk controller, which handles the error correction. RAID is generally used on network servers.

Regression Testing – The selective retesting of a software system that has been modified to ensure that any bugs have been fixed and that no other previously-working functions have failed as a result of the reparations and that newly added features have not created problems with previous versions of the software. Also referred to as verification testing, regression testing is initiated after a programmer has attempted to fix a recognized problem or has added source code to a program that may have inadvertently introduced errors.

Remote Procedural Call (RPC) – A mechanism to allow the execution of individual routines on remote computers across a network. Communication to these routines is via passing arguments so that, in contrast to using Sockets, the communication itself is hidden from the application. The programming model is that of the clients-servers.

Routers – A device that determines the next network point to which a data packet should be forwarded enroute toward its destination. The router is connected to at least two networks and determines which way to send each data packet based on its current understanding of the state of the networks it is connected to. Routers create or maintain a table of the available routes and use this information to determine the best route for a given data packet.

RAM – Random Access Memory is the most common computer memory which can be used by programs to perform necessary tasks while the computer is on. An integrated circuit memory chip allows information to be stored or accessed in any order, and all storage locations are equally accessible.

S

Secured Socket Layer (SSL) – A protocol developed by Netscape for transmitting private documents via the Internet. SSL works by using a private key to encrypt data that are transferred over the SSL connection. Both Netscape Navigator and Internet Explorer support SSL, and many Web sites use the protocol to obtain confidential user information such as credit card numbers.

Server – In the client/server programming model, a server is a program that awaits and fulfills requests from client programs in the same or other computers. A given application in a computer may function as a client with requests for services from other programs and also as a server of requests from other programs.

Servlet – Java programs that can be run dynamically from a Web server. Servlets are a server-side technology. A servlet is an intermediating layer between an HTTP request of a client and the Web server.

Simple Mail Transfer Protocol (SMTP) – A protocol for sending e-mail messages between servers. Most e-mail systems that send mail over the Internet use SMTP to send messages from one server to another; the messages can then be retrieved with an e-mail client using either POP or IMAP. In addition, SMTP is generally used to send messages from a mail client to a mail server. This is why the POP or IMAP server and the SMTP server need to be specified when users configure their e-mail applications.

Sniffer – An application or device that can read, monitor, and capture network data exchanges and read network packets. If the packets are not encrypted, a sniffer provides a full view of the data inside the packet.

Sniffing – Method of hacking using some scripting languages or technology.

Software Development Life Cycle – A process of developing a software system in an organized, controlled, and predictable way. The process starts at the conception of the project to its termination with the company, sometime called a cradle-to-grave process.

SQL injection – As the name suggests, an SQL injection attach "injects" or manipulates SQL code. By adding unexpected SQL to a query, it is possible to manipulate a database in many unanticipated ways.

Storage Area Network (SAN) – Collections of initiators, such as servers or individual "workstations," and storage devices, typically disk- or tape-based, that are connected over a specialized or private LAN.

Structured Query Language (SQL) – Pronounced as either see-kwell or as separate letters. SQL is a standardized query language for requesting information from a database. The original version called SEQUEL (structured English query language) was designed by an IBM research center in 1974 and 1975. SQL was first introduced as a commercial database system in 1979 by Oracle Corporation.

Subnet – A portion of a network, which may be a physically independent network, which shares a network address with other portions of the network and is distinguished by a subnet number. A subnet is to a network what a network is to an internet.

T

T-1 – A leased-line connection capable of carrying data at 1,544,000 bits-per-second. At maximum theoretical capacity, a T-1 line could move a megabyte in less than 10 seconds. That is still not fast enough for full-screen, full-motion video, for which at least 10,000,000 bits-per-second is needed. T-1 lines are commonly used to connect large LANs to the Internet.

TCP/IP (Transmission Control Protocol/Internet Protocol) – This is the suite of protocols that defines the Internet. Originally designed for the UNIX operating system, TCP/IP software is now included with every major kind of computer operating system. To be truly on the Internet, a computer must have TCP/IP software.

Test Bed – An execution environment configured for testing. May consist of specific hardware, OS, network topology, configuration of the product under test, other application or system software, etc. The Test Plan for a project should enumerate the test beds to be used.

Threads – Similar to processes, in that both represent a single sequence of instructions executed in parallel with other sequences, either by time slicing or multiprocessing. Threads are a way for a program to split itself into two or more simultaneously running tasks.

U

User Datagram Protocol (UDP) – Connectionless transport-layer protocol; part of the TCP/IP protocol stack. Exchanges datagrams/packets without guaranteed delivery or acknowledgments. Error processing and retransmission is handled by other protocols. Sometimes used in place of TCP where transaction-based application programs communicate; normally carries non-critical network information.

V

VBScript – Short for Visual Basic Scripting Edition, a scripting language developed by Microsoft and supported by Microsoft's Internet Explorer Web browser. VBScript is based on the Visual Basic programming language, but is much simpler. In many ways, it is similar to JavaScript. It enables Web authors to include interactive controls, such as buttons and scrollbars, on their Web pages

Virtual user – A software entity, internal to Web Performance Trainer and Trade, that simulates a real user by repeatedly performing a Business Case during a load test.

W

Web Application – A software program that uses Hypertext Transfer Protocol (HTTP) for its core communication protocol and that delivers Web-based information to the user in the Hypertext Markup Language (HTML) language.

Wide Area Network (WAN) – A computer network that spans a relatively large geographical area. Typically, a WAN consists of two or more local-area networks (LANs).

X

XML – Short for Extensible Markup Language, a specification developed by the W3C. XML is a pared-down version of SGML, designed especially for Web documents. It allows designers to create their own customized tags, enabling the definition, transmission, validation, and interpretation of data between applications and between organizations.

About the Author

Dr. Subraya (subraya@infosys.com), BM, Associative Vice President, currently works as a principal researcher for the Education and Research Department and as the head of the Global Education Center (GEC), Infosys Technologies Limited, Mysore, India. He is also responsible for the foundation level training at Global Education Center (GEC), Mysore. His areas of interest are Web performance, software engineering, and software testing. He has offered tutorials in Web performance testing in many preconference tutorials, including QAI, SEPG, and PSQT international conferences. He has published many papers in international conferences in the area of performance testing of Web applications.

Before he came to Infosys, he worked 18 years as a professor and head of the Computer Centre at S.J. College of Engineering, an affiliate college of the University of Mysore, a reputed engineering college in southern India.

Dr. Subraya holds a PhD from the Indian Institute of Technology, Delhi, Computer Science and Engineering Department, in the area of hardware verification.

Index

Symbols

.NET 72, 234
8 second rule 5

A

acceptance criteria 174
acceptance test 88
accuracy 2, 12
active server pages (ASP) 43, 72
active time 180
ad hoc queries 208
ADO 212
advertisements 11
allocation 248
AltaVista 7
ambiguities 78
analysis phase 125
analyzing requirements 78
AOL 7
Apache server 43
Apache Tomcat server 55
application server logs 168
application servers 205
application throughput 246
architectural level monitoring 234

architectural plan 88
architecture 3, 110, 175, 204
architecture level 175
array bound errors 31
asynchronous transfer mode 45
audience 173
authentication 83, 210
authenticity 156
automated system 79
automated testing 55
automation 203

B

B2B 1
B2C 1
background activities 172
bandwidth 4, 235
bandwidth soaked 112
bar charts 174
batch processing 81
behavior 105
benchmark design 102
black box method 19
bottleneck 174, 212, 235
broadband connection 8
broken page 189

disk usage 189
distributed data collection 246
distribution 209
domain specific 103
downloading 189
DSL (digital subscriber line) 131
dual port redundancy 42
dynamic behavior 89
dynamic link Library 57
dynamic page 174
dynamic pages 189
dynamic Web site 4

E

e-auctioning 1
e-commerce 1
eBay 7
efficiency 154
elaboration testing 156
electronic commerce 1
end results 174
end user requests 189
endurance test 15, 172
enterprise application 56
Enterprise Java Bean (EJB) 60
environment 206
error pages 189
ethernet 85
execution 153
exit criteria 152
expected behavior 105
extensible hypertext markup language
    (XHTML) 69
extensible markup language (XML) 69
external events 81

F

failed commands 180
fat server 39
fault tolerance 57
features testing 52
file access utilization 237
file requests 53
file servers 54
file transfer 38
file transfer protocol (FTP) 38

firewall 12, 192, 235
flexibility 68
front end monitoring 191
functional behavior 88
functional defect 153
functional design 88
functional regression testing 203
functional requirements 52
functional test automation 203
functionality 66

G

garbage collection (GC) 161, 187, 247, 252
goal oriented 110
goals 78
Google 9
graceful degradation 132
groupware server 54
GUIs (graphical user interface) 60

H

healthy state 153
heap memory 251
heap size 155, 161
heterogeneous 53
heterogeneous client 34
high level design (HLD) 77
horizontal scaling 54
HTML 32
HTTP 25
HTTP return code 172
hyper text markup language (HTML)
    32, 68
hyper text transfer protocol (HTTP) 25,
    172
hypertext preprocessor (PHP) 72

I

IMAP (Internet mail access protocol) 35
inactive time 180
incorrect configuration 112
information system (IS) 81
initial congestion window (ICW) 35
integrated services digital network (ISDN)
    44